THE STATE OF WELFARE

The State of Welfare

*The Welfare State in Britain
since 1974*

NICHOLAS BARR
FIONA COULTER
MARIA EVANDROU
JANE FALKINGHAM
HOWARD GLENNERSTER
JOHN HILLS (editor)
JULIAN LE GRAND
WILLIAM LOW
BEVERLEY MULLINGS
DAVID WINTER
FRANCES WOOLLEY

CLARENDON PRESS · OXFORD
1990

Oxford University Press, Walton Street, Oxford OX2 6DP
Oxford New York Toronto
Delhi Bombay Calcutta Madras Karachi
Petaling Jaya Singapore Hong Kong Tokyo
Nairobi Dar es Salaam Cape Town
Melbourne Auckland
and associated companies in
Berlin Ibadan

Oxford is a trade mark of Oxford University Press

Published in the United States
by Oxford University Press, New York

British Library Cataloguing in Publication Data
The state of Welfare: the welfare state in Britain since
1974.
1. Welfare State. Great Britain
I. Barr, N. A. (Nicholas Adrian), 1943– II. Hills,
John
361.650941
ISBN 0–19–823305–1

Library of Congress Cataloging in Publication Data
The State of welfare: the welfare state in Britain since 1974
Nicholas Barr ... [et al.]; John Hills, editor.
p. cm.
Includes bibliographical references (p.   ) and index.
1. Public welfare—Great Britain. 2. Great Britain—Social
policy. 3. Welfare state. I. Barr, N. A. II. Hills, John.
HV245.S72 1990 361.6'5'094109047—dc20 90-7648
ISBN 0–19–823305–1

Typeset in 10/12 pt Times
by Graphicraft Typesetters Ltd., Hong Kong

Printed and bound in
Great Britain by Biddles Ltd.
Guildford and King's Lynn

Acknowledgements

This book has been a collective enterprise, part of the Welfare State Programme at the London School of Economics. While the authors of each chapter are responsible for its contents, we have all benefited from the comments of other members of the team at various stages during the research and writing of each chapter. Particular contributions have also been made to the whole book by individuals outside the confines of their own chapters. Julian Le Grand and John Hills co-ordinated the project. Maria Evandrou and Jane Falkingham carried out the computer analysis of the General Household Survey, providing material for the chapters on education, the National Health Service, and housing as well as personal social services. John Hills acted as editor, supervised the production of the final manuscript, and with Beverley Mullings assembled the Bibliography.

Outside the project team we have many debts. The origins of this book lie in an earlier article by A. B. Atkinson, John Hills, and Julian Le Grand (1987) on health, housing, and social security policy between 1970 and 1985. We owe Tony Atkinson a great debt, not only for the material from that earlier study, but also for inspiration and support over the whole life of the LSE Welfare State Programme. In the analysis of public spending we were greatly assisted by data assembled at the start of the project by Chris Gordon (see Gordon 1988). We are also very grateful to Jane Dickson and Sue Coles, who came to our aid when the typing would otherwise have proved beyond us, and to the many people who have commented on drafts of various parts of the book, in particular Mark Kleinman, Anne Power, Holly Sutherland, Christine Whitehead, and participants in a series of Welfare State Programme Discussion Groups in the winter of 1988/9, when some of the ideas contained here were first presented. We have been assisted by government departments in the supply of data in all of the areas we have studied, in particular by the Office of Population Censuses and Surveys (with the ESRC Data Archive at Essex University) in making data available from the General Household Survey (in the form of SIR/DBMS and SPSS files from OPCS and Surrey University). The computing would have been impossible without the help of Brian Warren of the LSE and Steven Self at the University of London Computing Centre.

Much of the research for and writing of the book was made possible by financial support from Suntory Limited for the Welfare State Programme at the Suntory Toyota International Centre for Economics and Related Disciplines at the London School of Economics. The research on the distribution of the use of and need for welfare services forms the first part of the Economic and Social Research Council funded Welfare Research Programme (grant reference X206 32 2001). The work by John Hills and Beverley Mullings on housing was supported by the Joseph Rowntree Memorial Trust's Housing Finance Initiative. All this support is gratefully acknowledged.

London School of Economics
September 1989

Contents

List of Figures

List of Tables

Abbreviations

CIPFA	Chartered Institute of Public Finance and Accountancy
DES	Department of Education and Science
DHSS	Department of Health and Social Security
DoE	Department of the Environment
DoH	Department of Health
DSS	Department of Social Security
FES	Family Expenditure Survey
GDP	Gross Domestic Product
GGE	General Government Expenditure
GHS	General Household Survey
GNP	Gross National Product
HIP	Housing Investment Programme
HRA	Housing Revenue Account
LEA	local education authority
MHLG	Ministry of Housing and Local Government
MSC	Manpower Services Commission
n.a.	not available
NHS	National Health Service
OPCS	Office of Population Censuses and Surveys
PEWP	Public Expenditure White Paper
PSS	personal social services
RAWP	Resource Allocation Working Party
RFC	Rate Fund Contributions
RPI	Retail Price Index
SB	Supplementary Benefit
SEG	socio-economic group
SERPS	State Earnings-Related Pension Scheme
SSD	social service department
TOPS	Training Opportunities Scheme
UGC	University Grants Committee
YOP	Youth Opportunities Programme
YTS	Youth Training Scheme

1

Introduction

John Hills

This book is about what has happened to the welfare state in Britain over the last fifteen years. Some readers may expect to be reading an obituary. As we write, it is, after all, thirteen years since the package of public-spending cuts associated with the Labour government's agreement with the International Monetary Fund at the end of 1976, and ten since the election of a Conservative government with a strong ideological opposition to the public sector as a whole and deep suspicion of public 'welfare' in particular. The beginning of our period should therefore mark the end of the halcyon era of three decades during which the welfare state grew to maturity. Since then the picture should show the 'rolling back', one by one, of the cherished institutions which were once 'the envy of the rest of Europe'.

The detailed study which we report in these pages may come as a surprise to such readers. It is true that, by most measures, the welfare state has not grown since the mid-1970s in the way that it had before. It is also true, as we analyse in detail, that particular services within the welfare state have been reduced in extent. More generally, changes in service provision may have failed to keep up with the increasing needs for such services as, in particular, the elderly and unemployed populations have grown. This we also examine in detail where such indicators of 'need' can be constructed. Nor may expectations for service standards have been met over a period when material living standards rose by nearly a third (over the period 1974–88 as measured by real personal disposable income per capita). But, as a general proposition, reports of the death of the welfare state have, like Mark Twain's, been greatly exaggerated.

As well as examining the extent of the welfare state, we also examine the state of welfare itself as measured by various indicators. Here again, there may be a group of readers who expect to read a gloomy picture of failure to achieve improvements in the key indicators of the state of people's welfare which are—or which should be—the ultimate objectives of the welfare state. This group will include those who have in their minds what Titmuss (1968: 26) described as the 'burden' model of welfare, in which public spending on welfare services is simply money down an expensive drain. The very title of Bacon and Eltis's book, *Britain's Economic Problem: Too Few Producers* (1976), and the stark first paragraph of the incoming 1979 Conservative government's initial public spending White Paper—'Public expenditure is at the heart of Britain's present economic difficulties' (HM Treasury 1979*b*: 1)—both suggest this kind of model.

While such readers may be particularly disappointed not to be reading the story of the successful rolling back of what they see as a parasitic part of the economy, we hope that all will be cheered by the successes of welfare policy which we report in many areas. Even such successes do not, of course, end the political argument about whether a particular level of spending or particular approach is justified or affordable. The macroeconomic effects of changes in policy are outside the scope of our study (for an examination of economic policy as a whole over the overlapping period 1970–85 see Dornbusch and Layard 1987). There is also a considerable problem in allocating cause and effect, which we discuss below.

The scope of the book

The core of this book is concerned with five areas—education, the National Health Service, housing, personal social services, and social security. Together we take public policy in these areas to constitute 'the welfare state'. A primary focus is on public spending and the results of that spending. In 1987/8 (i.e. the financial year ending on 31 March 1988) total UK public spending on these areas came to £100 billion. If nothing else, its scale suggests that it is important to examine the way in which such a sum is spent.

At this point, we should make clear that 'the welfare state' is not a term that we are entirely happy to use. Like others before us (Titmuss 1958) we would rather consider the term within quotation marks. But the term does have a popular meaning and resonance, so we shall continue to use it, developing and expanding it as we go. However, there are other 'states of welfare' than that provided by public spending alone. These include what Titmuss identified as 'fiscal welfare', operating through what have come to be called 'tax expenditures' (income tax relief for mortgage interest payments being perhaps the best-known), and 'occupational welfare', operating through employers (e.g. in providing occupational pensions).

It would also be a mistake to look at public spending in isolation. While the public sector is dominant in many of the areas which we examine—education, health, and non-pension-related social security—it plays a smaller role than the private sector in others—housing and many areas covered by the personal social services (where unpaid informal carers carry out most of the work).

Even where the public sector is dominant, it is important to maintain a distinction between public *finance* (or resources provided in kind) and public *provision*. The National Health Service provides a model where provision is largely by public employees paid for through tax-financed public spending. However, this is by no means a universal feature of the welfare state. Where charges are made for publicly provided services— e.g. rents for local authority housing—it is private-sector resources which are paying for public provision. Meanwhile, public-sector finance of privately provided services is becoming more important: one example is 'contracting out' of services previously provided publicly; another is the use of social security payments to meet the costs of privately run residential homes. Even in areas where both provision of a service is private (profit-making or voluntary/informal) and it is paid for privately, public-sector regulation may still have very important effects. We have therefore looked at public-sector services where appropriate in the context of this 'mixed economy of welfare' (although we would not want to claim that our coverage of private/occupational welfare was complete).

We examine the period since 1974 for three reasons. The most important is that it bridges the gap between a period of continuous growth and development in social policy and that following the economic crisis and public expenditure cuts of the mid-1970s, marking a break in the history of ideas and discussion about social policy. Second—linked to the first—is that it covers the periods in office of the Labour governments from 1974 to 1979 and of the Conservative governments since then. This allows us to examine whether the election of 1979 really did cause a sudden discontinuity in welfare policy, or whether many policies continued, for a while at least, despite the change in rhetoric. A final reason is that we have been able to look at the use and distribution of many welfare services using data from the government's annual General Household Survey (GHS), which covers more than 10,000 households (containing more than 25,000 individuals) each year. We have used raw data from the survey for individuals and households for a number of years, using in particular the surveys carried out in 1974, 1979 (or 1980), and 1985 to compare the performance of the welfare state over the two political periods, supplemented by material from a wide range of other sources.

Public discussion of the welfare state is often confused by the messy state of the data describing it. Politicians can pick the figures to suit their case. We have attempted to provide consistent time series which we hope will provide a useful source of coherent data. In the analysis we therefore concentrate on quantitative measures and indicators. This should not be taken to imply that we regard qualitative analysis and information as unimportant, but rather reflects the constraints of length and our aim of providing directly comparable material on the different service areas and on trends over time. For similar reasons we provide little in the way of international comparisons; again, that is not to imply that they are unimportant, simply that they would require a second book.

Structure of the book

In Chapter 2, Howard Glennerster traces the development of the welfare state between the end of the Second World War (and, in some respects, before that) up to the start of our main period of study in 1974. This provides the background to the five core chapters of the book, in which we look in turn at education, health, housing, personal social services, and social security. Finally, in Chapter 8 Julian Le Grand brings together some of the key findings of the earlier chapters to provide an overview of the 'state of welfare' and to speculate about its future.

The separation of the five service areas into different chapters will be convenient to those readers who have a particular interest in, say, education or social security. We have also tried, where this is possible without putting a strait-jacket on what are sometimes heterogeneous areas, to answer common questions about each area within a common format. The logic behind that format is sketched out in Fig. 1.1. Thus, for instance,

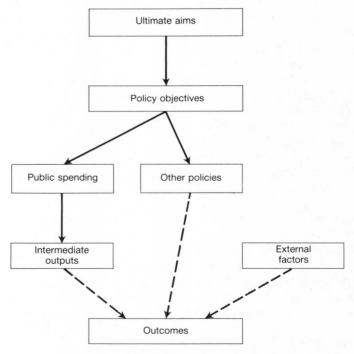

FIG. 1.1. Policy and outcomes

someone who wanted to examine the way in which policy towards the whole of the welfare state had developed could read Chapter 2 and then the policy sections of the five succeeding chapters. Similarly, each of the core chapters contains sections on public expenditure, on the 'outputs' from that spending, and on 'outcomes' in terms of indicators of individual welfare. The book is thus designed to be read 'horizontally' as well as vertically. Someone who did not want to read very much could content themselves with the 'In brief' sections at the end of each chapter and with Chapter 8.

Ultimate aims

At the start of each of the core chapters we discuss the ultimate aims of welfare policy in that area. What is the result of all this activity supposed to be, and why is the state involved in this area, rather than leaving it to the unaided market? This may seem unnecessary, but it often seems to be forgotten that the *objective* of health policy, for instance, is to do with *health*, not—ultimately—with the amount of *health care* provided. This specification of objectives helps to provide a framework against which outcomes can be measured at the end of each chapter. A recurring problem, however, is the vagueness or blandness of the specification of such objectives—'a healthy population' or 'a decent home for all at a price within their means', to give two examples. We have tried to tie such statements down in ways in which we can at least measure progress in the direction of their attainment, even where we cannot specify precisely what full achievement would entail. A further problem is that some of the objectives conflict, and in some areas (such as education) there has been considerable disagreement about the objectives of policy and changes in declared policy aims over time.

While there is some dispute, it will be evident from the discussion throughout the book that neither we, nor those who have shaped the welfare state, see its sole aim (or even in many cases its main aim) as being the provision of services for the poor. Even in the case of social security, where one might expect this to apply most clearly, Nicholas Barr and Fiona Coulter identify in Chapter 7 a series of aims, including economic efficiency, social integration, the protection of accustomed living standards, and the smoothing-out of income over the life-cycle, which go well beyond the relief of poverty. Other chapters provide a similar range of objectives in their area.

Policy objectives

However clouded their ultimate aims, governments more often specify their objectives for particular services in more concrete terms, through specific White Papers and through statements on individual programmes in the annual Public Expenditure White Papers. These objectives have a tendency to focus on public spending priorities and on the 'throughputs' (numbers of operations carried out or lengths of waiting lists) or 'outputs' (numbers of houses built) resulting from public spending, rather than on what we call 'outcomes'. As well as allowing us to examine progress in terms of each government's own stated objectives, the account of policy in each chapter shows the extent to which, for instance, 1979 did mark the end of a previous consensus, or whether there was continuity in some respects throughout the period.

Public spending

Each of the core chapters contains a careful examination of public spending since the financial year 1973/4 (which provides the base for the examination of trends over the 'Labour' period up to its final full year of 1978/9). This is not an entirely straightforward exercise. First, there are problems of data. In a few cases detailed and consistent data for spending in the whole of the United Kingdom are available from the Central Statistical Office's *Annual Abstract of Statistics* or from Public Expenditure White Papers. In most cases they are not. Particular items move from programme to programme, or disappear entirely as a once-explicit spending item is transformed into a tax expenditure (Housing Benefit illustrates both problems). Some detailed information is available only for Great Britain excluding Northern Ireland, or for England and Wales but not for Scotland, or even only for England. We have used a variety of sources in order to present series which are as consistent as possible, and have tried to present most information on at least a Great Britain basis, but the latter has not always been possible.

A second problem relates to the *measurement* of public spending. Presentation of figures for spending in *cash* terms may be useful for accounting purposes, or even as political propaganda, but has few merits as a way of showing trends over a period when prices have changed as much as they have over the last fifteen years. Much of the information we provide is therefore shown in *real* terms (sometimes called 'cost' terms), that is, with the cash figures adjusted by an index of general inflation (specifically by the 'GDP deflator' calculated by the Central Statistical Office, which measures inflation throughout the economy). This gives the best guide to trends in the resources going to a particular area in terms of their opportunity cost to the rest of the economy, and is most useful as a way of measuring how resources going *into* a particular service are changing, and thus how priorities are changing.

Real spending does not necessarily tell us, however, what is coming *out* of a particular spending programme. This is because the prices of what is being purchased by that programme (which could be goods such as school textbooks, or services such as paying for teachers) may not have changed by the same proportion as prices as a whole—the *relative* price of what is being purchased may have changed. Thus, to take a hypothetical example, spending on doctors' salaries may have increased by 2 per cent per year over some period, but this may have meant no change in the number of doctors being employed if all that happened was that their real salaries also increased by 2 per cent per year. In order to measure what *volume* of services is being provided by a particular programme, the cash spending figures have to be adjusted using an index for the prices of whatever it is spent on—an 'own-price deflator'. Where this is possible and appropriate we also provide information on this basis.

Until 1982, public spending was planned in volume terms, with the figures presented in what were called 'Survey Prices' (once less kindly referred to as 'funny money'). The problem with planning in this way was that while it gave a good guide to, say, the number of doctors being provided, it did not necessarily give a good guide to how much tax revenue would be needed to pay for them. What became known as the 'Relative Price Effect'—a change in real spending which was invisible in the volume figures—undermined their credibility. The problem was not that the volume information was wrong or uninteresting, but rather that it shed light on only some of the important questions about public spending. To get a clear picture, one really needs *both* real *and* volume information, which is what we have tried to provide. We also show changes in spending in relation to the whole of general government expenditure (i.e. by central government and local authorities, but not including public corporations) and as a share of Gross Domestic Product.

We have presented figures up to the most recent year for which reasonable estimates of out-turn spending were available at the time of writing (usually either 1987/8 or 1988/9) but have not paid a great deal of attention to the spending *plans* for future years. Such plans have proved unreliable guides in the past, and estimates of the price adjustments which would be needed to make sense of them are subject to considerable uncertainty.

Real and volume information together still do not give the whole picture. A first problem is that it is very hard to measure the *quality* of what is being provided. To return to the example above, there may have been no change in the *number* of doctors employed, but it may be that their higher salaries reflect a higher level of training and quality of service. In this case, the volume figures could be misleading as a guide to the output of health care. One reason why some branches of the social services show much slower growth in volume terms than in real terms is that they are highly labour-intensive, and salaries tend to rise in real terms over time. The reasons for this lie partly in the need of the public sector to compete with increasing salaries elsewhere even if there is no productivity improvement possible in that particular service, but also in productivity improvement within the public sector itself. There is little we can do to measure this, however, other than to jump all the way to the kind of outcome measures which should reflect both quantity and quality of the service provided (but also reflect many other factors).

The second problem is somewhat more tractable. This is that one is interested not only in the volume of service being provided, but also in the relationship between this supply and the demand or *need* for it. Thus, for instance, much of the debate about spending on the National Health Service has concerned the extent to which spending has kept up with the increasing needs of an ageing population. If such needs are increasing, a constant total volume of spending will imply a declining level of service for equivalent conditions (as there are, for instance, more or more difficult cases to cope with). Again, where possible, we present figures on a per capita or demographically adjusted basis to give some idea of the relationship between the volume of service provided and such needs.

A third point to bear in mind is related to the difference between public funding and public provision which was noted above. Figures for public spending can be on a *gross* basis, or they can be *net* of charges. Where there is a change over time in the extent to which finance comes from charges, the gross and net figures will change in different directions, the gross figure giving a guide to public *provision*, but the net figure to public *funding*. Chapter 5, for instance, examines the differences in trend between the net figure for current public spending on housing—including subsidies to public housing—and the gross amounts actually being spent on its day-to-day management and maintenance. Once again, figures on both bases are more illuminating than either by itself.

Finally, the discussion of public spending in each area includes an examination of the *tax expenditures* which parallel (and often exceed) the explicit public spending programmes.

Intermediate policy objectives

Following the discussion of public spending we look at the *outputs* which result from that spending—numbers of houses built, numbers of meals on wheels delivered, and so on. These are closely related to the volume of spending (indeed, if there was only one variety of output and its price was calculated correctly, the two would show identical trends). Such measures are often used to formulate policy objectives—targets for nursery places in relation to the number of children under five, to give an example from education policy. As well as looking at trends in the totals of such outputs, it is often possible to look at their *distribution* (and that of the 'outcomes' discussed below)—e.g. by income group or by region. This is of interest not only because policy objectives may have been stated for distribution (e.g. through the Resource Allocation Working Party system in the NHS), but also because concepts of *equity* in access to public services may form part of the ultimate objectives of policy in the area.

In four of the five areas (it was not possible for data reasons in the case of social security) we have been able to draw on the General Household Survey (GHS) as part of this exercise. This allows us to examine the distribution of the use of welfare services, or status in relation to the targets of those services, in a variety of ways, such as distribution by tenure, by region, by age, by socio-economic group, by parent's or head of household's birthplace (as a proxy for ethnic origin), and by income.

Distributional results by income are shown in relation to quintile groups, that is, successive fifths of the population arranged by income. There are many ways in which this could be done. We have used gross family income, that is, including social security benefits but before deducting taxes. We have also adjusted for family size, recognizing that a family of four with a particular income will not be as well-off as a single person with the same income. This adjustment produces equivalent income to that of a single person (the scale used being to divide by 1 where the 'family unit' is a single person, and by 1.61 for a couple, adding 0.44 for each child; these relativities are a simplified version of those embodied in what used to be the 'ordinary' Supplementary Benefit scale rates). In the analysis, this level of gross equivalent family income was allocated to each individual (including children) within the family, and each individual was then allocated to one of the five quintile groups, each containing 20 per cent of the individuals within each year of the GHS used.

This procedure gives a consistent way of allocating individuals by income over the period of study, except in one respect. The inconsistency results from the change in the Housing Benefit system in 1982/3. Before then, those receiving Supplementary Benefit would have included in their benefit payment—and hence in their gross incomes on our basis—an amount reflecting their rates and rent (if tenants). After the 1982/3 change, these rebates were in most cases netted off rent and rates demands rather than being included in Supplementary Benefit payments. The rent and rates element thus disappears from our definition of gross income used in, for instance, allocating individuals to income quintile groups for 1985. This has advantages in bringing the treatment of those receiving Supplementary Benefit (now Income Support) into line with that of those receiving partial rent and rate rebates (which have always been netted off rent and rates demands and would not be included in gross income for earlier years either). It does mean, however, that the allocation of individuals between the first and second income quintile groups is not entirely comparable between 1975 and 1979 (or 1980) on the one hand and 1985 on the other. Comparisons on this basis between the two dates therefore have to be interpreted with some caution. Unfortunately the data did not permit a consistent definition of gross income, either including or excluding all Housing Benefit throughout.

Final outcomes

In Fig. 1.1 the final part of the picture is the box of what we call *outcomes*. The difference between these and the outputs discussed above is best explained with some examples. In education, the number of teachers per pupil would be given as an output from public spending, but the educational qualifications of the population would be an 'outcome'. In health, the number of operations carried out would be an output (sometimes called a throughput), but levels of morbidity and mortality would be outcomes. Of necessity, the accounts of outcomes in the different areas are fairly heterogeneous. However, we have tried to provide figures which match the objectives identified at the start of each chapter, and which give a guide to distribution as well as average or total levels of achievement.

In the figure the line linking the outputs from welfare spending and such outcomes is dashed to stress that the link between the two may be tenuous. Mortality may be more related to public health in a wider sense than to health care by itself, for instance, and educational achievement may be influenced as much by home environment as by teacher/pupil ratios. A full analysis of causality would have to specify counterfactuals as to what would have happened in the absence of the particular part of the welfare state, an exercise we have not been able to carry out. It should not be forgotten either that some of the other links in the figure are tenuous too—governments may set policy objectives, but the bureaucratic machine may be able to pursue others, so that public spending may not change automatically in the way in which the policy pronouncements would suggest.

IN BRIEF

● In this book we attempt to provide a consistent picture of what has happened to the 'welfare state' as represented by public spending on and policy towards education, health, housing, personal social services, and social security (examining, where possible, comparable trends in private-sector activity). We examine the data available on such services both in terms of their extent and in terms of the ultimate outcomes which they are intended to influence. The picture we present will be a disappointment to those looking for simple overarching trends. The welfare state is not homogeneous; nor is what has happened to its component parts since 1974.

2

Social Policy since the Second World War

Howard Glennerster

I. SUSTAINING A MYTH

There is a widely accepted mythology about social policy that television producers and the media more generally reinforce when new social legislation is discussed. The same theme was orchestrated in the publicity that surrounded the review of social security in the mid-1980s. The essential myth is that during and immediately after the Second World War the Coalition and Labour governments created a set of new social institutions that were designed to look after citizens 'from the cradle to the grave'. They were the outcome of the shared sacrifices of war borne by the whole population. The invention of Sir William Beveridge, this massive new system secured bipartisan and popular support which was sustained through to the 1970s, when economic crisis and Mrs Thatcher's radical new government began to question whether the economy could afford to sustain such an expensive, outdated system of largess. Intended as an instrument to achieve a more equal society, it has failed, as even its supporters agree.

Like any myth it has an element of truth embedded in it. The Second World War did provide a catalytic environment in which plans for social reconstruction were drawn up, and perhaps the most influential was the Beveridge Report (1942). Yet almost all the ideas and proposals for reform in social security and education, for example, had been long discussed in the 1920s and 1930s (Harris 1977; Gosden 1976). The new structures built on or simplified many of the systems that preceded them. In many cases they extended to a national scale experiments which had been introduced by some local authorities. The clear distinction between primary and secondary education and free access to grammar schools are examples. It was a very British evolution, but the changes never were, and rarely have been since, a matter of consensus (Deakin 1989). The National Health Service was most bitterly fought over in Parliament and outside (Foot 1975; Webster 1988). The Beveridge Report was never meant to be more than a limited technical job and the Treasury and the Prime Minister, when they saw it, tried to bury it (Harris 1977). The National Health Service that emerged from Bevan's discussions in the Ministry of Health after 1945 was very different from the Coalition government's White Paper (Webster 1988). The biggest difference was the nationalization of the hospitals. The new Labour government's determination to change the old public assistance committees and the system of health insurance was driven more by the class memories and ideological battles of the 1930s than by the 'quickening sense of altruism' during the war, which Titmuss (1950) saw as so central. As we shall see, the history of social policy in the 1940s, 1950s, and 1960s is one of continuous debate about the appropriate extent of state action.

Later in this volume we shall question whether the changes in social policy from 1974 to 1988 do reflect as big a break with the past as is popularly thought. The year 1988 may turn out to mark a more decisive change. In order to put the policy changes of this later period into perspective we shall look at the fluctuations that preceded it and at some of the common themes of debate.

II. COMMON THEMES IN POST-WAR LEGISLATION

Probably the most important social policy of the post-war period was never formulated as legislation—the commitment to a high and stable level of employment. This was spelt out in the 1944 White Paper on *Employment Policy* (Ministry of Reconstruction 1944). It was the essential underpinning for the social security system, which assumed only short-term temporary periods of unemployment, and it provided the essential means for achieving the goals of social solidarity which we find running through the legislation of the period. Thus the welfare state of the 1940s had twin pillars—a commitment to full employment *and* the range of social legislation that came immediately afterwards.

The years irom 1944 to 1948 were remarkable for the range of social legislation that was passed and the profound and lasting effect it had on the structure of social service administration for the next forty years. Merely to list these Acts is to remind ourselves of the significance of this period. The Education Act 1944 established free secondary education as a universal right. It remained, until the Education Reform Act of 1988, the primary statute setting the administrative structure and guiding principles of education policy. The Family Allowances Act 1946 created the first universal cash benefit (for second and subsequent children) paid to the mother. Though extended by the Child Benefit system in 1975, it was this Act which established the principle of paying a *cash* benefit to *mothers* to help defray the costs of a child. The 1946 National Insurance Act did largely implement the structural changes recommended in the Beveridge Report. The Report set out its fundamental principles—flat-rate subsistence benefits (enough to live at a tolerable standard of living), flat-rate contributions, a single unified administrative structure for social insurance, adequate benefits, a scheme that was adjusted to different kinds of employment. Above all it was comprehensive:

It should not leave either to national assistance or to voluntary insurance any risk so general or so uniform that social insurance can be justified. (para. 308)

The insurance scheme is one for all citizens irrespective of their means. (para. 309)

Though *adequacy* of benefits was left to be reached in stages, the Act did essentially legislate the other principles set out by Beveridge. The National Health Service Act 1946 was also, until the 1989 White Paper (DoH 1989*a*) and subsequent legislation, *the* essential foundation stone for the administration of health care in the United Kingdom. In setting out his objectives for the new service to his Cabinet colleagues in 1945, Aneurin Bevan wrote:

We have got to achieve as nearly as possible a uniform standard of service for all and to ensure that an equally good service is available everywhere. (Cabinet minutes for 5 Oct. 1945, quoted by Buxton and Klein 1978)

The National Assistance Act 1948 created a single, national, means-tested allowance available to all those not in employment whose financial resources fell below a standard set by Parliament. The Children's Act of 1948, the Housing Act of 1949, and the Town and Country Planning Act of 1947 complete the list of fundamental and long-lasting statutes.

Since they were all passed in such a short space of time, mainly by one government, they contain common values and assumptions. First, they embodied the principle of a citizen's universal right of access to services of an equal standard regardless of geography or income. This principle differed sharply from practices in the 1930s, against which politicians of the Centre as well as the Left were reacting. There were sharp geographical inequalities. There were the indignities of public assistance. There was unequal access to health care, which depended on gender (women and children had very little access to the national insurance panel doctor), on generation, and on occupation (which affected the financial viability of workers' insurance schemes). These were all strongly felt injustices. Social services were primarily concentrated on some sections of the working class and on men, who were the insurance beneficiaries (Glynn and Oxborrow 1976). But in the new legislation, family allowances went to *all* mothers with two or more children. Every worker had to be a member of the National Insurance scheme. The National Health Service was available for all, not just those below average incomes. The Children's Act created a service for all children in need of care and protection. The Education Act embodied the principle of free secondary education for all. Fees had been charged until then. The aim was to 'widen educational opportunity and at the same time to raise standards' (see Kogan 1978).

The powers given to central departments enabled them to ration resources between local authorities. Local education authorities had to submit development plans to ensure there would be comparable standards of provision in different areas. Capital building was regulated and priorities set by central departments (Griffith 1965). Quotas were set to limit the employment of doctors and teachers in favoured areas. How effective these powers were we shall discuss later.

A second common principle was the setting of minimum standards. The National Insurance scheme sought to ensure that during periods of predictable income loss, when earnings were interrupted because of sickness or unemployment or more permanently after retirement, the citizen's standard of living did not fall below a minimum. Housing and public health legislation and regulations set minimum standards of fitness and overcrowding. Maximum class sizes were set by national regulations. This legislation was not, in short, concerned to create an egalitarian society. Beveridge was absolutely clear on this. Everyone should *contribute* the *same* amount regardless of income, so that all citizens should feel themselves equally entitled to the benefits (this was, of course, a considerable fiction in one sense because the taxpayer was to contribute a substantial portion of the eventual costs under the scheme's actuarial assumptions). However, the purpose and structure of the scheme were not designed to achieve redistribution from the rich to the poor. It *was* designed to achieve redistribution through a family's or individual's lifetime, to even out periods of misfortune or non-earning capacity. Indeed the *inclusion* of the middle classes for the first time as major beneficiaries inevitably made the post-war welfare state even less redistributive in overall terms than its 1930s predecessor, which had embodied the principle of 'targeting'. The point was made powerfully in Abel-Smith's essay (1958) in *Conviction*. Goodin and Le Grand (1987) suggest that middle-class take-over is a common feature of welfare states. Those just excluded from the benefits press to be included and the service gradually becomes more universal. The providing professions such as the doctors in poor areas, despite their leaders' protestations, were happy to have their livelihoods put on a more secure footing by being part of a national service. It was only in the 1950s and 1960s that the Labour Party and academic social reformers came to see equality or redistribution as a goal of the welfare state, distinct, that is, from security and free access, which had been at the centre of campaigns of the 1930s and 1940s.

The structure of the welfare state and its financing mechanisms were ill fitted to deliver equality. They had never been designed to do so. As those on the Left began to expect welfare institutions to deliver egalitarian goals, they were to be increasingly disillusioned (Bosanquet and Townsend 1972; Le Grand 1982).

The third common characteristic of the statutes of this period was stronger central power and administrative rationalization. Beveridge's national scheme replaced a multiplicity of tiny schemes and a mass of administrative complexity. Complex though the modern welfare state may look, it is simplicity itself compared with the schemes that preceded it. Eckstein (1959) maintained this was the main thrust of the reforms. Small district councils lost powers to county and county borough councils. The central departments assumed stronger powers of oversight and direction. Local authorities lost both public assistance powers and their hospitals. Centralization of welfare is nothing new.

So far, we have been concerned with that spate of post-war legislation which has never been matched until 1988. But politics did not stand still in the interim. Indeed, as empire declined and the United Kingdom's international role diminished, 'social politics', as Crosland (1956) the socialist philosopher and politician called it, prospered. Social policy became the stuff of politics. The notion that somehow both parties agreed on the broad structure of the welfare state is far from the case. It may have been true for a time in the early 1960s, but it was never true for the period as a whole. Debates about the appropriate scale of state activity, between universal or targeted benefits, and about the economic impact of social policy recurred throughout.

III. THE SWING OF THE SOCIAL POLICY PENDULUM

Consolidation and reaction: 1948–1951

If the previous three years had been ones of legislative activity, the period from 1948 to 1951 saw a growing economic crisis and relative inactivity in legislative terms. It might be called a period of consolidation. Most of the new services—National Health Service (NHS), National Insurance, National Assistance—came into being on 1 July 1948. They involved a period of enormous administrative upheaval as the new authorities took over responsibility and much wider powers. Meanwhile, however, a political reaction was developing to these big changes. In opposition, the Conservative Party became increasingly critical at the whole trend to welfare statism. This was reflected publicly in their criticism and questioning of ministers in the House of Commons and in public speeches. In the debate on the 1949 devaluation of the pound the main target of attack was not the Chancellor but Aneurin Bevan, whose profligacy as Minister of Health was seen to be the main reason for the country's economic plight. This became a recurrent theme in Conservatives' speeches in the country. Moreover, the Conservative Party was developing a consistent alternative approach to social policy. Two men who later became famous in their own right were at work in the research department of the Conservative Central Office, Ian Macleod and Enoch Powell, both of whom were later to become Ministers of Health. The results of their work could be seen in a pamphlet produced by the Conservative Political Centre called *The Social Services: Needs and Means* (Macleod and Powell 1952). They argued that the multiplication of statutory social services had produced a decline in individual initiative and a reduction of personal and family responsibility. This had led to unnecessarily high levels of taxation and disincentives to work. The trend of post-war legislation had been fundamentally mistaken. Two major weaknesses were identified.

First, policy had moved away from the principle of insurance, for example in the health service, towards increasing levels of Exchequer contributions out of tax. What was needed, they argued, was a return to the insurance principle to finance the NHS. Secondly, they argued that post-war legislation had systematically moved away from charging. Hospital care was free, secondary education was free, and the effect was to involve an element of redistribution from the rich to the poor. This, they argued, should have no place in social policy philosophy. They concluded: 'The question which therefore poses itself is not should a means-test be applied to a social service, but why should any service be provided without a test of need?' Criticism of the way in which social welfare services were developing was summed up in an article by a Cambridge economist in the *Lloyds Bank Review* (Hagenbuch 1953): 'Social services were originally intended to provide services for the poorest members of society; now they have become the providers of universal services, free for everyone, on an ever-increasing scale.' We see developing in the late 1940s an alternative philosophical position. Several studies by economists showed, or purported to show, that there had been a rapid redistribution of income since the 1930s away from the upper income groups. Neither rich nor poor any longer existed in Britain, and indeed, if the process of redistribution continued, the economic health of the country would be endangered. The Labour Party responded to these kinds of attack by defending rather uncritically the institutions it had created. The new social services, it was often implied, were well-nigh perfect. They had eliminated poverty. They would provide a better life if only the Conservatives would leave them alone.

Retrenchment: 1951–1958

The return of the Conservative government in 1951 was part of the reassertion of individualistic values and the shift away from the universalist model of social policy. The government began a whole series of policy reviews attempting to reflect that shift of emphasis. The government set up a Committee of Enquiry on the cost of the NHS. The aim was to see what limitations could be placed on the growth of health expenditure, of which the Conservatives had been critical in opposition. They set up a parallel Committee of Enquiry to consider financial provisions for old age. The first committee was chaired by a Cambridge economist, Professor Guillebaud. The second looked at provision for the elderly, and an internal review was being undertaken on housing policy. It was the first to report. A White Paper on housing in 1953 set out a long-term strategy for Conservative housing policy: *Houses: The Next Step* (MHLG 1953). The aim was to reduce drastically the role of local authorities in housing provision and to rely instead on the private market to meet the needs of working people who required rented accommodation. Councils should be confined, it argued, to the role of replacing unfit property, and the free market should be re-established in private rented accommodation. The Phillips Committee (Ministry of Social Security 1954) recommended the government abandon any long-term aim of raising retirement pensions to a subsistence or adequacy level. It argued that in view of the rising numbers of retirement pensioners this would present an unduly heavy burden on the Exchequer. It was accepted by government twelve years after the Beveridge Report had been published. His essential principle was abandoned. Flat-rate benefits were no longer to be gradually raised to subsistence level. Instead, pensioners who had to rely on state aid alone would have their pensions brought to subsistence level by the National Assistance Board. The government's housing White Paper was followed by two complementary measures, the first was the withdrawal of council house subsidies by the Exchequer except in instances where local authorities were to replace slums or provide accommodation for old people. This process was begun in 1956. In the following year the Rent Act 1957 decontrolled higher-rented properties and provided for the gradual decontrol of any unfurnished property when a tenant moved. The aim was to restore, over a period, free market forces in housing once again.

It is enough to note here that at least for a period the government succeeded in checking the rising cost of Exchequer aid to local authorities for housing. Even while the Guillebaud Committee was sitting the government·had put a strict limit on NHS spending, and in the early 1950s the proportion of the Gross National Product (GNP) devoted to health fell year by year. All these measures can therefore be seen as part and parcel of an attempt to reduce the scale of state activity, which has close parallels to what Mrs Thatcher's administration was attempting to do thirty years later. In 1957/8 the government sought to reduce public spending on the social services still further. The White Paper on *Local Government Finance* (MHLG 1957) argued that percentage grants should be replaced because they encouraged too much local authority spending. Under this system local authorities were given grants that met a percentage of their spending on a particular service. Under the new arrangement a flat sum of money would be given for a range of services in the hope that those authorities who spent more would be discouraged from doing so since the grant would not rise to meet additional spending. The National Insurance Act of 1959 introduced graduated contributions, which were an attempt to raise more money to meet the cost of pensions without putting an additional burden on general taxation. Thus for a period there was a real attempt to hold down the scale of welfare state spending, as two decades or more later. However, the commitment to full employment was still strong. Anything else was seen to be political suicide. Hence the active reflation that followed any rise in the number of unemployed.

Restriction on social service spending in the early 1950s was beginning to show its effects in increasing frustration and criticisms of the welfare system. In 1956 the Guillebaud Committee reported, and although its original intention had been to suggest areas for economy, what it did, in fact, was to suggest that the NHS was being *starved* of funds and that more should be spent on it. Unlike the Phillips Committee, which had drawn on advice from within government, the Guillebaud Committee had gone outside to appoint as its advisers the new Professor of Social Administration at the London School of Economics, Professor Richard Titmuss, and a young research worker called Brian Abel-Smith. The evidence which they presented to the Committee, and which can be read summarized at the beginning of the report, drew attention to the fact that the NHS was taking a declining share of the GNP, lower even than in the 1930s. This neglect was nowhere more obvious than in hospital building. No new hospital had been built since the war and capital expenditure was running at about a third of the level achieved by the numerous voluntary hospitals and small local authorities throughout the country in the 1930s. The Guillebaud Committee (MoH 1956) therefore recommended a major new hospital-building programme and the retention of the NHS on broadly the same pattern as then existed. Enoch Powell, the backroom boy in Central Office who had doubted the wisdom of the NHS, announced in 1962 the largest hospital-building programme since the Victorian era.

Expansion and convergence: 1959–1970

This was the first example of many committees of enquiry that were to focus attention on deficiencies in service provision and propose improve-

ments. The organized providing professions—the BMA, the Royal Colleges, the teachers' unions, the local authority associations—mobilized
opinion and built links with the spending departments (Kogan 1978; Klein
1983; Beer 1982). The spending departments appointed a series of expert
committees which produced volumes of research and began to win support in Cabinet (Heclo and Wildavsky 1974). After the Suez fiasco, social
politics moved to the centre of the stage. The new generation of social
scientists began to explore educational opportunity and the outcome of
the 1944 Education Act (Floud, Halsey, and Martin 1956), the reality of
family life and the incomes of old people (Townsend 1957), the declining
nutritional standards of families (Lambert 1964), and the extent of family
poverty (Abel-Smith and Townsend 1965). Above all it was a period of
major demographic change. After fears of population decline in the
1940s, births rose steadily. The number of schoolchildren began to rise.
More children stayed on longer at school. More acquired qualifications
that would gain entry to universities if only the places were available. The
Russians' successful launch of the first space satellite provoked fears of a
Soviet domination and set off a rise in scientific and education spending
throughout the Western world.

The elderly who had acquired rights under the post-war legislation
were reaching retiring age. The country would be asked to deliver the
fruits of those reforms and they would be costly. Thus, despite a decade
in which a Conservative government had sought to contain and reduce
social spending, and with initial success, the dam began to break in the
late 1950s and finally gave way in the early 1960s. If any period fits the
myth it is this. It was the period of expansion for higher education, and of
massive council-house building. The reorganization of the social work
services and the NHS was largely bipartisan.

Re-establishing the private sector aborted: 1970–1974

Yet this period was relatively brief. In opposition in the late 1960s, the
Conservatives began to develop a divergent philosophy reminiscent of
the late 1940s. The public sector was making excessive demands on the
economy. Levels of personal taxation were too high. Taxable capacity
was insufficient to finance major improvements in *all* the social services.
It was therefore better to concentrate public funds on the major services
for which there was at present no private alternative—health and education. But in the fields of income maintenance and housing, measures were
taken to build up alternatives to public provision. The two major Acts
which gave legislative form to this new strategy were the Housing Finance
Act of 1972 and the Pensions Act of 1973. The Housing Finance Act was
designed to end the complex system of general Exchequer aid to housing
authorities based on the number of houses they had built at various times

in the past and replace it by a government subsidy which would give aid only to poorer tenants. A national system of reasonable rents would be fixed and rent rebates and allowances given to poorer tenants. This was accompanied by a policy of selling council houses to tenants to reduce the stock of public housing in general. In parallel with this was the Pensions Act. Its purpose was to rely on private occupational pension schemes. These would be regulated by government but provision would be private. In the long run this would mean a declining role for National Insurance and leave employers with the primary responsibility for providing pensions for their workers. Thus, the twin strategies of a more managerial structure in the NHS and local government and the stabilization and long-term reduction of spending on housing and pensions did constitute a coherent selective strategy. In the end the pensions legislation was never implemented. It was to have come into force in 1975, but by that time a Labour government had taken office and repealed it. The housing legislation was also repealed by the incoming Labour government and there followed a brief last fling for that part of the 1960s agenda that remained uncompleted. Child Benefit replaced tax relief for children, a major new pensions scheme was introduced. House-building increased. The economic crisis of 1976 put an end to all that.

Social policy and the role of the state

Social policy, in short, has always been controversial, but in the 1960s and 1970s it became more so. The Labour Party moved from espousing a basic citizenship model of welfare to more egalitarian aspirations, abolishing grammar schools, toying with positive discrimination, and introducing measures to redistribute health-care resources more equally and to abolish tax reliefs for children, all measures which began to hurt middle-class, middle-income voters and articulate professionals. Above all, the rising tax rates began to hit not merely average earners but poor ones too. The Conservatives had several times sought to push back the scope of state provision, to re-establish the market in private rented houses and occupational pensions. Yet, the reality was that a quarter of the population worked in the public sector, about half the population drew some kind of benefit, and most received services in kind. Though people objected to high taxes, they would also object to their jobs and services being attacked. That would be the balancing trick government would have to try as their predecessors had.

The scale of the social service sector

Behind the political rhetoric and the swing of political intentions, there were major social and economic changes in progress that drove social spending along, and economic crises which restrained it. From any perspective, the growth of the social welfare sector in the United Kingdom was spectacular. From the turn of the century, when social provision consisted largely of poor-law provisions and elementary education, there were added health care, insurance benefits, and public housing. All these services were at first for the poor, but later (as we have described) they became universal in scope. The share of the nation's income that was taxed away or borrowed to finance education, housing, health, income maintenance, and social care services grew from about 2.6 per cent at the beginning of the century to about 25 per cent in the mid-1970s when this study begins (see Fig. 2.1).

In one important respect these figures are misleading. They do not mean that 25 per cent of the nation's economic production in 1976 was taken up providing social welfare services. Roughly half that total was allocated to cash benefits. These transfer payments were used to buy goods and services in the market economy and it was these transfer items that had increased fastest. The use of real resources by the welfare sector had remained much more stable as a share of the total economic activity (see Table 2.1). Nevertheless, over the period since the Second World War, roughly half of the additional purchasing power of the nation had gone to buy public services of one kind or another and a rising share of these had been social services. As can be seen from Table 2.2, this

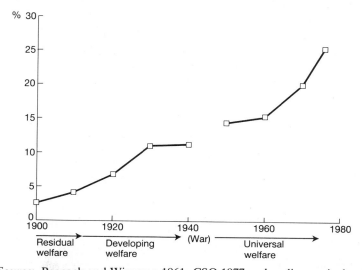

Source: Peacock and Wiseman 1961; CSO 1977 and earlier equivalents

Fig. 2.1. Social spending and the economy: the cost of social services as a percentage of GDP

Table 2.1. *Social services and the economy*

	1951	1961	1971	1981
Final consumption of goods and services and capital formation as % of GDP:				
All general government	25.4	22.3	26.1	29.3
Social services	9.9	9.5	12.4	15.1
Current government grants to personal sector as % of personal income	6.0	7.5	10.0	11.4

Sources: CSO 1983 and earlier equivalents.

Table 2.2. *Social expenditures[a] in OECD countries as percentage of GDP, 1960 and 1981[b]*

	1960	1981
Denmark	n.a.	33.3
Germany	20.5	31.5
Austria	17.9	27.7
Belgium	17.4	37.6
Italy	16.8	29.1
Netherlands	16.2	36.1
Sweden	15.4	33.4
Finland	15.4	25.9
United Kingdom	13.9	23.7
France	13.4	29.5
New Zealand	13.0	19.6
Canada	12.1	21.5
Ireland	11.7	28.4
Norway	11.7	27.1
United States	10.9	20.8
Australia	10.2	18.8
Greece	8.5	13.4
Japan	8.0	17.5
Switzerland	7.7	14.9
OECD average (unweighted)	13.1	25.6

[a] Direct public expenditure on education, health services, pensions, unemployment compensation and other income maintenance programmes, and welfare services. Note that housing is excluded from this list, in contrast to the treatment of welfare services elsewhere in this book.

[b] Or nearest available year.

Source: OECD 1985: table 1.

pattern of growth in the United Kingdom was very much in line (between 1960 and 1981, at least) with the experience in other OECD countries. Indeed, the share of GDP taken by 'social expenditures' (excluding housing) in the United Kingdom had fallen slightly behind the OECD average by 1981, having been very close to it in 1960.

Numerous 'explanations' of the 'inevitability' of this process were advanced by sociologists, political scientists, Marxists, and—rather tardily, considering the scale of the economic activity involved—economists. The literature of the time was succinctly reviewed by Judge (1982). Sociologists naturally concentrated on fundamental social changes that were tending to increase the scale of dependency—the extension of childhood and the reasons for the growth of an isolated elderly population in a mobile industrial society, the housing problems associated with urbanization. Much of this work assumed a logically untenable position that such 'problems' in some way required a collective or state response, whereas in fact different societies had responded in divergent ways and at different points in the process of industrialization. Political scientists tended to emphasize the pluralist bargaining process and the politics of budgeting. Once a public agency was created, it grew in an incremental way. Bureaucrats and service providers had privileged access to legislators and were able to establish a habit of growth (Wildavsky 1964; Niskanen 1971). Increasingly, these theoretical accounts came to emphasize the problems, the costs, and the potential crisis of funding that would arise if such growth continued (O'Connor 1973; Gough 1979; Beer 1982; Wright 1980). These accounts came to seem increasingly plausible as the first oil crisis hit the world's economies.

Perhaps the best way to incorporate all these strands of literature into a simple model is to see the process in terms of demand and supply factors interacting in the political market-place (Breton 1974). We can begin by taking as given the fact that certain services have traditionally come to be seen as appropriate for government either to provide or to finance. Demand for those services will be affected by factors very similar to those that affect the demand for any good or service—the number of people who wish to buy that service, the age group concerned, the incomes of those who have to pay, the taxpayers, their preferences for that service compared with others they could buy, and the cost of the services or their supply price.

If we further assume a competitive political process in which alternative political parties are competing for votes, it is possible to envisage voters being offered a variety of potential policy bundles, some involving more extensive or higher-quality services with higher rates of tax, or less extensive benefits and lower taxes. Where a citizen's ideal bundle differs from this the more coerced he or she will feel and switch his or her vote.

In practice, there are difficulties with this model, not least that elections are fought on issues other than social policy, but for much of the period we have been discussing, social policy *was* at the centre of politics. Again, the market is imperfect. Some voters have more power than others in the market-place because of their control of information and leverage. Service providers are in a good position to control information and manipulate it to advocate higher spending, reinforcing clients' demands. Some consumers have more effective watch-dogs. Some are less powerful. But over time the range of social-policy-based pressure groups grew and articulated group demands more effectively.

During the thirty years after the Second World War the population who stood to benefit most from public services—those of school age and over retirement age—grew faster than the population as a whole. In 1951 the number of people over the age of 65 constituted 11 per cent of the population. By 1971 the figure had risen to 13 per cent and would rise to 15 per cent in 1986. The population of compulsory school age (5–14 inclusive) was 14 per cent of the population in 1951 and 16 per cent in 1971, and that does not take into account the big increase in voluntary staying-on beyond the compulsory age.

At the same time the supply price was rising. As real increases in society at large rose so the labour-intensive social services had to raise the salaries they offered to remain competitive in the tight labour market. The relative price of social services thus increased. The same applied to benefit rates. Merely to hold benefits stable in real terms produced a decline in the relative purchasing power of pensions, for example. Economic growth did not make financing the social services easier as social democrats had hoped. The tax price of providing a larger basket of social service goods grew too. This might slow the demand for additional social services, but so long as a large range of services were provided free at the point of use and the political market was used to determine their supply, many politicians and economists feared that the scale of state activity would drift steadily upwards. It was only, some felt, by removing service provision from the voter market-place altogether that this could be avoided. Thus, privatization would be needed to achieve a really decisive reduction in the role of the state.

IV. OUTCOMES

Clearly one element on the demand side was the voters' perception of the quality of the output they were buying. Increasingly, a view gained ground that the quality of public services was not keeping pace with that in the private sector or with past standards in the public sector. This was perhaps most true of public housing, but it also extended to schools and local authority services more generally and the Supplementary Benefit system. The perception was aided by proponents of social welfare themselves producing a continual stream of criticisms of the failings of social welfare institutions. Most often these were couched in terms of their failure to achieve a more equal distribution of income or educational attainments. We have suggested earlier that equality had not been one of the main goals of the post-war legislators, but this literature did serve to reinforce the sense of failure. (For a critical but balanced review of the period, see Abel-Smith 1983; and Klein and O'Higgins 1985.)

In fact, measured against the kinds of objectives the politicians of the mid-1940s had set themselves, the achievements of these thirty years were considerable (George and Wilding 1984; Wilding 1986). As Bradshaw and Deacon (1986) point out, egalitarian goals were discussed very little in the debates on National Insurance. James Griffiths, in his second reading speech, saw the purpose as the creation of a 'National Minimum Standard'. The means-tested National Assistance and Supplementary Benefit schemes *were* to play a much larger role than Griffiths or Beveridge envisaged. But to a large extent, up to the mid-1970s cash benefits did manage to provide a floor under those whose income in the market-place would have been minimal. Supplementary Benefit and retirement pensions sustained their purchasing power relative to male manual earnings. That is to say, they roughly doubled in real terms. In 1973 the average private or original income of the poorest tenth of all households in Great Britain was about £19 *a year*—most, remember, were pensioners. The income of the next decile was £283 a year (CSO 1974). If we look at the situation *after* the welfare state did its job and we include benefits in cash and kind we find the poorest tenth of households had a standard of living not of £19 a year but of £777, and the next decile an income of £896 a year, not a princely sum even in 1973 but a lot better than without the welfare state. This is a vivid illustration of Griffiths's National Minimum. What had been achieved was not equality, but a floor nevertheless. As Townsend, Walker, and Lawson's study (1983) of European systems showed, the British social security system was more successful than most others in putting an effective National Minimum in place, albeit at a fairly tough poverty standard.

The same kind of story can be told of housing. If we take a combination of measures of inadequate housing—more than one household sharing a dwelling, overcrowding at $1\frac{1}{2}$ persons to a room, or lack of a basic amenity—we find from the 1951 Census that 70 per cent of all households suffered from at least one deficiency. By 1976 that was true of only 15 per cent of households. Indicators of maternal mortality, infant mortality, and perinatal mortality, all of which reflect on the standards of health provision as well as on nutrition and social conditions, had fallen dramatically in the thirty years. From 80 deaths of mothers per 100,000 live and still births in 1951 the figure fell to 14 in 1979, for example. In 1950 only one primary class in three had thirty pupils or less. By the mid-1970s the figure was more than two in three.

By the mid-1970s, however, people had come to demand more. It was not that the social services were failing to meet the objectives of the 1940s. The question was, how far were they meeting the new objectives of the 1970s and 1980s?

V. OTHER 'STATES OF WELFARE'

So far we have been largely concerned with describing changes in the state's role either in providing cash benefits itself and in providing services, or in regulating the private sector, for example occupational pensions. For much of the early period after the Second World War state provision in cash and kind *was* 'the welfare state' as popularly perceived. Gradually, however, it came to be understood that there were other 'states of welfare' (Digby 1989). There were other ways in which resources were allocated by the state to perform the same kind of functions as the formal welfare services. Not the least of these was tax relief for children, housing, and pension contributions (Titmuss 1958). Though voluntary or non-statutory non-profit organizations had long been part of the academic study of social policy, the shift in political preferences in the 1970s and 1980s was to concentrate much more attention on to the role they played and could play. The Wolfenden Committee (1978) set out the modern case for an enlarged and active voluntary sector. Then again, families and local informal support by friends and neighbours came to be seen as part of the fabric of welfare. This was fostered by a political suspicion of large bureaucracies on the Left of politics and a dislike of state provision on the Right. By the beginning of our period of study in the mid-1970s the welfare state began to be portrayed as a rather old-fashioned concept. The wave of the future lay with care by 'informal networks', 'voluntary action', and families as well as the private sector. All had the common attraction that they did not apparently need taxpayer's support. Here, at last, was something for nothing. The attraction of the idea grew through the 1980s.

The problem was that, though politicians might have forgotten about such forms of support, they had always taken a large part of the strain and cost of caring. It was their weakness that had, in many instances, brought the statutory services into being in the first place. How much scope for expansion was there in these other states of welfare?

VI. IN BRIEF

● In the period since the end of the Second World War there had been continuous debate about the scope and scale of public provision in the social services. It never was a period of consensus, but the economic crisis in the mid-1970s was to sharpen and deepen that debate. Much had also been achieved in those post-war years. We now go on to consider the changing goals of social policy in the 1970s and 1980s and the outcomes service by service. We begin with education.

3

Education and the Welfare State: Does it Add Up?

Howard Glennerster and William Low

I. GOALS AND POLICIES

This is not the place to begin a long philosophical discussion about the aims and purposes of education in a modern society. None the less, the aims and objectives of education are central to any evaluation of public spending on the service over the past two decades and they pose special difficulties. Education, more than any other of the services we discuss in this volume, provokes disagreement not just about means but about ends. No unambiguous statement of goals is possible. Different participants in the education process differ on the weight they give to divergent objectives. Using an economic framework we may distinguish the private benefits that education confers on people and the wider public benefits that are less easily produced for particular individuals. Education and training will probably increase a person's earning capacity. In the words of the Robbins Report on higher education (DES 1963), education 'imparts skills suitable to play a part in the general division of labour' (para. 25). But individuals may also enjoy learning, gaining the capacity to indulge in a wider range of leisure or cultural pursuits. As leisure time grows and working life shortens these may become of growing significance. If this were all there were to education it might well be left to the private market-place. Yet we collectively gain from living in a well-educated and law-abiding society in which others are able to converse with us, enjoy music and the theatre, and go about their lives peaceably. Society at large derives both production and social benefits from its schools and colleges (Barr 1987). Left to themselves, individuals might not invest sufficiently in their own or their children's education to reap these benefits, especially if their educational experience has been limited. It seems plausible to argue that any economy needs a critical mass of highly educated people to develop in a sophisticated way. Scientific, medical, or even economic research can increase production possibilities and the quality of life. Research findings are public goods which cannot simply be bought and held exclusively by a particular person or company. Public funding becomes necessary.

The American historian Martin Weiner (1981) has argued that Britain's economic decline can be traced to an élite culture essentially hostile to productive goals and industrialization. Such hostile values permeated our education system. These attitudes were common to aristocrats, traditional conservatives, liberals, and romantic socialists alike. As we shall see, the 1976 economic crisis forced both Labour and Conservative governments to take this message to heart. Both tried to shift the balance of emphasis towards economic goals (Marquand 1988).

Nevertheless, there are other kinds of goals that schools are called upon to pursue. To quote the Robbins Report again, society has an interest in ensuring 'the transmission of a common culture and common strands of citizenship' (para. 28).

One driving force behind the 1944 Education Act (see Chapter 2 above) had been belief that education was responsible for unnecessary social divisions but could become a force for social unity. The 1943 Coalition White Paper put it thus: 'Social unity within the education system . . . would open the way to a more closely knit society' (Board of Education 1943: para. 1). Tawney (1931) had expressed this view with typical fervour:

The fundamental aim of education is not difficult to state. It is simple because the needs of those it is designed to meet have themselves a terrible simplicity. Every year a new race of 400,000 souls slips quietly into the United Kingdom—the purpose of the educationalist is to aid their growth. It should be easy to regard them, not as employers or workmen or masters and servants or rich and poor, but merely as human beings. Here, if anywhere, the spirit of equality might be expected to establish its Kingdom. (p. 141)

Thus, any position on the map of educational values (Fig. 3.1) is possible. Some occupy a position at the north-western corner. For them, education is mainly about improving one's own or the population's earning capacity. At the other extreme, some believe that schools and colleges should be primarily concerned with promoting social equality. Politicians may differ from teachers, and the profession and politicians differ amongst themselves, while parents also take very different views. It is this very diversity of objectives and values that leads Coons and Sugarman (1978) to argue that parents are the best judges and should be free to choose any content for their children's schooling they wish. This runs counter to the belief that one of education's main purposes should be to build citizenship and social cohesion. This basic philosophical tension has been evident throughout the period of study, not just between governments but within the present Conservative government's own legislative programme. The Education Act 1988 seeks both to extend government control over what schools teach *and* to promote parental choice (Glennerster, Power, and Travers 1989).

In short, any unambiguous statement about the efficiency of education becomes impossible. So much depends on the value positions of the

Private benefits

Public benefits

Conservative/
liberal
values

Production
Preparation for work,
enhanced earning capacity.
(Rate of return to
education as a measure.)

Consumption
Education of one's children
with social equals. Present
pleasure, potential future
non-monetary gains from
extended leisure pursuits.
Simple capacity to acquire
knowledge. (Largely
immeasurable.)

Production
General benefit from a
highly trained labour force
with skills not specific to
one firm. Scientific and
other research with
commercial or industrial
applications. (Largely
immeasurable.)

Social goods
Respect for law and order;
socialization into existing
norms and values;
transmitting cultural
heritage; occupational
mobility and positions
open to the most able; an
informed electorate, mutual
benefits derived from living
in a culturally rich society;
promoting equal access
to education and a sense
of social justice; social
cohesion and a sense
of shared citizenship;
promoting social and racial
equality. (Some can be
measured.)

Private/public values

FIG. 3.1. An education values map: potential benefits from education

readers and their interpretations of what governments have really wanted to achieve. We seek to distinguish areas of policy where there has been some political consensus from those where there has not.

Convergent political concerns: basic standards and vocational 'relevance'

One striking feature of the period, especially since 1976, has been the extent to which common themes emerge. The economic crisis seems to have been the catalyst. Labour and Conservative governments became more concerned with shifting the emphasis to the productive goals of education—preparation for work, training, and modernizing the economy. Both produced White Papers which said very similar things:

Young people need to reach maturity with a basic understanding of the economy and its activities, especially manufacturing industry, which are necessary for the creation of Britain's economic wealth. (DES 1977*a*)

By the time they leave school, pupils need to have acquired, far more than at present, the qualities and skills required for work in a technological age. (DES 1985*a*)

The Government believes that it is vital for our higher education to contribute more effectively to the improvement of the performance of the economy. (DES 1985*b*)

If these statements represent a bipartisan shift in the values of governments, a similar cross-party concern was emerging about basic standards and the content of schooling. The Black Papers (Cox and Dyson 1969) caught press attention.

There appeared to be some basis for these fears in the results of the DES's own regular national monitoring of reading standards. This had been undertaken ever since the Second World War, usually on a four-yearly basis. The results reported from 1948 to 1964 showed a steady improvement (DES 1966). The average reading age of 11-year-olds had improved by 17 months and 15-year-olds by 20 to 30 months over that period. The 1971 results (Start and Wells 1972) appeared to show that reading standards had ceased to rise and at junior level had fallen slightly. The caveats in the research report were largely ignored. Mrs Thatcher, as Secretary of State for Education, appointed the Bullock Committee to investigate. Its Report (DES 1975) threw considerable doubt on the more alarmist inferences. Amongst a whole number of difficulties was the fact that many more children now found the tests, originally set in 1948, *too easy*. Many scores were bunched about the 100 per cent mark, creating a 'ceiling effect'. The best children could not get higher marks and thus pull up the mean scores.

There was other evidence. A study in Aberdeen (Nisbet, Watt, and Welsh 1972) analysed trends in reading standards by the social class of children's parents and found that, while children from professional and managerial homes had improved their standards, those from the lowest social status groups had declined. This could scarcely be blamed on the ceiling effect! Work in the education priority areas suggested this effect might be more widespread. The new Labour government in 1974 set up both the Assessment of Performance Unit to mount regular monitoring exercises across a range of subject areas and a unit to study ways of improving standards achieved by children suffering from various social disadvantages (DES 1974). After the economic crisis in 1976 concern about standards and economic failure came together.

In a well-publicized speech on 8 October 1976 at Ruskin College, James Callaghan, the new Prime Minister, both accepted that there was concern about basic standards of attainment and linked that with complaints by employers about the educational standards of young employees. A series of regional conferences was organized under the grandiloquent title of a 'Great Debate' about education. The DES began to work towards building a consensus around the notion of a common curriculum (DES 1978, 1979, 1985*d*). As a DES Consultation Document (1987*a*) put it:

Since Sir James Callaghan's speech as Prime Minister at Ruskin College in 1976, successive Secretaries of State have aimed to achieve agreement with their partners in the education service on policies for the School Curriculum which will develop the potential of all pupils and equip them for the responsibilities of citizenship and for the challenges of employment in tomorrow's world. (para. 4)

The time was ripe for the central department to pursue a long-term interest in the curriculum followed by schools that dated back to Sir David Eccles's attempt to create a curriculum study group in the old Ministry of Education in 1962. The origins of the National Curriculum and the assessment targets legislated in the 1988 Education Act can be traced to the Ruskin speech. So too can the concern with vocational relevance. A Committee of Enquiry was appointed by Callaghan to investigate mathematics teaching. It reported in 1982 (DES 1982). A substantial section was devoted to the needs of employers and the relevance of a mathematical training to the future needs of the economy. Junior ministers in the Labour government extended the message of relevance from schools to higher education: 'The economic difficulties of the country require an education system producing people the country really needs' (Crowther-Hunt's speech to the Association of Teachers in Technical Institutions, 24 May 1975).

Also of long-term significance was the creation of the Manpower Services Commission in 1974. Legislated by the Heath government, it was set up by the new Labour government. Its aim was to co-ordinate and develop a national strategy for vocational training previously pursued disparately by separate Industrial Training Boards. We discuss below its rapid development as a countervailing influence to the DES.

A centralizing tendency

Looking back over these areas of policy development we can trace, in common with other areas of social policy, a growing centralizing tendency. We see both a declining emphasis on public-sector provision *and* a growth in the role of central government promoting and implementing social policy (Glennerster, Power, and Travers 1989). It is a tendency that can be traced, as we have just illustrated, through both Labour and Conservative periods, though it becomes even more evident after 1985. The 1988 Education Act extends the nascent trends we have found in our period of study. It legislates for a National Curriculum whose content and assessment will be determined ultimately by the Secretary of State for Education. Under the 1944 Education Act these powers were pluralistically spread between governing bodies of schools, universities, examining bodies of various kinds, and above all heads of departments in schools. The University Funding Council appointed by the Secretary of State is to exert much tighter control on the nature of activities undertaken in universities. An uncertain but probably significant number of schools will come under the direct funding and potential control of the Secretary of State and his equivalent in Scotland.

It may seem paradoxical that a government dedicated to reducing the role of the state should be actively extending the powers of central government. Some see this as a strategy to curb the most active exponents of state expansion—the local authorities (Dearlove 1979; Newton and Karran 1985; Travers 1986). Another interpretation is possible. It lies nearer to public choice theory and the economics of bureaucracy. The hypothesis is that until the middle of the 1970s central departments in the United Kingdom, because of the nature of central–local relations, had a significant role to play in steering social policy through the activities of local government. Central departments created the 'Framework for Expansion', to use the title of Mrs Thatcher's education White Paper in 1972 (DES 1972). Local authorities merely filled it in. This gave central departments a major role. When education and housing capital spending was cut so severely, that part over which central departments had most say was cut most. There was, quite simply, very little left for the central departments to do! It is therefore not surprising that we find both education and other ministries looking for ways to justify their existence.

Divergent goals

Labour   Some differences between the parties remained. Looking back to the beginning of the 1974 Labour government, the Queen's Speech (12 March 1974) is reminiscent of a bygone age. It set the goal of a nation-wide system of free nursery education for all who wanted it.This echoed a commitment in Mrs Thatcher's own last expansionist White Paper (DES 1972). The system of mandatory grants was to be extended to Higher National Diploma and teacher-training courses. The Houghton Commit-tee recommended a major increase in teachers' salaries. The stock of teachers to be employed was to rise to 510,000 to ensure there would be no classes over thirty in primary or secondary schools. Circular 7/74 stated that the government expected all local authorities to avoid the selection of children at eleven plus. Grammar schools would go. When not all local education authorities (LEAs) obliged, the Education Act of 1976 required them to submit plans to the Department of Education to create a comprehensive system of schools. Grants to the Direct Grant Grammar Schools were phased out from 1976 onwards. Most of the schools became independent. Over a quarter, mainly Catholic, became LEA comprehensive schools. The government's plan to give grants to schoolchildren from low-income families to encourage them to stay at school had to be scrapped because of expenditure constraints. There was considerable concern about the poor achievements of West Indian chil-dren, not least expressed by organizations representing West Indian pa-rents. The House of Commons Select Committee on Race Relations called for a high-level inquiry. One was appointed, reporting finally in 1985 (DES 1985*c*). Another committee on special education for handicap-ped children was also appointed, chaired by Mary Warnock. Finally, a new capital building programme was to renovate and replace all old secondary schools.

Conservative   The first post-1979 Conservative administration did set a new direction for education policy, but only of a relatively modest kind. One of its first acts was to repeal the 1976 legislation compelling local authorities to go comprehensive. A new scheme of direct financial sup-port for independent schools was introduced to replace the direct-grant system. It was called the 'assisted places scheme', and under it selected private schools could offer places to children and charge reduced fees related to the income of the parents. The difference between those fees and the normal ones could be recovered from central government. The scheme began in a small way in September 1981; 5,300 places were made available but only 4,200 were taken up. Nevertheless, by 1987/8 the scheme offered 33,200 places. The eventual target was 35,000. The government claimed a 98 per cent take-up and that 40 per cent of pupils were receiving full fee remission.

The explicit goal of this policy was to widen the range of choice available to parents with lower incomes and with able children. Legislation in 1980 strengthened parents' rights to choose between state schools. At the same time, the duty of local authorities to provide nursery education was removed and LEAs were pressed to close schools and school places made unnecessary by declining numbers, pressures that tended to reduce effective choice. However, these were all relatively marginal changes. The years 1979–85 marked the end of the old order and a pause before the new thrust of Conservative ideas produced in the 1987 Election Manifesto and embodied in the 1988 Education Reform Act. The Act contained five main elements:

1. National Curriculum and common assessment targets set for children nation-wide, to be examined at ages 7, 11, 14, and the last year of schooling.
2. Provision for schools to opt out of local authority control and to be funded directly from central government.
3. Universities were to be funded by a Funding Council which would expect them to meet set conditions. Under separate proposals, students would be offered top-up loans while grants were limited (DES 1988*b*). Tenure for new academic staff ceased.
4. Polytechnics also became independent institutions.
5. The Inner London Education Authority was abolished.

These major changes would take a long time to have their full effects.

II. EXPENDITURE TRENDS

Theories of resources allocation

So far we have argued that there was a good deal more in common between the Labour and Conservative education policies than is often supposed. Can the same be said of public spending priorities?

There is a substantial body of literature which tends to suggest that public spending priorities have more to do with interdepartmental rivalries and broad economic trends than with party politics. With the exception of housing expenditure, which did vary between governments, the incrementalist pattern had applied to British social policy since 1950 (Judge 1982). Significant and similar rates of expansion in educational spending had occurred under all previous governments from the mid-1950s onwards, as the school population rose and as governments sought to reduce class sizes and improve buildings and equipment. Between 1950 and 1974 volume expenditure on education had trebled. Annual growth rates in the 1950s averaged 4.5 per cent, rising to 5.2 per cent in the 1960s (Peston 1982). Education spending was equivalent to 3.3 per cent of Gross Domestic Product (GDP) in 1950, 4.1 per cent in 1960, 5.8 per cent in 1970, and was 6.5 per cent in 1973/4. It is against this background of a generation of fast growth that we have to judge the impact of the cuts that came in the mid-1970s.

Until recently, nearly all the academic literature which sought to explain patterns of public spending has concentrated on explaining its growth (see a special edition of *Journal of Public Economics* devoted to theories of budgeting and public expenditure growth, no. 28 (1985)). More recently, various attempts have been made to analyse the politics of cuts. One early view was that the need to cut spending would break the pattern of incremental budgeting and bureaucratic bargaining which Wildavsky (1964) had observed, followed by many others. In its place, it was argued, departments would be forced to be more rational and analytical, reconsidering the goals of policy more rigorously (Hinings *et al.* 1980). Others argued that bureaucratic politics would simply be played out differently (Glennerster 1980). More formally, this theory predicted that bureaucrats would seek to minimize the long-term impact on the public service jobs and minimize bureaucratic stress, the pain of their own jobs. Cuts were more likely in capital expenditure than in current spending, which would involve staff. It was hypothesized that the principle of 'equal pain for all' would be more likely to apply to budget cuts than to major strategic changes in priorities. Budget shares would remain stable. Later commentators have argued that this was likely only as a temporary adjustment phase. In the longer term, if cuts continued, major changes of direction would take place.

Another prediction is suggested by public choice theory. Le Grand and Winter (1987) hypothesize that politicians will seek to minimize vote loss, first by modifying expenditure patterns so as to minimize the dissatisfaction of potential users by cutting services with lowest demand or demographic need. This will minimize the loss of service that voters perceive. They also predict that middle-class voters will exercise greater influence on the actual services which they use most or of which they are predominant suppliers. These will fare better in the battle for funds. Their modelling of this hypothesis suggested that middle-class-user services had been given preference by the first Conservative administration after 1979 but not in the previous Labour period. Education is a prime example of a middle-class-user service. On the Le Grand and Winter model, we should therefore expect university spending to do particularly well. With these models in mind we can begin to analyse the changes in public spending on education that took place from 1973/4 through to 1985/6 and beyond.

Resource allocation in practice

Education entered the bargaining arena in a poor strategic position. Whether in terms of a pure rational planning model or vote-loss minimizing, demography was not on its side (Fig. 3.2). The primary-school age group was falling fast, to recover only slightly by the mid-1980s. Though still rising in the 1970s, the secondary age group was set to fall after 1980, and steeply at that. It was only the 18–24-year-old age group that was rising until the mid-1980s. Only a few of that age group were in education and there was no statutory commitment to provide any particular level of access. In contrast, other services, such as health, could point to a demographic case for higher spending. The outcome can be seen from the last two columns of Table 3.1. Education spending fell as a share both of all public expenditure and of GDP. In 1973/4 education took over 13 per cent of all public expenditure. This share fell to about 12 per cent by the

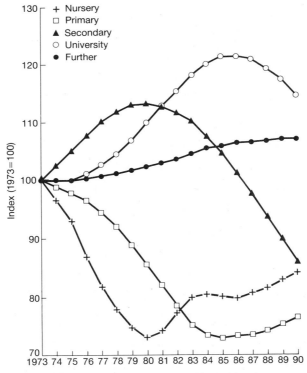

FIG. 3.2. Demographic change in educational groups

Table 3.1. *Real public expenditure on education, United Kingdom* (£ billion at 1987/8 prices, adjusted by GDP deflator)[a]

| | Current (net) | | | | | | | Total grants | Total capital | Total net spending | Total gross spending | Net spending | |
	Primary	Secondary	FE/AE[b]	University	Other	Related	Total current					% of GGE	% of GDP
1973/4	3.7	4.4	1.8	1.7	1.6	1.7	15.0	0.7	3.0	18.7	19.4	13.3	5.7
1974/5	4.4	5.3	2.1	1.7	1.9	1.8	17.2	0.8	2.5	20.5	21.1	13.0	6.3
1975/6	4.5	5.5	2.2	1.7	1.9	1.8	17.6	0.8	2.3	20.7	21.5	13.2	6.4
1976/7	4.4	5.5	2.4	1.8	1.6	1.9	17.6	0.9	2.0	20.5	21.2	13.3	6.1
1977/8	4.2	5.3	2.3	1.6	1.5	1.7	16.7	0.8	1.5	19.0	19.8	13.0	5.5
1978/9	4.2	5.4	2.3	1.7	1.5	1.7	16.8	0.9	1.2	18.9	19.8	12.3	5.3
1979/80	4.1	5.2	2.3	1.7	1.5	1.8	16.6	0.9	1.2	18.7	19.6	11.8	5.1
1980/1	4.2	5.5	2.4	1.9	1.6	1.7	17.3	0.9	1.2	19.4	20.2	12.0	5.5
1981/2	4.2	5.6	2.4	1.7	1.6	1.6	17.2	0.9	0.9	19.1	19.8	11.7	5.4
1982/3	4.1	5.6	2.5	1.7	1.7	1.7	17.3	1.0	0.9	19.1	19.9	11.4	5.3
1983/4	4.1	5.6	2.6	1.8	1.7	1.7	17.5	1.0	0.9	19.4	20.2	11.4	5.2
1984/5	4.0	5.6	2.6	1.8	1.7	1.7	17.4	1.0	0.8	19.2	20.0	11.0	5.1
1985/6	4.0	5.5	2.6	1.7	1.7	1.7	17.3	0.9	0.8	19.0	n.a.	10.9	4.8
1986/7	4.5	6.0	2.7	2.0	1.6	1.8	18.6	1.2	0.9	20.7	n.a.	11.6	5.1
1987/8	4.8	6.1	2.9	2.2	1.7	1.9	19.4	1.2	0.8	21.5	n.a.	12.1	5.1
1988/9	4.9	6.1	2.7	2.2	1.7	1.9	19.6	1.2	0.9	21.7	n.a.	12.3	4.9

[a] For detailed notes and sources, see the Annexe to this chapter, Table 3A.1.
[b] Further education/adult education.

end of the decade. In the first half of the 1980s, after Conservatives came to power, the share fell again, reflecting that government's concern to shift priorities further towards defence and law-and-order programmes and the need to raise spending on the unemployed. After Mr Baker's more successful battles in the Public Expenditure Survey Committee rounds of the late 1980s the share taken by education returned to 12 per cent by 1987/8.

The year-by-year level of net public spending relative to GDP is a result of the vagaries of the economy's performance, but these figures show that education spending has suffered a long-term decline relative to GDP as the economy has grown. From a high point of 6.4 per cent reached in 1975/6 the share fell to 5.1 per cent of GDP in 1979/80. It then rose as the economy declined and as a result of the teachers' salary awards in 1980, to fall back again to 4.8 per cent in 1985/6. The Public Expenditure White Paper of 1989 suggests the share could fall to 4.2 per cent by 1992, or roughly back to the level it was in 1960.

Spending in Table 3.1, as in comparable tables in the rest of this volume, is deflated by the general GDP deflator. It shows the opportunity cost of education to the rest of the economy. The substantial rises that took place in current spending both in 1974/5 and in 1980/1 reflect the long 'catch-up' salary increases awarded after several years in which teachers' salaries lagged behind those in competitive occupations. The same happened in 1987/8. The most striking change in real spending levels is the collapse in capital expenditure. This is net capital spending and hence to a limited extent reflects a rise in the sale of school sites in the later period (running at about £40 million), but the effect is small. The real fall in net capital spending has been dramatic, down to less than a third of its 1973 level in eight years. With declining pupil numbers, real spending on primary- and secondary-school building fell most. Nursery capital spending rose sharply in percentage points in the first few years, reflecting the initial commitment of the Labour government to universal provision (see above). This programme was a major casualty of the post-1976 cuts.

Spending on transfers, mainly student grants, also rose initially as the entitlement rules were relaxed and as student numbers rose. From 1976 on, the real level of spending then flattened out, despite the rise in student numbers after 1976. This was achieved partly by letting the real level of the maximum award fall by about 13 per cent between 1974 and 1987 (DES 1988*b*), but also by increasing the expected parental contribution after 1980. Average parental contributions nearly doubled in real terms from 1980/1 to 1986/7 (using the Retail Price Index). The real level of fee income increased only to a very small extent in comparison with total spending, except for the university sector, to which we shall return.

Thus the trends in overall *gross* expenditure are not substantially different from that already described.

As we move from real- to volume-terms expenditure (see Fig. 3.3) we see the rise in spending caused by salary increases smoothed out. We can see the total volume of resources available to public-sector education remaining relatively stable throughout the period, with the volume of current expenditure offset by the reduction in capital expenditure. By reanalysing the volume of current expenditure according to the level of education to which the spending was devoted, what is striking is the relative stability in the shares over time (see Fig. 3.4). This occurred despite the large variations that were taking place in the demography of the age groups concerned (see Fig. 3.2).

In order to get a picture of the responsiveness of education spending to these demographic need factors we have divided total volume spending

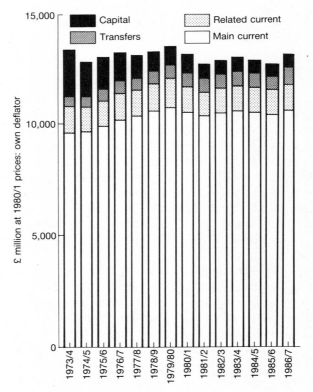

FIG. 3.3. Public expenditure on education by economic category, United Kingdom

over the period by the number of children or adults in the relevant age groups. What we illustrate in Fig. 3.5 is the trend in the volume of spending relative to the potential beneficiaries. If the index were to remain at 100 the educational resources available to that age group would remain unchanged.

Essentially, we find that during the period of adjustment to 1978/9 most sectors, except the polytechnics, stabilized their spending per capita despite the different demographic changes. The decline was least for primary schools, slightly more for secondary education, and most for universities and, after 1975, polytechnics. Some demographic rationality may be observed, but the fate of the sectors differs sharply. Spending per capita at primary level rises to recover and surpasses the 1973/4 level by 1978/9. Secondary spending recovers slightly but remains below its 1973 figure. University and polytechnic spending relative to the age group

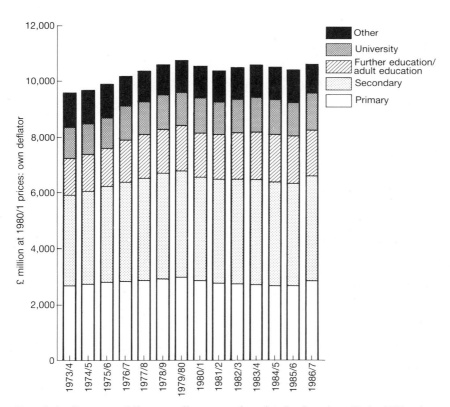

FIG. 3.4. Current public expenditure on education by function, United Kingdom

18–24-year-olds continues a precipitate decline, falling by a quarter by 1985/6.

How are we to explain these changes in the light of the theories with which we began? The relative stability in volume spending across age groups from 1974 to 1979 is consistent with what we know of the Labour government's attempt to spread the cuts according to some broad social planning indicators of need—broadly, the populations affected (Challis *et al.* 1988; CPRS 1975, 1977). Moreover, public expenditure planning was still being undertaken in volume terms even though cash limits were applied to each year's out-turn spending. The wide divergence in per capita spending in the Conservative period could reflect a conscious sense of priority, for example between primary and secondary schools and universities. However, if we look at the relative stability of spending by each sector another explanation appears. The government's main

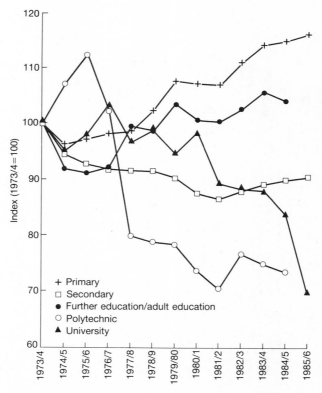

Fɪɢ. 3.5. Per capita volume spending on education, United Kingdom

concern was to limit cash spending. The minimum bureaucratic and political stress to local authorities and others resulted from their holding current spending fairly stable. Primary schools were difficult to close, for example. Thus, per capita spending figures may be the result of an interaction between demography and inertia. This still leaves the dramatic fall in higher education spending relative to the age group to be explained. It fits particularly poorly with the Le Grand and Winter (1987) thesis, though the age group they used was somewhat different. University spending is both concentrated on middle-class users and is provided by a social élite. If the Le Grand and Winter thesis were to hold anywhere, surely it should hold here?

One difficulty with the way the Le Grand and Winter model is formulated is that it takes the level of spending on a service as equivalent to the benefit received. This is, of course, merely a first approximation, which may be reasonable for a cash benefit. Universities are more complex. They are multi-product firms. One group of beneficiaries is overseas students. It was clearly possible to withdraw spending on them without damaging middle-class voters. Universities not only provide places for students, they also conduct research. If this failed to get done, middle-class students and parents would suffer no immediate loss, but academics would—and so would society in the long run. Hence the struggle by universities to sustain their level of resource per student even at the cost of accepting fewer students.

The trends in Fig. 3.5 relate to expenditure per capita for the whole relevant population. This is not to be confused with expenditure per student actually in the system. This is especially relevant beyond the school-leaving age. By reducing the intake of students, by charging overseas students the economic fee, and by raising other non-public sources of funds, universities and polytechnics sought to sustain spending *per pupil*. They failed, as we can see from Table 3.2, but universities sustained their gross spending per student more effectively.

So far we have been concerned with that element in the public expenditure accounts labelled 'education and science'. Yet it can be argued that this presents only part of the picture. From 1974 another institution enters the same or adjoining territory—the Manpower Services Commission. It was specifically concerned with training and later with the vocational relevance of education.

The training budget

It is difficult to draw a distinction between education and training, especially since governments have laid increasing stress on the vocational goals of education. Economists (Becker 1964) have long pointed out that the finance of general training poses problems in a competitive labour market. It is not in the interests of any one employer to give a basic training to employees because they can simply go to another firm when that training is complete. It is always in the interests of firms to free-ride on others' investment in training, unless that training is highly specific to the original firm. The costs of training thus tend to fall on the young employee, who is in a poor position to pay, leading to underconsumption or to not being incurred at all. The state can seek to remedy this situation either by subsidizing training from general taxation or by imposing a levy

Table 3.2. _Gross[a] recurrent expenditure per full-time-equivalent student:[b]_
Further and higher education (£ at 1985/6 prices)

	Maintained FE[c]	Polytechnic[c]	University[d]
Adjusted by GDP deflator			
1973/4	2,135	4,590	5,725
1975/6	2,205	5,055	6,550
1977/8	2,755	4,600	5,790
1979/80	2,835	4,615	6,425
1981/2	2,665	4,075	6,355
1983/4	2,565	3,360	6,120
1985/6	2,490	3,265	6,075
Adjusted by own-price deflator			
1973/4	2,465	5,305	5,940
1975/6	2,185	5,010	6,670
1977/8	2,650	4,425	5,655
1979/80	2,810	4,575	5,735
1981/2	2,555	3,905	6,075
1983/4	2,520	3,400	6,220
1985/6	2,520	3,265	6,075

[a] Spending for other further education and polytechnics is a weighted average of advanced further education and non-advanced further education unit costs, grossed up by assuming the same ratio of net to gross spending as the average for 1983/4 and 1985/6. University gross spending is income except specific income (e.g. research contracts). Rounded to nearest £5.

[b] In 1973/4 and 1975/6, for other further education and polytechnics, part-time students are assumed to be one-half of full-time-equivalent students and evening students to be one-third; similarly for part-time university students in 1973/4 and 1977/8.

[c] England and Wales until 1975/6, then England.

[d] United Kingdom throughout. Own-price deflator is the Tress–Brown price index (for May/July of each year).

Sources: DES 1987b: table 6 and equivalents for earlier years; DES 1977c: vol. 3, tables 14 and 21, and equivalents for earlier years; UGC 1987: vol. 3, table 2 and equivalents for earlier years.

on firms and forcing them to provide training programmes. It was the latter logic that had underpinned the Industrial Training Act of 1964 and the creation of Industrial Training Boards. They could impose levies on employers to finance approved training schemes. The Employment and Training Act of 1973 created the Manpower Services Commission (MSC), which had the dual job of co-ordinating the work of the Training Boards and running the Employment Service and Job Centres. (This latter function was handed back to the Department of Employment in 1987 and the remaining agency responsible for training was given the title of Training Commission.) Throughout our period of study, however, the newly created MSC not merely came to undertake a wider range of training functions, but also began to *finance* courses in schools and further education colleges. It was a separate bureaucracy created to pursue the training and 'vocational relevance' objectives of the government in parallel to what ministers perceived to be a somewhat reluctant DES. For completeness, therefore, we include in our public spending analysis those parts of the MSC's budget that relate to education and training objectives.

First, there was the function taken over from the previous legislation to co-ordinate and finance the activities of the Industrial Training Boards. This grew under the Labour government but was reduced and then eliminated by the Conservatives, who argued that industry was capable of looking after its own training needs.

Second, there was the responsibility to finance individuals, mainly adults, who wanted to acquire skills, retrain, or return to the work-force —the Training Opportunities Scheme (TOPS) and later variants.

Third, and introduced in 1978, were the programmes for school-leavers who had not managed to get ordinary jobs. They were both an emerging response to rising levels of unemployment and an attempt to provide some basic training and work experience. The original Youth Opportunities Programme (YOP) became the Youth Training Scheme (YTS) and the length of the period was extended from a maximum of one year to two. The training and formal education elements grew. The aim of the YTS, introduced in 1983, was to ensure that 'all young people should be able to enter either full-time education or planned training and work experience' (MSC 1984).

Fourth, in the later part of the period came a number of attempts to shift the emphasis of educational institutions towards vocational goals. The earliest of these was the Technical and Vocational Educational Initiative in schools. Schools and LEAs were asked to devise curriculum experiments that linked school and work more effectively and to bid for funds to support these experiments. In 1985/6 it was the turn of colleges of further education. A slice was taken off the rate support grant to local authorities that would have gone to those colleges. Instead the money was transferred to the MSC to support schemes for 'work-related' courses in those colleges. This approach was extended to universities and higher education. Institutions are asked to devise schemes that will 'develop qualities of enterprise in students'. The programme began in December 1987. These parts of the MSC budget added the equivalent of 0.2 per cent of GNP to the education and training budget in the 1970s and 0.3 per cent in the mid-1980s (see Table 3.3).

The private funding of the public sector

We have already seen that income to the public sector from fees and charges was still small in 1985/6 compared with the overall size of the public budget. Universities, however, were an exception. After the removal of Exchequer grant support for the overseas students, universities and colleges had to charge them the full economic fee and also developed income-generating courses. For some institutions the income was to become significant. None of these incentives applied to home students. It was this kind of perversity that led some to call for a new kind of funding arrangement altogether. Barnes and Barr (1988) argued that the government should give bursaries to a set number of home students with which college fees could be paid, while leaving institutions free to offer courses, charge fees, and set entry targets as they wished.

During the period from 1979/80, universities managed to increase the share of their total income from sources other than the basic UGC grant from 30 per cent to 43 per cent.

One way in which LEAs sought to continue to sustain standards was to charge for such items as materials used in domestic science, geography trips, outings, and even books. Some parents challenged this in the courts as counter to Section 61 of the 1944 Education Act, which prohibited charging fees in state schools. The 1988 Education Act defined circumstances in which trips outside school hours could be financed by parents and how far charges could be imposed on 'optional extras'. We have no reliable estimates of the sums involved (the issues are reviewed in Bull 1980 and CPAG 1987).

Private spending on private education

General educational spending   If the scale of public-sector education has declined relative to the economy as a whole, has it been replaced by private spending on private-sector provision? Some writers have explained the relative decline in the private sector since 1870 in terms of a 'crowding-out' effect. Forced to pay taxes to support state education, parents have not been able to reveal their true preferences for private education, so it is argued (West 1965, 1975). While we have reasonably

Table 3.3. *The training budget: Manpower Services Commission programmes, United Kingdom* (£ million at 1987/8 prices, adjusted by GDP deflator)

Programmes	1974/5	1975/6	1976/7	1977/8	1978/9	1979/80	1980/1	1981/2	1982/3	1983/4	1984/5	1985/6	1986/7	1987/8
Working experience and training for young people (YOP, YTS)	—	—	—	—	127	194	319	540	741	823	848	884	990	1,132
Training needs of workers (TOPS, YTP, YOTP)	264	386	494	450	414	385	367	317	292	160	229	237	332	312
Training needs of industry (Industrial Training Boards)	56	125	184	209	201	165	148	155	95	21	17	—	—	—
Technical and Vocational Education Initiative in schools (TVEI)	—	—	—	—	—	—	—	—	—	8	28	39	76	61
Work related non-advanced further education	—	—	—	—	—	—	—	—	—	—	—	63	119	115
Total training budget	320	511	678	658	742	745	833	1,012	1,128	1,012	1,122	1,224	1,517	1,620

Source: Training Commission 1988: table 1.1 and equivalents for earlier years.

accurate figures on the number of pupils in private-sector schools dating back to the early part of the century (Glennerster and Wilson 1970), we have only more tentative estimates of the scale of the private sector as a whole in money terms. Not least is it difficult to know exactly where to put the boundaries of the private sector.

One source does, however, enable us to create a series for household spending on education and training in the United Kingdom. That is the Family Expenditure Survey (FES). There are difficulties. The survey distinguishes between school fees and other education and training expenses such as music lessons, learning to drive a car, secretarial courses, and fees for evening classes. But it does not distinguish fees paid to public-sector institutions from fees paid to private-sector ones. Also, school fees are traditionally paid by a range of methods other than direct expenditure from current earnings. Parents use life assurance, capital schemes, and endowments from grandparents. It is unlikely that these would be returned on the FES questionnaire as expenditure on school fees. The survey is therefore likely to understate the total income of the private sector. Moreover, the income of the private schools is enhanced by their endowment incomes. Nevertheless, the FES does provide us with reasonable trend data on private spending, assuming that the deficiencies remain of similar importance over time. Subject to these caveats we present in Table 3.4 our estimates of cash and real-terms spending by households on education. (Erratic results were obtained by applying the 'volume' series, suggesting that it is not appropriate to private-sector spending, and we have excluded it.) Real private spending on all forms of education followed a pattern not that different from the public sector, falling in the aftermath of the squeeze on incomes in the mid-1970s, rising as the net incomes of the upper-income groups rose after 1980. Overall, private education spending remained at about 0.4 per cent of GDP over the period. This share was sustained while the public sector's share was falling.

It is instructive to consider how far public and private education spending has kept pace with gross disposable income over a longer period. What has happened to the income elasticity of education spending, as economists call it? Throughout the 1960s public expenditure on education rose roughly half as fast again as disposable incomes (see Table 3.5). In the early 1970s the rate of expansion slowed, but was still above unity. Then after 1975 public-sector spending rose at only 0.84 per cent of the growth in the economy generally. In the 1980s the income elasticity rose again but was still less than unity. In comparison, the income elasticity of private spending remained fairly near unity from 1960 through to 1980. Households increased their own spending on education in line with their incomes. Between 1980 and 1986 some increase is visible, but it should be remembered that the figures are still very small in relation to total weekly income for the average household (0.8 per cent). Only the highest income groups with children spend significant sums on private education. The figure reaches only £480 a year for a family with two children in the group with a household income of £19,500 or more in 1986.

Private schools Within the overall total of private spending on education no systematic survey of the finance of private schools has been undertaken between that of one of the authors (Glennerster and Wilson 1970) and a survey based on a stratified sample of schools' accounts in 1980–3 (Posnett and Chase 1985). For 1981/2 Posnett and Chase estimated that

Table 3.4. *Private household expenditure on education in the United Kingdom[a]*

	Current prices (£m.)	Index of real spending (1974 = 100)
1974	307	100
1975	348	96
1976	400	88
1977	525	99
1978	588	96
1979	641	91
1980	804	95
1981	1,087	112
1982	1,215	115
1983	1,132	98
1984	1,286	103
1985	1,234	92
1986	1,562	102

[a] Standard errors in the original survey vary from 3 to 12% for different elements in the fees paid.

Sources: DE 1988: annexe A and equivalents for earlier years; CSO 1988*a*: table 2.4 and equivalents for earlier years.

Table 3.5. *Income elasticity[a] of education expenditure, public and private, 1960–1986*

	1960–5	1965–70	1970–5	1975–80	1980–6
Public expenditure	1.57	1.44	1.15	0.84	0.91
Private expenditure	1.05	0.97	1.06	1.07	1.16

[a] Using growth in gross national disposable income.

Source: CSO 1987*b*: table 1.7 and equivalents for earlier years.

the total income of private schools was about £1.2 billion (with a 95 per cent confidence limit of ±11.4 per cent). Fees paid by parents and others constituted 87 per cent of the total. Using average fee levels given in the Independent Schools Information Service Annual Census and total pupil numbers in different categories of school, it is possible to derive an estimate of fee income within 2 per cent of Posnett and Chase. We have therefore estimated the current expenditure of private schools from 1976/7 to 1985/6 by assuming a constant ratio of fee income to total current spending (Table 3.6).

From 1951 to 1977 current expenditure on private schools fell steadily as a share of all current expenditure on schools in England and Wales. It fell from 18.6 per cent to 8.8 per cent in 1977/8. Then, as state spending is cut, private-school spending sustains its share of the total until 1979 and the new Conservative administration. Almost immediately we see a reversal of the thirty-year post-war trend. Private-school spending begins to rise as a proportion of the total. Whether this was a reflection of parents' fears about the falling standards in state schools resulting from the cuts, or whether it was a reflection of the shift in the income distribution to the higher-income groups must remain largely speculation. However, some work has been done at the Institute for Fiscal Studies which illuminates this question. FES data on private-school attendance was analysed with household characteristics. Preliminary findings (Pearson, Smith, and Watson 1988) suggest that a rise in income amongst households in professional and managerial groups produces a proportionate increase in private-school attendance. A 35 per cent rise in household income was associated with a 42 per cent increase in the probability that a profession-

Table 3.6. *Private-school current expenditure, 1951/2–1985/6, England and Wales*
(£ million)

	Current spending	As % of total current spending on schools
1951/2	51	18.6
1956/7	67	14.7
1962/3	91	12.5
1967/8	125	11.8
1976/7	100	8.9
1979/80	571	9.2
1982/3	1,228	12.9
1985/6	1,504	13.7

Sources: 1951/2–1967/8: Glennerster and Wilson 1970; 1976/7–1985/6: authors' calculations (see text); ISIS 1986*a*: tables 3 and 5 and equivalent for earlier years; ISIS 1986*b*.

al family will have children at private schools. On the other hand, a high level of local authority spending on schools offsets that effect.

The expenditure figures are only part of the story. The number of private-school pupils had also continued to fall from 1947, when it was 10.2 per cent, through to 1976, when it constituted 5.7 per cent of the total school population. The recovery to 6.4 per cent by 1986 is not as dramatic as the spending figures would lead us to expect. Numbers of pupils have remained little changed as the population has fallen (Tables 3A.4 and 3A.5 in the Annexe to this chapter). What seems to have happened is that much of the relative increase in private over state spending has been caused by a continued rise in private spending per pupil, while spending per pupil in the public sector was held down by successive governments.

The public funding of the private sector

Direct state support We saw that the Labour government both discouraged local authorities from paying fees for children to attend independent schools and began phasing out the direct grant from central government to the direct-grant schools. From 1976 onwards the scale of public funding of the private sector declines (see Fig. 3.6). The introduction of the Assisted Places Scheme gradually reversed that trend (Walford 1987; Tapper and Salter 1986) (our figures include grants paid to a small number of non-maintained special schools). By 1985/6 the real level of grants to private schools from all public sources had not quite recovered to reach the 1973/4 level. Our results appear to differ from Walford's (1987), who concludes that the private sector has gained increasing state support under the Conservative government since 1979. That is because his study concentrates on the Assisted Places Scheme and *central* government policy. Our figures are consistent with this account but include the reduced local authority support.

Indirect state support Families can arrange their finances in such a way as to attract tax relief on money set aside to pay for their children's education. This cannot strictly be classed as 'tax expenditure' on private schooling. The benefits could just as well have been spent on foreign holidays or BMWs. Tax expenditures can properly be said to exist only if the tax laws are so arranged as to benefit a particular kind of institution or spending category. Charities fall under the first heading, and educational institutions can claim charitable status simply by virtue of providing education. Virtually all the public schools have claimed charitable status. Of the remaining private schools, less than half have claimed it (Posnett and Chase 1985). The best review of tax policy and independent schools is that by Robson and Walford (1989), on which we draw.

Although committed to removing the charitable status of private schools, the 1974–9 Labour government left office without doing so. The Conservative government has sought to encourage charitable donations. In fact, the effects of various tax changes have moved in different directions:

1. Schools that are charities are exempt from income, capital gains, and corporation tax. If they make no profit this is not important, but schools may make surpluses to carry over for capital expenditure and, by virtue of charitable status, these do not attract tax. In 1982/3 this could have amounted to a benefit of £36 million. Since the small companies' tax rate fell from 42 per cent in 1978/9 to 25 per cent in 1988/9, so has the value of the relief.

2. More importantly, schools can recover tax paid by donors on the gifts they make to the schools. Changes in the tax laws since 1980 have encouraged such donations. First, tax relief could be claimed on covenanted income at the higher rates of income tax under the 1980 Finance Act from 1981/2 onwards. The limit on such covenants

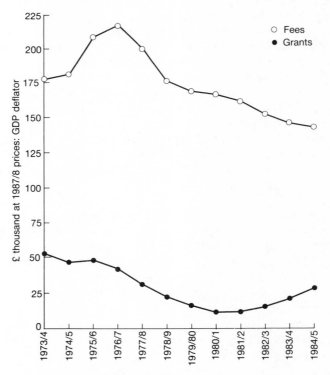

FIG. 3.6. Public funding of private schools

was raised in 1983/4 and 1985/6 and removed in 1986. Firms can, since 1986, set single donations against corporation tax. The 1986 Finance Act also introduced tax relief on payroll giving. All these moves enhance the value of donations made to schools. The reduction in the basic and higher tax rates does the reverse.

3. In the 1983 Budget, gifts to charities were made completely exempt from capital transfer tax. On the other hand, the capacity to avoid the tax by other means—giving to children or relatives seven years before death—makes giving to charities less attractive in comparison.

4. Value added tax rose to 15 per cent (nearly doubling) in 1979. Education is exempt. If VAT were charged on private schooling, as the provision of a service like any other, the impact would be considerable. Non-payment of VAT on items purchased—e.g. equipment—is quite small.

5. All charities carry a mandatory rate reduction of 50 per cent. This will rise to 80 per cent with the advent of the community charge and the Uniform Business Rate. Complete relief can be given by a local authority—'at its discretion'.

Robson and Walford (1989) conclude that the total level of relief was £190 million in 1982/3: £150 million in VAT exemption on fees and charges; £35 million in income tax/corporation tax exemption on profits; and £5 million in rates relief.

If we include exemption from VAT as a tax subsidy then this total is much more significant than other studies have suggested—it is roughly equivalent to 15 per cent of spending by the schools in 1982/3. Excluding VAT brings the tax relief down to about 3.5 per cent of the schools' income—not far short of the figure Glennerster and Wilson (1970) produced for 1965/6 (i.e. 4.5 per cent of total income).

III. INTERMEDIATE POLICY OUTPUTS

Politicians do not normally deal in ultimate goals and objectives. They do sometimes set more practical targets. A clear example was the White Paper for which Mrs Thatcher was responsible as Secretary of State for Education and Science in the Heath government, *Education: A Framework for Expansion* (DES 1972).

The 1970–4 Conservative government set out a programme of expansion for the next decade which was largely taken over by the Labour government in 1974. Though later events changed both parties' spending priorities, it is worth comparing the goals set at the outset of our period with what had actually been delivered by the end.

Nursery education

The 1972 White Paper stated: '[The government's] aim is that within the next ten years nursery education should become available without charge ... to those children of three and four whose parents wish them to benefit from it' (para. 17). The estimate was that the provision for 90 per cent of four-year-olds and 50 per cent of three-year-olds would meet the demand. The Labour government reiterated that pledge. In the event, as the House of Commons Select Committee on Education (1989) pointed out in January 1989, this was not achieved. The number of under-fives in maintained education rose from 17 per cent of three- to four-year olds in 1970 to 44 per cent in 1987, and much of that was in the form of places in primary schools for those just under five. Provision in the public and private sectors combined is lower than in most European countries.

School buildings

The next priority was to be a major renewal scheme for secondary-school buildings to complement the renewal plan for old primary schools, and a new special-school building programme. The programme of renewal was to be large enough to prevent the accumulation of a backlog of obsolete buildings. The DES undertook a national survey of school building standards in the mid-1970s to quantify this goal (DES 1977*b*). It was estimated that capital spending at the level then planned, if sustained, would go only half-way towards achieving the improvements needed by 1987/8. In the event, capital spending on schools more than halved over the period in volume terms, rather than doubled.

Class size

Mrs Thatcher's White Paper set a 10 per cent improvement in staffing standards as its goal by 1981. The Labour government promised to end classes over thirty. It can be seen from Table 3.7 that average class sizes fell until 1981. Then the primary pupil/teacher ratio worsened slightly and the secondary ratio stabilized. Within that overall trend the number of classes with over thirty pupils fell in both primary and secondary schools, but by 1986 19 per cent of English primary-school classes were still over the Labour government's 1974 target.

Staying on at school

All governments have sought to increase voluntary staying-on at school. Nevertheless, the proportion of children in the United Kingdom staying at school or college beyond 16 is one of the lowest in the industrialized world. In the European Community, only Greece has a lower staying-on rate. In the United States and Japan the comparable rate is nearly double that in the United Kingdom. Following the raising of the school-leaving age to 16 in 1972 the proportion staying on *did* rise from 35 to nearly 50 per cent, only to fall back again after 1982 to nearer 45 per cent. Micklewright, Pearson, and Smith (1989) show that this fall was associated with rising unemployment. Maximizing family income is particularly important, especially for low-income groups.

Higher education

Targets were also set in 1972 for higher education, assuming that staying-on rates would continue to rise and that about 22 per cent of the 18-year-old group would enter higher education. In fact, the percentage, which had been 13.7 in 1970, fell to 12.6 in 1980 and rose only to 14.1 by 1986/7. Changes in access to higher education were partly caused by deliberate decisions by the Labour government to reduce places in colleges of education, and by the Conservative government, who reduced the number of places universities could offer at a time when the 18–24-year-old age group was rising (HM Treasury, 1981). We examine the impact of labour market demand side-factors later.

IV. FINAL OUTCOMES

We have argued that governments after 1976 gave greater weight to raising basic standards of achievement and to the economic or productive efficiency goals of education. Equity goals have receded almost to

Table 3.7. *Class sizes as taught, England*

	Primary schools			Secondary schools		
	1977	1981	1986	1977	1981	1986
% of classes taught by: one teacher in classes with:						
1–20 pupils	16.1	20.0 ⎫		42.3	44.4 ⎫	
21–30 pupils	46.3	54.9 ⎭	75.1	41.7	45.1 ⎭	90.7
31 or more pupils	33.7	21.8	19.0	12.5	8.2	6.1
two or more teachers	4.0	3.3	5.9	3.5	2.4	3.2
Average size of class (nos.)	27.5	25.5	25.9	22.4	21.5	21.3

Source: CSO 1988*a*: table 3.6.

vanishing-point. The difficulties we have in judging the outcome of such a shift of priorities are several.

First, the time lag is bound to be long. It has taken a decade to legislate a National Curriculum. Effectively implementing it in the classroom will be difficult, as Her Majesty's Inspectors of Schools suggest and as the French have found (DES 1988*a*). Change, on this scale, has its costs. More specialist teachers will be needed. Teachers, publishers, examining bodies, all take time to adapt and may do less well in the interim. It will probably be well into the next century before we can really judge the impact.

Second, measuring changes in pupil performance over time is inherently difficult. We have already referred to the 'ceiling effect'. Moreover, as knowledge changes and as different kinds of knowledge are given more or less importance by society and the labour market, so teachers' emphasis and the curriculum will adapt. Mathematics, as taught in schools, has changed a great deal in the last thirty years. To give a repeat examination of the same questions a generation later might not reveal anything about the quality of maths teaching. If the same questions were answered just as well this could show the subject was dead and had not kept pace with the needs of society. A reduced capacity to answer thirty-year-old questions might even be a good sign!

Third, an extension of the previous point, we do not know what knowledge is important in economic or other terms. The Cockcroft Committee (DES 1982) was appointed because of press criticism and employers' complaints about the mathematical attainments of young workers. It turned out, on careful questioning, that employers had very few and very vague complaints and that their entrance tests seemed to have little relation to tasks actually required of employees. The Committee did its best to be helpful in indicating areas for the curriculum to develop, but it was all very general advice. Pioneering work at the National Institute of Social and Economic Research (Prais 1981, 1987; Prais and Steedman 1986; Prais and Wagner 1983, 1985, 1988) has pursued this question by comparing standards and types of education received by young workers in England, Germany, France, and Japan. Prais's most convincing point is that the English system is particularly deficient in equipping average and below-average pupils, and in giving them technical and vocational training.

Fourth, even if a change in, say, reading or mathematical standards were to be observed, it is difficult to know how far that would be the result of social factors or the schools. A long-term decline in attainments of US schoolchildren was observed amongst children born from the mid-1940s through to the mid-1960s. The Congressional Budget Office (1987) reviewed a wide range of explanations that had been advanced.

The most plausible linked the lower average attainment levels attained by third and fourth children in families to the rise in the number of three- and four-children families in the relevant twenty-year period. This merely illustrates the difficulty of disentangling social and school factors over time.

We know that social factors explain the greater part of variations in levels of attainment between schools and between LEAs in Britain. The same is likely to be true of trends in attainment over time. However, Smith and Tomlinson (1989) argue that the 'school effect' is larger than generally perceived. Their methodology considered the achievement of comparable individuals in different multiracial comprehensives. Progress can depend on the school attended, with the incremental change in performance being significant to the individual even if relatively unimportant in changing his or her relative position compared with the brightest pupils. School policies and practices, even down to the level of subject department, exert strong influence on the pattern and level of courses studied and grades achieved.

The interaction of changing social structures and educational performance is paralleled by the interaction of the labour market and education. Staying-on rates and participation in higher education may well have much more to do with relative shortages of labour and with private rates of return than with the performance of school sixth forms. We return to this below, and to the question of the economic returns to spending on education. Bearing these caveats in mind, we briefly review the limited research evidence on changes in basic levels of attainment in schools and then move on to discuss trends in examination results and link those to changes in the organization of secondary schools.

Overall attainments in schools

There is only one long-term follow-up study of basic attainment standards in this period and it is in mathematics. It compares scores achieved by schoolchildren aged 13 in 1964 and in 1981. It illustrates the kind of general difficulties we have mentioned and others besides. The study was part of an attempt to compare educational standards internationally (see below). Mathematics seemed to offer the most promising starting-place (Pidgeon 1967). Even so, elements of the subject covered in one country were not in others. Teaching of maths in England and Wales was transformed over the period. Other, more narrowly technical, problems arose (Cresswell and Gubb 1987). Since they turn out to be very important, readers are urged to refer to the original source.

The study selected thirty-seven 'anchor' questions from the 1964 survey which were repeated in 1981. As the authors admit, very few reflect the new approach to mathematics teaching introduced in the interim. The examinations took place three months earlier than in 1964, the questions were of a multiple-choice kind, and children were more used to such a format in 1964. The response rate from schools was less than 50 per cent in 1981. The results showed that the mean scores were lower in 1981 than in 1964, and this result was significant at the 5 per cent level: 52 per cent of the items were answered correctly in 1964 and 43 per cent in 1981. A more recent and much deeper study, specially designed for England and Wales by the Assessment of Performance Unit (APU), suggests that whatever the longer-term trend, recent maths standards have been improving. The APU surveyed 11- and 15-year-olds between 1978 and 1981. Their results show a 1.5 per cent improvement in scores gained by 11-year-olds and a 2.0 per cent improvement in those of 15-year-olds during that period. Since this happened in a period of declining resources per pupil, it must be counted a real gain in the efficiency of mathematics teaching!

A similar detailed study by the APU (1988) was undertaken of science attainments between 1980 and 1984. Results varied from year to year within the confidence limits. The overall conclusions from a report which should be read in detail suggest:

There is no evidence in the survey data of any underlying trend in ... performance levels of 15 year olds between 1980 and 1984 ... Nor is there any evidence of the changes in performance gaps between particular pupil groups ... or of different sexes.

The surveys show a persistently lower performance by children in Wales and Northern Ireland. Girls perform less well in physics (where teachers' expectations may well be an important factor). Elsewhere gender differences disappear when differential course take-up is taken into account. One of the more encouraging features of the surveys was the reduced drop-out from science subjects. Even before the National Curriculum the policy goal of wider access to science was being achieved, and especially by girls. The disparity between Northern Ireland, Wales, and England suggests a major inequality of opportunity which needs more investigation. It is worth reminding ourselves that performance levels in any one subject area cannot tell us about *overall* educational performance. Improvements in access to science may have been bought by reduction in access to other subjects.

International comparisons

So far we have discussed how far the attainments of British schoolchildren have changed over time. It is also relevant to know how they compare with those in other countries. This is no easy question to answer, as we explained earlier, but one major study has attempted an answer: the International Study in Educational Achievement. Its most recent survey was a repeat of one carried out twenty years ago. The mathematics results appeared first and are instructive (Garden 1987; Robitaille and Garden 1989). At the age of 13, children from England and Wales performed slightly less well than the average for arithmetic, algebra, and measurement, but did better at geometry and descriptive statistics. We did significantly less well than Japan, for example. By the time children were ready to go on to higher education, however, the story was different. Those taking maths at that point out-performed most countries at most elements of maths, with the exception of Japan and Hong Kong. The bad news was that so few children stayed on to that level. Our schools are capable of reaching the very highest standards in international terms. We need to encourage more to stay on to reach those standards.

The attainment of school-leavers

A traditional method of measuring the output of the school system is to compare trends in exam performance over time. The English examination system does not make that an easy task. There has not until recently been a common leaving examination. Most school-leavers took no examination at all. Moreover, the examiners' main task was to compare pupils' relative performance—'norm-referencing', as the jargon has it. To compare standards over time a system of criterion-referencing is necessary. This means measuring a pupil's performance against some absolute yardstick, irrespective of the performance of other pupils. This is the aim of the new national system of assessment. No such system has existed before. Since the O-level exams were designed for the top 20 per cent of the ability range, for example, there was a natural tendency for teachers to ration entrants to O-level courses and for examiners to raise pass marks as standards improved. Exam results may, therefore, reflect these rationing devices rather than any deficiency or achievement in the education system. This is all quite apart from the impact of wider social and economic change we discussed earlier.

National figures for school-leaving exams should be approached with caution. With these caveats in mind we can see from Table 3.8 that there has been a not insignificant increase in the proportion of young people gaining A-levels in the ten years after 1975—from 19 to 23 per cent. There has been a much larger increase in the percentage of pupils passing CSEs, and an increase in those gaining five O-levels. At the same time, the numbers leaving school with no qualifications fell sharply. It is noticeable, however, that a peak was reached in 1985/6. It could be that the resource constraints of the 1980s were beginning to have an effect.

The impact of comprehensive reorganization

What impact did the reorganization of secondary education have on these outcomes? It was one of the more contentious policies pursued and it came to fruition during this period. Over 85 per cent of English state school pupils were in comprehensive schools by 1986, 99 per cent of Welsh schoolchildren, and 96 per cent of those in Scotland. These crude figures may overstate the position. In 1976, one study concluded that only one in three LEAs was fully comprehensive (Gray, Jesson, and Jones 1984), that is, they had no selective schools at all.

What impact did the change have on pupils' performance? Attempts to answer that question have caused fierce debate. See, for example, two whole issues of academic journals on this debate (*Journal of the Royal Statistical Society*, Ser. A, 147/4 (1984); *Oxford Review of Education*, 10/1 (1984)). It was tempting to conclude that the easy way to test the impact of comprehensive schooling was to compare the performance of children in LEAs that had gone comprehensive with those that had not. However, this path was littered with traps. Those authorities which retained grammar schools tended to be those with more middle-class parents (Heath 1984). Not fully standardizing for this and for the effects of remaining grammar schools led some commentators to suggest that the selective grammar/secondary modern system produced superior results (Marks, Cox, and Pomian-Srzednicki 1983). Adopting a much fuller analysis of

Table 3.8. *Attainments of young people as a percentage of relevant population, United Kingdom*

	1970/1	1975/6	1980/1	1985/6	1986/7
GCE A-levels or SCE H grades					
17-year-olds achieving:					
1 or more passes	—	19	20	22	23
GCE O-levels and CSE but no A-levels or SCE					
15-year-olds achieving:					
5 or more higher grades[a]	7.1	8.2	8.9	10.5	10.3
1–4 higher grades[a]	16.8	23.9	24.8	26.7	26.6
1 or more other grades[b]	9.8	27.8	30.6	32.7	32.5
No graded results	44.0	18.7	13.5	11.7	10.9

[a] Grades A–C at GCE O-level and grade 1 at CSE. Includes Scottish O grades A–C.
[b] Grades D and E at O-level (except 1970–1), grades 2–5 at CSE, Scottish O grades D and E.
Source: DES 1989: table 6.

the social composition of local authority areas, Gray, Jesson, and Jones (1984) concluded that they 'could find no overall trend to suggest that once differences in social composition had been taken into account, LEAs which had retained selection to a greater or lesser extent achieved better results than those that were fully comprehensive' (p. 45). The DES study (1984*b*) of variations in exam performance between LEAs which standardizes for social factors does show a small but statistically significant relationship between remaining grammar schools and exam performance.

A study in Scotland uses a quite different and richer data base (Gray, McPherson, and Raffe 1983). It was a large national survey of school-leavers in 1975/6. Their experience coincided with Scotland's move to abolish selection. It was possible to compare the achievements of those in comprehensive, mixed, and selective areas. The results show that, over-all, pupils from the uncreamed comprehensive areas performed rather better in examinations than those in the selective areas including the Scottish equivalent of direct-grant schools. The top-ability pupils did slightly better in the selective system. Those lower down the ability range did much better in the comprehensive system. These results are compatible with the original findings of the Swedish experiments in the 1960s (see a summary of this research in Public Schools Commission 1970). The uncreamed comprehensives also had less class differentiation, and less truancy. Unlike England, Scotland already had a tradition of 'omnibus' schools, especially in the rural areas and smaller towns. Gray *et al.* conclude that the new comprehensive system worked best where it was building on older traditions and was working with the grain of social solidarity. It could not readily create it.

Finally, there is a third source of evidence. Heath (1984) used the British Election Survey to investigate the exam performance of those in the sample. He compared two cohorts, those who were between 31 and 45 in 1979 and those who were between 18 and 30. The first group were products of the pre-1965 selective system and the latter had experienced the comprehensive change, and some the longer period of compulsory schooling. Overall, the numbers gaining CSE and O-levels rose substantially, A-levels somewhat less, which fits with the national data. What Heath's analysis does is to show through which types of school this increase was 'channelled', as he puts it. The comprehensives contributed 17 per cent more qualified leavers, the secondary moderns 7 per cent, and the grammar schools 7 per cent. A-level achievers rose by nearly 6 per cent and the grammar schools contributed half of that rise.

The pattern that emerges is therefore reasonably consistent. The main and really major improvements in exam performance were achieved by the average-ability students and they were achieved mostly in the comprehensive schools. These changes might have taken place anyway under the old system, hence Heath's cautious use of the word 'channelled'. But it is a tribute to the state schools that they produced both more qualified leavers and the structural changes politicians were demanding. Once more this is a measure of improved effectiveness.

A more qualified labour force

If we merely consider trends in exam performance over time we thus see some improvement at the higher levels, but it is scarcely dramatic. In an important respect this 'official' view understates the achievements of the education system over the period. It does so for two reasons. First, there is a demographic factor—a much larger cohort was passing through higher education compared with earlier decades. Second, there is the fact that the sixth forms, universities, and polytechnics were catering for a higher *proportion* of the age group than their predecessors in the 1950s and early 1960s. The percentages staying on to gain A-levels were double for men and nearly quadruple for women what they had been in the late 1950s. Thus, simply by continuing to 'process' a constant but a historically high portion of the population, the stock of human capital being created was much larger than in the 1950s. As older people from an even earlier educational system retired, the transformation in the human capital content of the labour force has been quite dramatic. Our analysis of the General Household Survey (GHS) data shows the big change that has occurred in the educational qualifications of the work-force in only a decade (see Table 3.9). The proportion of the sample with degrees rose by 150 per cent. Those with A-levels or post-A-level qualifications increased by 60 per cent, those with O-levels by nearly half. The number with no qualifications has fallen from about 60 to 40 per cent.

A separate analysis of the trends for men and women shows that more women reached O-level standard in 1985, whereas the reverse was true in 1974. Women were catching up at degree level (a 2:1 disadvantage compared to 3.3:1). This was less true at A-level.

The raising of the school-leaving age to 16 in 1972 has also been feeding through the system. In 1974, 40 per cent of the population between 16 and 49 had left school before they were 15. By 1985 the figure was half that. Successive governments have urged educational institutions to take more mature entrants. In Table 3.10 we compare the proportion of the various age groups who were actually attending an educational establishment or were on an Open University or correspondence course. The numbers in touch with the education system after the age of 21 is still very small, but there is evidence of growth over the decade.

The relevance of possessing a qualification to gaining or keeping a job can be seen in Table 3.11. In 1974, when less than 2 per cent of the GHS sample (16–49) were unemployed, the incidence was spread fairly evenly. In 1985, over 7 per cent were unemployed. Only 3 per cent of those with degrees were unemployed and over 8 per cent of those with no qualifica-

Table 3.9. *Labour force human capital: Highest level of qualification of 16–49-year-olds, Great Britain* (% of age group)

Qualification	1974	1979	1985
Degree	2.7	4.8	6.7
Other post-A-level	5.1	6.4	8.2
A-level	4.9	5.6	7.9
O-level	13.2	14.9	19.1
CSE, commercial and other qualifications	13.5	15.0	15.5
No qualifications	60.7	53.3	42.6
All 16–49-year-olds	100	100	100
Base (no.)	18,507	19,245	16,096
$\chi^2 (10) = 1{,}335.2\,^a$			

[a] Chi-square statistic to test for independence (with ten degrees of freedom).
Source: Own calculations from GHS raw data files.

Table 3.10. *Continuing education: Percentage of 16–49-year-olds taking an education or training course, Great Britain*

Age	1974		1985	
	Full-time	Part-time	Full-time	Part-time
16–21	28.6	11.1	28.2	16.7
22–29	1.8	5.2	4.5	8.6
30–49	0.3	2.5	1.2	4.5
All	5.7	4.7	6.5	7.6
Base (no.)	721	598	397	461
	$\chi^2 (2) = 335.7$		$\chi^2 (2) = 115.1$	
Men	6.5	6.5	5.1	8.6
Women	5.0	3.0	8.1	6.3
	$\chi^2 (1) = 18.3$		$\chi^2 (1) = 45.5$	

Source: Own calculations from GHS raw data files.

Table 3.11. *Work status and education, Great Britain* (%)

Work Status	Highest level of education						All	Base (no.)
	Degree	Other post-A-level	A-level	O-level	CSE/apprent.	No qual.		
1974								
Working	88.0	77.9	77.2	74.9	73.9	65.4	69.6	12,884
Unemployed	1.8	0.6	1.0	1.1	1.3	1.9	1.6	296
Economically inactive	10.2	21.4	21.8	24.0	24.8	32.7	28.8	5,333
All	100	100	100	100	100	100	100	
Base (no.)	497	952	902	2,435	2,495	11,283	18,513	
$\chi^2 (12) = 281.0$								
1985								
Working	83.6	78.6	78.5	68.9	61.0	50.7	62.4	10,051
Unemployed	3.3	2.9	4.4	7.2	8.8	8.4	7.1	1,144
Economically inactive	13.0	18.4	17.0	22.1	29.0	40.6	29.7	4,786
All[a]	100	100	100	100	100	100	100	
Base (no.)	1,076	1,317	1,278	3,014	2,462	6,834	15,981	
$\chi^2 (12) = 1,005.0$								

[a] Includes those on YTS. Separate analysis too small for significance.

Source: Own calculations from GHS raw data files.

tions. Degrees are also important in determining incomes. In our 1985 GHS survey analysis we found that 66 per cent of those in the top quintile of gross incomes had degrees. Only 12 per cent of those with no post-school qualifications were in that income group.

Nickell (1979*c*), analysing lifetime patterns of unemployment and education using the GHS for 1972, concluded that the level of education an individual achieved strongly influenced the probability of becoming unemployed and weakly affected the length of time without a job once unemployed. Our figures bear out that conclusion for a later period.

Rates of return to education

We have just seen that the educational qualifications of the labour force rose steadily during the post-war period and especially fast during the 1970s and 1980s. This does not of itself prove that this was a good thing in economic terms. That turns on the relative costs and benefits to the economy and is a matter of dispute.

During the 1960s the idea that it was possible to measure the rate of return to spending on additional years of schooling became firmly established in the economics of education (Becker 1964; Blaug 1970). We can compare the lifetime earnings of a matched group of school-leavers with similar school-leaving qualifications, one group who continued education for *x* further years, the other who did not. On average the incomes of the first group are higher than the second.

We can also calculate the cost of that extra education. It is of two kinds: first, the cost of instruction—formal education provision—and second, the loss of earnings involved in undertaking the education. By expressing the extra earnings as a rate of return on the additional re-source costs of the extra *x* years we get a traditional rate of return on educational investment. This may be expressed as a private rate of return on the individual's own investment or as a social rate of return on the costs to the whole economy. Various adjustments have to be made to take account of the fact that more able people tend to stay on at school. These are always extremely crude adjustments.

By using the GHS data, which include incomes and school-leaving qualifications, we can approach this kind of analysis. As we have seen, there are two kinds of rates of return. One compares the costs actually born by the individual with his or her enhanced future earnings. This private rate of return reflects an individual's judgement about continuing education. The social rate of return relates the economic costs, teaching resources, buildings, and the opportunity cost of the student's labour, to the extra output generated, and this is measured by the additional earnings generated. We shall not dwell on the perfect labour market assumptions built into such an analysis. The claim is that sufficient competition exists for the results to have validity.

All such studies also have to rely on cross-section data about differences in earnings *today*. We cannot know what a lifetime earnings profile of a current school-leaver would *actually* look like.

In the 1970s critics of this approach advanced a more fundamental criticism. The earnings differentials being observed, they argued, were a reflection of employers' use of the education system to select people they considered more able or better motivated. Education was merely, or largely, a screening device (Taubman and Wales 1974). Those who stay at school longer give more signals about their potential productivity. Argument followed about how much weight to give to these different explanations of the differential earnings we observe. Layard and Psacharopoulos (1974, 1979) played down the screening hypothesis. Riley (1979) has presented evidence of its importance, at least in some occupations.

Bearing these theoretical interpretations in mind we can turn to examining the trends in rates of return over time. While the social rates of return may be problematic, private rates of return may help explain trends in the demand for higher education.

The DES has calculated social rates of return using data on male university graduates from the GHS survey, and it has recalculated that figure using each GHS survey from 1971 to 1984 (Clark and Tarsh 1987; DES 1988*b*). The 'comparison group' were males with any A-levels. More recent calculations by the DES give a comparison of graduate earnings with those gained by school-leavers with two A-levels. The calculations were undertaken on two assumptions about teaching costs in universities. One was that all university costs should be ascribed to the output of students, the other was that 30 per cent of university costs were devoted to research activities. Two further assumptions were made: one that all extra earnings observed were the result of education's contribution, and the other that only two-thirds was, the rest being the result of graduates' higher ability. The results, for what they are worth, show a decline in the average rate of return in the late 1970s and early 1980s, with a certain recovery by 1984. It should be stressed that these results only apply to men and for all first degrees (see Table 3.12). Such overall trends tell us nothing about the causes, in particular, how much declining rates of return are the result of demography or the labour market.

In a very interesting study of young people's perceptions of the returns to post-school education, Williams and Gordon (1981) show that at the end of schooling pupils *are* aware of the differential earnings that flow from staying on. Moreover, their ideas conform very closely to the actual differential earnings of graduates. They rate their earnings higher if their actual and perceived abilities are greater. Women rate their chances of better earnings lower than men. For all groups the intention to enter higher education is associated with higher expected earnings—a high private rate of return. Bosworth and Ford (1985) found the same. Those from manual backgrounds expect a higher earnings differential. In order to be persuaded to enter higher education, 'boys and girls from manual homes need the expectations of a higher potential earnings advantage than their non-manual counterparts' (Williams and Gordon 1981: 210). The higher the private costs imposed on students by the government, the more the differential effect on access.

This more sociological work is confirmed by econometric analysis. Pissarides (1982) sought to explain the rise that took place in staying-on rates and university entry from 1955 to 1970 and the stabilization through the 1970s. He demonstrated a clear link between the school staying-on

Table 3.12. *Rates of return to first degrees,[a] 1971–1984, male graduates, Great Britain* (%)

| | Total cost minus research | | Total cost | |
| | Education factor[b] | | Education factor[b] | |
	1.0	0.67	1.0	0.67
1971	10	8	9	7
1972	9	6	7	5
1973	9	7	8	6
1974	10	7	8	6
1975	9	7	8	6
1976	9	7	8	6
1977	8	6	7	5
1978	8	6	7	5
1979	8	6	7	6
1980	7	5	6	4
1981	6	5	6	4
1982	8	6	7	5
1983	9	7	8	6
1984	10	7	8	6

[a] Including postgraduate teaching diplomas, polytechnic and university degrees, but assuming university costs.

[b] The extent to which education is considered to contribute to the differential in earnings: 1.0 assumes it is the whole explanation, 0.67 assumes that a third reflects the higher ability of graduates.

Source: Clark and Tarsh 1987.

rate, which in turn affects the numbers gaining two A-levels, and the present values of graduate earnings compared with non-graduates. He argued that the plateau in demand for higher education was thus the result of two factors—manual earnings had risen faster than graduate earnings in the 1970s, and overall real permanent earnings growth had slowed down. Both trends have now been reversed. We would therefore expect a rise in the staying-on rate, in A-level performance, and in the demand for university and other places in higher education. This is beginning to happen, as we have already shown.

Equity considerations

We have argued that traditional equity goals, though evident in government pronouncements in 1974, had ceased to be given much, if any, prominence by 1988. That should not divert us from considering various measures of equity over the period, if only because they have traditionally featured in the rationale for state involvement in education. We look at a number of interpretations of equity in turn.

Equality of access by area   A weak definition of equality of opportunity is that children in different areas of the country should have access to equal levels of educational resources. Governments from 1945 to 1975 had taken measures to ration capital and teaching resources between different LEAs. In the early post-war years the aim was to divert capital resources to areas of new population growth, then in the 1960s to areas with older school buildings and social deprivation. The teacher quota was used to limit the extent to which favoured areas could attract teachers from areas of acute shortage. After the Plowden Report (DES 1967) additional payments were given to teachers in 'stress' schools. This probably had only a weak impact on variations in spending. More important, the various equalization elements in grants to local government did even out LEAs' capacity to spend on education. Over time, for a mixture of these reasons, education became the most equally distributed of local services (Davies 1968). The trend to more equality in spending patterns between LEAs continued until the early 1970s (Glennerster 1972; Foster, Jackman, and Perlman 1980). There was some sign of growing disparities between the larger cities in the late 1960s. But in 1976 the quota restrictions on LEAs' employment of teachers were removed. Shortages were deemed to be a thing of the past! Then, as we have seen, capital spending was severely restricted and local authorities encouraged to sell sites to finance new building. Central government's main concern shifted to trying to reduce spending, and it had more success with some authorities than with others. Thus central pressures to equalize spending were relaxed, though not eliminated. The post-1980 block-grant formula did contain an element which reflected school population and low resources.

What impact did these changes make? From 1974 onwards new and larger LEAs took on education powers. We can compare the variations in spending patterns and pupil/teacher ratios across the new education authorities in England and Wales. Over the period 1974/5–1985/6 no major reorganization of boundaries took place. For example, at the beginning of the period, average current spending per primary-school pupil varied from £191 per annum (in Wigan and Cornwall) to £300 per pupil in the ILEA. Nevertheless, the standard deviation was about £20. Secondary-school expenditure, which is over half as costly again on average, had a standard deviation of £32—a roughly equivalent dispersion. The best way to standardize the measures of variation to take account of the rising mean value of spending is the coefficient of variation used by Foster, Jackman, and Perlman (1980). The higher the score, the more inequality. As Table 3.13 shows, the variation in LEA unit costs for both primary and secondary schools increased between 1974/5 and 1980/81, quite sharply reversing the previous decades of gradual equalization. Secondary-school spending per pupil continued to widen between 1980 and 1985.

Table 3.13. *Variations in average local education authority spending per pupil, England and Wales*

	All authorities outside London	England and Wales including London	
	All schools	Primary	Secondary
Coefficient of variation			
1959/60	12.39		
1965/6	7.92		
1971/2	7.88		
1974/5		9.2[a]	8.83
1980/1		12.9	11.3
1985/6		12.1	12.9
Standard deviation in pupil/teacher ratios			
1974/5		1.61	1.14
1980/1		1.61	0.96
1985/6		1.75	1.07

[a] 1974/5 has eleven missing returns from LEAs. The effect of missing out these same authorities in 1980/1 was to increase the coefficient by 0.2 and 0.03.

Sources: Figures for 1959/60–1971/2 from Foster, Jackman, and Perlman 1980. Other figures from own calculations from raw data, CIPFA 1988*b*: tables 3 and 5 and equivalents for earlier years.

Equally effective education   It is one thing to have access to schools with
the same pupil/teacher ratios, quite another to have access to equally
effective schools. We could call this a 'stronger' definition of equality of
opportunity. That is a difficult concept to operationalize. So much of the
variation in school performance relates to social class variables, and the
same is true at the more aggregated level of a local authority. However,
recent work by DES statisticians (DES 1983, 1984*b*) and by the National
Institute for Social and Economic Research (Levitt and Joyce 1987) has
attempted to standardize the 'performance of LEAs', taking into account
the different social class and deprivation factors in each area that are
found to be associated with pupils' performance. Six measures of examination success were used, from one or more A-levels down to a
non-graded result at O-level or CSE. Twelve socio-economic variables
were entered into the regression equation, including social class, country
of birth, household composition, unemployment, the infant mortality
rate, and other measures of poverty. Two variables measured expenditure
on schools. Eight variables were included that related to school inputs or
organization (we have mentioned the grammar-school variable earlier).

As in earlier work, the socio-economic variables accounted for nearly
all the variation that could be explained. Higher teacher expenditure was
associated with some higher performance. Levitt and Joyce (1987) use the
data to examine the inequalities in performance that exist once these
social factors are taken into account. They compared *predicted* results,
given the social variables, with *actual* results. For example, an average
22.7 per cent of English school-leavers passed five or more O-levels.
Harrow, which gained 37.2 compared with its expected 31.0 per cent,
was the most divergently effective; Bromley, the most divergently 'ineffective', gained 28.8, not 32.8 per cent. Of greater significance, most
LEAs cluster within one or two percentage points of the average and
the most divergent in *both directions* contain rich and poor areas without
distinction.

Access to higher education   It is only when we move on to the most
Utopian definition of equality—equality of outcome regardless of social
background—that we find grounds for disappointment. Yet as Warnock
(1975) has argued, anyone who wants to apply Utopian yardsticks is
bound to be disappointed. Jencks (1972) made the same point in a
different way. Given the powerful forces that social class exerts on
schoolchildren's achievements, and the weak impact schools have on
changing those inequalities overall, one cannot expect much leverage
on social inequality through the education system. Despite some interpretations to the contrary, Rutter's work (Rutter *et al.* 1979) does not

change that conclusion for the schools he investigated in south London (see the penultimate chapter of his book).

If we turn from measures of exam performance at one point in time and examine trends over time, the picture changes. As schooling has lengthened and as higher education has expanded, the highest social classes' take-up rate has begun to slacken. Longer education is, after all, not costless, especially for the less able child. Meanwhile, take-up by the poorer groups in society grew as financial and other barriers were removed. Through this century, although the fastest *rates* of growth were experienced by the working class, the biggest *absolute* increases were gained by the upper middle classes (Halsey, Heath, and Ridge 1980). How has that changed in the 1970s and 1980s? The normal statistics that are quoted are taken from the University Central Council on Admissions, which analyses the social class of entrants. They show little change in the relative share of places taken by different social groups. Indeed, the recent figures for the 1980s show more entrants from the highest social classes. The pessimistic conclusion is drawn that there has been no change or a worsening in the relative chances of children from manual social backgrounds getting to university. However, there is a major flaw in that argument. The social composition of the population has been changing. There are *more* families who fall into the non-manual groups and fewer in the manual. Stability in the shares going to university implies a relative *growth* in the chances of manual-class children going to university. The second flaw is that the obsession with universities overlooks the more rapid expansion of the polytechnics since the early 1970s. We can rectify both errors by using the General Household Survey.

The GHS data give us the percentage of the population aged 16–49 who have achieved different qualifications. We can compare the percentage who gained degrees from both universities and polytechnics analysed by their father's occupation (Table 3.14). If 10 per cent of degree-holders' fathers were professionals and 10 per cent of all people's fathers were professionals they would score a ratio of 1.0. We can see from Table 3.14 that in 1974 the ratio for those with professional- and managerial-class fathers was 2.7. They were nearly three times as likely to be degree-holders as their numbers in the population. The score for the semi- and unskilled manual group was 0.2. Those who had skilled manual-worker fathers were half as likely to possess degrees in 1974 as their numbers in the population would lead one to expect. For qualifications below degree level the differences between the ratios are not as great, but are still considerable. By 1985 we do see a change. The ratios for the professional and managerial groups have declined at every level, while the ratios for the manual groups have improved. Notice that the absolute numbers are much larger for the manual groups. Thus a small increase in the ratio implies a large increase in achievers compared to the highest social groups.

What has happened is that the number of entrants to higher education from the *non-manual* groups has risen, but not as fast as their representation in the population. Moreover, non-university degree-granting institutions have been playing a more important role. Once again the reforms of the 1960s are having their effect in the 1970s and 1980s.

Achievement and ethnicity   At the beginning of the chapter we referred to the unease amongst the West Indian community at what was seen to be the underachievement of many children from that community. The ILEA literacy survey (1981) showed that black British children's reading attainment was low at age 8 and remained low at 16. Concern has more recently been expressed about the school achievements of the Bangladeshi community. The Swann Report (DES 1985c) summarized the

Table 3.14. *Highest level of qualifications gained (population aged 16–49), by social class of father, Great Britain* (equal proportionate achievement = 1.0)

Highest qualification	Ratio of achievers to their social class representation in the population			
	Professional and managerial	Intermediate non-manual	Skilled manual	Semi-skilled and unskilled manual
Degree				
1974	2.7	1.7	0.5	0.2
1985	2.1	1.6	0.5	0.4
Post A-level				
1974	1.9	1.5	0.8	0.5
1985	1.4	1.4	0.9	0.6
A-level				
1974	1.8	1.5	0.8	0.5
1985	1.5	1.3	0.8	0.8
O-level				
1974	1.4	2.1	0.7	0.6
1985	1.2	1.3	0.9	0.8

1974: χ^2 (9) = 143.9
1985: χ^2 (9) = 204.2

Source: Own calculations from GHS raw data files.

research evidence available. It showed that it was very important to take into account the interaction between ethnicity and social class and to distinguish between the achievements of boys and girls and between ethnic groups, which show striking differences, many performing better than the white community.

It is not relevant or necessary to repeat that work here, for we are concerned with whether any changes are discernible over time. One of the more encouraging parts of the report was the evidence of some improvement in the relative performance of various groups between 1978/9 and 1981/2, which was the only period for which trend data were available from the School-Leavers Survey. For example, the percentage of West Indians gaining five or more higher grades at CSE and O-level had risen from 3 to 6 per cent and at A-level from 2 to 5 per cent in that three-year period. Research at the ILEA Research and Statistics Branch (ILEA 1987) has compared the school-leaving examination performance of ethnic minority pupils in London between 1976 and 1985. The overall performance score improved from 13.7 to 15.6. Each ethnic group's score improved. The Asian, already high, improved least, but the Caribbean score rose from 10.3 to 13.6. The O-level performance of that group more than doubled. Once more the gradual process of improvement and equality of outcomes is visible. The importance of not associating 'immigrants' and those from the 'New Commonwealth' with low performance is reinforced by the DES survey (1984*b*) of LEA performance which we quoted earlier. Though entered as a measure of 'social deprivation', the proportion of the local population coming from New Commonwealth backgrounds proved to be *positively* associated with examination performance once the other factors had been standardized.

Evidence that ethnic minority children score lower on reading and maths tests at ages 7–10 is presented by Smith and Tomlinson (1989). However, their study also points to a narrowing gap in achievement at later ages. By the fourth and fifth forms, exam results tend to be better than the level predicted from earlier results, hence some 'catching-up' occurs. Minority children still tend to be allocated to lower course levels, but this appears to be based on past attainment and socio-economic group rather than on race. Interestingly, differences between ethnic groups should continue to narrow in adulthood, as Asians and West Indians make more use of post-school further education (but not of higher education) than do whites.

Our own GHS analysis of the educational levels achieved, by father's birthplace, shows that students with parents born outside the United Kingdom do relatively well at the higher levels and fewer non-white children end up with no qualifications (see Table 3.15).

Utilization and expenditure Another way to look at the equity of public expenditure is to consider on whom it is spent. If public revenues are proportionate to income, as they broadly are, whom do they benefit? Over the years it has been shown many times that post-school expenditure disproportionately benefits the higher-income groups or the higher social classes (Glennerster 1972; Le Grand 1982). Again the GHS data help us explore the latest trends. We analysed the 16–24-year-old age group separately. We were able to calculate the total years of education beyond 16 that respondents had received. We then calculated what share of that total had been received by students from different social class backgrounds. We further compared that with the share they would have received if all groups had been equally fortunate. We repeated the same calculations, this time weighting the years of education received by its cost. Table 3.16 shows the results. In 1974 the professional-class children had had 3.0 times the amount of post-school education than their num-

Table 3.15. *Country of origin and educational qualifications, 1985,*
Great Britain (%)

Educational level	Father from			
	UK	Europe or N. America	Elsewhere	All
Degree	6.6	8.5	7.5	6.7
Higher qualification	8.1	10.4	8.2	8.2
A-level	8.0	6.3	8.4	8.0
O-level	19.3	14.6	17.9	19.0
CSE/appr.	15.0	16.8	24.5	15.5
No qualifications	43.0	43.3	33.6	42.6
Base (no.) χ^2 (10) = 75.1	14,542	796	682	16,020
	White	Non-white	All (16 years and older)	
Degree	6.7	6.1	6.7	
Higher qualification	8.2	7.8	8.2	
A-level	7.9	6.3	7.9	
O-level	19.1	16.8	19.1	
CSE/appr.	15.2	25.8	15.5	
No qualifications	42.8	37.1	42.7	
Base (no.) χ^2 (5) = 44.3	15,442	523	15,965	

Source: Own calculations from GHS raw data files.

bers pure and simple would have merited. By 1985 this ratio had fallen to 2.8. More significantly, the managerial-class ratio had fallen from 2.4 to 1.6. The major beneficiaries of the change were the non-manual intermediate groups. The semi- and unskilled group did not gain. If anything, they lost relatively. These are significant findings and suggest that higher education has been more effective in widening access than many critics have realized.

V. IN BRIEF

● Compulsory education between the ages of 5 and 16 places a huge resource burden on government. Further and higher education, serving perhaps only a third of those in the relevant age range, adds half as much again to government expenditure. Such a burden is borne because education is deemed to generate socially desirable objectives. Yet there is much disagreement about those goals, and the influence of wider social changes on the outcomes of the educational process is profound. No straightforward cost-benefit analysis is therefore possible. At most we can set out how far the resources allocated to education have increased or decreased and measure changes in outcomes which different participants consider important. We can thus summarize the period 1974–89 in terms of policy, resources, and outcomes.

Table 3.16. *Years of post-school education received by the population aged 16–24 in 1974 and 1985, Great Britain*

Father's social class	Ratio of share of extra years received to share of population[a]			
	1974		1985	
	Unweighted	Weighted by cost	Unweighted	Weighted by cost
Professional	3.0	4.3	2.8	3.4
Managerial	2.4	2.6	1.6	1.6
Intermediate	1.0	0.9	1.5	1.5
Skilled manual	0.8	0.7	0.8	0.7
Semi-skilled	0.5	0.7	0.4	0.3
Unskilled	0.3	0.2	0.3	0.3

[a] Equal shares = 1.0.

Source: Own calculations from GHS raw data files.

• During our period a shift in emphasis was evident in the proclaimed policy goals of government:

  * Greater emphasis on basic standards of achievement;
  * Greater emphasis on economic relevance and training;
  * Less emphasis on equity.

• Such general policy objectives say little about the level of resources necessary for their achievement, nor about the mix between public and private finance. In practice, expenditure trends owed more to interdepartmental budgetary politics and institutional inertia than a clear reflection of these priorities:

  * Education's share of public spending fell from 13 to 11 per cent.
  * The volume of resources fell from 1975, stabilized by 1985, and has risen slightly since then.
  * Demographic shifts seem to have most influenced levels of per capita spending on relevant age groups.
  * Private spending on education, while rising slightly since 1980, has done little to offset the fall in public spending.
  * Public finance for private schools fell under the Labour government and has been revived by the Conservative government.
  * The range of spending between local authorities widened.
  * Expenditure on training through the Manpower Services Commission did rise but spending per head on 18–24-year-olds, when arguably the greatest economic value of education occurs, fell sharply.

• Cuts in resources undoubtedly affected the policy goals of the early 1970s. A programme to improve school buildings reached only a quarter of the way to its target. One in five primary-school children remained in classes over thirty, instead of none. Nursery-school places were available for less than half the relevant population, not for all of it. Places in higher education failed to keep pace with the number of young people gaining two A-levels.

• Less clear are the effects of shrinking resources on broader outcomes. There is evidence that the education system continued to perform surprisingly well, though this reflected the policy goals and expenditure of previous decades:

  * Human capital content of the labour force has been raised substantially.
  * Exam performance of average and below average children particularly has risen.
  * A considerable degree of equity in education was achieved, both between sexes, between socio-economic groups, and to a lesser extent between ethnic groups.

It may be that the bitter outcome of the cuts in the late 1970s and early 1980s has yet to be tasted. One worrying pointer to the future could be the stagnation of staying-on after 16 and the declining entry to higher education that occurred through much of this period. The end of the 1980s saw the introduction of a National Curriculum and 'opting-out' by state schools. What the effects of these policies will be and when they will be felt must remain a matter for speculation.

Annexe

Table 3A.1. *Education expenditure, United Kingdom* (£ million at 1987/8 prices, adjusted by GDP deflator)

	1973/4	1974/5	1975/6	1976/7	1977/8	1978/9	1979/80	1980/1	1981/2	1982/3	1983/4	1984/5	1985/6	1986/7	1987/8	1988/9
Current																
Nursery	53	66	73	80	68	68	75	77	77	79	81	80	81	90	96	99
Primary	3,684	4,415	4,491	4,421	4,166	4,168	4,072	4,207	4,174	4,099	4,069	3,994	4,032	4,492	4,795	4,945
Secondary	4,425	5,335	5,477	5,494	5,273	5,357	5,186	5,474	5,591	5,586	5,633	5,562	5,513	5,965	6,155	6,114
Special	430	511	547	571	564	608	614	656	675	684	702	711	726	702	731	738
Further education/adult education[a]	1,825	2,132	2,202	2,393	2,318	2,283	2,282	2,357	2,445	2,503	2,599	2,593	2,589	2,660	2,684	2,714
Teachers[b]	500	537	459	176	152	133	133	138	132	140	128	127	140	66	67	67
University[a]	1,711	1,706	1,690	1,760	1,645	1,696	1,721	1,873	1,723	1,748	1,804	1,791	1,750	2,053	2,157	2,174
Other	662	765	789	793	750	713	711	764	746	754	790	799	801	757	800	840
Total	13,289	15,467	15,728	15,687	14,936	15,027	14,795	15,547	15,564	15,593	15,805	15,658	15,630	16,783	17,486	17,691
Education-related																
Health[c]	212	20	26	26	26	27	28	30	32	34	36	38	40	n.a.	n.a.	n.a.
Meals and milk	898	1,097	1,120	1,174	986	960	891	710	648	628	625	604	579	581	624	584
Youth service	179	190	211	206	198	209	213	219	228	242	252	260	260	266	270	268
Transport	239	257	291	302	298	318	318	319	315	319	316	308	304	273	268	260
Miscellaneous	28	0	1	0	4	4	4	4	4	5	5	6	5	154	161	193
VAT[d]	127	206	196	189	216	236	372	443	395	452	482	510	519	558	598	622
Total	1,684	1,770	1,845	1,897	1,727	1,754	1,826	1,725	1,623	1,680	1,716	1,726	1,707	1,833	1,921	1,927
Total current	14,973	17,237	17,573	17,584	16,664	16,781	16,620	17,272	17,187	17,273	17,521	17,385	17,337	18,616	19,407	19,618
Capital[e]																
Nursery	13	11	35	28	14	10	11	9	5	5	7	8	9	8	8	10
Primary	838	618	512	434	282	242	232	258	184	161	170	165	178	154	154	190
Secondary	1,088	915	784	693	598	489	412	406	314	301	280	241	243	210	210	260
Special	92	88	102	90	52	31	32	39	30	26	24	16	18	0	0	0
Further education/adult education	298	257	249	230	182	152	163	191	146	175	170	159	90	189	138	77

Teachers	44	33	18	8	2	2	5	3	3	4	2	3	3	n.a.	n.a.	n.a.
University	360	301	310	269	177	172	186	173	158	146	167	139	152	202	196	201
Other	18	110	117	101	77	53	54	49	39	42	43	39	37	121	121	130
Education-related[f]	212	167	169	158	122	94	96	85	72	65	65	64	63	23	12	15
Total capital	2,962	2,501	2,295	2,011	1,506	1,246	1,191	1,212	951	925	929	835	795	906	837	883
Transfers																
Grants[g]	727	758	832	868	827	895	914	934	948	956	994	975	912	1,185	1,216	1,185
Total net	18,662	20,497	20,700	20,464	18,996	18,922	18,725	19,418	19,086	19,154	19,443	19,195	19,043	20,797	21,460	21,687
Recurrent income[h,i]	694	625	665	610	650	716	677	664	594	644	687	674	n.a.	n.a.	n.a.	n.a.
Capital receipts[h]	n.a.	n.a.	106	97	119	147	161	135	108	102	106	142	n.a.	n.a.	n.a.	n.a.
Total gross expenditure	19,356	21,122	21,471	21,171	19,765	19,785	19,564	20,217	19,788	19,899	20,237	20,011	n.a.	n.a.	n.a.	n.a.
Net expenditure as:																
% of public expend.	13.3	13.0	13.2	13.3	13.0	12.3	11.8	12.0	11.7	11.4	11.4	11.0	10.9	11.6	12.1	12.3
% of GDP	5.7	6.3	6.4	6.1	5.5	5.3	5.1	5.5	5.4	5.3	5.2	5.1	4.8	5.1	5.1	4.9

[a] Includes tuition fees.

[b] Tuition fees and residence costs.

[c] From 1 Apr. 1974, expenditure on school health service was included in the NHS.

[d] VAT paid by local authorities; estimated for 1986/7–1988/9.

[e] Includes loan charges.

[f] Aggregate of education-related categories as above in current spending.

[g] Refers to mandatory and discretionary awards for further and higher education plus grants for school uniforms etc.

[h] England and Wales between 1973/4 and 1979/80, then a grossed-up figure (assuming the same proportion of England and Wales to England only as in 1979/80) applied thereafter. No figures available after 1984/5.

[i] Recurrent income net of tuition fees (see note *a* above). University income is the difference between UGC total expenditure and net expenditure figure from *Annual Abstract of Statistics*.

Sources: DES 1987c: tables 6 and D5 and equivalents for earlier years; CSO 1988c: table 3.2 and equivalents for earlier years; HM Treasury 1989: tables 12.1, 16.1, 17.1, 18.1; UGC 1987: table 6 and equivalents for earlier years.

Table 3A.2. *Education expenditure, United Kingdom (£ million at 1980/1 prices, adjusted by own-price deflator)*[a]

	1973/4	1974/5	1975/6	1976/7	1977/8	1978/9	1979/80	1980/1	1981/2	1982/3	1983/4	1984/5	1985/6	1986/7
Current														
Nursery	38	41	46	51	47	47	55	52	51	53	54	53	53	56
Primary	2,675	2,736	2,798	2,833	2,864	2,921	2,972	2,840	2,762	2,735	2,702	2,659	2,665	2,826
Secondary	3,213	3,305	3,412	3,520	3,625	3,754	3,785	3,695	3,699	3,727	3,740	3,702	3,645	3,753
Special	312	317	341	366	388	426	448	443	446	456	466	473	480	442
Further education/adult education[b]	1,325	1,321	1,372	1,533	1,594	1,600	1,666	1,591	1,618	1,670	1,726	1,726	1,712	1,673
Teachers[c]	363	333	286	113	105	94	97	93	88	93	85	85	93	41
University[b]	1,154	1,113	1,118	1,223	1,187	1,220	1,168	1,264	1,172	1,218	1,248	1,240	1,200	1,309
Other	481	474	492	508	516	499	519	516	494	503	525	532	529	476
Total	9,561	9,639	9,863	10,146	10,324	10,561	10,709	10,494	10,329	10,455	10,544	10,470	10,377	10,576
Education-related														
Health[d]	154	12	16	17	18	19	20	21	21	23	24	25	26	n.a.
Meals and milk	652	679	698	752	678	672	650	479	429	419	415	402	383	366
Youth service	130	118	132	132	136	146	155	148	151	161	167	173	172	167
Transport	174	159	181	193	205	223	232	215	209	213	210	205	201	172
Miscellaneous	20	0	0	0	3	3	3	3	3	3	3	3	4	3
VAT[e]	73	128	122	121	148	165	271	299	262	302	320	340	343	351
Total	1,204	1,097	1,149	1,216	1,188	1,229	1,332	1,165	1,074	1,121	1,139	1,149	1,128	1,153
Total current	10,765	10,736	11,012	11,362	11,512	11,790	12,042	11,658	11,402	11,576	11,684	11,619	11,505	11,730
Capital[f]														
Nursery	9	7	22	18	9	7	8	6	4	3	5	5	6	5
Primary	608	383	319	278	194	170	169	174	121	108	113	110	118	97
Secondary	790	567	488	444	411	342	301	274	208	201	186	160	160	132
Special	67	55	64	58	36	22	23	26	20	18	16	11	12	n.a.
Further education/adult education	217	159	155	147	125	106	119	129	96	117	113	106	60	119
Teachers	32	21	11	5	2	1	4	2	2	3	2	2	2	n.a.
University	207	163	187	160	109	105	116	117	107	101	115	94	104	137
Other	13	68	73	65	53	37	40	33	26	28	29	26	24	76
Education-related[g]	154	103	105	101	84	66	70	57	48	43	43	43	42	15
Total capital	2,097	1,526	1,423	1,276	1,022	857	850	818	632	621	620	558	528	580

Transfers													
Grants[h]	467	492	545	559	531	588	605	631	630	638	660	649	603	785
Total net	13,329	12,755	12,981	13,197	13,065	13,235	13,497	13,107	12,664	12,834	12,964	12,826	12,637	13,094

[a] Own-price deflator is the CIPFA education price deflator, except for universities, where we have used the CVCP's (formerly Tress–Brown) price index (May or July) for recurrent expenditure and the DTI's price index (July) for equipment purchases. Grants are adjusted by the Retail Price Index (fiscal years).

[b] Includes tuition fees.

[c] Tuition fees and residence costs.

[d] From 1 Apr. 1974, expenditure on school health service was included in the NHS.

[e] VAT paid by local authorities; estimated for 1986/7–1988/9.

[f] |Includes loan charges.

[g] Aggregate of education-related categories as above in current spending.

[h] Refers to mandatory and discretionary awards for further and higher education plus grants for school uniforms etc.

Sources: CIPFA 1988*b*: table 8 and equivalents for earlier years; DES 1987*c*: tables 6 and D5 and equivalents for earlier years; CSO 1988*c*: table 3.2 and equivalents for earlier years; HM Treasury 1989: tables 12.1, 16.1, 17.1, 18.1; UGC 1987: table 5 and appendix III, and equivalents for earlier years.

Table 3A.3. *Education spending per capita*

	Nursery	Primary	Secondary	FE/AE	Polytechnic	University
£ at 1987/8 prices, adjusted by GDP deflator						
1973/4	24	685	953	23	50	169
1974/5	30	772	1,054	24	61	191
1975/6	43	776	1,030	26	70	191
1976/7	46	762	992	28	65	190
1977/8	37	713	922	36	57	180
1978/9	37	726	904	36	57	180
1979/80	43	734	856	41	61	172
1980/1	44	790	898	48	67	179
1981/2	41	804	906	48	64	179
1982/3	41	828	914	51	74	176
1983/4	41	855	931	52	70	175
1984/5	41	859	937	51	68	168
1985/6	41	874	955	n.a.	n.a.	166
1986/7	41	851	1,062	n.a.	n.a.	179
1987/8	43	904	1,134	n.a.	n.a.	184
1988/9	44	928	1,182	n.a.	n.a.	183
Index numbers: 1973/4 = 100						
1973/4	100	100	100	100	100	100
1974/5	122	113	111	103	123	113
1975/6	177	113	108	112	141	113
1976/7	190	111	104	119	132	112
1977/8	152	104	97	153	116	107
1978/9	152	106	95	154	115	107
1979/80	175	107	90	174	122	102
1980/1	179	115	94	204	135	106
1981/2	169	117	95	206	129	106
1982/3	166	121	96	217	148	104
1983/4	167	125	98	224	141	103
1984/5	167	125	98	220	137	99
1985/6	169	128	100	n.a.	n.a.	98
1986/7	166	124	111	n.a.	n.a.	106
1987/8	175	132	119	n.a.	n.a.	109
1988/9	181	136	124	n.a.	n.a.	108

Note: Age groups are: nursery (2–4), primary (5–11), secondary (12–18), further education/adult education (16–64), polytechnic (18–24), and university (18–24).

Sources: Table 3A.1 above; unpublished data provided by the Office of Population Censuses and Surveys.

Table 3A.4. *Pupils in private-sector schools, 1947–1986, United Kingdom*

	1947[a]	1957[a]	1961	1971	1976	1981	1986
Total pupils in assisted and independent schools ('000)	576	591	680	621	629	619	607
Private pupils as % of all school pupils	10.2	8.0	7.7	6.1	5.7	5.8	6.4

[a] England and Wales figures.

Sources: CSO 1988*a*; 1947 and 1957 figures from Glennerster and Wilson 1970.

Table 3A.5. *Full-time pupils in private-sector schools, by age,*
England and Wales[a] ('000)

	Age group			
	2–4	5–11	12–15	16 and over
Independent schools				
1973/4	17	211	143	48
1974/5	12	209	147	49
1975/6	17	200	149	49
1976/7	16	193	153	51
1977/8	16	189	155	53
1978/9	17	193	158	56
1979/80[b]	26	202	159	47
1980/1[c]	26	231	204	69
1981/2	27	227	201	69
1982/3	25	223	200	68
1983/4	26	218	201	68
1984/5	27	217	202	68
1985/6	28	218	202	68
Direct-grant schools and non-maintained special schools				
1973/4	1	32	68	30
1974/5	1	31	69	31
1975/6	1	31	69	31
1976/7	1	30	67	31
1977/8	1	24	65	28
1978/9	1	32	59	27
1979/80[b]	1	36	56	21
1980/1[c]	0.3	4	4	1
1981/2	0.3	3	4	1
1982/3	0.3	3	4	1

Table 3A.5. (*cont.*)

	Age group			
	2–4	5–11	12–15	16 and over
1983/4	0.2	3	4	1
1984/5	0.3	2	4	1
1985/6	0.2	2	4	1
All non-maintained schools				
1973/4	18	242	211	78
1974/5	13	240	215	80
1975/6	18	231	217	79
1976/7	17	223	220	81
1977/8	17	213	220	82
1978/9	18	225	217	83
1979/80[b]	27	238	215	68
1980/1[c]	26	235	208	69
1981/2	27	230	206	70
1982/3	25	226	204	69
1983/4	27	221	205	70
1984/5	28	220	206	69
1985/6	28	220	206	70

[a] Estimated from an England-only figure after 1976/7.
[b] For 1973/4–1978/9, age at 31 Jan.; thereafter age at 31 Aug.
[c] From Jan. 1980, most direct-grant schools became registered independent schools.
Source: DES 1988c: tables A10 and A11 and equivalents for earlier years.

Table 3A.6. *Universities: Home candidates accepted, by social class, United Kingdom* (%)

Social class	1977	1981	1986
I	20.9	24.5	20.4
II	41.2	48.9	48.2
III non-manual	14.8	9.7	10.7
III manual	16.6	12.3	12.5
IV	5.2	4.2	6.9
V	1.2	1.0	1.2

Source: UCCA 1987: table E8 and equivalents for earlier years.

Table 3A.7. *Highest qualification attained by the population aged 16–69 in 1985, Great Britain* (%)

Qualification	Year of birth					All (16–69)
	Pre-1921	1921–35	1936–55	1956–63		
Higher degree	0.5	0.5	1.4	0.6		0.8
First degree	2.2	4.3	7.7	9.3		5.8
Other post-A-level	4.2	6.1	11.3	10.1		8.1
A-level	1.9	2.2	8.2	13.2		7.9
O-level (5+ or matric.)	5.7	6.8	8.5	10.8		9.5
Other O-levels	1.0	1.1	8.2	18.1		9.5
Commercial	3.0	5.1	5.8	2.1		4.4
CSE	—	—	1.0	8.5		3.7
Apprenticeship						
all	8.1	7.4	4.5	1.3		4.4
(men)	(14.4)	(14.0)	(7.7)	(2.2)		(7.9)
Other	2.4	3.3	3.7	1.9		3.4
No qualifications	69.6	62.2	39.4	23.8		42.4

Source: Own calculations from GHS raw data files.

Table 3A.8. *Highest educational level achieved, by father's socio-economic group (16–49-year-olds) (%)*

	Professional (i)	Managerial (ii)	Intermed. (iii¹)	Skilled manual (iii²)	Semi-skilled (iv)	Unskilled (v)
1985						
Degree	28.8	13.3	12.4	4.1	3.1	2.2
Other higher	13.5	13.0	13.4	7.9	5.4	4.0
A-level	20.0	14.8	14.3	8.9	7.2	7.4
O-level	22.9	29.4	30.9	23.1	21.3	14.5
CSE etc.	7.3	13.0	13.0	17.9	17.3	14.0
No qual.	7.6	16.4	16.0	38.1	45.7	57.8
All	100	100	100	100	100	100
1974						
Degree	16.7	5.5	4.4	1.3	0.6	0.7
Other higher	14.2	8.8	7.3	3.8	2.4	2.0
A-level	14.8	8.5	8.5	3.8	2.7	2.3
O-level	27.3	15.8	26.9	9.5	7.9	5.5
CSE etc.	13.6	15.3	15.4	14.1	11.2	10.2
No qual.	13.3	45.9	37.5	67.5	75.2	79.3
All	100	100	100	100	100	100

Source: Own calculations from GHS raw data files.

Table 3A.9. *Highest level of education of 16–69-year-olds in 1974, 1979, and 1985, by sex* (%)

| | 1974 | | 1979 | | 1985 | |
	Men	Women	Men	Women	Men	Women
Degree	4.2	1.3	7.1	2.7	9.3	4.3
Other higher	5.1	5.2	6.5	6.3	8.6	7.8
A-level	7.0	3.0	8.2	3.2	10.4	5.8
O-level	13.8	12.6	14.6	15.2	17.7	20.3
CSE/Appr.	15.2	12.0	16.0	14.1	15.3	15.7
No qual.	54.8	65.9	47.6	58.5	38.7	46.2

Source: Own calculations from GHS raw data files.

4

The National Health Service: Safe in Whose Hands?

Julian Le Grand, David Winter, and Frances Woolley

If the British welfare state has a jewel in its crown, it is the National Health Service (NHS). Immensely popular at home, attracting both admiration and hostility abroad, it seems to be a permanent focus of political, media, and popular attention. In consequence, government policies towards the NHS have become central issues in political controversies concerning the welfare state, with politicians vying with each other to reassure the electorate that the NHS is 'safe' in their hands. In this chapter we address some of these issues, beginning with the aims and evolution of government policy towards the NHS over the last two decades (section I) and the resources devoted to it (section II). Section III discusses the 'output' of the NHS, interpreted here as its performance relative to certain policy goals concerning efficiency and equity. Section IV considers health outcomes, concentrating on mortality and self-reported morbidity. The chapter's principal conclusions are summarized in section V.

I. GOALS AND POLICIES

Governments rarely have clearly defined, consistent policy goals; perhaps in consequence they rarely have consistent, well-defined policies. However, the NHS may be something of an exception to this pattern. There was some specification of policy goals by both governments in our period; and perhaps in consequence there also seems to have been some consistency in policy.

Goals

The ultimate aim of policies directed towards health care has to be the promotion of health itself. More specifically, it is difficult to imagine a health-care system that did not have as its principal goal that of effecting an improvement in the health of the individuals who use the system. The very name of the National Health Service implies a concern with health; it is not, after all, called a National Health-Care Service, or even a National Medical Service. However obvious the overriding priority of health itself may appear, it seems worth emphasizing, for it is too often ignored in the controversies that frequently engulf the NHS.

It is also obvious, but also often ignored, that health care is not the only factor that affects health. Improvements in nutrition, in sanitation, and in environmental quality have historically proved to be of far greater importance in raising the national health than advances in medical care (McKeown 1976). Much current medical care is of unproven effectiveness; some may be actually harmful. Hence any assessment of health-care policies over a period has to take account of changes in individuals' health states over that period, but also must be aware of the danger of ascribing those changes wholly, or even in large part, to those policies.

The most comprehensive official statement of the importance of health as an objective (as well as the most comprehensive definition of health itself) is enshrined in the Constitution of the World Health Organization (WHO), whose first two principles state that:

— Health is a state of complete physical, mental and social well-being and not merely the absence of diseases and infirmity; and
— The enjoyment of the highest attainable standard of health is one of the fundamental rights of every human being without distinction of race, religion, political belief, economic or social condition. (WHO 1958: 459)

British examples include the original White Paper on the creation of a National Health Service, which described the 'real need' for the service as 'being to bring the country's full resources to bear upon reducing ill-health and promoting good health in all its citizens' (MoH 1944: 1). The Royal Commission on the National Health Service (1979) listed first among seven aims for the NHS that it should 'encourage and assist individuals to remain healthy' (p. 9). The government's Expenditure Plans also make reference to the importance of health; two of the more recent, for example, stated that, among other things, 'the NHS aims to improve and promote health' (HM Treasury 1988: ii. 242; HM Treasury 1989: ch. 14, p. 4).

Most of these statements can be interpreted as reflecting a concern about the average or *mean* level of health. The WHO reference to human beings' rights to the highest standards of health without distinction of religion, political belief, or economic or social condition can also be taken to imply a concern about variations or *inequality* in health. So can the more explicit statement of David Ennals, Secretary of State for Health in the Labour government during part of its term, who drew attention to the importance of 'narrowing the gap in health standards between different social classes' (Black 1980: 1). Hence in our assessment of the overall outcomes of health policy in the penultimate section of this chapter, we shall look at changes in various measures of both mean health states and inequalities in those states.

However, most statements concerning policy objectives of the period under review have concerned health care rather than health. Indeed, they generally focus on one particular form of health care: the medical and other services provided under the NHS. As the official documents produced during the period indicate, the Labour government had a variety of aims for the NHS. These include both *efficiency* goals, such as the providing of 'a broad range of services to a high standard' (Royal Commission on the NHS 1979: 9), and *equity* goals, such as providing 'equality of access' (ibid.) or 'equality of opportunity of access to health care for people at equal risk' (DHSS 1976a: 7). The Conservative government's aims are perhaps best summarized in their Public Expenditure White Papers; to the improvement and promotion of health, they add the aims of providing 'necessary treatment for illness and care for those in need, while making the best use of available resources' (HM Treasury 1988: ii. 242).[1]

How can we assess the extent to which these goals have been achieved? Terms such as 'broad range' or 'high standard of services' are not easy to define, let alone measure; nor is the 'necessary treatment for those in need'. However, it is likely that the standard and availability of services depend, for the most part, on the resources devoted to them. In the next section, we examine what happened to those resources over the period, and compare trends in resources with trends in demographic indicators of need.

The aim of making 'the best use of available resources' is an efficiency objective. The concept of efficiency in the NHS can have a number of different dimensions. Given that very little internal costing of NHS services occurs, it is extremely difficult to measure any possible change in efficiency. As a result we confine ourselves to a brief discussion of some of the 'micro-efficiency' programmes instituted by the Conservative government. Similarly, we limit our discussion of the breadth of services to developments in one area that has been a major concern of both governments: that of the so-called 'Cinderella' or priority services of the elderly, the mentally ill, and the mentally handicapped.

The 'equity' objectives are also ill defined. However, they seem to have been operationalized—again by both governments—into a concern with regional and social inequalities in the use and provision of services. We examine trends in both these types of inequality.

An essential preliminary to these analyses, however, is a brief description of policy developments during the period with which we are concerned. That is the task of the next section.

---

[1] The 1989 White Paper has the same wording except that, for reasons known only to its authors, it drops the phrase 'for those in need' (HM Treasury 1989: ch. 14, p. 4).

The evolution of policy[2]

The Labour government elected in February 1974, and re-elected in October of that year, was seen by many of its supporters as having the opportunity to make the radical changes in key areas of society which eluded the 1964–70 administration. However, this opportunity, if such it was, was not exploited in the case of health. Some of the changes, such as the decision to phase out private beds in NHS hospitals, or the taxing as an employee benefit, at all levels of remuneration, of medical insurance paid for by the employer, represented a definite reversal of policy, but others reflected the concerns of the previous Conservative government.

This was particularly the case with two out of the three principal concerns of policy during the period: the reallocation of resources to the relatively deprived regions and to the priority services—for the elderly, the mentally ill, and the mentally handicapped (the third was pay-beds in NHS hospitals). In 1976 the Resource Allocation Working Party (RAWP) recommended the adoption of a new formula for allocating NHS resources between the regions (DHSS 1976a). The principal innovation was the inclusion of measures of need (chiefly demographic factors and mortality rates) among the factors used to determine the allocation of funds. The effect of this was to divert resources that would otherwise have gone to regions that, relative to need, were well endowed (primarily, London and other south-eastern regions) to poorly endowed regions (most of the rest of the country). Despite obvious problems (such as the omission of morbidity as an indicator of need, the existence of extensive areas of deprivation even within the wealthier regions, and the neglect of inequalities other than geographical ones), the operation of RAWP during the period did manage a measure of redistribution between regions, as we shall see.

The attempt to reallocate resources to the Cinderella services met with more mixed success, as is discussed in the next section. Perhaps part of the reason for the mixed performance was the government's preoccupation with the third major issue of the period: that of the removal of private beds from NHS hospitals. Despite the bitterness of the struggle, the success of this too was very limited, as is also discussed below.

One of the by-products of the eventual compromise over pay-beds was the setting up of a Royal Commission to examine the overall state of the NHS. This reported in 1979, and provided, in the words of one commentator 'an overwhelming—though not uncritical—endorsement of the NHS's achievements' (Klein 1983: 133). It was the last such endorsement the NHS would receive for some time. Another important inquiry initi-

[2] This section draws on Atkinson, Hills, and Le Grand (1987).

ated in this period was a response to one of the criticisms of RAWP: that it concentrated too heavily on regional differences, and did not address possibly more fundamental inequalities, particularly those associated with social class and income. In 1977 a DHSS Working Party was set up under the chairmanship of Sir Douglas Black to investigate these 'social' inequalities in health. However, it did not produce its Report (Black 1980) until after the Conservative government had taken office, and its conclusions did not fit in with the philosophy of the new government. Only a few copies were made available, and for a few years the Report 'acquired something of the novelty of an underground samizdat publication from Eastern Europe' (Paterson 1981). However, the Report became more widely available with the eventual publication of a commercial edition (Townsend and Davidson 1982).

The Conservative government that took office in 1979 did not intend to dismantle the NHS. The 1979 Conservative Manifesto stated: 'we do not intend to reduce resources going to the National Health Service'. The 1983 Manifesto was not quite so explicit as the 1979 one in terms of overall resources going to the NHS, but made a number of specific spending commitments (notably, to hospital building and maintenance, to the priority services, and to the underprovided regions); and the 1987 Manifesto made specific commitments to nurses, prevention, community care, management, and modernization, all within a general commitment to 'continue to improve the service'. None made any reference to large-scale privatization of the service, although the 1983 Manifesto did 'welcome the growth in private health insurance in recent year'.

It is therefore not surprising that at least in the earlier years the policy interventions in the health field by the Conservative government were in part a continuation of earlier concerns. For example, there were two major organizational changes, both in the name of efficiency. The 1982 reorganization removed one tier of administration; the changes following the NHS Management Inquiry (1983) by Sir Roy Griffiths increased the role of professional management. Also, prescription, dental, and ophthalmic charges were raised considerably, a development discussed in detail in a subsequent section.

There were some other changes. There was the contracting out of catering and cleaning services. Perhaps more significantly, there were measures to stimulate the private medical sector, through abolition of the Health Services Board that had regulated its activities, through changes in consultants' contracts that increased the opportunities for private practice, and through the restoration of exemption of employer-provided medical insurance from tax for employees below a certain level of remuneration. In the early years the effect of these latter changes was spectacular, with 26 per cent increase in the number of subscribers to private medical insurance in 1980, followed by 13 per cent increase in 1981. The rate of increase has now fallen sharply: by 1985 it was about 2 per cent, although in 1986 it rose again to 5 per cent (CSO 1988*a*: 128). Also, the entry of commercial, and chiefly American, firms into the market for providing hospital care has had the paradoxical effect of driving *up* the costs of private care, prompting the memorable complaint by the Chief Executive of BUPA that 'private medicine is threatened by commercialism' (*Daily Telegraph*, 8 Jan. 1986). However, despite the reversal of the pay-beds policy, the average daily bed occupation by private patients in NHS hospitals continued to fall. Overall, the private sector remains small, but continues to make a significant contribution in the areas of acute care and elective surgery (Propper 1989*a*).

But overall the most striking feature of policy towards the NHS, at least until 1988, was its continuity (an interpretation also supported by Klein 1985). There were ideological skirmishes on the periphery (over pay-beds, tax concessions to private medicine, and contracting out), but the main concerns of all the governments involved were broadly the same: managerial reorganization, regional and other inequalities, and the Cinderella services.

However, all this was apparently to change in 1988. In that year, in response to one of the perennial outcries concerning allegedly low levels of NHS funding, the government set up a review of the NHS as a whole. The review took longer than expected (perhaps delayed by the splitting up during the year of the Department of Health and Social Security into its component parts, and the consequent appointment of a new Secretary of State for Health, Kenneth Clarke), but eventually a White Paper, *Working for Patients*, appeared in January 1989 (DoH 1989*a*).

Given its genesis in the middle of an NHS funding crisis and given the ideology of the government that produced it, the White Paper was an astonishing document, at least in terms of its omissions. It contained virtually no proposals for increased resources; and, with the exception of the introduction of tax relief for private health insurance for the elderly, it contained no proposals for expanding the role of private funding for health care. Instead the NHS would, in the words of the Prime Minister's foreword to the White Paper, 'continue to be available to all, regardless of income, and to be financed mainly out of general taxation'. At least as far as the level and sources of funding were concerned, continuity of policy was to be maintained.

However, the document was more radical on the delivery side. Its key proposals included provisions for:

hospitals to 'opt out' of local health authority control;
district health authorities to contract with the newly independent hos-

pitals to provide services; they could also contract with other health authorities;

large GP practices to be given budgets for the care of their patients; again they would contract with hospitals or with different health authorities for services;

capital charging and the extension of medical 'audit'; and

changes in the composition of health authorities to make them more 'managerial'.

Assessment of the impact of these reforms will have to wait until they have been in place for several years. However, it is important to note how they parallel changes recently initiated by the Thatcher government in other areas of the welfare state, such as education and personal social services, all of which involve changes in the organization of the *delivery* of services rather than in the level or sources of *finance*. This is a point to which we shall return in Chapter 8.

II. TRENDS IN EXPENDITURE ON HEALTH CARE

The bulk of public discussion of expenditure on health care concerns central government expenditure on the NHS. This is indeed by far the largest component of total expenditure on health care, and we begin by examining it in some detail. However, it is not the only one. Even within the services provided by the NHS, patients are charged for prescriptions and these prescription charges have for long been a subject of political controversy. In addition NHS patients may face implicit costs in using the service, arising from the time spent travelling to NHS facilities and the costs of waiting for services to be delivered to them. Thus there are costs of the NHS that are paid for by patients, as well as those that are met by the government; these are also discussed below.

Health-care services are also provided by the private sector. The relationship between these two sectors has often been the subject of government policy, and it is in this area that there is the sharpest difference between Conservative and Labour governments. The private sector has been encouraged to grow in the last ten years and it has done so. We therefore end this section with a discussion of that growth.

Trends in government expenditure

Expenditure in real terms   The first step in analysing the trends in central government expenditure is to deflate figures in current prices by a measure of inflation. As mentioned in the Introduction, there are a number of ways of doing this. We begin by using a general measure of the rate of inflation: the Gross Domestic Product (GDP) price deflator. Using this deflator provides a measure of the resources devoted to the NHS in terms of the value of those resources had they been spent elsewhere in the economy. We call this total 'real NHS expenditure', and it is shown in the first column of Table 4.1. It grew by 29 per cent during the Labour government (1973/4–1978/9) and 28 per cent under the Conservatives (1978/9–1987/8), with corresponding constant annual growth rates of 5.2 and 2.8 per cent respectively.

Both Labour and Conservative governments rapidly increased real expenditures shortly after they came to power. Under Labour, total real expenditure rose by over 20 per cent in 1974/5. Under the Conservatives it rose by nearly 10 per cent in 1980/1. Both these large increases may partly reflect comparatively generous pay awards. After these sharp initial increases, the pattern of growth is rather different under the two governments. The growth rate under Labour declines until there is an actual fall of 2.9 per cent in 1977/8. This decrease was partly made up by a resumption of growth in 1978/9. Under the Conservatives, real expenditure rises for every year for which we have data. For some of these years the

Table 4.1. *The National Health Service: Growth in resources and needs*

	Expenditures			
	£bn. (real)	As % of GDP	Volume (1973/4 = 100)	Needs (1973/4 = 100)
1973/4	12.5	3.8	100	100
1974/5	15.1	4.6	113	100
1975/6	16.0	4.9	122	100
1976/7	16.1	4.8	123	100
1977/8	15.7	4.6	122	101
1978/9	16.1	4.5	124	101
1979/80	16.1	4.4	124	103
1980/1	17.7	5.0	130	104
1981/2	17.9	5.1	131	104
1982/3	18.1	5.1	133	105
1983/4	18.5	5.0	131	105
1984/5	18.7	4.9	133	106
1985/6	18.9	4.8	134	107
1986/7	19.7	4.8	133	108
1987/8	20.6[a]	4.9	n.a.	109

[a] Provisional.

Sources: Real expenditures: Table 4.A1; % of GDP: calculated from Table 4.A1 and CSO 1988*b*; volume: calculated from Table 4.A2; needs: *Official Report*, 26 Mar. 1984, WA, col. 60, and *Official Report*, 23 June 1986, WA, col. 66–7.

growth rate is comparatively small (approximately 1 per cent for 1981/2, 1982/3, 1984/5, and 1985/6), but in three of them it is notably higher: 2.3 per cent for 1983/4, 4.4 per cent for 1986/7, and 4.6 per cent in 1987/8.

An alternative way of looking at these figures is to examine the share of total national resources, as measured by GDP, devoted to the NHS. The relevant percentages are given in the second column of Table 4.1. Looking at the two periods as a whole, the share rose by 0.7 percentage points under Labour and by 0.4 percentage points under the Conservatives. As one might expect from the expenditure figures, the timing of these increases is entirely concentrated in the earlier years of office of each government.

One explanation for this 'hump-shaped' time path lies in the large pay awards that the governments concerned apparently felt it was necessary to grant or to promise to health-service workers during election periods. For instance, qualified nurses received pay increases of 21.5 per cent in 1974/5 and of 12.5 per cent in 1980/1 (Trinder 1987). The latter were a part of the Clegg award to nurses that was promised by Labour and paid for by the Conservatives after the 1979 election.

Expenditure in volume terms   These above-average wage increases show that it is possible for input prices to change in the health-service sector at different rates from those in the rest of the economy. As a result, real expenditure as we have defined it may not be a good measure of the actual volume of health-care services provided by the NHS. To analyse this, we need to use a deflator specifically constructed for the NHS. A number of deflators are available that attempt to take these further considerations into account. Only one of these, taken from the National Income Blue Book, covers the whole of our period. A volume index based on this deflator is given in the third column of Table 4.1.

Again we find a similar time path. The bulk of the growth is concentrated in the early years of each government. For Labour we have three years of growth, followed by one year of decline (1977/8), followed by a year of further growth which, on these figures, more than offsets the earlier decline. The volume of total expenditure rose by 23 per cent in the first three years, declined by 0.8 per cent, and finally rose by 1.6 per cent. The overall growth was 24 per cent, or 4.4 per cent at constant annual rates.

For the Conservatives, after a year of no growth, we have a growth rate of 4.8 per cent for 1980/1, followed by six years of low growth or in two cases (1983/4 and 1986/7) decline. Over the whole Conservative period for which we have data, we find total growth of 7.3 per cent, at an average annual rate of 0.9 per cent.

Thus the evidence from the volume estimates suggests that, although the very sharp rates of growth of real expenditure are partly attributable to factors such as increases in pay that do not themselves constitute increases in volume, nevertheless part of the comparatively sharp growth in real expenditure in the early years of each government actually reflected a growth in volume (about two-thirds for both governments).

Given the relatively high rates of growth in volume in the first two years of each party in office, it follows that the pattern of growth is roughly similar in the two periods. It appears that the bulk of the total volume growth in both periods occurs during the first two years: over 90 per cent for Labour and over 65 per cent for the Conservatives. The constant annual growth rate thereafter is extremely low: 0.5 per cent for both periods.

Nevertheless these figures also point to differences in overall growth between the two periods. They confirm that total growth was higher in the Labour period, whether real or volume expenditure is used. Using constant annual growth rates which take into account the fact that the Labour period is shorter than the Conservative period, we find that the annual growth rate under Labour was approximately twice as high as under the Conservatives if the real-expenditure measure is used, and over four times as high if the volume measure is used.

An alternative volume deflator has also been provided since 1978/9 by the House of Commons Select Committee on Social Services. The deflator covers only England rather than the whole of the United Kingdom, though there is no evidence that costs rose at a different rate in England from the rest of the country. The Select Committee also provides deflators which cover different components of NHS expenditure. We have compared three different volume estimates: one derived from the deflators for the components of NHS expenditures; one derived from the total Social Services Committee (SS) deflator; and a third derived from the Blue Book deflator.

The pattern of volume growth is different using the SS deflators. After a decline in 1979/80 (as with the estimates using the GDP deflator), volume grows in every year thereafter. The concentration of growth in the first two years is now no longer present. In addition, overall growth in the Conservative period is slightly different if the SS deflators are used (7.6 per cent using the component deflators, 6.2 per cent using the total).

The discrepancies between the calculations of the total volume of expenditures by using different deflators, while they may not seem large, illustrate the difficulties of determining the rate of growth of expenditure at constant prices. It is therefore difficult to make very definite statements about whether the volume of NHS expenditure rose or fell in a particular year in the 1980s. However, there is a rough agreement between the different indices over the rate of growth during the Conservative period— at least in comparison with the rate of growth in the Labour period.

While the volume deflators attempt to take into account specific increases in NHS input prices, they do not take into account improvements in the quality of those inputs, or any increases in the efficiency with which those inputs are used (CSO 1985*a*; Robinson and Judge 1987). As a result, it is extremely difficult to make very precise statements on the basis of these deflators; it is possible only to draw broad conclusions.

Composition of government expenditure   The proportions of expenditure devoted to the various components of spending are given in Table 4.2. The main feature of this table is the stability of the proportions over the period. The most substantial change took place in the first two years, where the proportion of total spending on hospitals rose 5 percentage points, chiefly at the expense of GPs (general medical) and capital expenditure. Thereafter the share going to hospitals remained roughly constant, with an increase of over a percentage point in 1980/1 probably reflecting pay settlements in that year. It is also of interest that the share going to pharmaceuticals fell substantially in 1975/6, and thereafter rose slowly. Fears of dramatically increasing drug costs do not seem to be borne out by these figures, though the slow growth may reflect the success of policies that were designed to prevent sharp increases in pharmaceutical costs.

The other substantial change in expenditure shares concerned the share of capital expenditure. This fell by nearly 40 per cent from 1973/4 to 1979/80. Thereafter the share increased slightly, but never regained the ground it had lost under Labour. Finally, it is worth noting that the share of total NHS costs paid for by patients also remained comparatively small throughout the period. The share fell under Labour, and then rose under the Conservatives, though it has yet to reach its level in 1973/4. These trends and the possibility of future growth in patient charges are discussed further below.

It is worth remembering that the percentages given in Table 4.2 only show changes in the proportions of the various components as they are usually defined in NHS data sources. It is, of course, quite possible that there were more substantial changes within these components, particularly within the largest component, namely hospital and community care services (see the section below on 'priority services').

Need and demand

So far our discussion has centred on the changes in the quantity of services provided by the NHS. It is important to compare these changes with changes in the demand and needs for these services. Just as it is difficult to measure accurately the growth in the volume of services provided, so it is also difficult to measure the growth in both need and demand.

Table 4.2. *Composition of NHS expenditure* (%; years ending 31 Mar.)

| | Hospitals | Family practitioner[a] | | | | Administration | Patients' payments | Other | Total current | Capital expenditure |
		General medical	Pharmaceutical	General dental	Ophthalmic					
1973/4	62.4	8.0	11.0	5.2	1.2	3.0	-3.5	3.1	90.5	9.5
1974/5	65.0	6.5	10.7	5.0	1.3	3.8	-2.7	3.1	92.6	7.4
1975/6	67.4	6.2	8.9	4.4	1.4	3.9	-2.0	2.5	92.6	7.4
1976/7	66.9	6.1	9.9	4.2	1.3	3.9	-2.1	3.0	93.2	6.8
1977/8	67.6	5.9	10.8	4.0	1.2	3.9	-2.1	2.9	94.1	6.0
1978/9	66.9	5.9	11.2	4.2	1.2	3.8	-2.0	2.9	94.1	6.0
1979/80	67.1	6.2	10.7	4.4	1.2	4.0	-2.2	3.0	94.3	5.7
1980/1	68.3	6.3	10.2	4.1	1.0	3.8	-2.4	2.9	94.2	5.8
1981/2	68.1	6.5	10.5	4.2	1.1	3.6	-2.6	2.3	93.7	6.3
1982/3	67.4	6.8	11.1	4.4	1.2	3.4	-2.8	2.2	94.0	6.0
1983/4	67.9	6.8	11.5	4.4	1.2	2.9	-2.9	2.3	94.0	5.8
1984/5	66.9	7.3	11.8	4.6	1.3	2.9	-3.0	2.2	93.9	6.1
1985/6	66.7	7.4	11.8	4.5	1.0	2.7	-2.8	2.5	93.7	6.3
1986/7	66.2	7.4	12.0	4.7	0.8	3.1	-3.0	2.8	93.8	6.2
1987/8	66.2	7.4	12.0	4.8	0.8	2.9	-3.2	2.7	93.7	6.3

[a] Gross figures (i.e. not net of patients' payments).

Source: Table 4A.1.

The distinction between need and demand is often arbitrary. Here we simply describe changes in the potential use of the NHS that arise from changes in the demographic structure of the population as changes in need, and those that arise because tastes and perceptions may have changed as changes in demand. Since the latter are extremely difficult to observe directly, we associate demand changes with changes in personal incomes.

The Department of Health (DoH) calculates an index of need based on the changing demographic structure of the population. It is constructed to apply to the Hospital and Community Health Service, but we see no reason why it cannot be applied to the whole of the NHS. The validity of this index has been challenged by a number of writers. Certainly it appears to be based on a very limited concept of need. It makes no attempt to take into account, for instance, any increase in morbidity which may have arisen as a result of the sharp increase in unemployment in the 1980s (see Smith 1987). In fact, there now seems to be a consensus that the DoH measure provides the lowest probable figure for the effects of the changing demographic structure on the NHS (Robinson and Judge 1987; Radical Statistics Health Group 1987).

Bearing this in mind, we give the DoH index from 1973/4 to 1987/8 in the last column of Table 4.1. As will be seen, the index grows slowly, reflecting the increase in the age of the population as a whole. The rate of growth accelerates during the 1980s. The index grew by only 1 per cent under Labour but by 8 per cent under the Conservatives. At constant annual rates, the growth in need is 0.2 per cent for Labour and a little over 0.8 per cent for the Conservatives. This suggests that, using the Department's own figures for the growth in need, the growth in the volume of services under the Conservatives was only slightly higher than the growth in need (0.9 per cent as against 0.8 per cent at annual rates). For Labour, when the annual growth in volume was higher (4.4 per cent per year as against 0.2 per cent), there was a much bigger difference between the two.

It is reasonable to assume that there has been an increase in the demand for health care in this period as a result of the rise in personal incomes. If we assume that the taxes which pay the NHS costs are borne entirely by households, we can compare the shares of gross household income devoted to NHS expenditure. Under Labour this share rose from 4.6 to 5.8 per cent, while under the Conservatives the share increased only slightly from 5.8 to 6.0 per cent.

There are conflicting estimates of the income elasticity of demand for health care. Aggregate time series analysis suggests that it is larger than one, cross-section micro-studies indicate that it may be less than one (see Parkin, McGuire, and Yule 1987; Newhouse 1987). Relative prices may also have changed. But these figures further suggest that, under the Conservatives, the balance between the growth in volume and the growth in need and demand was not maintained.

As we have stressed, these calculations do not take into account possible improvements in efficiency. These are discussed in the next section. In addition, there may have been increases in costs owing to the introduction of new techniques, although the latter might also be expected to be accompanied by increase in the quality of services provided. A government minister has indeed suggested that additional spending of 0.5 per cent per year is necessary on account of medical advance (letter from Mr B. Hayhoe to the Chairman of the Institute of Health Services Management, 28 Jan. 1986; see also Robinson and Judge 1987).

Underfunding of the NHS?

Before concluding our discussion of central government expenditure on the NHS, it is worth noting that our analysis may go some way to explain why rising real spending on health care (albeit at a comparatively low rate) is clearly at variance with the widespread perception in the late 1980s that the NHS was in serious decline. This was not a new phenomenon, and a number of different explanations can be offered for it. Klein (1983) noted the recurrent discrepancy between the rhetoric of crisis and increasing real resources; he ascribed it to a number of factors, including the demands of technological developments and international comparisons with the health systems of wealthier countries. Another possible explanation, discussed by Robinson (1986), concerns changes in the *composition* of spending, though as we have noted, if fairly broad categories of NHS expenditure are used, there have been no large changes in the composition of expenditure since the 1970s. The success of the reallocations to the deprived regions and the priority services has also created tensions; in each case, the losers are acute hospitals in the South-East, institutions with powerful friends and loud voices.

No doubt some or all of these factors were at work in the late 1980s. In particular, much political mileage was made of the fact that Britain spends a relatively low proportion of GDP on health care compared with other countries—although some commentators regarded this as a tribute to the ability of the NHS to control costs (Barr, Glennerster, and Le Grand 1988).

Our analysis also points to another factor that might explain the perception of crisis: a change in the rate of growth of supply relative to need or demand. The behaviour over time of the main variables which determine the balance between supply and need and demand is shown in Fig. 4.1. In the figure we also attempt to take into account the possible increase in the volume of NHS resources that may have arisen through efficiency savings (volume with augmented improvements). They have been calculated from the savings given in Table 4.4 and 4.5 and are discussed in more detail below.

The growth in supply has had a different pattern from the growth in demand. Under Labour, personal income rose, fell, and then rose again. It had a milder fall under the Conservatives in 1981/2 and then rose steadily. Our needs indicator shows slow growth, with the rate tending to rise over time. On the supply side there was continuity in terms of the overall growth of volume between the two governments after 1975/6. Since there had been rapid growth just before that, it took some time before slower growth in volume was overtaken by the higher growth on the demand side. Thus it is not hard to understand the widespread feeling of a growing pressure on NHS resources during the 1980s.

The amount of extra funding required to restore a rough balance between supply and need or demand depends on a number of factors—increases in NHS efficiency, the rise in personal incomes, changes in technology and personal tastes, etc. However, the latest government plans for spending as given in HM Treasury (1989) imply an average

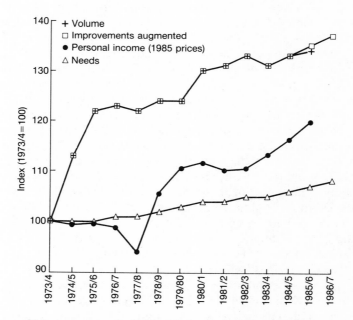

Sources: Volume and needs: Table 4.1; income: CSO 1988*b*; improvements: Table 4.5

FIG. 4.1. Trends in personal income, NHS volume, and needs

annual rate of growth of 2.3 per cent in real terms for the four financial years after 1987/8. This is rather less than the comparable figure for the period 1978/9 to 1987/8 (2.8 per cent), but very slightly larger than the annual growth from 1980/1 to 1987/8 (2.2 per cent). It would appear, therefore, that there is no plan to change the Conservative policies towards overall funding of the NHS. This implies that the government is unwilling to make the effort, in terms of total spending, to restore an approximate balance between the supply of health-care services provided by the NHS on the one hand and the need and the demand for those services on the other. A perceived 'crisis' of underfunding is therefore likely to continue.

Private costs of public health care

As we have already mentioned, although most health care is provided by the NHS and is funded by central government, there are significant private expenditures on health care. These include not only payments for private health care, but, within the NHS, the payment of prescription and other charges. There are also private non-monetary costs of waiting for NHS treatment. Here we discuss the private costs (monetary and non-monetary) of using the NHS (the private costs of public health care); in the next section, we consider the growth of the private sector (the private costs of private health care).

Charges   The NHS charges for certain pharmaceutical, dental, and ophthalmic services. The amount of revenue raised from charges is relatively small. In 1987/8, revenue from charges met 2.7 per cent of NHS costs. Prescription charges accounted for 10 per cent of pharmaceutical expenditures. The majority of prescriptions are exempt from charges, and charges are less than the cost of treatment. For example, in 1987 the average net cost of a prescription was £5.47, compared with prescription charges of £2.80 per item (as of April 1988). Patients' payments are, nevertheless, highly political. Labour and Conservative governments have differed radically on their policy towards charges.

The Labour government was reluctant to raise charges. Prescription charges remained constant in nominal terms at 20p per item. Charges for ophthalmic and dental services were increased once, in April 1977. The combination of constant or slowly increasing nominal charges and rapid inflation meant that charges fell in real terms. During the Labour government, the total amount paid in charges fell by 29 per cent from £439 million to £322 million (1987/8 prices); as a proportion of NHS expenditures it fell from 3.5 per cent in 1973/4 to 2.0 per cent in 1978/9. The most dramatic decrease occurred in payments for pharmaceuticals, which more than halved (Table 4A.1).

The Conservative government reversed the trend in patients' payments. Since coming to office in 1979 the Conservative government has adopted a policy of continually increasing the real value of patient charges (Ryan and Birch 1989). In July 1979, prescription charges more than doubled to 45p per item. By April 1988, prescription charges stood at £2.80 per item, 540 per cent more in real terms than when the Conservative government came into power. New dental treatment charges were introduced in April 1988, and charges for dental examinations were introduced in January 1989. From April 1989, charges for sight-tests were introduced (HM Treasury 1989).

Total revenue from patients' payments has risen more slowly than charges. This is for two reasons. First, owing in part to an increase in the number of exempt prescriptions for those over retirement age and those with a low income, the proportion of prescriptions exempt from charges in England and Wales has risen from 65 per cent in 1979 to 82 per cent in 1986 (Office of Health Economics 1987). Second, from April 1985, spectacles under the General Ophthalmic Services were made available only to children, people on a low income, and the users of certain complex lenses. Because fewer people were using them, total patients' payments for ophthalmic services fell, in real terms at 1987/8 prices, from £60 million in 1984/5 to £15 million in 1985/6 and £1 million in 1987/8 (Table 4A.1).

Over the period of Conservative government from 1978/9 to 1987/8, revenue raised from charges more than doubled in real terms. Charges now finance 2.7 per cent of NHS expenditures, compared with 2.0 per cent in 1978/9. With the introduction of new charges in April 1988 and January 1989, revenue from charges will probably continue to rise.

Non-monetary costs   There are two major non-monetary costs of using the NHS. The first is the cost of keeping an appointment, for example the cost of travelling to the GP, and the time cost of being in the doctor's surgery. Because these costs are lower for certain groups of people—for example people with cars or workers on a monthly salary—they may lead to social inequality in access to the NHS, discussed later in this chapter. The second non-monetary cost of using the NHS is the cost of waiting for treatment, both in terms of the suffering and incapacity experienced while waiting, and in terms of the decline in the value of the treatment as it is delayed. The mean waiting time for NHS treatment rose in the second half of the 1970s from 13.8 weeks in 1974 to 15.7 weeks in 1976 and 17.5 weeks in 1979. Since then it has remained at about 17 weeks. The latest figures available, for 1985, give a mean waiting time of 17.3 weeks.[3]

---

[3] These figures come from the *Hospital In-Patient Enquiry* series MB4 for various years. A recent example is OPCS 1989.

The mean waiting time measures only one dimension of the cost of waiting for treatment. As important is the amount of welfare lost each day spent waiting. The amount of welfare lost each day is difficult to measure directly. For example, consider an elderly person waiting for a cataract operation. If the patient is not engaged in paid employment, standard economic criteria do not associate any costs with time spent waiting, let alone make any allowance for inconvenience and suffering. Yet a service which is provided promptly is clearly of more value than one for which the patient has to wait.

One approach to estimating the cost of waiting begins with the observation that a person has an alternative to waiting, that is, jumping the queue by going private. A person will only join the waiting list if the cost of waiting is less than the cost of going private. The cost of going private can be used, therefore, as an upper limit on the cost to each person of waiting. Using this methodology, Cullis and Jones (1986) estimated aggregate NHS waiting costs at £1.2 to £2.1 billion, or between 7 and 13 per cent of NHS expenditures.

An alternative approach, used in Propper (1989*b*), is the 'stated preference' methodology. Propper surveyed 1,360 people, chosen at random from the population. She presented each with a hypothetical choice between immediate treatment at a specified cost, or free treatment after a certain length of time. By presenting people with several such choices, she was able to estimate the cost of waiting. Using the same waiting-list data as Cullis and Jones, she estimated the cost of waiting at about £370 million per annum (at 1987 prices), or 2 per cent of total NHS expenditures.

With costs of this magnitude, it is not surprising that waiting lists have been an important policy issue. At the end of 1986, the Conservative government launched its waiting-list initiative, aimed at reducing the time people wait for treatment. The initiative was backed by a Waiting List Fund of £25 million for 1987/8 (£30 million for 1988/9), which was used by health authorities to provide, for example, extra operating sessions and beds, to bring forward medical appointments, to buy or make use of spare capacity in other NHS or non-NHS facilities (HM Treasury 1989). Government estimates put the number of additional in-patients and day cases treated using the fund at 100,000, and the number of additional out-patients treated at 44,000.

It is as yet too early to assess the overall impact of the waiting-list initiative. One interesting question, however, is the effect of the initiative on the balance between public and private health care. By shortening waiting lists, the initiative will make public health care more attractive. On the other hand, the initiative provides private hospitals with access to public funds, and utilizes excess capacity in the private sector. This may decrease average costs in the private sector, enabling the sector to lower charges and attract more patients. Furthermore, the possibility of 'selling' excess capacity to the NHS may encourage the growth of the private hospitals.

Private costs of private health care

An increasing number of people are opting out of public health care. Some use NHS facilities as private patients, others use purely private facilities. In each case, each person's care is paid for privately, through the individual's own insurance policy, through one provided by his or her employer, or by the individual on a one-off basis.

Mixed health care   Much of so-called private health care is provided using a mix of private and public facilities. A classic example is pay-beds in NHS hospitals. The physical capital, such as beds and other facilities, is provided by the NHS, which charges private patients for its use. The consultant seen by private patients will usually be employed concurrently, on either a full- or a part-time basis, in the NHS.

This mix of public and private care has been viewed differently by Labour and Conservative governments. The Labour government discouraged mixed public/private provision, attempting to phase out private beds in NHS hospitals. The Conservative government has taken measures to redress the situation, notably by changing the conditions of employment for NHS consultants in 1981 to increase their incentive to undertake work in the private sector (Propper 1989*a*).

Table 4.3 shows trends in private health care within NHS hospitals over

Table 4.3. *Mixed and purely private health care, England and Wales* ('000)

	1976	1980	1984	1986
NHS hospitals				
Average daily bed occupation				
Private	1.7	1.5	1.2	1.0
All departments	330	307	287	272
Out-patient attendances				
Private	91.4[a]	153.4	215.6	261.6
Total	47,997	50,994	53,842	54,616
Registered nursing homes and private hospitals				
Beds available	30.6	32.9	44.5	65.1
Private medical insurance				
Persons covered	2,251	3,577	4,400	5,250

[a] England only.

Sources: CSO 1979, 1986*a*, 1988*a*, 1988*c*, 1989*a*.

the period 1976–86. A number of interesting patterns emerge. First, although the Labour government was committed to phasing out pay-beds and the Conservatives to maintaining them, the average number of beds occupied by private patients each day fell by 12 per cent during the primarily Labour period 1976–80, and by one-third during the Conservative period 1980–6. Second, over the entire 1976–86 period, there is a striking increase in the number of private patients at out-patient clinics. Private attendances increased 68 per cent between 1976 and 1980, and 70 per cent between 1980 and 1986. The trends in out-patient attendances and bed occupation follow those for the NHS as a whole, but are much more pronounced.

An alternative measure of the treatment and growth of the mixed public/private sector is the value of patients' payments for hospital treatment, which consist mainly of charges to private patients. The real value of private patients' payments fell from £83 million in 1973/4 to £70 million in 1978/9 (at 1987/8 prices)—a fall of 16 per cent (see Table 4A.1). The Conservative government has seen the real value of private patients' payments rise to £106 million in 1987/8—an increase of 51 per cent. This rise in revenue can be explained by an increase in the number of private out-patient attendances, possibly combined with an increase in the real value of charges. While it may seem odd that the Conservative government, after instituting policies to encourage the mixed private/public sector, should increase charges on private patients, it is worth noting that the increase in private patients' payments is substantially less than the rise in revenue from prescription charges (349 per cent) or dental charges (118 per cent).

Private health care An increasing number of patients are being cared for in private hospitals, some of which are run for profit. The number of beds available in registered nursing homes and private hospitals grew at an average annual rate of 12 per cent between 1980 and 1986, rising to 65,100 (Table 4.3). The growth in the private sector can be attributed to increased demand stemming from a number of sources. The RAWP programme has put pressure on NHS services in traditionally well-funded areas, such as the South-East, possibly encouraging people to seek private care. Demographic changes have led to greater demand for nursing homes. Finally, the favourable tax treatment of private insurance has led to an increase in demand for private services.

Health insurance The Conservative government has used tax concessions to encourage the growth of private insurance. Tax concessions have been given since 1980 on employer-paid medical insurance premiums for people earning less than £8,500 per year. The effect of these concessions, coupled perhaps with a change in perception of the relative merits of public and private health care, was immediate. The number of people covered by private health insurance increased from 2.3 million in 1976 to 3.6 million in 1980. By 1986, 5.3 million people, or about 9 per cent of the population, were covered by private health insurance (Table 4.3). The 1989 White Paper (DoH 1989*a*) announced tax concessions on non-corporate medical insurance to those over the age of 60. These further concessions may well prompt another increase in the demand for medical insurance (Propper 1989*a*).

The link between tax concessions and the demand for insurance can be established by comparing the period of Conservative government with the Labour period. Under Labour, with no tax concessions, private medical insurance coverage rose, on average, by 4.7 per cent a year, while under the Conservatives it grew at an average annual rate of 8.3 per cent.

However, it is easy to overestimate the importance of private medical care. Insurance schemes provide a service mainly in the area of elective surgery rather than emergency care or treatment for long-term chronic illnesses. So while 9 per cent of the population had private health insurance in 1987, benefits paid were less than 3 per cent of NHS expenditures (CSO 1989*a*; Office of Health Economics 1987). At the same time, private health care is important in providing treatment for certain groups of people—27 per cent of professionals aged 45–64 had private health insurance in 1986. It makes a significant contribution to the provision of facilities for acute care in general, and elective surgery in particular. In some regions and for some specialities, 25 per cent of care is provided by the private sector (Propper 1990).

The policies of Labour and Conservative governments towards the private costs of health care have been more at odds than their policies in any other area. The Labour government restricted the role of private finance, allowing charges to fall in real terms, and attempting to eliminate pay-beds. The Conservative government has pursued a policy of relating private costs to ability to pay. Charges have risen substantially in real terms, but exemptions for the elderly and those on low income have broadened. The private/public and pure private sectors have been encouraged. Those who can afford to buy private insurance have been given incentives to do so. However, despite these developments, the bulk of health care—care for the poor, the aged, and the chronically ill—is the province of the NHS, and is likely to remain so for the foreseeable future.

III. OUTPUTS

The 'outputs' of the NHS are notoriously difficult to define. Here we confine ourselves to a discussion of the success of policies towards the NHS in terms of certain policy goals, relating to efficiency and equity.

Efficiency

A major priority of both the Labour and Conservative governments has been the efficient use of resources within the NHS. But the concept of efficiency in an institution like the NHS is not entirely a straightforward one. This is quite apart from the very considerable problems of measurement of the quantity and quality of the services provided.

It is possible to distinguish three different dimensions to the concept of efficiency in the NHS. First, there is what we might term 'output efficiency'. This involves adjusting the mix of service outputs so that the net social benefit from these services is at its greatest. This means directing resources into the areas where more resources will make the most difference to people's health. Considerations of this kind, along with equity concerns, arguably motivated both governments' policies towards the regions and towards the priority services.

Second, there is what is often termed 'input efficiency'. This involves adjusting the mix of inputs to reflect changes in relative costs. If one kind of input becomes relatively more expensive (e.g. residential care), it may be efficiency to substitute a different kind of input (e.g. 'community' care). Third, there is 'technical efficiency' which simply means producing the maximum possible outputs from a given amount of resource inputs.

A major difficulty with all three kinds of efficiency in the context of the NHS is that they may be very hard to measure. What constitutes an improvement in output efficiency will depend on social priorities. If it is considered important that geriatric care should become a priority, then moving NHS resources in that direction, other things being equal, achieves an improvement in output efficiency. But from the perspective of someone who disagrees with this priority, this change will represent a reduction in efficiency.

Input efficiency suffers from similar problems. Changing the input mix that produces a particular health-care service may be thought to change its quality as well as its quantity. Such a change may suit certain kinds of patients more than others—in which case a change in output efficiency may be involved as well. Finally, improvements in technical efficiency may come about as a result of increases in inputs, such as work activity, which are not adequately recorded. In this case the supposed improvement in efficiency actually involves increases in inputs rather than an improvement in technical efficiency.

In some cases it may be difficult to distinguish between changes in input and technical efficiency. Often increases in throughputs are claimed when the increase in output is linked to only one input (such as nurses or doctors). It is not clear whether the increase in efficiency is then the result of substitution between inputs, is a result of gains in technical efficiency from all inputs, or, possibly, is quite spurious, being the result of an increase in other inputs. The problem is aggravated by the difficulty of measuring the capital inputs in NHS services, and the ease with which costs can be passed on to patients by reducing the quality of the services provided.

A final difficulty in adequately accounting for improvements in efficiency is presented by technological change. This may take the form of technical improvements in acute medical care, but it may also be the discovery of new ways of delivering services for the mentally ill and the elderly. The shift towards community care in both these areas may be the result of such a process.

All these problems aside, it is probably a fair generalization to say that while Labour policy was most concerned with increasing both input and output efficiency, the Conservatives have tended to emphasize input and technical efficiency. *The Government's Expenditure Plans 1980–81 to 1983–84* (HM Treasury 1980) contains an early Conservative commitment to input and technical efficiency. It announced changes in the administrative structure of the NHS which were implemented in 1982 after the Griffiths Report. It also called for other changes, for example in procurement policies, which were intended to assist the Health Service in the task of achieving a better use of available resources in order to ensure that more of the funds provided went to patient care. *The Government's Expenditure Plans 1989–90 to 1991–92* (HM Treasury 1989) states that 'the NHS aims to improve and promote health, to provide necessary treatment for illness and care *while making the best use of available resources*' (ch. 14, p. 4, emphasis added).

One of the best sources of information on input and technical efficiency is the House of Commons Social Services Committee's reports on public expenditure on the social services (for a recent example, see HC, Social Services Committee, 1987). They consider two types of efficiency measures: 'throughput' measures, and measures of 'cash-releasing cost improvements'. Increased throughput means that the same resources are producing more outputs; it is thus a form of technical efficiency. Cash-releasing cost improvement programmes mean that less cash is needed to produce the same outputs. Cost improvements may be achieved by increasing technical efficiency, that is, improving the use of existing resources; or by increasing input efficiency, for example by shifting from more to less expensive inputs.

The figures provided by the Select Committee give one estimate of the overall improvement in efficiency. Cost improvement programmes for 1986/7 are estimated to produce £408 million, compared with total Hospital and Community Health Services current net spending of £10,269 million (HC, Social Services Committee, 1987). While the savings themselves may not be large, they represent a significant amount of the resources supposedly available for improvements in services. The Social Services Committee estimated in 1984 that, during the previous two years, the growth in services had come more from efficiency savings than from growth in input volume (Table 4.4). Moreover, the source of the savings is revealing in terms of government employment policy.

Table 4.5 shows the source of savings for the years 1985/6 to 1987/8. The Social Services Committee report does not describe the nature of the savings achieved by 'rationalisation of patient services'; and a recent study of these and the other forms of savings suggests that the estimates should be treated with caution, indeed scepticism (Kings Fund Institute 1989). However, a large amount of the savings appears to come from reductions in labour costs, either directly or by competitive tendering to private companies (who will, in general, pay lower wages). The majority

Table 4.4. *Growth in hospital and community services* (%)

	Growth in input volume	Efficiency savings	Growth in services
1979/80	0.1	—	0.3
1980/1	0.9	—	0.9
1981/2	2.5	0.2	2.7
1982/3	0.2	0.3	0.5
1983/4	0.3	0.5	0.8

Source: HC, Social Services Committee, 1984.

Table 4.5. *Cost-improvement programmes: Analysis by source of savings*
(£ million)

	1985/6	1986/7[a]	1987/8[a]
Rationalization of patient services	29.8	37.3	35.9
Competitive tendering	16.3	48.4	39.0
Other reductions in labour cost	38.3	23.6	26.2
Rayner scrutiny savings	7.3	7.6	7.0
Supply cost savings	9.5	7.8	8.7
Energy savings	6.8	8.7	6.5
Other savings	30.2	25.0	28.7
Total	138.4	158.4	152.1
HCHS[b] current net spending	9,574	10,269	11,179

[a] Plans only.
[b] Hospital and community health services.
Source: HC, Social Services Committee, 1987: 10.

of contracted-out services are labour-intensive, e.g. domestic services, laundry, and catering (Pirie 1988).

Priority services

Since 1975, a continuing aim of government policy has been to direct resources to the 'Cinderella' or priority services. There are three main priority services: care for the elderly, the mentally handicapped, and the mentally ill—areas where there was either growing demand, a history of neglect, or both.

The need to set priorities in health care was first recognized in the Labour government's 1976 White Paper, *Priorities for Health and Personal Social Services in England* (DHSS 1976c). The document, written at a time of fiscal crisis, asked how funds could be used most effectively. Besides pin-pointing priority groups, it set out strategies for meeting the needs of those groups using low-cost solutions (p. 12), and with an emphasis on increasing community care. For the elderly, this meant an expansion of the home-nursing and health-visiting services; for the mentally handicapped, growth in local authority training centres and residential homes; and for the mentally ill, an increase in local authority day care and residential accommodation. While services directed at the elderly, such as geriatric in-patient and out-patient services, were projected to grow faster than the Health Service as a whole, they were not given as high a priority as community care. Hospital services for the mentally handicapped and mentally ill were seen as segregating and distancing the handicapped and ill from the community, and were targeted to grow at less than the rate of overall health spending.

The Conservative government continued Labour's commitment to the priority services. For example, the 1988 Public Expenditure White Paper recognized the elderly, the mentally ill, and the mentally handicapped as priority groups, and placed special emphasis on developing community-based services (HM Treasury 1988: ii. 244). Like its Labour predecessors, the government realized the need to respond to demographic change: 'The main objective of the NHS in the coming years is to respond to the increased demand for a greater volume of health care arising from demographic and technical pressures' (HM Treasury 1984: ii. 76).

Table 4.6 documents the level of spending on the priority services in volume terms over the period 1976/7–1985/6. It tells only part of the story; developments in personal social services, described in Chapter 6, complement the changes chronicled here. The Labour years of 1976/7–1978/9 saw substantial growth in spending on hospital services for the elderly, and significant growth in health visiting and district nursing. Spending on hospital services for the mentally ill and mentally handicapped grew substantially during 1976/7–1978/9, but fell off during 1978/9–

1979/80. The year 1979/80 saw a cut in the volume of hospital spending on the elderly and mentally handicapped. Of the services shown, only health visiting and district nursing were able to maintain their rate of growth. Except for the year 1980/1 (which may be atypical because of the Clegg pay award), the Conservative government has limited the growth in spending on geriatric in-patients and out-patients to a rate comparable with the overall growth in the total hospital and community health-care budget. Spending on the mentally ill and the mentally handicapped (in-patients and out-patients) has fallen in some years, and grown at a lower rate than the total hospital and community care budget throughout (except for spending on the mentally handicapped in 1982/3). The one area where there has been consistent and high growth in spending, however, is in health visiting and district nursing.

Table 4.7 allows us to examine to what extent these changes were in line with policy. The first column shows Labour's target growth rates set out in *Priorities for Health and Personal Social Services in England* (DHSS 1976c). The second column shows average annual growth rates for each sector under the Labour government. It is clear that the targets were broadly achieved. Comparable figures for the Conservative government are given in the third column. Growth rates are lower than under

Table 4.6. *Programme budget, hospital and community health services, England* (£ million at 1986/7 prices[a])

	In-patient and out-patient			Visiting and nursing	All HCHS[b]
	Geriatric	Mental handicap	Mental illness		
1976/7	797.7	479.9	986.7	344.4	9,290.1
1977/8	839.7	499.8	1,031.7	354.0	9,576.1
1978/9	876.5	508.1	1,036.9	367.4	9,829.0
1979/80	872.1	507.1	1,042.4	378.0	9,833.9
1980/1	898.3	510.8	1,057.8	403.4	9,922.6
1981/2	911.4	518.1	1,082.3	422.2	10,163.1
1982/3	912.4	523.3	1,081.3	435.4	10,176.6
1983/4	914.2	520.1	1,077.6	439.6	10,264.2
1984/5	923.0	519.3	1,083.4	455.4	10,276.6
1985/6	920.6	511.0	1,074.3	472.0	10,272.4
1986/7[c]	933.5	496.6	1,069.6	495.9	10,317.2

[a] Adjusted to take account of changes in services' pay and price inflation.
[b] Hospital and community health services.
[c] Provisional estimate only.

Source: HC, Social Services Committee, 1988.

Table 4.7. *Effectiveness of priority-service expenditures*

	Target[a] growth rate p.a. (%)	Actual[b] growth p.a. (%)			Percentage change in share of all hospital and community health expenditure[c]			Percentage change in share of population in client group[c]	
	1975–80	1976–80	1980–7	1976–87	1976–80	1980–7	1976–87	1976–80	1976–86
Geriatric[d]	3.5	3.01	0.98	1.59	3.28	2.03	5.37	1.04	5.38
Mental handicap[d]	1.6	1.85	–0.30	0.34					
Mental illness[d]	1.3	1.85	0.37	0.81					
Visiting/nursing	6.0	3.15	3.95	3.71	3.70	25.05	29.67	1.04	5.38
Total hospital and community health	1.5	1.91	0.69	1.05					

[a] From DHSS 1975a, 1976c.
[b] Average annual rate of growth.
[c] Total change over period specified.
[d] In-patient and out-patient.

Source: HC, Social Services Committee, 1988.

Labour for all sectors, except health visiting/district nursing. Expenditures on hospital services for the mentally handicapped actually fell, on average, over the period. The Conservative government's performance may be viewed in two lights: as a cut in services or as a successful 'de-institutionalization' of the mentally handicapped. The key question here is whether community-based services stepped in as hospital services were cut back—a question addressed in Chapter 6.

The remaining columns of Table 4.7 show the change in the share of all Hospital and Community Health expenditure going to geriatric in-patients and out-patients under each government, and compare these with the change in the percentage of elderly in the population. The share of spending on geriatric hospital services increased by more than required by demographic changes under Labour, but by less than required by demographic changes under the Conservatives. In consequence, over the total period from 1976, resources devoted to geriatric hospital services have almost kept pace with demographic change.

An alternative measure of the level of spending on priority groups is provided in the government's annual estimates in its *Expenditure Plans* of the average cost of care for an elderly person. These estimates include personal social services spending in addition to NHS expenditures, and therefore can be used to evaluate the overall success of the community care strategy. There was a steady increase in expenditures (measured in volume terms using the Blue Book deflator) during the Labour government, and a more erratic performance during the Conservative period, with substantial gains in the 1982/3–1984/5 period being offset by a sharp downturn in 1985/6.

Both Labour and Conservative governments have made commitments to spending on priority groups—the elderly, mentally ill, and mentally handicapped—and to developing community care. The Labour government increased spending on hospital-based in-patient and out-patient services, and also increased the volume of spending on each elderly person. The Conservative government spent less on hospital services for the elderly than did Labour. Hospital services for the mentally handicapped were cut back, but spending on health visiting and district nursing increased substantially. The pattern of spending may mean successful de-institutionalization or neglect: to know which, we have to consider health and personal social services spending simultaneously.

Equity

There is no universally agreed interpretation of equity for the allocation of health service resources (see Le Grand 1987, essay I, for discussion of some of the alternatives). However, the two areas of policy concern in the period that most obviously had implications for equity were the regional distribution of resources and inequalities in access and utilization between socio-economic groups.

The regional distribution of resources   In 1975, the Labour government set up the Resource Allocation Working Party (RAWP) to establish 'a method of securing, as soon as practicable, a pattern of distribution responsive objectively, equitably and efficiently to relative need'. RAWP responded with a revenue allocation formula intended 'to reduce progressively, and as far as is feasible, the disparities between the different parts of the country in terms of opportunity for access to health care of people at equal risk' (DHSS 1976c: 1). The RAWP formula has attracted much criticism but, at the same time, has been effective in reducing regional inequality.

The RAWP formula was described in the *Report of the Resource Allocation Working Party* (DHSS 1976a). A region's target resource allocation was determined by its population, weighted by age and sex, and, for certain conditions, regional variations in morbidity were adjusted by using standardized mortality ratios (SMRs). Later adjustments were made to account for the inter-regional flow patients and the number of 'old long-stay' patients, and teaching hospitals received a special increment for teaching (SIFT) (Allsop 1984).

The RAWP targets differed significantly from regions' actual allocations. For the four Thames regions, the RAWP targets were substantially below actual allocations: for other regions, particularly the Trent, North-Western, and Northern regions, RAWP targets were above allocations (DHSS 1976c). Table 4.8 shows the distance between regions' actual revenue allocations and RAWP targets. It can be seen that, over time, there has been a narrowing of the distance between actual and target allocations. Table 4.9 gives some idea of what the reallocation of resources means in terms of per capita expenditures. The relatively deprived regions have experienced steadily increasing per capita expenditures, whereas the better-provided regions, such as North-West Thames, have seen expenditures stay constant or fall. The variance in expenditures has fallen in every year since the inception of RAWP, with the exception of 1980/1 and 1982/3.

However, if we look not at total expenditures but at GPs as an index of access to health care, a somewhat different picture emerges. Table 4.10 shows the number of GPs in each Regional Health Authority (RHA) per 100,000 in the population. As in the case of overall facilities, the Thames areas are well-provided and the northern areas are not. However, there is far less evidence of an equalizing trend. Consider, for example, the North-Western RHA. Its distance from RAWP target has decreased from

Table 4.8. *Distances of regions from revenue RAWP target* (% of regional allocation)

	1979/80	1980/1	1981/2	1982/3	1983/4	1984/5	1985/6	1986/7	1987/8
Northern	-7	-6	-5	-5	-4	-4	-3	-2	-2
Yorkshire	-4	-4	-4	-4	-4	-4	-3	-2	-2
Trent	-7	-8	-7	-6	-5	-5	-5	-4	-3
E. Anglian	-5	-6	-6	-6	-6	-4	-4	-4	-4
NW Thames	13	13	12	12	11	8	7	8	6
NE Thames	11	10	9	9	9	9	10	6	9
SE Thames	10	11	9	8	6	7	6	4	3
SW Thames	6	5	6	6	6	7	4	2	0
Wessex	-4	-4	-5	-6	-5	-5	-4	-1	-1
Oxford[a]	1	0	-1	-2	0	-2	-3	-2	-2
South-Western	-4	-4	-5	-5	-4	-4	-2	-2	-1
W. Midlands	-6	-5	-4	-4	-4	-4	-5	-4	-2
Mersey	-1	-1	0	-1	-1	-1	0	0	0
North-Western	-9	-8	-6	-6	-4	-4	-2	-1	-2
Mean distance	6.29	6.07	5.64	5.71	4.93	4.86	4.14	3.00	2.64

[a] In 1983/4 Oxford region's resources were built up in preparation for the opening of a new district general hospital in May 1984.

Source: Calculated from HC, Social Services Committee, 1988.

Table 4.9. *Regional health authority expenditures per capita (volume[a])* (£)

	1974/5	1975/6	1976/7	1977/8	1978/9	1979/80	1980/1	1981/2	1982/3	1983/4	1984/5	1985/6
Northern	173	176	178	178	188	189	196	196	203	197	204	206
Yorkshire	168	176	176	176	181	184	193	194	197	192	197	204
Trent	155	163	167	170	174	175	181	182	184	181	187	190
E. Anglian	168	172	169	172	178	181	187	188	189	183	190	192
NW Thames	216	221	216	219	220	217	224	226	216	210	214	213
NE Thames	208	208	209	206	208	212	227	223	241	233	238	236
SE Thames	201	212	212	210	214	217	223	221	225	218	220	221
SW Thames	206	215	212	207	207	201	219	213	209	204	208	208
Wessex	165	172	171	173	175	176	185	184	187	185	193	193
Oxford	175	174	171	168	169	169	173	174	175	171	175	175
South-Western	173	174	175	175	179	192	188	201	203	200	204	205
W. Midlands	160	168	166	165	171	177	185	184	187	185	193	199
Mersey	188	192	193	194	197	198	206	206	211	204	210	211
North-Western	173	180	182	188	194	200	209	215	219	211	219	220
England	183	188	187	188	192	195	203	204	207	202	208	209
Wales	193	206	203	199	204	206	213	214	223	218	224	224
Scotland	206	219	220	223	233	235	242	248	252	247	255	255
N. Ireland	234	274	283	232	237	246	253	263	260	257	259	270
UK	185	194	194	193	198	201	208	210	214	208	214	216
Variance[b]	360.2	363.6	332.8	308.1	275.9	246.4	312.9	282.4	323.9	274.3	261.6	230.5

[a] Deflated using NHS specific deflator calculated from CSO 1983, 1987b.
[b] England only.

Source: Office of Health Economics 1987: table 2.6a.

Table 4.10. *GPs in each regional health authority per 100,000 home population (1 Oct. each year)*

	1975	1978	1979	1980	1981	1982	1983	1984	1985	1986
Northern	45	48	48	48	49	51	52	53	54	55
Yorkshire	45	47	48	50	51	52	54	54	55	56
Trent	43	46	47	48	48	50	51	51	52	53
E. Anglian	46	49	50	51	53	52	56	55	55	57
NW Thames	53	55	55	57	58	59	61	61	61	61
NE Thames	50	52	51	52	52	54	55	55	55	56
SE Thames	49	50	52	52	53	54	56	55	56	57
SW Thames	50	51	50	54	53	54	55	55	56	57
Wessex	47	49	50	51	53	54	56	56	57	56
Oxford	46	48	48	49	51	51	55	54	54	56
South-Western	50	52	56	54	58	60	62	62	63	64
W. Midlands	45	46	48	49	50	51	53	53	54	55
Mersey	44	48	49	50	52	52	54	55	55	56
North-Western	44	47	47	50	51	51	53	53	54	54
England	47	49	50	51	52	53	55	55	56	56
Wales	49	51	52	53	55	56	59	59	60	62
Scotland	58	61	62	63	65	66	69	69	70	71
N. Ireland	49	48	49	50	53	55	54	54	57	58
UK	48	50	51	52	53	54	55	56	57	58
Variance	8.21	6.29	7.21	6.07	7.71	8.36	8.79	8.29	7.93	7.64

Source: Office of Health Economics 1987: table 4.4a.

9 per cent below target in 1979/80 to 2 per cent below in 1985/6. In terms of GPs per 100,000 home population, however, it had two less than the English average in 1978 *and* in 1986. Table 4.10 shows that the experience of North-Western is typical; the variance remains virtually constant throughout.

A reallocation of resources which benefits certain regions at the expense of others is bound to create opposition, and RAWP has been no exception. It might be hypothesized that it is easier to reallocate resources in a period of growth, when redistribution may be achieved by holding the share of richer regions constant, rather than actually making cuts. Comparing the annual percentage change in the average distance from RAWP target with the percentage change in NHS volume (Social Services deflator), we find a pattern similar to the one expected: years of higher growth in volume are accompanied by larger falls in the average distance of regions from RAWP targets. The relationship does not appear to be so straightforward if a different deflator is used.

Concentration on resource distribution at a regional level can hide substantial inequalities within regions. The Social Services Committee has, since 1982/3, analysed the distance from RAWP target at the District Health Authority (DHA) level for four regions: North-East Thames, Oxford, Trent, and Yorkshire. The variation within regions can be impressive. Within the North-East Thames region, for example, we find Islington DHA at 28 per cent above its RAWP target in 1982/3, and Mid Essex DHA at 22 per cent below. Within Yorkshire we have Wakefield DHA at 2.8 per cent above target, and Scarborough at 19.6 per cent below for 1982/3. Allsop (1984) argues that in fact RAWP has achieved little success in reducing inequalities within RHAs. She notes that 'Structured inequalities in needs and provision, by their nature, are reinforced by structured interest groups which slow down and modify the pace of change' (p. 99). RHAs are committed to funding the revenue requirements of capital projects already in place, which leads to the maintenance of expenditure differentials.

RAWP applies only within England. Scotland, Northern Ireland, and Wales had in 1975/6, and still have, higher per capita expenditures than the England average. Scotland is particularly well provided; for instance, in 1986 it had 71 GPs per 100,000 population, compared with the England average of 56. Birch and Maynard (1986) estimate that, had the RAWP formula been applied to the United Kingdom as a whole, England's share of the total health budget would have been £398 million higher in 1985/6. However, the increase in England's budget would be financed by a fall in the Scottish budget of 19 per cent, and of 27 per cent in the Welsh. Birch and Maynard, after considering possible explanations for the between-country differentials, conclude that they 'are difficult to substantiate on anything other than political grounds' (p. 15).

Social inequality in access and utilization   The General Household Survey (GHS) provides information on people's perceptions of their own health (self-reported morbidity), and the use they make of the services provided by the NHS, including GP, in-patient, and out-patient services. The GHS allows us to compare the health (as measured by self-reported morbidity) and health care of people in different socio-economic classes and of different income levels.

People get access to the NHS through visiting their GP, who acts as 'gatekeeper' to the rest of the system. Hence we can obtain an indication of the extent to which there is social equality or inequality in access from data on the distribution (by socio-economic group or income group) of GP visits.

Table 4.11 shows visits to the GP by socio-economic group (SEG). Semi- and unskilled manual workers are more likely to visit their doctor than the population as a whole. In the two weeks prior to the 1985 GHS survey, 17.3 per cent of unskilled manual workers and their families (SEG VI) and 15.9 per cent of semi-skilled manual workers and their families (SEG V) had visited their GP, compared with 14.4 per cent in the population as a whole. In the same period, only 8.5 per cent of professionals and their families (SEG I) visited their GP. Interestingly, this represents an increase since 1974 for unskilled and semi-skilled families (15.8 per cent and 14.3 per cent respectively in 1974), and a fall for professionals (10.0 per cent in 1974); moreover, as the age-specific columns of the table indicate, these changes seem mostly to have occurred among the over-65s.

Table 4.12 shows visits to the GP by income group. In 1985, 18 per cent of the lowest group and nearly 17 per cent of the next lowest consulted a GP, compared with 12 per cent for the top group. Again, this difference (which is much less marked in 1974 and 1979) appears to be in part the consequence of an increase in consulting rates by the over-65s in the lower groups.

Equality or inequality of access for the population as a whole, however, is not a very sensible interpretation of equity, for it takes no account of differences in need. The poor may consult the doctor more than the better-off, but they are also generally less healthy. A more interesting question, therefore, is whether the pro-poor pattern of access matches the pro-poor distribution of illness. Or, to put it another way, is there equal access for those in equal need?

The GHS includes data on two kinds of self-reported morbidity: chronic and acute sickness that limits activity. If those who report either or both of these are taken to be in 'need' of health care (a not uncontroversial definition of need), then the degree of equality of access relative to need can be obtained by looking at the proportions of these in the different groups who have consulted the doctor. The relevant figures are shown in

Table 4.11. *Percentage of population who have consulted a doctor in the last two weeks, by socio-economic group*

Socio-economic group	All ages			16–65			Over 65		
	1974	1979	1985	1974	1979	1985	1974	1979	1985
I	10.0	10.1	8.5	9.0	9.7	8.0	16.9	13.3	13.6
II	11.2	10.9	12.3	9.5	9.8	11.4	18.3	16.2	16.2
III	12.6	13.9	15.2	12.3	13.0	14.7	14.4	19.1	17.7
IV	12.2	13.8	13.0	11.7	12.8	11.9	14.9	18.5	18.0
V	14.3	15.8	15.9	13.8	15.4	15.0	16.0	16.9	19.3
VI	15.8	16.4	17.3	15.3	15.5	15.3	17.0	18.4	23.0
All	12.9	14.1	14.4	12.3	13.2	13.5	15.7	17.8	18.4

Source: Own calculations from GHS raw data files.

Table 4.12. *Percentage of population who have consulted a doctor in the last two weeks, by income quintile*

Quintile	All ages			16–65			Over 65		
	1974	1979	1985	1974	1979	1985	1974	1979	1985
Bottom	13.9	13.8	18.2	15.2	14.1	17.4	16.6	17.2	20.0
2	12.6	15.4	16.7	13.5	15.1	16.2	15.4	19.8	19.3
3	11.8	13.4	14.3	11.6	14.2	13.6	15.4	18.2	18.4
4	11.3	12.8	13.3	11.6	13.1	12.8	15.5	12.6	17.8
Top	11.1	11.4	11.9	11.1	11.6	11.5	15.9	15.3	13.0
All	12.1	13.4	14.8	12.2	13.3	13.8	16.0	18.1	18.9

Source: Own calculations from GHS raw data files.

Tables 4.13 (for SEGs) and 4.14 (for income groups). It is apparent that the pro-poor pattern becomes much less pronounced than in Table 4.12, suggesting that there is something close to equality of access for equal need, and that this has not changed greatly over the eleven years for which our data are available.

This finding has been confirmed by a more sophisticated multi-variate analysis of the determinants of GP consultations carried out by Le Grand and Winter (1989) using GHS data from 1980. For a majority of people the only significant determinant of visits to the doctor was self-reported

Table 4.13. *Percentage of population reporting acute or chronic illness that limits their activity who have consulted a doctor in the last two weeks, by socio-economic group*

Socio-economic group	All ages		16–65		Over 65	
	1974	1985	1974	1985	1974	1985
I	25.2	27.2	23.6	26.2	31.8	31.6
II	27.2	27.8	25.4	29.0	30.7	25.6
III	31.0	32.1	33.1	32.7	25.1	30.3
IV	32.9	29.4	35.9	30.0	26.0	28.1
V	32.5	29.9	36.0	31.3	26.4	27.6
VI	31.4	34.0	33.3	31.1	28.3	38.9
Total	31.5	30.5	33.7	31.1	26.6	29.3

Source: Own calculations from GHS raw data files.

Table 4.14. *Percentage of population reporting acute or chronic illness that limits their activity who have consulted a doctor in the last two weeks, by income quintile*

Quintile	All ages		16–65		Over 65	
	1974	1985	1974	1985	1974	1985[a]
Bottom	31.0	32.6	36.5	29.8	25.7	29.7
2	32.7	33.0	35.7	34.4	23.6	29.8
3	34.5	33.9	32.8	32.9	29.6	30.5
4	31.3	32.1	30.3	28.8	27.9	30.4
Top	31.6	30.1	30.4	29.1	25.3	25.8
All	32.1	32.5	32.8	30.9	25.6	29.7

[a] For the over-65s, cell-counts for quintile groups 4 and 5 are less than 21 observations (1985).

Source: Own calculations from GHS raw data files.

morbidity; all of the other socio-economic variables tried (including income and occupation) were insignificant. There were only two exceptions to this: poor elderly men, and women between 16 and 40, who appeared to visit less often than their level of morbidity suggests that they should. In the latter case the determining factors appeared to be whether the woman had children and/or was employed.

These kinds of analysis deal only with access to the NHS through initial contact with a GP. They do not take account of 'total' utilization of the NHS: that is, all GP visits, out-patient visits, and in-patient stays. Although useful for attempting to discover whether there is equal *access* for equal need, they cannot be used to answer the question whether there is equal *treatment* for equal need.

In an early study that attempted to explore this question, Le Grand (1978) used GHS data from the early 1970s on GP consultations, out-patient consultations, and in-patient days to construct estimates of total NHS expenditures per person reporting illness for different socio-economic groups. The results showed that the distribution favoured the better-off, with, on an age-standardized basis, the families of professionals, employers, and managers receiving nearly 40 per cent more NHS expenditure per person ill than the families of semi- and unskilled manual workers.

However, a similar analysis of the GHS data for 1985 carried out for the Welfare State Programme by O'Donnell and Propper (1989) came to rather different conclusions. This found no evidence of a bias in favour of the better-off, whether defined in terms of income or socio-economic group—indeed, if anything rather the reverse. The difference between their findings and those of the earlier study appears to derive, not from any significant changes in the pattern of utilization by different social groups, but from an increase in self-reported morbidity by the higher SEGs relative to the lower ones. Whatever the explanation, the results suggest that, if need is defined in terms of self-reported morbidity, there has been some movement towards greater equality of treatment relative to need over the period.

Safe in whose hands?

We began this chapter by discussing the evolution of policy during the period. The conclusion there, given that we have no data on the effects of the implementation of the 1989 White Paper, was that there appeared to be a striking continuity in policy over the twelve years we have studied. The main areas of policy initiative and conflict seemed to be in places peripheral to the central concerns of the NHS.

We have examined in some detail the overall trends in resources devoted to the NHS, and the effects of such policy changes as there were on efficiency, regional disparities, and the priority services. We are now in a position to answer the question whether this considerable body of data and analysis leads us to confirm our preliminary conclusions about the NHS during this period. We can also draw some tentative conclusions as to whether health-care policies can be said to have been 'successful' over the period. Have the aims of policy that we discussed at the beginning of the chapter been fulfilled?

We begin with the aims of policy towards health care, and, in particular, towards the NHS. The first of these, it will be recalled, was to improve the 'range' and 'standard' of services provided. These characteristics we assessed by examining the trends in overall resources devoted to the NHS. Our conclusion there was clear. Both governments increased the overall volume of resources going to the NHS. However, the annual growth rate in resources was higher under Labour than under the Conservatives—according to one measure, over four times as high—while the growth in need (or demand) was higher under the Conservatives than under Labour. Hence the increase in resources relative to need was substantially greater under Labour than under the Conservatives.

Much of the growth in resources under Labour came during their first two years of office. After that the performance of both governments was similar. Our interpretation of the overall expenditure data is that the growth in resources has not matched the growth in needs and demand since about 1976/7. Thus the pressure on NHS resources has steadily increased since then. The government's expenditure plans show little sign of trying to reverse this trend.

The next aim to be considered concerned efficiency. One indicator of this that we were able to obtain concerned savings due to the cost-improvement programmes introduced under the Conservative government. However, whether these savings exist at all is controversial; even if they do exist, they are relatively small, amounting to 2 per cent of the overall NHS budget.

A broader, allocative efficiency objective concerned the diversion of resources towards the priority services. Here both governments succeeded in increasing the proportion of health-service resources devoted to the elderly, although the Conservatives by much less than Labour. The proportions going to the mentally ill and mentally handicapped hospital services fell under both governments, although by much more under the Conservatives than under Labour. The proportion going to health visiting and district nursing increased under both governments, but this time by substantially more under the Conservatives.

The next set of aims concerned equity, particularly with respect to the allocation of resources between regions and the use of services by different social groups. So far as the regions are concerned, the RAWP reallocations, introduced under Labour and, until 1989, continued under the Conservatives, have been a major success story, at least in redistributing resources *between* regions. However, there remained substantial inequalities *within* regions; there was also no improvement in regional inequalities in access to care, as measured by the availability of GPs.

The picture is less clear with respect to the use of services by social class. It appears that over the whole period, there has been little difference between socio-economic groups in the extent to which they consult GPs when they are ill. There is evidence that, at least in the early 1970s, the better-off received more by way of treatment relative to self-reported morbidity than the poor; however, this difference seemed to be no longer apparent in the 1980s.

What is the overall conclusion of all this? Both governments can chalk up some policy successes over the period, particularly with respect to maintaining the overall level of resources, with respect to regional re-allocation, to some extent with respect to the priority services, and with respect to health outcomes. There are differences between the governments; in particular, it is clear that the NHS was safer in the hands of Labour than it has been under the Conservatives, at least so far as the volume of resources relative to need was concerned. However, the Conservative government has maintained the level of resources going to the NHS, has maintained a commitment to funding from general taxation, and, to judge from the outcome of the 1988/9 Review, will continue with both of these commitments in the future. Where things will change following the Review is in the delivery of services; how this will affect the achievement of policy objectives (particularly with respect to efficiency in service delivery) remains to be seen.

IV. OUTCOMES

The 'outcomes' of health policy are notoriously difficult to measure. The DHSS (now Department of Health) has produced a series of 'performance indicators', designed 'to help managers compare aspects of their services with other authorities' (HM Treasury 1986: ii. 216). But these in general refer to 'throughputs', and are therefore closer to measures of inputs than of outcomes. More sophisticated outcome measures are currently under development—notably the Quality-Adjusted-Life-Year or QALY (Gudex and Kind 1988)—but these are not available at an aggregate level. There are a number of simpler outcome measures, including mortality levels or rates, days off work and National Insurance incapacity certificates, and self-reported morbidity based on household interviews. The ones with data most readily available at an aggregate level are mortality and self-reported morbidity, and it is on these that we concentrate.

As illustrated in the Black Report (Black 1980), epidemiologists or medical sociologists conventionally use mortality data to construct and compare mortality rates for different groups in the population, such as social classes. This has a number of difficulties (detailed in Le Grand 1985 and Illsley and Le Grand 1987), particularly when comparisons over time are concerned. In particular, the fact that the size of the classes (and sometimes the classification scheme itself) can change significantly over time implies that like is not being compared with like. Also, social class can be confidently ascribed only to males aged 15–64; hence class analyses are mostly confined to deaths for that group, which in 1983 were less than 20 per cent of all deaths.

An approach that does not suffer from these problems is to choose an indicator that can be attached to individuals rather than to groups, and then to examine trends in that indicator's mean and dispersion. Thus, for instance, economists exploring changes in income inequality over time have not compared, say, changes in the difference between the average income of SEGs I and V; rather, they have examined changes in a summary statistic, such as the variance or the Gini coefficient, based on differences between individual incomes throughout the population. This approach can be applied to mortality by using as an indicator an individual's length of life or age at death.

Results employing this approach are provided in Table 4.15. This shows the mean, variance and Gini coefficient for the distribution of age at death in England and Wales. The data are taken from the Office of Population Censuses and Surveys' annual publication *Mortality Statistics: General* for the relevant years. Estimates are provided for males, females, and the total of males and females from 1974 to 1985. The data in Table 4.15 are calculated from standardized deaths, i.e. those that would have occurred at each age if the age distribution for each year had been the same; the procedure is designed to overcome the difficulty that observed changes in the distribution of age at death can be the product of changes in the age distribution itself.

Table 4.15 provides two measures of dispersion: the variance and the Gini coefficient. Each of these has different properties. Of particular importance, given the change in the mean over the period, one (the variance) is translation-independent (i.e. independent of translation by a constant) and the other is scale-independent (independent of multiplication by a constant). Further discussion of the methodology involved can be found in Le Grand and Rabin (1987) and Illsley and Le Grand (1987).

It is apparent from Table 4.15 that two things have happened over the period: there has been a steady rise in the mean age at death, and there

Table 4.15. *Inequality in age at death, England and Wales*

	Males			Females			All		
	Mean	Variance[a]	Gini	Mean	Variance[a]	Gini	Mean	Variance[a]	Gini
1974	68.71	284.5	0.123	75.10	260.2	0.106	71.90	282.6	0.117
1975	68.91	278.4	0.121	75.17	259.4	0.106	72.03	278.7	0.117
1976	69.14	272.0	0.120	75.50	247.5	0.104	72.33	269.8	0.114
1977	69.42	278.5	0.121	75.26	253.1	0.105	72.31	274.4	0.116
1978	68.96	272.5	0.120	75.18	256.3	0.106	72.05	274.2	0.116
1979	69.12	268.1	0.120	75.37	247.2	0.104	72.23	267.4	0.114
1980	69.20	264.0	0.118	75.36	248.6	0.105	72.27	265.8	0.114
1981	69.28	263.6	0.118	75.47	240.1	0.103	72.37	261.4	0.113
1982	69.36	259.4	0.117	75.42	237.4	0.103	72.39	257.6	0.112
1983	69.44	253.9	0.116	75.47	235.8	0.102	72.45	254.0	0.117
1984[b]	69.37	253.8	0.116	75.39	235.3	0.103	74.38	253.6	0.112
1985	69.70	250.6	0.115	75.66	231.0	0.101	72.70	249.6	0.110

[a] Calculated as the product of the square of the mean and the square of the coefficient of variation.
[b] Table 10a (Deaths) of OPCS 1984 does not include data on deaths in the 55–9 age group. Deaths in this group were taken to be an average of the number of deaths for the same cohort in 1983 and in 1985.

Source: Own calculations. Mortality data taken from OPCS 1984 and equivalents for other years.

has been a fall in its dispersion, as measured by either summary statistic. The latter is of particular interest since, as we have seen, it was one of the main contentions of the Black Report that, at least until 1971, inequalities in health as measured by differences in the (male) mortality experiences of the social classes were getting wider rather than narrower. The data that would permit comparisons between the social classes over our period have not been published in a form that makes such comparisons easy (OPCS 1986); however, it appears that the widening has continued (Marmot and McDowall 1986). But it is important to note that it is quite possible for there to have been a fall in measures of inequality between individuals while there was an increase in the gaps between the social classes. There may have been a fall in inequality within each social class whose aggregate effect outweighed the widening between the classes. Also, as noted above, the social class data refer only to a minority of deaths, whereas the individualistic measures take account of all mortality.

The interpretation of this evidence poses several problems. First, they relate to *ex post* realizations, whereas our concern may be with the *ex ante* position. That is, the policy aim may be either that of equalizing the age of death for all people of the same sex or that of securing equal chances of attaining a given age at death, regardless of social or economic position. Each is problematic as an objective. The first is obviously unrealistic, given that there will always be an irreducible minimum of stochastic variation in mortality. The second may allow 'too much' variation in actual mortality outcomes to be socially acceptable. In any case, the fall in inequality we observe could be due to a component common to all (thus contributing to *ex post* inequality) or to one specific to particular groups (thus contributing to both). From the data presented, we cannot determine which.

Secondly, since mortality is heavily affected by factors other than curative health policy, it is difficult to link directly any changes we may observe with changes in policy. Because of the absence of a proper counterfactual hypothesis as to what would have happened to mortality in the absence of the relevant policy (or under different policies), we cannot draw any unequivocal conclusions from this concerning the effectiveness or ineffectiveness of health policy over the period. However, trends in mortality inequalities have been used in the past to criticize the performance of the Health Service (as in the Introduction to Townsend and Davidson 1982). Hence it is worth noting that this evidence suggests that there have been improvements in some key aspects of mortality outcomes, and therefore that criticism of the effectiveness of the welfare state based on the proposition that there has been a deterioration in these respects may be ill founded.

What of morbidity? GHS data show that people in the professional and managerial social classes are less likely to report long-standing or restricting illnesses, while manual workers and workers in the social services are more likely to report illnesses, as compared with the population as a whole. In 1974, unskilled manual workers were 34 per cent more likely to report illness than the average individual; in 1979, 25 per cent; and in 1985, 19 per cent. Professional workers were 28 per cent less likely to report illness in 1974, and 33 per cent less likely in 1985. Unskilled manual workers are coming closer to the average illness rate, but professional workers are increasing their advantage.

Another general finding from the GHS is that more and more people are reporting chronic illness—up from 26.5 per cent in 1974 to 32.6 per cent in 1985. This conflicts with the evidence of a continuous fall in the mean age at death, suggesting an improvement in health over the period.

There are three possible explanations for the disparity. First, the population as a whole is ageing, which in so far as increasing age is correlated with increasing ill-health should lead to a rise in the latter (the mortality data were age-standardized, so this effect should not appear there). However, Winter (1989), in an analysis of the changing self-reported morbidity rates for different cohorts of males, was able to reject this hypothesis. Second, people may be more willing to report illness today than in 1974, but the illness may be of a less significant kind (and in particular may have a lower impact on mortality). That this may be a factor is indicated by data from the GHS showing that, between 1974 and 1985, the number of people who report that their illness limits their activity has decreased. Although this may be due to the increasing mobility of a more affluent society, it may also indicate that the illnesses being reported are less severe. Finally, Winter found some evidence that the increase in self-reported morbidity was linked with unemployment, the impact of which on mortality may have yet to appear.

This leads us to a final point. Again, it should be emphasized with respect to health outcomes that the changes observed are almost certainly the result of changes in a large number of other factors in addition to those that relate directly to the NHS. Moreover, it is possible that the influence of some of these factors is in the long term. In particular, whether and when the effects of increasing dispersion of disposable income and of the high levels of unemployment that have characterized the 1980s will have a measurable impact on morbidity and mortality remains to be seen.

V. IN BRIEF

● Both governments increased the overall volume of resources going to the NHS. However, the annual growth rate in resources was higher under Labour than under the Conservatives—according to one measure, over four times as high—while the growth in need (or demand) was higher under the Conservatives than under Labour. Hence the increase in resources relative to need was substantially greater under Labour than under the Conservatives.

● There appear to have been gains in efficiency that can be attributed to the Conservative cost-improvement programmes. However, as yet the savings are relatively small, amounting to 2 per cent of the overall NHS budget.

● Both governments succeeded in increasing the proportion of health-service resources devoted to the elderly, although the Conservatives by much less than Labour. The proportions going to the mentally ill and mentally handicapped hospital services fell under both governments, although by much more under the Conservatives than under Labour. The proportion going to health visiting and district nursing increased under both governments, but this time by substantially more under the Conservatives.

● The RAWP reallocations, introduced under Labour and, until 1989, continued under the Conservatives, have been a major success story, at least so far as the reallocation of expenditures between regions is concerned. However, there remained substantial inequalities within regions; there was also no improvement in regional inequalities in access to care, as measured by the availability of GPs.

● Over the whole period, there has been little difference between socio-economic groups in the extent to which they consult GPs when they are ill. Moreover, there is evidence of some equalization across socio-economic groups in the overall use of the NHS per person reporting illness; but this seems to be due to a rise in the numbers of the higher SEGs reporting illness, rather than a change in the pattern of utilization.

● As the above suggests, there appears to have been an increase in self-reported morbidity, although there is some evidence that this does not represent an increase in illness that limits activities. Mortality indicators that are possibly more reliable suggest there has been both a steady improvement in the mean level of health and a reduction in inequality in health, at least between individuals. There seems to be no particular difference between the Labour and Conservative periods in this respect; however, the high levels of unemployment and the widening of income inequality that have characterized the 1980s may have an impact on health that is yet to appear.

Annexe

Table 4A.1. *NHS real expenditure (gross), United Kingdom* (£ million at 1987/8 prices, adjusted using GDP deflator)

	1973/4	1974/5	1975/6	1976/7	1977/8	1978/9	1979/80	1980/1	1981/2	1982/3	1983/4	1984/5	1985/6	1986/7	1987/8ᵃ
Hospitals, running[b]	7,781	9,787	10,781	10,806	10,595	10,762	10,821	12,092	12,190	12,205	12,588	12,514	12,590	13,006	13,635
Family practitioner															
General medical[c]	1,000	974	997	992	923	951	1,000	1,117	1,169	1,225	1,264	1,367	1,405	1,445	1,528
Pharmaceutical[c]	1,373	1,618	1,418	1,597	1,693	1,807	1,730	1,797	1,881	2,014	2,129	2,201	2,221	2,353	2,464
General dental[c]	645	750	699	685	620	678	702	732	758	792	820	857	844	923	990
Ophthalmic[c]	154	188	222	204	182	185	188	182	200	300	230	236	185	163	182
Administration	377	577	617	633	605	610	640	667	640	615	545	542	517	582	602
Patients' payments															
Hospital	−83	−74	−73	−83	−75	−70	−74	−84	−93	−91	−98	−96	−100	−104	−106
Pharmaceutical	−127	−118	−79	−70	−61	−57	−86	−130	−144	−157	−161	−171	−172	−215	−256
Dental	−149	−143	−108	−121	−139	−133	−137	−157	−178	−205	−216	−226	−245	−275	−290
Ophthalmic	−79	−77	−61	−67	−61	−62	−58	−50	−51	−57	−61	−60	−15	−1	−1
Total	−439	−412	−322	−341	−336	−322	−354	−422	−467	−510	−536	−553	−532	−595	−653
Other	386	463	398	478	459	462	489	511	410	397	427	407	462	544	546
Total current	11,276	13,945	14,810	15,054	14,741	15,131	15,216	16,676	16,781	17,038	17,466	17,571	17,692	18,422	19,294
Capital expenditure	1,189	1,110	1,184	1,093	932	957	916	1,019	1,123	1,079	1,067	1,135	1,181	1,211	1,304
Total expenditure	12,465ᵈ	15,055	15,994	16,147	15,673	16,088	16,132	17,695	17,904	18,117	18,534	18,706	18,873	19,633	20,598
GDP deflator	22.8	27.2	34.2	38.7	44.0	48.7	57.0	67.5	74.1	79.4	83.0	87.2	91.9	95.0	100

[a] Provisional figures.
[b] Including the school health service from 1 Apr. 1974, previously included in education.
[c] Before deducting payments by patients.
[d] Excluding £934 million of local authority health services expenditures (at 1987/8 prices).

Source: Expenditures: CSO 1982, 1988c, 1989c; GDP deflator: HM Treasury 1989: table 21.4.1.

Table 4A.2. *NHS volume expenditure (gross), United Kingdom* (£ million at 1980 prices, using Blue Book deflators)

	1973/4	1974/5	1975/6	1976/7	1977/8	1978/9	1979/80	1980/1	1981/2	1982/3	1983/4	1984/5	1985/6	1986/7
Hospitals, running[a]	5,724	6,757	7,533	7,528	7,549	7,578	7,601	8,162	8,164	8,211	8,147	8,177	8,176	8,108
Family practitioner														
General medical[b]	736	673	697	691	657	669	702	754	783	824	818	893	912	901
Pharmaceutical[b]	1,010	1,117	991	1,112	1,206	1,272	1,215	1,213	1,260	1,355	1,378	1,438	1,442	1,467
General dental[b]	474	518	488	477	442	477	493	494	508	533	531	560	548	575
Ophthalmic[b]	113	129	155	142	130	130	132	123	134	202	149	154	120	102
Administration[b]	277	398	431	441	431	429	450	450	428	413	352	354	336	363
Patients' payments														
Hospital	−61	−51	−51	−58	−53	−49	−52	−57	−62	−61	−63	−63	−65	−65
Pharmaceutical	−94	−81	−55	−49	−44	−40	−60	−88	−97	−106	−104	−112	−112	−134
Dental	−110	−99	−76	−85	−99	−94	−96	−106	−119	−138	−140	−148	−159	−171
Ophthalmic	−58	−53	−43	−47	−44	−43	−41	−34	−34	−38	−40	−39	−10	−1
Total	−323	−284	−225	−238	−240	−227	−249	−285	−313	−343	−347	−361	−346	−371
Other	284	320	278	333	327	325	344	345	275	267	276	266	300	339
Total current	8,296	9,627	10,349	10,488	10,502	10,655	10,689	11,256	11,239	11,462	11,304	11,482	11,490	11,484
Capital expenditure	874	767	827	761	664	674	643	688	752	726	691	742	767	755
Total expenditure	9,170[c]	10,394	11,176	11,249	11,166	11,329	11,332	11,944	11,991	12,188	11,995	12,224	12,257	12,238

[a] Including the school health service from 1 Apr. 1974, previously included in education.

[b] Before deducting payments by patients.

[c] Excluding local authority health services expenditures in 1973/4.

Sources: Expenditures: CSO 1982, 1988c; deflator: calculated from CSO 1983 for 1973–5; CSO 1987b for 1976–86; CSO 1988b for 1987.

5

Housing: A Decent Home for All at a Price within their Means?

John Hills and Beverley Mullings

I. GOALS AND POLICIES

Government has never seen its role as being a universal provider or funder of housing in the same way as it has for education or health. One consequence of this is that policy goals in the sector have to be pursued by less direct methods than in others. In terms of the matrix of provision and funding shown in Fig. 5.1, a much greater proportion of the sector's activity by value occurs in the private/private quadrant than for most of the other activities examined in this book.

None the less, as the figure also shows, the public sector plays a substantial role in the housing market, both through provision of housing

	Public provision	Private provision
Public funding	Subsidies to council housing Housing Benefit for council rents	Housing Benefit for private rents Tax expenditures on owner-occupation Grants to housing associations Tax expenditures on private landlords (BES) Improvement grants
Private funding	Net rents paid by council tenants	Owner-occupiers' housing costs (net of tax expenditures) Net rents paid to private landlords and housing associations

FIG. 5.1. Housing: provision and funding

for which individuals pay rent and through a range of subsidies, including Housing Benefit, subsidies to local authorities and housing associations, and tax expenditures for owner-occupiers. It has also played a substantial role in the regulation of the housing market, both as far as the enforcement of minimum standards is concerned, and in controlling rents charged in the private sector.

Housing remains part of the welfare state not just because of inertia. There are continuing positive reasons for government intervention, for instance because of market failure, or at least the presumption of market failure. Because housing has such a long life, the service it provides depends on a stock of assets whose size is very large in relation to the rate at which new investment can be made. Unlike most other commodities, the supply of housing is therefore very slow to adjust to changes in price. This can leave tenants open to exploitation by landlords in times of shortage, providing the rationale for rent controls and security-of-tenure legislation. Another effect of the cost of housing in relation to current income is that capital market failure becomes important: purchasers may have difficulties in borrowing against their future incomes, particularly where these are low and uncertain.

Another kind of market failure stems from the externalities resulting from private housing consumption. The condition of one house affects its neighbours and, indeed, its whole neighbourhood. A private market is unlikely to allow for the 'spill-over' effects of improvement in its investment decisions. Historically, much housing legislation has its origins in public health legislation—overcrowding and squalor breed disease for the whole population, not just for the residents affected.

Once a floor is put to the quality of housing which is allowed, something has to be done for those whose incomes are too low to choose housing of that standard at unsubsidized prices. Combined with more general distributional concerns this has led to a series of interventions aimed at those with low incomes. Specific subsidies have been given to keep down the rents of housing, primarily aimed at those on low incomes, while they have also received housing benefits whose size has been directly tied to their spending on housing. This contrasts with the policy generally adopted towards income support, under which benefits take the form of cash, which the recipient then uses to buy food, clothing, or whatever. There seem to be two reasons for this difference. First, housing is seen as a 'merit good' whose consumption by the poor is more readily supported by society (partly because of the externalities described above) than, say, the consumption of alcohol or tobacco. Secondly, the housing market is so distorted in terms of the relationship between price and quality of service received that it has been seen as impossible (or very expensive) to give a standard allowance for housing as part of general cash benefits:

Any such proposal would fail to take account of the very wide variations that exist in the cost of similar housing throughout the country. It would also fail to recognise that for a number of reasons many households on low incomes have unavoidably high housing costs in proportion to their disposable income. (DHSS 1985*d*: p. v)

A similarly pragmatic reason for continued intervention in the housing market is that everyone has adjusted their behaviour (and the prices they are prepared to pay) in the light of that intervention. The Housing Policy Review established by the Labour government in 1975 to sort out what was described by the then Secretary of State for the Environment, Anthony Crosland, as the 'dog's breakfast' of housing finance (Lansley 1979: 104) resulted in a Green Paper whose foreword explicitly defended the status quo on the grounds that

we certainly do not believe that the household budgets of millions of families—which have been planned in good faith in the reasonable expectation that present arrangements would broadly continue—should be overturned, in pursuit of some theoretical or academic dogma. (DoE 1977*a*: p. iv)

Further, since some people already benefit from such arrangements, equity requires that others should too—if owner-occupiers have a favourable tax treatment, should not tenants receive comparable concessions, quite apart from any additional help that might be going to those on low incomes? From this observation come notions that tax and subsidy arrangements should start from the idea of 'tenure neutrality'.

Finally, housing policy has been seen as an instrument by which wider social aims can be achieved. These have varied over the years. Immediately after the war, the government saw the private landlord as inherently incapable of providing housing on the scale which was required; by contrast, local authorities were 'plannable instruments' through which investment should be channelled. At the same time, it was hoped to promote social integration through developments which would house those of all incomes. Aneurin Bevan hoped that council housing would have 'the lovely feature of English and Welsh villages, where the doctor, the grocer, the butcher and the farm labourer all lived in the same street' (Foot 1975: 76). More recently, policies such as the 'Right to Buy' have stressed the promotion of self-sufficiency and wider consumer choice.

The expression of policy aims

The phrase which gives this chapter its title has recurred as the stated overall aim of housing policy in many official documents since the Second World War. The Heath government's 1971 White Paper, *Fair Deal for Housing*, gave the aim as 'a decent home for every family at a price within their means', followed by the equity aims of 'a fairer choice between owning a home and renting one' and 'fairness between one citizen and another in giving and receiving help towards housing costs' (DoE 1971). Similarly, the opening sentence of the Labour government's 1977 Green Paper was that 'The Government believe that all families should be able to obtain a decent home at a price within their means' (DoE 1977*a*: 1). We explore later in this chapter what might be meant by the perhaps rather vague formulations of 'a decent home' and 'within their means'.

By contrast, after 1979 the promotion of owner-occupation became a much more dominant aim of policy. For instance, the Department of the Environment's part of the 1986 Public Expenditure White Paper baldly stated that 'The Government's leading housing policy aim is to encourage the widest opportunities for home ownership' (HM Treasury 1986: ii. 142).

More recently, this exclusive emphasis appears to have relaxed. The 1987 White Paper, *Housing: The Government's Proposals*, gave a much wider formulation of objectives:

The Government has four principal aims. First, to reverse the decline of rented housing and to improve its quality; second, to give council tenants the right to transfer to other landlords if they choose to do so; third, to target money more accurately on the most acute problems; and fourth, to continue to encourage the growth of home ownership. (DoE 1987: 1)

and in November 1988 Lord Caithness, the minister responsible for housing, said in a speech to the National House-Building Council that 'The government's aim in housing is no different from those of any other post-war government. We want decent, affordable, suitable housing to be within the reach of all families.'

This shift-back in emphasis appears partly to be a result of the government's having decided that its main objective had been substantially achieved by 1987—with a rise in owner-occupation from 55 per cent of dwellings in Great Britain at the end of 1978 to 65 per cent ten years later (see Table 5.14). It may also reflect a change in its perception of the universal applicability of that objective.

Policy: Labour government 1974–1979

Some of the Labour government's first acts on return to office were direct reversals of the policies of its Conservative predecessor. In particular, the 1972 Housing Finance Act was repealed, and with it the attempt to take council rents out of the control of the local authorities. That Act had been an attempt to force local authorities to charge 'fair rents', set by local rent officers in the same way as for regulated rents in the private sector, rather than rents being at each authority's discretion and depending heavily on the state of the authority's Housing Revenue Account (HRA), which carries current income and expenditure relating to its direct provision of housing. The government restored the 'no profit rule', outlawing again transfers of surpluses from HRAs to General Rate Funds. Council rents were initially frozen in nominal terms as part of the general 'Social Contract' anti-inflation policy and were subsequently increased by amounts which did not keep up with general inflation.

The 1974 Budget again removed the tax deductibility of interest payments on forms of personal borrowing *except* for housing (as had been the position from 1969/70 to 1971/2), this time subject to a limit of £25,000 on the amount of a mortgage on which relief could be given. This limit has been raised in cash terms only once, to £30,000 in 1983, which has acted as some restraint on the growing cost of tax relief (see Whitehead 1978 for a discussion of the issues involved). In 1974, the limit affected only 0.1 per cent of new building-society advances; by 1987 more than 38 per cent were above the limit (DoE 1985: table 10.10; DoE 1988a: table 10.10). However, the excess over the limit is not large, even for new mortgages, and others date from earlier years, so the overwhelming bulk of mortgage interest continues to receive relief.

By contrast, the Housing Finance Act's national scheme of income-related rent rebates (for council tenants) and rent allowances (for private tenants in unfurnished accommodation) remained in place, although its cost has varied substantially since 1974 as policies towards gross rents changed (see section II below).

The 1974 Housing Act included two measures which continued the general policy shift towards renovation of the existing stock rather than clearance and redevelopment, a shift first signalled by the 1968 White Paper, *Old Houses into New Homes* (MHLG 1968) and the 1973 White Paper, *Better Homes: The Next Priorities* (DoE 1973). The first of these measures was the introduction of Housing Action Areas, as a more intensive focus for area improvement and rehabilitation activity than the General Improvement Areas introduced in 1969. The second was the establishment of the Housing Association Grant system, under which associations (non-profit organizations run by voluntary committees) could receive generous enough capital grants to allow them to break even while charging fair rents on newly rehabilitated or constructed property. Under this financial regime the total housing association stock has more than doubled.

More significant moves on housing finance were postponed until the conclusion of the Housing Policy Review; the subsidies to local authorities introduced by the 1975 Housing Rents and Subsidies Act were intended to be temporary arrangements until a new system was designed. In the event, the system proposed in the 1977 Green Paper (DoE 1977a:

83) was actually introduced by the next government's 1980 Housing Act.

Between 1969 and 1976 local authorities were free to make their own decisions about how many new houses to construct, subject to minimum *standards* (the 'Parker Morris' standards) and limits on *costs* (the 'Housing Costs Yardstick'). But from 1977/8, controls on local authority borrowing for capital spending were extended to include the construction of new dwellings under the Housing Investment Programme (HIP) system (renovation spending was already controlled). This system was originally presented in the 1977 Green Paper as

a means of controlling public expenditure while allowing resources to be allocated selectively with regard to variations in local housing requirements. Within the context of national policies and standards it will increase local discretion by putting greater responsibility for deciding the right mix of investment on the local authorities. (DoE 1977a: 77)

In the event, 'local discretion' has not figured prominently in the way the system has operated:

The local autonomy and planning objectives of the system have been almost fully subservient to central decisions on the distribution of resources, strong encouragement to follow national policy initiatives and a tightly controlled and uncertain financial climate. (Leather 1983: 223–4)

As can be seen from Table 5.5, gross capital spending on housing fell substantially after 1976; indeed, the volume of spending on new local authority construction has fallen continuously ever since then.

The final major policy initiative of the Labour government's period in office was the introduction of the Housing (Homeless Persons) Act of 1977. Originally a (Liberal) Private Member's Bill, this placed a legal duty on local authorities to secure housing for priority cases, such as families with children, pregnant women, or the elderly, who came within a new, statutory, definition of being 'homeless'. We discuss the numbers housed under this provision, and the meaning which can be attached to such statistics, below.

Policy: Conservative government since 1979

In looking at housing policy in the decade since 1979, it is striking that there have been two waves of policy-making. The first wave was embodied in the 1980 Housing Act and the 1980 Local Government Planning and Land Act, introducing the Right to Buy for local authority tenants and changing the system of subsidies to HRAs and the general system of Rate Support Grant to authorities. The second wave—whose effects it is too early to judge—is embodied in the provisions of the 1988 Housing Act and the 1989 Local Government and Housing Act, combined with the reform of Housing Benefit introduced in April 1988 (following an earlier, much less fundamental, change in 1982).

The first major policy mechanism in the 1980 Housing Act aimed at enhancing the drive towards home ownership through the Right to Buy. While mechanisms for council-house sales to sitting tenants had always existed at the discretion of the authority (with discounts which had been allowed up to 30 per cent between 1970 and 1974), the 1980 Act made the major change of granting public-sector tenants of at least three years' standing the personal right to purchase the freehold of a house or the 125-year lease of a flat. Tenants were entitled to discounts on the market value of the property, depending on the length of time for which they had been a council tenant. If this was less than four years, the discount was a third of the value as assessed by the District Valuer, increasing by 1 per cent for each additional year up to a maximum of 50 per cent and a maximum discount of £25,000 (subsequently increased to a maximum of 70 per cent in some circumstances, and up to £50,000 from 1989). The effect of the legislation has been far-reaching: about 1.2 million public-sector dwellings were sold (not all under the Right to Buy) in Great Britain between 1979 and 1987, more than a sixth of the stock at the end of 1978 (DoE 1988a: tables 9.6 and 9.3).

The 1980 Act introduced a new subsidy system for local authorities in England and Wales containing mechanisms to withdraw subsidy from them on the *assumption* that they increase their rents in line with an annual 'ministerial determination' or rent guide-line. It has not been compulsory to raise rents, avoiding the strategy that had led to direct confrontation with recalcitrant councils such as Clay Cross following the Heath government's 1972 Housing Finance Act (Malpass 1989). Instead, the combination of the Housing Subsidy system and the Block Grant system also introduced in 1980 makes it very expensive for authorities to choose not to increase rents. In aggregate, rents have risen substantially in real terms (see Table 5.2), and roughly in line with the annual guide-lines, but the strength of central government's 'leverage' over rents has declined as more and more authorities have fallen out of subsidy altogether—only a quarter of English authorities remained entitled to Housing Subsidy by 1986/7.

As general subsidies have been cut and rents increased, so Housing Benefit has become of much greater importance. This does not, however, reflect increased generosity in the formula by which benefit entitlement is calculated; indeed, it has become less generous in most cases. The system in place up until 1981/2 was essentially unchanged from that established soon after the Housing Finance Act. Then in 1982/3 the system under which Supplementary Benefit (now Income Support) covered the housing costs of its recipients in full was amalgamated with the rent and rate rebate and rent allowance systems (which gave partial assistance to those not on Supplementary Benefit) to produce a combined 'Housing Benefit'. The main effects of the change were administrative. Supplementary Benefit recipients no longer received cash from the DHSS with which to pay their rents and rates. Instead, 'certificates' would be sent to the local authorities, telling them to give rebates on rent and rates in full. In effect, however, two separate systems remained—one based on 100 per cent of housing costs, the other on a formula depending on 60 per cent of costs (see section IV below). As Berthoud (1989) puts its, 'Housing benefit . . . never looked like living up to its advance billing as a "comprehensive" solution. It was just the two old schemes tied together—with red tape.' At the same time as the change was being made, local authority rents were being increased—under the influence of the new Housing Subsidy system—by 50 per cent in real terms, and unemployment was rising rapidly, both factors bringing many more tenants within the system, and increasing the work-load which hit local authority offices still further.

The 1988 Housing Act included two new mechanisms designed to reduce the importance of local authorities as direct providers of housing. Under the first, other landlords will be able to bid to take over local authority housing, with tenants voting on whether this should go ahead, subject to the controversial condition that abstentions count as votes in favour (councils have been able to make 'voluntary disposals' to other landlords at their own discretion since 1985). Under the second, central government can establish 'Housing Action Trusts' (HATs) to take over the running of particular estates directly. At the time of writing it is not at all clear what—if any—effect these initiatives will have (see Glennerster, Power, and Travers 1989 for a further discussion).

Under the same legislation, the system of grants to housing associations has also been reformed. New housing association tenancies will no longer be at fair rents, and the system under which enough capital grant is given to allow the association to break even by charging such rents will be changed. Instead, the capital grant will be at a fixed level, and the association will have to charge rents which cover whatever costs are left over. At the same time, associations will have to make provisions out of rents to build up funds to cover future periodic major repairs (previously covered by grant). In combination, these measures look likely to bring about a significant increase in the rents which associations charge new tenants (existing tenants retain the right to a fair rent, although these also appear to be increasing in real terms). Quite how much the increase will be is not yet clear; all that the government has said is that rents should remain 'at levels within the reach of those in low paid employment' (Housing Corporation 1988).

For private tenants, the 1980 Housing Act introduced new kinds of tenancy which came outside the 'fair rent' regulatory regime established in 1965. These 'assured' and 'shorthold' tenancies never became significant in numerical terms, but they paved the way for the large-scale changes of the 1988 Housing Act, which has made all *new* tenancies either assured or 'assured/shorthold'. Rents will be set at market levels, with the tenant retaining permanent security of tenure in the first case (with Rent Assessment Committees taking on a new role of preventing increases to *above* market levels for sitting tenants) or for a fixed term in the latter case. Fair rents are retained for tenancies already covered by them.

As far as subsidies to local authorities are concerned, the proposals included in the 1989 Local Government and Housing Act and outlined in an earlier consultation paper (DoE 1988*b*) will ensure that nearly all authorities will be in receipt of the new Housing Revenue Account Subsidy (an amalgamation of Housing Subsidy and the grants paid to authorities in respect of Housing Benefit for their tenants), and so will come under the leverage of the DoE's rent guide-lines once more. At the same time local authorities will lose their ability to make discretionary transfers from their general funds to their HRAs. In most cases they will also lose the ability (restored in 1980) to make transfers in the other direction. This 'ring fencing' will leave local authority housing departments looking much more like separate housing organizations than simply part of the council's general activities.

After a series of reductions in the generosity of the Housing Benefit formula through increases in the 'tapers' under which benefit is withdrawn from those with higher incomes, the system was more fundamentally reformed as part of the 'Fowler reforms' to social security in April 1988. The new system genuinely brings the treatment of those receiving Income Support and other recipients into line with one another. However, the result of this is to extend the phenomenon that Housing Benefit now changes pound for pound with any change in rent (up to certain limits) for all recipients (previously this was only true of recipients of Supplementary Benefit). This sits rather oddly with the moves towards deregulation of private rents and increases in local authority and housing association rents which the 1988 and 1989 legislation is intended to bring about. On the one hand, rents are being moved more towards 'market' levels, while on the other, the benefit system largely subverts any attempt to establish a functioning market.

Consistency and change in housing policy

There are several ways in which there has been a high degree of continuity in the direction of housing policy over the last twenty years. First, tax concessions for owner-occupiers have remained largely intact. The abolition of the taxation of owner-occupiers' 'imputed rents' under Schedule A of income tax in 1963 was not reversed by the 1964–70 Labour government. Nor did that government impose its new capital gains tax on housing. When the tax deductibility of interest payments on other forms of personal borrowing was removed in 1974, mortgage interest continued to receive tax relief, albeit subject to a limit. More recently, there has been some attempt to rein back the cost of the relief. Not only is the limit now considerably lower in real terms than when it was introduced, but also tax relief on loans for repairs and improvements has been withdrawn, and the possibility of 'multiple tax relief' on the same dwelling has been removed. Just as significantly, the fall in income tax rates after 1977/8 has reduced the rate at which relief is given. On the other hand, the abolition of domestic rates in Scotland in 1989 and in England and Wales in 1990 removes a tax which has acted (with stamp duty) as virtually the only offset to the tax advantages of housing as a whole.

Secondly, since the late 1960s there has been a continuing shift of emphasis away from new local authority construction as the main form of capital spending on housing: the 'numbers game' of successive governments vying with one another over who could achieve the largest number of new housing starts was abandoned, both in response to disillusion with some of the products of wide-scale clearance and redevelopment, and as the 'crude shortage' of dwellings in relation to the number of households disappeared (see Table 5.11). Instead, there has been a steadily increasing emphasis on renovation of the existing stock through a redirection of local authority spending, through housing association rehabilitation activity, and through improvement grants.

Where there has been less consistency has been in the balance between 'general assistance', designed to keep down rents for all local authority tenants, and income-related housing benefits. While the national system of rent rebates and allowances introduced in 1972 was maintained by the 1974 Labour government, its policies on rents and subsidies as a whole meant that the public expenditure cost of the rebate system did not increase—in sharp contrast to the experience since 1979. Similarly, the Right to Buy marked a decisive change in the view of the role of local authorities as general providers of rented housing. As section III below shows, its introduction marked the point at which the proportion of housing provided by local authorities had passed its peak.

Perhaps the biggest change is the extent to which housing as an issue has moved down the political agenda—the public reaction to the substantial reduction in public spending described below has been much more muted than the reaction against constraints on a health budget whose cost has grown in real terms (see Chapter 4).

II. EXPENDITURE TRENDS AND INTERMEDIATE POLICY OUTPUTS

The figures conventionally given as representing public expenditure on housing are in some ways unsatisfactory. The Public Expenditure White Paper's figure for total spending on housing includes, amongst other items: current subsidies to local authority HRAs (the difference between current spending, including servicing of historic debt, and rental and other income); grants to the private sector for improvement and insulation; capital expenditure by local authorities financed by loans from central government or the private sector; and the total of net loans and grants paid to housing associations for capital development. Even in conventional accounting terms, the total given for these items involves much adding together of apples and pears, with current spending added to capital items fully covered by borrowing and future debt repayment.

The conventional totals are net of receipts from rents (for current spending) and from sales of assets (for capital). While these net figures are of interest in terms of the new public resources which are being channelled into housing, they can—as is explained below—be seriously misleading as a guide to how much is actually being spent on public housing. In addition, the cost of Housing Benefit—intimately related to the level of rents and hence to that of general subsidies—has been counted as part of the social security programme, and the cost of tax expenditures on housing is counted entirely separately.

Fig. 5.2 brings together the main elements of public spending on housing with the cost of Housing Benefit. The figures are for Great Britain and are expressed at 1987/8 prices (cash spending adjusted by the GDP deflator). The net capital and net current figures are drawn from successive Public Expenditure White Papers for England and from other sources for Wales and Scotland, with the exception of the period 1973/4–1975/6, where the figures are (roughly) adjusted from information originally given in survey price (volume) terms for Great Britain. The Housing Benefit totals are on a basis consistent with current White Paper presentation, that is, they include payments relating to the rent of public and private tenants on 'standard' Housing Benefit (rent rebates and allowances until 1982/3) and the equivalent of the whole of the rent of Income Support recipients (estimated for Supplementary Benefit recipients up to 1982/3 and excluding other elements of housing costs like rates or water charges).

The trends shown by the figure and given in more detail in Table 5.1 and Table 5A.1 in the Annexe to this chapter are clear. Even including spending on Housing Benefit, following an initial rise there is a substantial fall over the period in the GB total, particularly after 1979/80. Those tables also include total spending in Northern Ireland (although without a split between capital and current spending), and it is notable that the fall in this component has been much less than for the rest of the United Kingdom. The UK total reached a peak in 1974/5, both in real terms and as percentages of UK Gross Domestic Product (GDP) (4.3 per cent) and General Government Expenditure (GGE) (8.9 per cent). By the end of the period, the total had fallen to half of its maximum in real terms and to only 1.6 per cent of UK GDP and 4.0 per cent of GGE. More than any other public spending programme explored in this book, the housing programme has clearly been substantially cut since 1978/9.

Within this total, the relationship between net current expenditure (mostly Rate Fund Contributions and Housing Subsidy or equivalent payments to HRAs) and Housing Benefit is of particular interest. Throughout the period their combined cost in Great Britain is remarkably constant at about £5 billion (at 1987/8 prices). As general subsidies were cut back between 1978/9 and 1982/3, the cost of Housing Benefit rose by an equivalent amount. Much of this was cause and effect. General subsidies fell as local authority rents increased by 49 per cent in real terms between 1979/80 and 1982/3 (see Table 5.2). Meanwhile, the number of

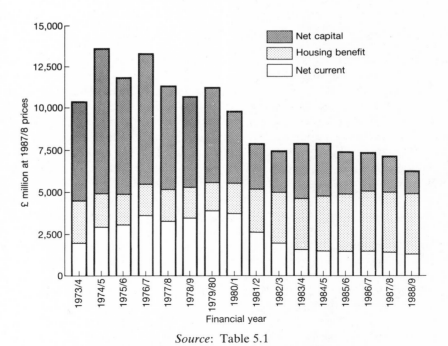

Source: Table 5.1

Fig. 5.2. Public expenditure on housing, Great Britain

Table 5.1. *Real net public expenditure on housing, Great Britain and United Kingdom* (£ billion at 1987/8 prices)

	Net current (GB)	Housing Benefit[a] (GB)	Net capital (GB)	Total public spending (UK)	Mortgage interest tax relief	Public spending on housing % of GDP[b]	Public spending on housing % of GGE[c]
1973/4	2.0	2.6	5.9	10.8	2.4	3.3	7.7
1974/5	3.0	2.0	8.6	14.0	2.8	4.3	8.9
1975/6	3.1	1.8	6.9	12.2	2.8	3.8	7.8
1976/7	3.6	1.9	7.7	13.8	3.2	4.1	9.0
1977/8	3.2	1.9	6.1	11.8	2.7	3.4	8.1
1978/9	3.5	1.8	5.3	11.2	2.6	3.2	7.3
1979/80	4.0	1.7	5.6	11.8	2.9	3.2	7.4
1980/1	3.8	1.8	4.2	10.3	3.2	2.9	6.4
1981/2	2.7	2.6	2.7	8.4	3.1	2.4	5.2
1982/3	2.0	3.1	2.4	8.1	3.1	2.3	4.8
1983/4	1.7	3.0	3.2	8.4	3.4	2.3	5.0
1984/5	1.6	3.3	3.1	8.5	4.1	2.3	4.9
1985/6	1.6	3.4	2.5	8.1	5.2	2.1	4.6
1986/7	1.6	3.6	2.2	8.0	5.0	2.0	4.5
1987/8	1.5	3.6	2.1	7.8	4.9	1.8	4.4
1988/9	1.4	3.6	1.3	7.0	5.2	1.6	4.0
Real growth rates (% per year)							
1973/4–1978/9	11.8	−6.4	−1.9	0.7	1.1		
1978/9–1988/9	−8.7	7.0	−13.1	−4.6	7.2		
1973/4–1988/9	−2.4	2.3	−9.5	−2.9	5.1		

[a] On current definitions.
[b] Gross Domestic Product.
[c] General Government Expenditure.

Sources: see Table 5A.1. Cash figures adjusted by GDP deflator.

Table 5.2. *Housing Benefit recipients (local authority tenants), Great Britain*

	Housing Benefit recipients as % of all local authority tenants[a]			Index of real local authority rents[b]	Rents as % of average earnings[c]	Index of value of needs allowance[d]
	Certif./Supp. Ben.	Standard/rebates	All			
1973/4	22	17	39	100	7.8	100
1974/5	22	16	38	92	7.5	112
1975/6	21	18	39	82	6.5	109
1976/7	21	19	40	82	6.3	105
1977/8	22	19	41	83	6.7	101
1978/9	22	18	40	82	6.3	102
1979/80	22	18	40	78	6.1	102
1980/1	23	20	43	80	6.0	101
1981/2	27	24	51	105	7.7	99
1982/3	31	26	58	116	8.2	101
1983/4	30	30	59	115	8.1	101
1984/5	32	29	62	115	7.8	101
1985/6	33	28	62	116	7.7	102
1986/7	35	29	64	119	7.6	100
1987/8	36	29	65	122	7.5	99

[a] Recipients as percentage of number of dwellings owned by local authorities; percentage of tenants will be slightly higher.
[b] Adjusted by Retail Price Index (financial year average).
[c] Average male earnings in April each year (men over 21 before 1983; men on adult rates since 1983).
[d] Needs allowance for married couple adjusted by Retail Price Index (excluding housing costs).

Sources: DoE 1988a: tables 9.3, 11.1, and 11.3, and equivalents for earlier years; DSS 1988: tables 35.02 and 35.05; Scottish Development Department 1987.

local authority tenants receiving Housing Benefit rose from 40 per cent in 1979/80 to nearly 60 per cent by 1982/3, the increased numbers being partly a result of the higher rents. Given that recipients of Supplementary Benefit would have had the whole of these rent increases covered by benefit and that other recipients would have had 60 per cent covered (as a result of the pre-1988 formula), this meant that approaching half of the increased rents would have re-emerged immediately as higher Housing Benefit. At the same time, the increase in unemployment was leading to greater numbers of benefit recipients as well.

It should also be noted from the table that the increased number of recipients occurred despite a reduction in the overall generosity of the benefit system. Before April 1988 this depended on the value of the 'needs allowance'. For a married couple without children the allowance (adjusted by the Retail Price Index excluding housing costs) was virtually unchanged between 1977/8 and 1987/8; in relation to earnings, its value fell significantly. The relationship between rents, the benefit system, and 'affordability' is explored in more detail in section IV below.

The fall in the real value of net capital spending was even more dramatic than in net current spending. This fall started from 1976/7, after which the housing capital programme was a significant casualty of the cuts following the agreement with the International Monetary Fund. By 1987/8, real net capital spending (in Great Britain) was only 17 per cent of the level it had been in 1976/7. As is discussed below, what happened to *gross* spending was somewhat different.

For comparison, Table 5.1 also shows the cost of mortgage interest tax relief (including Option Mortgage Subsidy before this was subsumed into the Mortgage Interest Relief at Source arrangements in 1983/4). This has risen almost continuously over the period as the number of owner-occupiers, house prices, and interest rates have risen, offset to some extent by falling income tax rates (from 34 per cent in 1977/8 to 25 per cent in 1988/9 for most mortgagors) and the effects of the limit on the mortgage eligible for relief. The real cost of the relief was more than twice as high in 1988/9 as in 1973/4. Indeed, by 1988/9 the estimated cost of the relief (£5.5 billion in cash) was equivalent to nearly three-quarters of the total of public expenditure on housing, including Housing Benefit. If one adds the cost of the relief to the other items, the real total in 1988/9 is higher than in 1981/2 and is only 8 per cent lower than in 1973/4, which puts a rather different perspective on what has happened to the net public resources going to housing from that given by the spending figures alone. The extent to which mortgage interest tax relief is an appropriate measure of the advantages of owner-occupation is discussed below.

Current spending

The bulk of current public spending on housing is made up of central government (Exchequer) subsidies to local authority or new town HRAs and Rate Fund Contributions (RFCs) made from the local authorities' general funds to their HRAs. As can be seen in Table 5A.1, there has been a much faster fall in the real value of Exchequer subsidies—from £3.0 billion in 1979/80 to £0.7 billion in 1988/9 (at 1987/8 prices)—than in RFCs—from £0.7 to £0.4 billion over the same period. The relationship between these items and the total of current spending and income on local authority HRAs is shown in Table 5.3 and Fig. 5.3.

What is clear from these is that the dramatic fall in public spending (subsidies) after 1980/1 does not correspond to a similar fall in the total amount spent on the management and maintenance of local authority housing. This grew continuously over the period. If one looks at real spending per unit (Table 5.4) allowing for changes in the size of the stock, this increased by 78 per cent between 1973/4 and 1986/7, with the 4.4 per cent annual growth rate after 1978/9 only just below the 4.8 per cent for the 1973/4–1978/9 period.

Ideally, it would be useful to relate this real growth to changes in the relative costs of providing management and maintenance, to give an indication of the growth in the volume of services. Unfortunately, a suitable index is not available, but these costs mainly depend on earnings growth, of manual workers for actual repairs and of white-collar workers for other elements of the service. With average earnings (for men working full-time) virtually constant relative to the GDP deflator over the earlier period and growing at just under 2 per cent per year over the later one (and at only 0.8 per cent per year for manual workers), it would appear that spending on management and maintenance per unit also grew significantly in volume terms during both periods, although more rapidly in the first one.

What is also interesting from Table 5.3 is what has happened to the real cost of debt servicing. This rose somewhat between 1973/4 and 1979/80, but since then has fallen back substantially. Spending per unit was 15 per cent lower in 1986/7 than in 1973/4 (Table 5.4). What has happened is that local authority housing as a whole has been in the position of an owner-occupier with a mortgage, whose mortgage payments fall in real terms as a result of inflation more quickly than they rise as a result of new borrowing. The effect has been particularly marked since 1979 as a result of the tightening restraints on new local authority borrowing imposed through the HIP system. It follows from this that roughly half of the fall in the real value of housing subsidies since 1979 could be justified on the grounds that greater subsidy was needed when the real cost of servicing

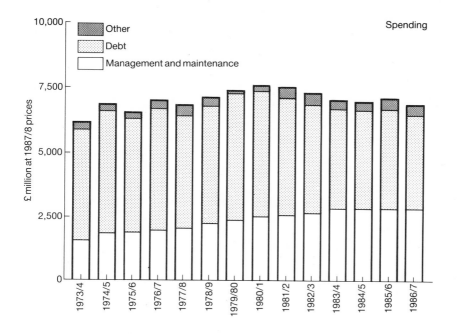

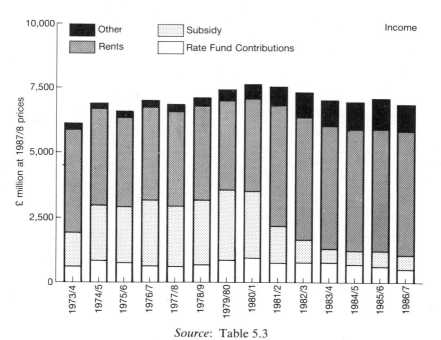

Source: Table 5.3

FIG. 5.3. Local authority Housing Revenue Account, Great Britain

Table 5.3. *Local authority Housing Revenue Account, Great Britain* (£ billion at 1987/8 prices)

	Expenditure				Income			
	Management and maintenance	Debt charges	Other	Total[a]	Gross rents[b]	Rate Fund Contributions	Housing Subsidy	Other
1973/4	1.6	4.3	0.2	6.1	4.0	0.6	1.3	0.2
1974/5	1.9	4.7	0.2	6.9	3.7	0.9	2.1	0.2
1975/6	2.0	4.4	0.2	6.6	3.4	0.8	2.1	0.2
1976/7	2.0	4.7	0.3	7.0	3.6	0.7	2.5	0.2
1977/8	2.1	4.4	0.4	6.9	3.7	0.6	2.3	0.3
1978/9	2.3	4.6	0.3	7.1	3.6	0.7	2.5	0.3
1979/80	2.4	4.9	0.1	7.4	3.5	0.9	2.7	0.4
1980/1	2.6	4.9	0.2	7.7	3.6	1.0	2.5	0.5
1981/2	2.6	4.5	0.4	7.6	4.6	0.8	1.4	0.7
1982/3	2.7	4.2	0.4	7.3	4.7	0.8	0.9	0.9
1983/4	2.9	3.8	0.3	7.1	4.8	0.8	0.5	1.0
1984/5	2.9	3.8	0.3	7.0	4.7	0.7	0.5	1.0
1985/6	2.9	3.8	0.4	7.1	4.7	0.6	0.6	1.1
1986/7	2.9	3.6	0.4	6.9	4.8	0.6	0.5	1.0

[a] Total expenditure includes change in balances and therefore equals total income.
[b] Including rent rebates.

Sources: DoE 1988a: table 10.26; Scottish Development Department 1987 and equivalents for earlier years. Cash figures adjusted by GDP deflator.

Table 5.4. *Indices of real Housing Revenue Account spending and income per unit, Great Britain (1973/4 = 100)*

	Expenditure				Income			
	Management and maintenance	Debt charges	Other	Total	Gross rents	Rate Fund Contributions	Housing Subsidy	Other
1973/4	100	100	100	100	100	100	100	100
1974/5	115	109	103	110	93	132	159	68
1975/6	113	98	96	102	83	117	157	80
1976/7	115	103	115	107	85	97	180	91
1977/8	117	93	163	102	84	91	· 163	100
1978/9	126	96	116	105	83	103	170	126
1979/80	133	103	45	109	79	127	185	151
1980/1	141	102	92	112	82	137	176	209
1981/2	145	97	160	112	107	110	100	279
1982/3	155	92	183	112	112	117	62	389
1983/4	169	86	137	110	115	123	37	411
1984/5	172	86	128	111	116	111	38	444
1985/6	174	89	158	114	118	97	46	492
1986/7	178	85	160	112	122	86	42	432
Growth rates of real spending and income per unit								
1973/4–1978/9	4.8	–0.7	2.9	1.0	–3.7	0.7	11.2	4.8
1978/9–1986/7	4.4	–1.6	4.2	0.8	4.9	–2.3	–16.1	16.6
1973/4–1986/7	4.5	–1.3	3.7	0.9	1.5	–1.1	–6.5	11.9

Sources: Table 5.3; DoE 1988*a*: table 9.3 and equivalents for earlier years.

debt was at its highest, but less is needed now (that is, greater subsidy was needed to cope with the 'front loading' problem, but this has now receded).

As the second part of the table makes clear, however, this is only part of the story. While aggregate debt charges fell by £1.3 billion at 1987/8 prices between 1979/80 and 1986/7, the total of RFCs and Exchequer subsidies fell by £2.5 billion, with the fall in the latter being particularly rapid. As a result, rents had to rise, with gross rents collected per unit being 54 per cent higher in 1986/7 than in 1979/80 (in real terms, adjusted by GDP deflator). Meanwhile, there was also a significant rise in 'other' income, mainly interest credited to HRAs in respect of accumulated capital receipts from Right to Buy sales, which authorities are allowed to spend only gradually.

Looking in detail at these figures using the typology of Fig. 5.1 thus indicates that the fall in net current 'public spending' on housing represents a switch from public funding through subsidies towards a mixture of private and public funding (through rents and housing benefit) of gross public *provision*, which has actually *increased* in real terms per unit over the period (Table 5.4). Within that gross total, the fall in the cost of debt servicing has allowed a substantial rise in real spending on services to tenants through management and maintenance.

Capital spending

With capital spending, one also has to make a distinction between what is actually spent on public provision and the way in which it is financed. It is also important to note the switch which has occurred between new building and renovation of the existing public-sector stock. Table 5.5 and Fig. 5.4 show what has happened to gross and net public capital spending and to the components of the former in England since 1976/7 (figures on a wider basis and for the period before 1976/7 are not readily available in this form).

As discussed above, net capital spending has collapsed—by 1988/9 it had fallen to a tenth of its 1976/7 real level in England. From being 4.3 per cent of UK GGE and 2.0 per cent of GDP in 1976/7, the English total had fallen to a mere 0.4 per cent of GGE and 0.2 per cent of GDP by 1988/9. The fall in the gross total is not quite so dramatic, although the 46 per cent real drop would be striking in most other contexts. The difference in the behaviour of the two totals after 1980/1 is particularly interesting: the net total continues to fall, but the gross total has been higher since 1982/3 than it was in 1981/2 (the same can be seen to be true of GB gross capital spending in Table 5A.1). The reason for the difference lies, of course, in what has happened to capital receipts. These nearly quadru-

Table 5.5. *Real public gross capital spending on housing, England* (£ billion at 1987/8 prices)

	Local authorities and new towns		Housing associations (to rent)	Other	Total gross spending	Capital receipts	Total net spending
	New build	Capital repairs					
1976/7	4.4	0.9	1.2	0.8	7.3	0.7	6.6
1977/8	3.5	0.9	1.2	0.5	6.0	0.9	5.2
1978/9	2.8	1.0	1.0	0.7	5.5	1.1	4.5
1979/80	2.3	1.3	1.0	0.9	5.5	0.8	4.7
1980/1	1.7	1.0	1.0	0.6	4.3	0.9	3.5
1981/2	1.2	0.9	0.8	0.6	3.5	1.4	2.0
1982/3	1.0	1.2	1.0	1.0	4.2	2.4	1.8
1983/4	0.9	1.4	0.8	1.7	4.8	2.4	2.5
1984/5	0.9	1.5	0.8	1.4	4.6	2.1	2.5
1985/6	0.8	1.4	0.7	1.0	3.9	1.9	1.9
1986/7	0.7	1.6	0.7	0.8	3.8	2.2	1.6
1987/8	0.6	1.7	0.7	0.8	3.8	2.5	1.4
1988/9	0.6	1.9	0.7	0.8	3.9	3.2	0.7

Sources: HM Treasury 1989: table 9.1 and earlier equivalents. Cash figures adjusted by GDP deflator.

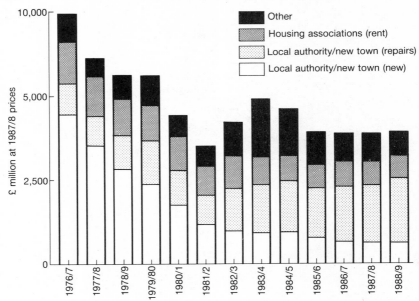

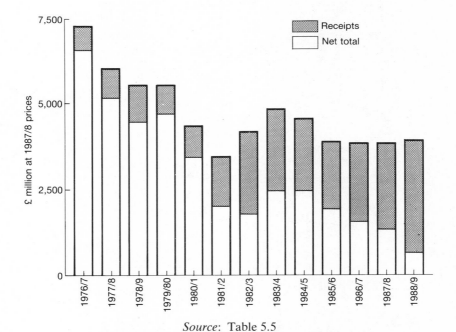

Source: Table 5.5

FIG. 5.4. Gross capital spending on housing, England

pled in real terms between 1979/80 and 1988/9 as properties were sold under the Right to Buy.

Again in terms of the breakdown shown in Fig. 5.1, the simple fall in the net amount of public funding of new provision masks a more complicated picture, with a much slower fall in capital resources devoted to public provision as a whole, but an increasing amount of this being financed by the proceeds from transferring existing provision to the private sector via sales.

Within the gross total, particular components have fared very differently. Real spending on new local authority and new town construction fell continuously over the period, the 1988/9 English total being 86 per cent lower than in 1976/7. Real spending on housing association housing to rent (either through new construction—'new build'—or rehabilitation of existing buildings) also fell, though the smaller 44 per cent fall meant that by 1986/7 spending on housing association rented housing exceeded spending on new council housing. However, the position looks very different if one takes account of spending on the renovation of existing council housing. This more than doubled over the period, so that total gross capital spending on local authority housing has actually grown in recent years—by 23 per cent since the low point of 1981/2, although this does not make up for the rapid falls between 1976/7 and 1981/2. The other items, reflecting support for the private-sector or home ownership schemes (some organized through housing associations), have had a much more variable history. The main part of this spending is on improvement grants. This increased rapidly during the 'boom' in grants between 1981/2 and 1983/4 but has subsequently fallen back again, taking the total of 'other' spending by 1988/9 below its real level in 1976/7.

A further perspective on the figures is given by Table 5.6, which gives indices for the *volume* of spending, adjusted by the output price index for new public-sector housing (this does not allow for the effects of changes in land costs). Construction costs for new public-sector housing rose less rapidly over the period than prices as a whole as measured by the GDP deflator. As a result, capital spending in volume terms fell less rapidly than real spending. Taking the period 1976/7–1987/8, the total volume of gross capital spending fell by 37 per cent, compared with the 46 per cent fall in real terms. Within this total, that on new council housing fell by 83 per cent (compared with 86 per cent in real terms), that on renovation of existing council dwellings rose by 126 per cent (against 88 per cent in real terms), while the fall in housing association rental provision was 29 per cent (against 41 per cent in real terms).

Outputs from public spending

The previous subsection has looked at the volume of public capital spending on housing. Table 5.7 shows the most straightforward measure of the output from this spending, the numbers of new dwellings completed each year between 1973 and 1988. In line with the figures for the volume of spending, it shows local authority and new town completions rising to a peak of 146,000 in 1975 and then collapsing to less than 19,000 by 1988, a fall of 87 per cent. Housing association completions of new dwellings rise rapidly between 1973 and 1977, reaching a maximum of over 25,000, but then fall back again to 11,000 in 1987, a fall of 56 per cent from the peak. The pattern of private-sector completions is also erratic, falling between 1973 and 1974 and then again after 1979, but recovering by the end of the period to almost as high a level as in 1973.

All of this resulted in a total of completions averaging about 300,000 each year between 1973 and 1977, then falling to stabilize again at about 200,000 between 1983 and 1988. The composition change was, of course, dramatic—the public sector was responsible for more than half of completions in the mid-1970s, but for only a seventh in 1988.

As we have stressed above, however, new building represents only a part of what was going on: during the period there was a significant switch

Table 5.6. *Indices of volume of capital spending on housing, England (adjusted by public housing output price index) (1976/7 = 100)*

	Local authorities and new towns		Housing associations (to rent)	Other	Total gross spending
	New build	Capital repairs			
1976/7	100	100	100	100	100
1977/8	85	104	103	72	89
1978/9	70	123	96	99	84
1979/80	57	156	92	119	82
1980/1	41	117	86	78	62
1981/2	28	101	73	78	50
1982/3	25	159	91	141	65
1983/4	24	183	77	243	76
1984/5	25	196	72	197	73
1985/6	21	193	67	144	63
1986/7	18	216	73	123	63
1987/8	17	226	71	122	63

Sources: Table 5.5; DoE 1988*a*: table A and equivalents for earlier years.

towards renovation and rehabilitation to improve the standards of existing dwellings. Some measures of this activity are given in Table 5.8.

The number of completed housing association rehabilitations mostly represents an addition to the numbers of dwellings in that sector (mainly at the expense of the private rented sector). Spending per unit rehabilitated—£16,700 in England in 1987 (DoE 1988a: table 7.1)—is substantial. Taking both forms of housing association completions together, the total peaked at nearly 45,000 units in 1977, but had fallen back to under 25,000 by 1987.

The figures shown for local authority renovations in Table 5.8 only account for about a third of their total spending on capital repairs as listed in Table 5.5, the balance being accounted for by items which come outside the capital control system (e.g. where the amount spent per dwelling comes below certain limits). Spending on renovation of council houses does not increase the number of units in the sector; rather it improves their quality. With spending of about £3,500 per dwelling in 1987 (in England—DoE 1988a: table 7.1), this is a much smaller amount of activity per unit than building a whole new dwelling. The notable features are the rapid fall in numbers between 1973 and 1975—capital

Table 5.7. *New housing completions, Great Britain* ('000)

	Local authority and new town	Housing associations	Central government	Total public	Private	Total
1973	96.6	8.9	2.0	107.5	186.6	294.1
1974	115.6	9.9	3.1	128.6	140.9	269.5
1975	145.6	14.7	1.9	162.3	150.8	313.0
1976	145.3	15.8	1.9	163.0	152.2	315.2
1977	135.6	25.1	1.8	162.5	140.8	303.3
1978	106.7	22.8	1.3	130.7	149.0	279.8
1979	85.0	17.8	1.1	104.0	140.5	244.5
1980	85.5	21.1	0.6	107.1	128.1	235.2
1981	65.3	19.2	0.3	84.8	115.0	199.8
1982	37.1	13.0	0.1	50.2	124.8	175.0
1983	34.8	15.8	0.2	50.9	146.1	196.9
1984	33.8	16.7	0.2	50.7	157.2	207.9
1985	27.1	12.9	0.1	40.0	152.1	192.1
1986	22.3	12.2	0.4	34.8	163.2	198.0
1987	19.5	11.9	0.7	32.1	170.7	202.8
1988	18.9	11.1	0.3	30.3	181.1	211.4

Sources: DoE 1988a: table 6.1 and equivalents for earlier years; DoE 1989a.

controls were applied to renovation activity of local authorities in advance of the general HIP system—but rapid growth to more than 200,000 units per year by the end of the period.

The pattern of grants for the renovation of privately owned property (including grants to tenants) shows very marked differences between the periods of different governments. A minority of these grants have been mandatory, available for the provision of missing standard amenities and for certain repairs to pre-1919 dwellings (see Walentowicz 1988 for a description of the system). Others are provided at the discretion of the local authority. Until 1989, grants have been set at varying percentages of the cost of the work done according to the category of dwelling, rather than according to the income of the occupant. Under the 1989 Local Government and Housing Act, grants will become available for a somewhat wider range of improvements from mid-1990, but on a means-tested basis.

As the table shows, from a peak of 245,000 in 1974, the total number of grants dropped to below 100,000 between 1976 and 1981. The numbers then jumped rapidly to reach a peak of over 300,000 in 1984, before falling back again, at the end of the 'grants boom' when the grants available were temporarily made more generous. Average spending per dwelling, about £3,400 in 1987 (DoE 1988a: table 7.3), was comparable

Table 5.8. *Publicly funded housing renovations, Great Britain* ('000)

	Local authority[a] and new town	Housing associations	Grants to private owners
1973	188.1	3.4	199.6
1974	121.1	4.1	245.8
1975	61.8	5.1	102.2
1976	74.8	13.5	82.5
1977	94.0	19.6	71.0
1978	105.6	14.7	70.3
1979	110.8	20.1	80.2
1980	99.6	17.7	95.2
1981	79.0	13.8	94.1
1982	108.3	21.8	139.0
1983	126.4	18.0	292.7
1984	123.3	20.7	319.7
1985	157.1	13.4	199.9
1986	207.4	14.1	163.3
1987	234.1	12.8	160.1

[a] Figures for 1977–83 omit Wales.

Source: DoE 1988a: table 7.4 and equivalents for earlier years.

to that on renovating local authority dwellings (the kind of work under-taken is rather different), although it had been higher in real terms in earlier years.

Tax expenditures

This is not the place to go into the argument about what precisely represents the true tax expenditure on owner-occupation, the answer depending on what bench-mark one compares the actual treatment with (see Whitehead 1977; Hills 1989). The conventional use of mortgage interest tax relief (as in Table 5.1) implicitly takes a bench-mark of the tax treatment of other forms of consumer spending, for which interest has not been tax-deductible since 1974.

Alternatively, if the tax treatment of private landlords is taken as the bench-mark, it can be argued that it is the lack of taxation of capital gains and the lack of taxation of owner-occupiers' imputed rents (the value of living in their own homes rent-free) which represents the true tax expend-iture, not the cost of mortgage tax relief. The value of the tax expenditure measured this way would also be substantial—£7.5 billion in 1989/90 if the combination of the two gives owner-occupiers an untaxed real return of 3.5 per cent on the trend capital value of their dwellings (Hills 1989). This kind of hypothetical cost does not allow for the way in which house prices—and capital gains—would be lower if such taxation really were imposed. On the other hand, the number would be higher if the bench-mark taken were a system in which nominal gains were taxable (see King and Atkinson 1980 for a calculation on this basis).

As well as deciding the bench-mark to be used to measure the advan-tages of owner-occupation within the income tax system, one also has to decide whether the lack of VAT on housing should be taken as a tax expenditure (on all housing, not just owner-occupied housing) and whether domestic rates should (until their abolition) be taken as an offset to these tax advantages.

Whichever choice of bench-mark one takes, none of the answers is going to be any *lower* than the simple total of mortgage tax relief. (A way of investigating the relativities between rented and owner-occupied sec-tors which bypasses the need to produce a 'true' tax expenditure on owner-occupation is described in section IV below.) The switch away from explicit public spending on housing towards tax expenditures raises questions of both effectiveness and equity. The effect of tax expenditures on creating new supply is much less direct than capital spending on new construction, and much of their effect may be dissipated on raising the price of the existing stock. As far as equity is concerned, advantages which increase with marginal tax rate and with the value of the dwelling occupied clearly have very different distributional effects from direct subsidies or Housing Benefit going to those on low incomes.

Private spending

As we said at the start of this chapter, a substantial part of housing activity occurs as a result of either private funding or private provision. Some indications of the scale of this are given in Tables 5.9 and 5.10. Table 5.9 shows consumers' expenditure on housing as defined for the national accounts. This includes owner-occupiers' imputed rents (based on the rateable value of the property they occupy) rather than mortgage interest payments, and also includes items such as net local authority rates and sewerage and water charges. Rents are shown gross, before allowing for rent rebates and allowances.

A measure of the relative scale of public and private funding can be derived by comparison with various items shown in Table 5.1. For tenants, the total of net current public spending (mostly subsidies to tenants) and Housing Benefit remained constant at about £5 billion (in 1987/8 prices) between 1973/4 and 1988/9. Between 1974 and 1987, the total amount paid in rent (roughly netting off Housing Benefit) fluctuated around £4.5 billion. In other words, public funding covered a little more than half of current expenses connected with rented housing throughout the period, with no clear trend in either direction. As there were about 13 per cent fewer tenants at the start of the period than at the end, payments per tenant from both public and private sources were correspondingly higher by the end of the period.

For owner-occupiers, the Central Statistical Office (CSO) figures for imputed rents plus maintenance, insurance, etc. rose from £15 billion (at 1987/8 prices) between 1974 and 1978 to £22 billion by 1987. This rise in real terms of 50 per cent compares with an increase in the number of owner-occupiers of about 37 per cent between the ends of 1974 and 1987, giving an increase of just under 10 per cent per owner-occupier. By comparison with this, the cost of mortgage interest tax relief doubled from £2.4 billion in 1973/4 to £4.9 billion in 1987/8. If this is taken as a measure of the share of owner-occupiers' current expenses which are publicly funded, it rose from about 16 per cent to about 22 per cent between 1974 and 1987. Public funding is thus proportionately less important for owners than for tenants, but it is on a rising trend for the former, despite the fact that their expenses (on CSO definitions) have risen a little less rapidly per household.

Table 5.10 allows a similar comparison to be made for construction activity. As far as new housing is concerned, there was a dramatic shift. Between 1974 and 1978, almost half of new housing was publicly funded; by 1987, only a seventh was publicly funded. A similar breakdown is not available for repairs and maintenance, but from Tables 5.3 and 5.5 it would appear that local authority current and capital repairs both in-

Table 5.9. *Consumers' expenditure on housing, United Kingdom* (£ billion at 1987/8 prices)

	Owner-occupiers		Other rents (gross)	Rates (net), sewerage, and water	Total housing	Total as % of consumers' expenditure
	Imputed rents	Maintenance etc.				
1974	10.9	4.1	6.7	5.9	27.6	13.4
1975	10.6	4.0	6.2	6.0	26.8	13.4
1976	11.0	3.8	6.2	6.0	27.1	13.4
1977	10.9	3.8	6.2	6.2	27.1	13.3
1978	11.3	3.8	6.3	6.3	27.6	13.1
1979	12.0	4.1	6.2	6.4	28.6	13.1
1980	12.0	4.3	5.9	6.7	28.9	13.7
1981	12.6	4.3	6.9	7.3	31.1	14.7
1982	13.0	4.5	7.7	8.0	33.2	15.4
1983	13.6	4.9	7.7	7.5	33.8	15.0
1984	13.8	5.3	7.6	7.7	34.4	15.0
1985	14.1	5.7	7.7	7.9	35.4	14.9
1986	14.7	6.7	7.9	8.5	37.8	15.0
1987	14.8	7.5	8.1	9.0	39.4	15.0

Sources: CSO 1988*b*: table 4.7 and earlier equivalents; CSO 1989*b*: table 1.

creased rather more rapidly than the UK total shown in Table 5.10. This suggests that the public share of repair and maintenance spending rose over the period, by contrast with its share of new building.

Table 5.10. *Construction output, Great Britain*

	New housing		Repair and maintenance	Total housing	Total as % of GDP (market prices)
	Public	Private			
Real spending on housing (£ billion at 1987/8 prices)					
1974	4.3	5.6	5.7	15.6	4.8
1975	4.5	4.6	5.0	14.1	4.3
1976	4.7	4.7	4.7	14.1	4.2
1977	4.0	4.3	4.8	13.1	3.9
1978	3.7	5.0	5.4	14.1	4.0
1979	3.1	4.9	6.6	14.7	4.0
1980	2.6	4.0	6.9	13.5	3.8
1981	1.7	3.5	6.3	11.4	3.3
1982	1.3	3.7	6.4	11.4	3.2
1983	1.4	4.5	6.8	12.7	3.5
1984	1.3	4.5	7.3	13.0	3.4
1985	1.0	4.2	7.5	12.7	3.3
1986	0.9	5.0	7.9	13.8	3.4
1987	0.9	5.9	8.5	15.3	3.6
Volume index at 1985 prices (1974 = 100)					
1974	100	100	100	100	
1975	110	90	88	89	
1976	122	96	81	88	
1977	111	91	84	87	
1978	104	103	97	100	
1979	86	95	118	108	
1980	70	75	123	101	
1981	46	68	111	92	
1982	39	78	111	96	
1983	41	94	118	107	
1984	37	91	124	109	
1985	31	86	128	109	
1986	28	96	134	117	
1987	29	107	143	126	

Sources: DoE 1988*a*: table 1.6 and equivalents for earlier years; CSO 1989*b*. Real spending figures are from cash adjusted by GDP deflator. Volume indices based on construction prices.

III. POLICY OUTCOMES: DECENT HOMES FOR ALL?

Households and dwellings

The most obvious measure of the outcome of housing policies is the relationship between the number of households and the number of dwellings available for them. Whereas there had been fewer dwellings than households after the war, new construction had meant that by the late 1960s the 'crude shortage' of dwellings in relation to households had been eliminated (CSO 1987a: fig. 8.3).

Table 5.11 shows what has happened since 1971 in England and Wales. Between 1971 and 1981 the increase of more than 2 million in the number of dwellings outstripped the growth in the number of households, taking the crude surplus of dwellings over households towards a million (although the census definitions of a 'household' changed between 1971 and 1981, which means that the figures are not wholly comparable). After 1981 household formation accelerated and completions fell back, so that by 1986 the crude surplus was a little smaller than it had been in 1981.

Not all dwellings are in satisfactory condition, however. The table shows how many were estimated to be statutorily unfit at each date, that is, so far defective on one or more of nine specified grounds as to be unsuitable for occupation (the grounds being repair, stability, damp, natural lighting, ventilation, water supply, sewerage, internal arrange-

Table 5.11. *Households and dwellings in England and Wales* ('000)

	1971 (April)	1981 (mid-year)	1986 (mid-year)
Households[a]	16,779	18,196	19,094
Dwellings	17,024	19,111	19,944
Crude surplus	245	915	850
Unfit dwellings	1,364[b]	1,253	1,125
Deficit allowing for unfit dwellings	1,119	338	275
'Concealed' households[c]	426	349	262
Deficit allowing for concealed households	1,545	687	537

[a] On census definition. This changed between 1971 and 1981 from a 'common cooking-pot' definition of a household to shared living space (see Murphy 1989). This will have reduced the number of households in the later years, which are therefore not strictly comparable.

[b] Using 1973 estimate for Wales.

[c] Families headed by married couples or lone parents which do not form separate households.

Sources: DoE 1977b: tables I.1 and I.5; DoE 1988a: tables 9.1 and 9.9.

ment, and kitchen facilities). A substantial number of dwellings still fall into this category, although there has been a reduction over the period. As a result, the number of households exceeds the number of fit dwellings, but the deficit fell from over a million in 1971 to less than 300,000 in 1986.

The DoE also publishes estimates of the number of 'concealed households', that is, families headed by married couples or lone parents who through choice or necessity do not set up their own household. These numbers fell throughout the period. If one therefore compares the total number of households, including 'concealed' ones, with the number of fit dwellings, there was a deficit of more than 1.5 million in 1971, but this had fallen by over a million by 1986, although the pace of improvement slowed considerably after 1981.

As Murphy points out, this is not the only aspect of the relationship between the size of the dwelling stock and the number of households. For instance, 'the relatively late age at which British children leave home compared to many other countries is probably tied up with the lack of suitable type and tenure of housing for young single people' (1989: 98). The increase in the number of households is to some extent an effect of the increase in the number of dwellings relaxing this kind of constraint. It is not just the differential between numbers of households and dwellings which is important, but also the absolute number of households which are able to form.

Even with the adjustments to give the final row of Table 5.11, there remain problems with this kind of measure of deficit or surplus. First, there is no allowance for second homes in the figures; nor is there one for vacancies which occur while people move house. Each 1 per cent of the stock allowed for vacancies (4 per cent is often used as a conventional allowance) adds 190,000 to the estimated deficit. Second, the aggregate figures do not allow for differences in the location of households and dwellings. Here the same sources as used in Table 5.11 show a variation in the crude surplus of households over dwellings in mid-1986 which ranged from 3.4 per cent in the West Midlands to 7.2 per cent in Wales (compared with the England and Wales average of 4.4 per cent). These figures do not, of course, tell one much about the location of dwellings in relation to where people would *like* to live.

Despite these shortcomings, the trends in Table 5.11 remain clear and, overall, one would expect that people would experience much less difficulty in getting housed now than they did in the early 1970s.

Homelessness

The figures shown in Table 5.12 present an apparent contradiction of this overall picture of success. Between 1978 (the first year after the Housing

(Homeless Persons) Act) and 1988, the number of households accepted by local authorities in England for rehousing because they were homeless doubled. The overall housing shortage may have reduced, but more families are 'homeless'.

Part of the reason for this contradiction lies in the interpretation to be put on the statistics for homelessness. First, the statistics relate to a *flow* of households rehoused during a year, not to the *stock* of households without a home at any one time. Second, homelessness has a statutory meaning here: it does not correspond to 'rooflessness' in the sense of being out in the streets (for which reliable statistics are scarce). The difference between the two works both ways. Single people do not qualify as being 'in priority need' under the 1977 Act, so the single people who sleep in cardboard boxes in London's parks are not part of the totals shown in the table. On the other hand, other groups can qualify as homeless on the grounds that they are threatened with entering one of the statutory categories within the next twenty-eight days. The distinction between homelessness in statutory terms and in terms of popular definition is illustrated by the group who are classed as 'homeless at home'—the local authority accepts that they have a right to be rehoused as homeless, but they remain where they are, that being preferable to alternatives such as temporary bed-and-breakfast accommodation.

The homelessness figures give an index to the numbers entering local authority housing via a particular route, one which has risen steadily in

Table 5.12. *Homelessness: Enquiries made by homeless households to local authorities, England* ('000 of households)

	Result			Total enquiries
	Accepted	Given advice and assistance only	Found not homeless	
1978	53	n.a.	n.a.	n.a.
1979	57	n.a.	n.a.	n.a.
1980	63	n.a.	n.a.	n.a.
1981	70	n.a.	n.a.	n.a.
1982	75	n.a.	n.a.	n.a.
1983	78	41	50	170
1984	83	44	53	180
1985	94	50	60	203
1986	103	55	62	219
1987	113	56	60	228
1988	116	63	63	242

Sources: DoE 1989c: table 8 and equivalents for earlier years.

importance relative to acceptances from the waiting list. But as Niner and others have discussed,

it is important to note that the homeless and waiting list applicants are similar in many ways. . . . it is possible to argue that it does not matter very much if local authorities can house no-one but the homeless, since council housing will still be serving essentially the same purpose as before. The major issue becomes one of fairness between applicants in roughly comparable circumstances, one of whom, either as a result of knowing the system or of genuine necessity becomes homeless, and one of whom does not. (Niner 1989: 98–9)

Similarly, the Audit Commission reported from its survey of the problem that 'all the [council] officers interviewed during the study believed that the great majority of homeless households currently being accepted for housing in their authority were people to whom the council would in any event have given priority' (1989: 19).

This is not to argue that those classified as homeless are not in desperate need, but it does mean that the trends shown in Table 5.12 have to be interpreted with a degree of caution. They show a change in the route by which people gain access to council housing as much as giving an index of the failure of supply in relation to demand.

Rooflessness

While a national time series for the numbers literally roofless does not exist, Canter *et al.* (1989) present the results of a survey carried out for the Salvation Army in London on a cold night in April 1989. They found 753 people openly out on the streets or in stations. This figure is three times the equivalent figure found by a National Assistance Board survey in December 1965. The April 1989 figure does not include those in derelict buildings or covered basements. The authors suggest that the numbers sleeping rough fluctuate considerably: a pilot study in November 1988 had found 514 people at three central London locations, compared with 366 at the same places in April 1989. The study also estimated the numbers in hostels, in temporary accommodation in bed-and-breakfast hotels, and in squats as totalling 75,000 'overtly homeless' in London on the same night. Those literally out on the street thus represented a 1 per cent tip of this iceberg.

Temporary accommodation

A further index of the stress being experienced by the housing system—and by those whom it fails—is given by the rising numbers placed by local authorities in temporary accommodation (shown in Table 5.13), of which, in the Audit Commission's words, 'Bed and breakfast (B&B) hotels usually offer the lowest standards at the highest costs' (1989: 2). The number of households reported by local authorities in England and Wales as being placed in bed and breakfast multiplied more than eightfold between the end of 1978 and the end of 1988, with the major rise occurring after 1982. Between 1974 and 1978 the number of households in temporary accommodation had, by contrast, fallen (ibid.: 10).

Here again one has to be careful with interpretation of the trends. In some authorities a shortage of properties available for letting means that there is little alternative to the use of temporary accommodation. In others, better management of the stock and shorter intervals between properties falling vacant and being relet could eliminate the need for temporary solutions. According to the Audit Commission, faster relets could have reduced the numbers in bed and breakfast by 2,500 in 1987. Thirdly, it should be recognized that forcing households accepted as homeless to go through bed and breakfast, before permanent rehousing, is used by some authorities as a deliberate rationing device: 'several authorities also pointed out that B&B may deter applications and encourage households to seek alternative housing after they have been accepted if they are faced with long stays in hotels' (Audit Commission 1989: 21).

Again, the qualification of the reasons for the statistics does not subtract from the observation that the policy objective of providing a decent home for all has not been met for an increasing number of households.

Nor does it indicate an effective use of resources. The Audit Commission estimated the annual cost of keeping a family in bed-and-breakfast accommodation in 1986–7 as ranging from £5,000 in non-metropolitan

Table 5.13. *Households in temporary accommodation, England and Wales*
(end year)

	Bed and breakfast	Hostels (inc. women's refuges)	Short-life tenancies and other	Total
1978	1,270	2,524	n.a.	n.a.
1979	2,052	3,680	n.a.	n.a.
1980	1,397	3,527	n.a.	n.a.
1981	1,583	3,494	n.a.	n.a.
1982	1,661	3,613	n.a.	n.a.
1983	2,677	3,511	4,102	10,290
1984	3,301	4,119	4,874	12,294
1985	4,290	4,697	5,695	14,682
1986	9,025	4,758	7,500	21,283
1987	10,415	5,369	9,635	25,419
1988	11,011	6,523	13,220	30,754

Sources: DoE 1989c: table 8 and equivalents for earlier years; Welsh Office 1989: table 7.10.

districts to over £11,000 in London, with an aggregate cost in England as a whole of more than £90 million (1989: 12, 21). Meanwhile, in 1987 the total of land plus construction tender costs for a complete new local authority dwelling averaged £37,500 in England as a whole and £69,000 in Greater London (DoE 1988*a*: table 6.19).

Housing tenure

In terms of the policy objective of encouraging the growth of home ownership, Table 5.14 shows a much less ambiguous level of success. From just over half of all dwellings at the end of 1973, the owner-occupied sector was approaching two-thirds of the total fifteen years later, with particularly rapid growth after 1978. Part of this reflects the long-standing continued trend away from the private rented sector into much more favourably treated owner-occupation. But since 1980 it has also resulted from the transfer of dwellings out of the council sector. Whereas council housing accounted for nearly 32 per cent of the GB stock at the end of 1978, its share was below 25 per cent by the end of 1988. The impact of the Right to Buy can be seen in Table 5.15. In the peak year of 1982, nearly a quarter of a million public-sector dwellings were sold. In all, 1.2 million public-sector dwellings were sold between 1979 and 1987, most of them to sitting council tenants and accounting for a substantial share of the 3 million growth in the number of owner-occupied dwellings (although some sales were to other landlords).

This rapid change in tenure shares has been accompanied by the extent to which different tenures are polarized in terms of income, as can be seen from Table 5.16. In 1974, 17 per cent of individuals in the top income quintile group and 33 per cent of those in the next group were local authority tenants. These proportions had changed little by 1979, but in 1985 only 5 per cent of the top quintile group and 14 per cent of the next group were local authority tenants. The Right to Buy had clearly been used extensively by tenants with the highest incomes. As a result, in 1985, 90 per cent of the top group and 78 per cent of the next were owner-occupiers. Meanwhile, the proportion of the bottom quintile group who were owner-occupiers *fell* from 44 per cent in 1979 to 29 per cent in 1985, while the proportion who were local authority tenants rose corres-pondingly from 43 per cent to 57 per cent. Although a part of this may be a result of the change in the definition of income used to classify the groups as a result of the 1982/3 Housing Benefit changes (see Chapter 1), it is clear that the rapid growth in owner-occupation has mostly occurred in the top three quintile groups.

Meanwhile, the local authority sector is becoming increasingly residual-ized. To look at the General Household Survey (GHS) figures in a differ-ent way, while 50 per cent of individuals in local authority housing were in the bottom two quintile groups in 1974 (and 51 per cent in 1979), the proportion had risen to 68 per cent in 1985. Only 3 per cent of local authority tenants were in the top-income quintile group in 1985, compared with 10 per cent in 1974 and 11 per cent in 1979. The post-war aim of a range of groups being housed by local authorities has most decidedly been abandoned.

Table 5.14. *Housing tenure, Great Britain* (stock of dwellings; end-year figures)

	Number of dwellings (millions)	Percentage			
		Local authority/ new town	Owner-occupied	Housing association	Private rented and other
1973	19.4	30.5	52.3	17.2[a]	
1978	20.6	31.7	54.7	13.7[a]	
1983	21.5	28.7	59.9	2.2	9.2
1988	22.5	24.9	65.4	2.5	7.1

[a] Combines 'housing association' and 'private rented and other'.

Sources: DoE 1988*a*: table 9.3 and equivalents for earlier years; DoE 1989*b*: table 2.22.

Table 5.15. *Sales of public-sector dwellings* ('000)

	Total		Of which to sitting local-authority tenants, including Right to Buy (GB)
	England and Wales	Great Britain	
1973	41.8	n.a.	n.a.
1974	5.4	n.a.	n.a.
1975	3.0	n.a.	n.a.
1976	5.4	n.a.	n.a.
1977	13.4	n.a.	n.a.
1978	30.6	n.a.	n.a.
1979	42.6	44.0	n.a.
1980	85.7	92.2	n.a.
1981	113.8	124.8	105.7
1982	225.3	240.4	209.6
1983	165.9	184.3	149.3
1984	118.7	136.0	112.5
1985	105.5	121.3	101.1
1986	100.7	115.3	96.6
1987	115.1	132.8	109.4

Source: DoE 1988*a*: table 9.6 and equivalents for earlier years.

It is tempting to see the effects of the Right to Buy combined with the rapid fall in new local authority completions as causing a drop in the supply of local authority housing and therefore the rise in homelessness acceptances. The situation is rather more complicated, however. The key variable is the number of lettings which authorities can make. If, for instance, someone who would not otherwise have moved out of the sector for several years purchases under the Right to Buy, there will be no immediate change in the number of new lettings the authority can make. New completions are only part of the supply of new lettings—authorities can also relet property whose tenants move elsewhere or die. This last factor makes the age structure of local authority tenants shown in Table

Table 5.16. *Income quintile groups analysed by tenure composition, Great Britain* (% of individuals)

Quintile group	Owners with mortgage	Outright owners	Local authority tenants	Housing association tenants	Other
1974					
Bottom	16	23	43	1.3	18
2	24	16	44	1.7	15
3	33	15	37	1.6	13
4	40	15	33	1.4	11
Top	49	21	17	1.0	12
All	32	18	35	1.4	14
1979					
Bottom	24	20	43	1.6	11
2	22	20	45	1.4	12
3	40	14	36	1.6	9
4	47	14	30	1.5	8
Top	56	15	19	1.4	9
All	38	17	35	1.5	10
1985					
Bottom	13	16	57	3.9	10
2	24	23	40	3.0	10
3	48	17	26	1.7	8
4	63	15	14	1.2	7
Top	73	17	5	0.5	6
All	44	18	28	2.1	9

Source: Own calculations from GHS raw data files.

5.17 of some significance. The age of household heads and of all individuals housed by local authorities rose steadily between 1974 and 1985.

Kleinman (1988) has looked at the combined effects of all these factors. While the supply of lettings from new completions more than halved in England between 1976/7 and 1984/5, the number of relets of existing properties rose. As a result, the total number of lettings to new tenants was constant at about 270,000 between 1976/7 and 1980/1, falling to 240,000 in 1984/5. The effects varied greatly by region, however. In London, where half of lettings had resulted from new completions in 1976/7, the decline was greatest, total lettings falling by a third between 1980/1 and 1984/5. The comparable fall was 10 per cent in the North, 8 per cent in the South outside London, and 7 per cent in the Midlands.

The physical condition of the stock: House Condition Survey results

So far in this section we have looked at housing conditions in terms of simple numbers of dwellings available. Information from the successive English House Condition Surveys carried out by the DoE gives some information about the quality of that stock. The main results of those surveys are summarized in Table 5.18. It should be noted that the latest survey (1986) used different methods to decide whether dwellings were unsatisfactory and to gross up the results for the sample surveyed to the

Table 5.17. *Age profile of local authority tenants*

	1974	1979	1985
	% of households		
Age of household head			
Up to 44	32	31	31
45–64	40	37	34
65–74	17[a]	20	20
75 and over	11[a]	13	15
	% of individuals		
Age of individuals			
Under 16	29.3	24.8	22.4
16–64	58.3	59.7	58.7
65 and over	12.4	15.5	18.9

[a] Estimated.

Sources: Households: published GHS (OPCS 1977, 1981, 1987); individuals: own calculations from GHS raw data files.

whole stock. Two sets of results are therefore shown for 1986. The first are roughly on the same basis as the previous surveys and therefore give the best guide to trends over time (albeit based on a rather small sample for 1986). The second are based on a larger sample and give the DoE's best estimate of the position in 1986, but give a worse guide to trends.

The table shows that there has been very rapid progress in reducing the number of dwellings lacking one or more of the standard amenities (bath or shower, kitchen sink, and wash-hand basin with hot and cold water to each, and an indoor WC). Between 1971 and 1986, the number fell by 80 per cent and the proportion of dwellings affected fell from 17.4 per cent to 2.9 per cent. Similar figures for Wales show a drop in the proportion from 20.9 per cent in 1973 to 4.1 per cent in 1986 (Welsh Office 1982, 1988). Clearance, rehabilitation, and mandatory improvement grants to provide missing amenities have clearly had a major effect.

Table 5.18. *Unsatisfactory housing conditions, England*

	Unfit	Lacking one or more amenities	In serious disrepair[a]	Unsatisfactory in one of these respects	In poor repair[b]	In poor condition[c]
Nos. of dwellings ('000)						
1971	1,216	2,815	864	3,184	n.a.	n.a.
1976	1,162	1,531	859	2,223	n.a.	n.a.
1981[d]	1,116	910	1,049	2,006	n.a.	n.a.
1981[e]	1,138	905	1,178	n.a.	n.a.	n.a.
1986[f]	1,053	543	1,113	n.a.	n.a.	n.a.
1986[g]	909	463	n.a.	n.a.	2,430	2,868
Percentage of dwellings						
1971	7.5	17.4	5.4	19.7	n.a.	n.a.
1976	6.8	8.9	5.0	13.0	n.a.	n.a.
1981[d]	6.2	5.0	5.8	11.1	n.a.	n.a.
1981[e]	6.3		6.5	11.4	n.a.	n.a.
1986[f]	5.6	2.9	5.9	9.0	n.a.	n.a.
1986[g]	4.8	2.5	n.a.	n.a.	12.9	15.2

[a] Requiring repairs costing more than £7,000 at 1981 prices.
[b] Requiring 'urgent' repairs costing more than £1,000 in 1986.
[c] Unfit, lacking amenities, or in poor repair.
[d] As published in DoE 1982.
[e] As recalculated in DoE 1988c.
[f] On consistent basis with earlier years.
[g] Preferred estimates for 1986.

Sources: DoE 1982: tables B, H, J, K, and N; DoE 1988c: table 9.1 and fig. 5.1.

Progress in eliminating unfit dwellings has been slower. From an original total of more than 1.2 million in 1971, the number dropped by only about 10,000 each year until 1986. With the stock itself increasing, the proportion affected fell from 7.5 per cent to 5.6 per cent over the same period. Between 1973 and 1986 the fall in Wales was more rapid, but from a higher starting-point: from 15 per cent to 7 per cent.

The number of dwellings in 'serious disrepair' (requiring repairs costing more than £7,000 at 1981 prices) has by contrast increased over the period as a whole. The latest DoE figures suggest that there was a slight improvement in the position between 1981 and 1986, although the 1986 figures are worse than those originally published for 1981.

Many of the same dwellings are affected by more than one of these defects. As a result, the total that is unsatisfactory in one or more of these three respects is smaller than that given by simply adding the three categories together. This proportion more than halved over the period, from nearly 20 per cent to 9 per cent, although nearly 15 per cent of dwellings were 'in poor condition' on the DoE's new basis (unfit, lacking amenities, or requiring *urgent* repairs costing more than £1,000 in 1986).

Table 5.19 gives a breakdown of these results by tenure. It can be seen that the worst conditions are concentrated in the private rented sector (and also amongst vacant dwellings). Over time, all tenures have experienced a fall in the proportion lacking amenities, but it is interesting that the proportions of owner-occupied and local authority dwellings which are unfit or in serious disrepair have increased over the period. The shift in the relative balance between the tenures means that overall unfitness has declined none the less (especially if one excludes unoccupied dwellings) and that disrepair increased only slightly.

An equivalent result can be seen if one looks at the state of the stock built at different times. The proportions of the inter-war and post-1944 stock which were unfit rose between 1971 and 1986 (DoE 1988c: fig. 9.2; DoE 1982), but the decline in the proportion of the stock built before 1919 allowed a reduction overall.

Some indication of the way different income groups were affected in 1981 and 1986 is given in Table 5.20. What is striking is that the improvement has apparently been concentrated at the *bottom* of the income distribution, the differential between the lowest quarter (roughly) of the distribution and the highest quarter declining very markedly in all three respects. On these figures, not only were conditions improving, but they were also doing so most rapidly for those on the lowest incomes (this contrasts with findings from the GHS discussed below).

On a different dimension of inequality—race—narrowing of differentials is less evident from the evidence in the 1976 and 1986 House Condition Surveys. Of those households whose head was born outside

Table 5.19. *Unsatisfactory housing conditions in England, by tenure*
(% of dwellings)

	Owner-occupiers	Local authority and new town	Private rented and housing association	All (including vacant)
Unfit				
1971	4.2	1.5	21.7	7.5
1976	4.2	1.3	20.5	6.8
1981	4.7	1.3	17.7	6.2
1986[a]	5.1	2.7	15.4	5.6
Lacking one or more amenities				
1971	11.2	11.1	40.3	17.4
1976	4.9	5.5	25.2	8.9
1981	3.3	2.8	13.5	5.0
1986[a]	2.1	2.0	8.3	2.9
In serious disrepair				
1971	3.7	0.8	16.0	5.4
1976	3.9	1.0	15.6	5.0
1981	5.3	1.0	16.4	5.9
1986[a]	7.4	2.2	17.1	5.9

[a] Estimated from DoE 1988*c*: fig. 9.3.
Sources: DoE 1982: tables 5, 13, 21, 30, 32, 35, 39, 41, 44; DoE 1988*c*: fig. 9.3 and table 9.1.

Europe (using birthplace as a proxy for race), the proportion in unfit dwellings was twice that of households whose head was born in the United Kingdom, in both 1976 and 1986 (DoE 1988*c*: table 6.2; DoE 1983: table D.2.7). The proportion of households in dwellings in 'poor repair' in 1986 was 20.3 per cent of those with the head born outside Europe, against 12.5 per cent of those with the head born in the United Kingdom. The ratio between the two groups in 1986 was greater than that shown for the 1976 survey's category of 'in need of rehabilitation' (lacking amenities or needing 'essential' repairs), where the proportions were 29.0 per cent and 15.4 per cent.

The quality of the stock: General Household Survey results

Further indications whether people do have a 'decent' home can be derived from the results of the GHS, and are shown in Tables 5.21, 5.22, and 5.23. The first of these shows what proportion of individuals (adults and children) either do not have sole use of an inside WC or do not have sole use of a bath, the second what proportion live in households where there is one or more persons per room, and the third the proportion living without central heating. The latter category illustrates a general problem with looking at subjective concepts like a 'decent home' over time. In 1974 most individuals lived in dwellings without central heating. By 1985 only a quarter lacked it, making it a much more plausible candidate for assessing the quality of housing than it would have been eleven years before.

The tables give breakdowns which allow one to track the changes in the relative position of individuals broken down by five different classifications—tenure, socio-economic group, age, income, and birthplace of household head. It should be borne in mind that the GHS covers only those living in private households, excluding those in institutions and those who are literally roofless.

Lack of amenities Looking first at the lack of amenities in Table 5.21, the results broadly confirm the picture given by the House Condition Surveys, remembering that the latter refer to dwellings, many of which

Table 5.20. *Unsatisfactory housing conditions in England, by income group, 1981 and 1986* (% of households)

Income group[a]	Unfit	Lacking amenities	In serious disrepair	% of all households in group
1981				
Lowest	8.1	8.2	9.0	27.5
Second	6.5	5.0	7.2	19.6
Third	4.5	2.3	4.7	27.7
Highest	1.7	0.9	3.9	25.2
All	5.1	4.1	6.2	100
1986				
Lowest	4.5	3.1	6.3	29.3
Second	4.5	2.4	6.3	26.4
Third	3.5	0.9	4.6	20.9
Highest	3.1	1.0	5.1	23.4
All	4.1	2.0	5.8	100

[a] The 1981 survey was based on gross income from all sources of head of household and spouse. The 1986 survey asked about specific sources of incomes, including benefits, but not Housing Benefit.

Source: DoE 1988c: table A9.5.

John Hills and Beverley Mullings

Table 5.21. *Missing amenities (either without sole use of inside WC or without sole use of bath), Great Britain* (% of individuals)

(a) BY TENURE

	Owner with mortgage	Outright owner	Local authority	Housing association	Other	All (inc. missing categories)
1974	3.4	13.5	6.4	10.0	36.0	11.0
1979	1.3	6.4	3.7	8.8	24.8	5.5
1985	0.7	2.7	1.1	2.2	10.7	2.0

(b) BY SOCIO-ECONOMIC GROUP (ADULTS ONLY)

	I	II	III	IV	V	VI
1974	5.1	5.6	9.0	12.7	15.8	19.1
1979	3.7	2.9	4.1	7.1	8.2	10.1
1985	1.8	0.8	1.8	2.0	3.1	2.8

(c) BY AGE

	Under 16	16–64	65 and over
1974	8.5	10.4	18.3
1979	3.2	5.1	10.9
1985	1.2	1.8	3.7

(d) BY INCOME QUINTILE

	Bottom	2	3	4	Top
1974	18.2	13.4	8.5	8.0	7.3
1979	7.8	7.9	3.8	3.3	4.1
1985	4.0	2.8	1.5	1.0	1.0

(e) BY BIRTHPLACE (ADULTS ONLY)

	UK	Europe or N. America	Elsewhere	All
1974	11.4	16.9	23.4	11.9
1979	6.0	8.5	10.7	6.2
1985	2.0	4.8	3.6	2.2

Source: Own calculations from GHS raw data files.

are vacant if unsatisfactory, and to a slightly wider range of amenities. Between 1974 and 1985 the proportion of individuals either without sole use of a bath or without sole use of an inside WC fell from 11 per cent to 2 per cent. The proportionate decline in percentages affected was roughly uniform across tenures, although more than 10 per cent of those in 'other' tenures (mainly the private rented sector) still lacked amenities in 1985. Looked at by socio-economic group (for adults only), differentials decreased in magnitude. Interestingly, the same was not true by income group, where the proportion of the bottom income group lacking amenities was four times that of the top group in 1985, a larger ratio than in 1974 or 1979 (although the absolute improvement for the bottom group was much larger). The relative position of the elderly deteriorated by comparison with the population as a whole, but again the absolute improvement for those aged over 65 was much larger. Looking at birthplace, adults born outside the United Kingdom were much more likely to lack amenities than the average in all three years (again, comparable results for all three years are available only for adults). The proportionate differential between those born outside the United Kingdom and the average stayed much the same (implying again a more rapid absolute improvement for the disadvantaged group).

Density of occupation　Another area where the GHS provides evidence of improving living standards is the number of people per room of their accommodation. Table 5.22 shows how many people lived at a density of one or more person per room (including kitchens but excluding bathrooms and lavatories). This measure has no statutory force, but is a convenient, if crude, measure of the living conditions of different groups which is available for all three years. It should be noted that it does not allow for any difference in needs per person between, say, a single adult and a couple with children. A measure which would allow for this—density in relation to the official 'bedroom standard'—is not available for 1974.

It should also be noted that most of these figures, for the proportions of *individuals* living in crowded conditions, are necessarily higher than the corresponding figures for the proportions of *households* affected. The number of individuals affected seems in many ways a preferable measure of the problem. However, results by socio-economic group and birthplace are again available for all three years only for adults. Because households with children are much more likely to be crowded, a smaller proportion of adults than of all individuals are affected in each year. The effects of this can be gauged from the results for all individuals shown in parentheses for 1985.

Over the whole period, the proportion of individuals affected fell by

Table 5.22. *Crowded conditions (1.0 or more persons per room), Great Britain*
(% of individuals)

(*a*) BY TENURE

	Owner with mortgage	Outright owner	Local authority	Housing association	Other	All (inc. missing categories)
1974	16.6	7.4	35.1	33.2	23.4	22.2
1979	13.2	6.2	27.1	29.5	15.4	17.3
1985	10.7	5.2	24.0	20.1	10.0	13.3

(*b*) BY SOCIO-ECONOMIC GROUP (ADULTS ONLY)

	I	II	III	IV	V	VI
1974	5.6	8.6	12.4	18.8	19.0	18.1
1979	3.6	6.5	9.1	15.0	15.7	14.8
1985	3.9	4.6	6.9	11.3	12.3	12.4
(1985*a*	7.1	7.5	7.9	19.3	16.8	16.7)

(*c*) BY AGE

	Under 16	16–64	65 and over
1974	40.8	18.6	2.2
1979	32.0	15.2	1.1
1985	26.8	11.3	1.1

(*d*) BY INCOME QUINTILE

	Bottom	2	3	4	Top
1974	30.2	34.8	26.0	15.3	5.2
1979	24.7	22.3	25.5	14.2	4.4
1985	22.3	16.0	15.3	7.8	2.4

(*e*) BY BIRTHPLACE (ADULTS ONLY)

	UK	Europe or N. America	Elsewhere	All
1974	14.5	26.4	34.3	15.3
1979	11.9	15.5	28.3	12.6
1985	8.8	11.9	22.5	9.4
(1985*b*	12.9	12.1	23.3	13.2)

[a] All individuals; children given social class of head of household.
[b] All individuals, including children.

Source: Own calculations from GHS raw data files.

roughly a third in each tenure, and by 40 per cent overall (thanks to the composition change towards owner-occupation). The best improvements were in the housing association and 'other' tenures, which started with the worst conditions. Again, while the class gradient changed little between 1974 and 1985, the ratio between those affected in the bottom and top income quintiles increased sharply after 1979. Despite its poor starting position, the absolute improvement for the bottom quintile group between 1979 and 1985 (from 24.7 per cent to 22.3 per cent) was slower than for individuals as a whole (from 17.3 per cent to 13.3 per cent). As one would expect, those over 65 lived in much less crowded conditions, while children were much more likely to live at high densities. High densities affected those born outside Europe or North America quite disproportionately, with much the same proportionate differential to the average in all three years (but therefore again a larger absolute improvement).

Central heating   Table 5.23 shows that the proportions of individuals without central heating halved between 1974 and 1985. The pattern of decline was much more uneven between different groups than for the other indicators, however, being particularly rapid for owner-occupiers with a mortgage, the professional and managerial socio-economic group, and the top two income quintiles. The difference in the experience of the top and bottom income quintiles between 1979 and 1985 is particularly marked, with the absolute improvement of the former from an already better position much larger than that of the latter. By 1985, only 14 per cent of the top income group did not have central heating, compared with 45 per cent of the bottom group. By contrast with the two other indicators of housing quality, birthplace made little difference to the presence of central heating in 1974, and the position of those born outside Europe or North America actually improved more rapidly than the average after 1979.

Housing conditions overall   Putting the results of the three tables together, it is clear that overall housing conditions improved greatly over the period. By and large this improvement affected all groups in proportion to the scale of their original problems, so that *absolute* differentials between the percentage of each group affected in each group declined, but *proportionate* differentials remained roughly the same. The main exception to this pattern is the experience of the poorest income quintile between 1979 and 1985, whose absolute improvement in terms of the proportion who were missing amenities was only just greater than the average for all individuals, but was actually smaller than the average in respect of those in crowded conditions or lacking central heating. As a

Table 5.23. *Absence of central heating (including night storage), Great Britain*
(% of individuals)

(a) BY TENURE

	Owner with mortgage	Outright owner	Local authority	Housing association	Other	All (inc. missing categories)
1974	32.2	52.1	66.2	62.4	79.1	54.5
1979	23.3	41.0	54.0	45.4	71.1	42.1
1985	14.8	26.0	42.3	40.0	52.2	27.6

(b) BY SOCIO-ECONOMIC GROUP (ADULTS ONLY)

	I	II	III	IV	V	VI
1974	26.5	36.0	47.5	62.8	67.2	72.8
1979	17.9	26.6	33.9	49.7	54.8	60.3
1985	11.9	16.7	23.2	33.2	37.2	41.6

(c) BY AGE

	Under 16	16–64	65 and over
1974	49.4	54.2	65.2
1979	37.0	41.2	54.5
1985	23.5	27.0	36.3

(d) BY INCOME QUINTILE

	Bottom	2	3	4	Top
1974	69.5	63.3	56.1	46.7	38.5
1979	49.9	51.3	43.6	36.2	27.8
1985	44.5	36.7	26.9	19.7	14.0

(e) BY BIRTHPLACE OF HOUSEHOLD HEAD (ADULTS ONLY)

	UK	Europe or N. America	Elsewhere	All
1974	56.2	55.3	59.3	56.3
1979	43.6	40.1	48.0	43.7
1985	28.9	31.8	23.9	28.8

Source: Own calculations from GHS raw data files.

result, its position relative to the population as a whole worsened in all three respects.

Differences in the way income is defined between the two years make it impossible to be certain, but these results tend to suggest that the bottom income group was being left behind after 1979. This contrasts with the picture shown in Table 5.20, which indicated a relative improvement in the conditions of those in the bottom income group between 1981 and 1986 (although that comparison has problems as well, and its income groups are not of equal size).

The standard of service received by tenants

So far this section has concentrated on physical standards of housing. Until recently housing policy has shown a similar bias. But for tenants in particular, housing has another dimension—that of the repair and management service which they receive in return for their rent. As statistics and surveys tend to follow policy concerns, this means that there is a great paucity of statistics on standards of landlord services. This illustrates a general danger in using the statistics thrown up by the operation of policy to judge that policy—if an area is being neglected, it may be hard to gauge the extent of the problems in it.

There have, however, been some recent surveys which have collected information about repair services and tenant satisfaction with them, although they do not allow an assessment of trends over time. The 1986 English House Condition Survey asked tenants who had requested that repairs should be done whether they had experienced any difficulty in getting them done (DoE 1988*c*: table A7.10). More than half (51.7 per cent) of local authority tenants had experienced difficulty, compared with only 16.0 per cent of housing association tenants and 15.6 per cent of private tenants.

A similar differential emerges in the University of Glasgow's Centre for Housing Research report on *The Nature and Effectiveness of Housing Management in England* (CHR 1989). A third of local authority tenants and 20 per cent of housing association tenants surveyed rated the service they received as unsatisfactory (CHR 1989: table 7.3; the kinds of areas covered by the two kinds of organization in the survey are not the same—Inner London not being covered for local authorities—so that the results are not truly comparable). For 32 per cent of the tenants of large local authorities (managing over 20,000 dwellings), the last repair carried out had been completed more than a month after it was requested, compared with 23 per cent for smaller local authorities, 11 per cent for national/regional housing associations, and 5 per cent for local housing associations (ibid.: table 6.7). 27 per cent of the local authority tenants in the sample said that they received poor value for the money they paid in rent, compared with 13 per cent of the housing association tenants (ibid.: table 7.3; both groups paid much the same in rent, but the housing associations spent more on management services than the local authorities).

Asked whether they agreed with the more general statement that 'councils give a poor standard of repairs and maintenace' (without it being specified what this standard was being compared with), 70 per cent of local authority tenants responding to the British Social Attitudes Survey in 1983 agreed, and much the same, 68 per cent, in 1985 (Jowell, Witherspoon, and Brook 1986).

Overall satisfaction with housing

All of the features discussed above feed into general feelings of satisfaction or dissatisfaction with housing. A measure of whether people have a 'decent' home is whether they themselves are happy with it. The results of surveys which have explored this question are shown in Table 5.24. The table shows the proportions of household heads expressing some dissatisfaction with their accommodation. It should be noted that the phrasing of the question asked varied between surveys, so that they are not completely comparable.

The first feature to note is the low level of overall dissatisfaction, roughly one household in ten in each of the surveys. Second, despite the ways described above in which housing has clearly improved since the

Table 5.24. *Dissatisfaction with accommodation, by tenure*
(% of households dissatisfied)[a]

Coverage	Date of survey	All	Owner-occupiers	Local authority tenants	Housing association tenants	Other
England (NDHS)	1977 (end)	9	4	14	11	15
GB (GHS)	1978	11	6	16	17	17
GB (BSAS)	1983	9	4	19	21[b]	
GB (BSAS)	1985	9	n.a.	17	n.a.	14

[a] National Dwelling and Housing Survey (NDHS) categories: 'dissatisfied' or 'very dissatisfied'; GHS categories: 'a little dissatisfied' and 'very dissatisfied'; British Social Attitudes Survey (BSAS) categories: 'quite dissatisfied' and 'very dissatisfied'.
[b] Combines 'housing association tenants' and 'others'.

Sources: DoE 1978; OPCS 1980; Jowell and Airey 1984; Jowell, Witherspoon, and Brook 1986.

mid-1970s, there is no clear trend over time in the picture shown. This may reflect changing standards as conditions improve generally: features which might not have led to dissatisfaction ten years ago may cause it now. What the table does show, however, is a clear difference between tenures which remains pretty well constant over time. In view of the results described above, the pattern is hardly surprising, with the least dissatisfaction expressed by owner-occupiers and the most by tenants.

Tenure is not the only important variable, however. Satisfaction also depends on the type of house, with those living in detached houses expressing much less dissatisfaction than those living in flats within each tenure, for instance. Given that a much greater proportion of the local-authority than the owner-occupied stock consists of flats and a much lower proportion of detached houses, this composition effect accounts for part of the differential in dissatisfaction between the two tenures shown in Table 5.24. From analysis of the GHS raw data files for 1978, the proportion of individuals in households where the head expressed dissatisfaction was three times as high (18.9 per cent) for local authority households as for owner-occupiers (6.3 per cent). (The slightly different figures from the published 1978 GHS results in Table 5.24 refer to numbers of households.) However, given the proportions expressing dissatisfaction for each dwelling type within the two tenures, it is possible to produce a 'standardized' measure of dissatisfaction. This gives the result which would be expected if the dwelling-type composition of each tenure matched the national pattern. Dissatisfaction standardized in this way falls to 17.3 per cent for the local authority sector and rises to 7.5 per cent for owner-occupiers. The ratio between the two falls, but only to 2.3. Differences in dwelling type by themselves therefore appear to explain only a relatively small proportion of the overall difference between the tenures.

The various surveys also revealed clear differences in satisfaction by age and by ethnic group. In the case of the former, 20 per cent of household heads aged under 25 responding to the 1978 GHS expressed dissatisfaction, compared with only 8 per cent of those over 60. Meanwhile, in the 1977 National Dwelling and Housing Survey (NDHS), 17 per cent of those describing themselves as non-white expressed dissatisfaction, compared with 8 per cent of those describing themselves as white (DoE 1978: table 8).

Satisfaction with area and environment

Another, wider, feature of whether people have a 'decent home' is the state of the area in which it is located. The physical standard and amenities of a council flat may be very good in themselves, but vandalism, graffiti, and litter may mean that its environment is squalid (although often poor condition and poor environment go together). Again, measuring this aspect of housing policy has attracted more attention in the 1980s than the 1970s, and it is not easy to judge trends over time.

The 1986 English House Condition Survey did make an assessment, concluding that 10.6 per cent of all dwellings were in 'poor environments', that is, in areas where action was needed on four or more specified measures of environmental improvement (DoE 1988c: 27). The survey looked at blocks of flats which were affected by vandalism, graffiti, litter, and dumping of rubbish in common areas, finding that half of all local authority flats were affected to some extent, and that in 10 per cent of them 'vandalism, graffiti, litter and dumped rubbish was extensive' (ibid.: 39). Less than 20 per cent of flats with other owners were affected to some extent, and for less than 2 per cent of them was misuse of communal areas extensive (information supplied by Building Research Establishment).

The survey also showed that dwellings in poor environments were much more likely to be in poor condition than others—more than twice as likely to be in poor repair, more than three times as likely to lack amenities, and nearly four times as likely to be unfit (ibid.: table A5.6).

Both the 1977 NDHS and 1978 GHS asked about satisfaction with the area. In the first case, this was a separate question from that about satisfaction with accommodation. More households expressed dissatisfaction (11.2 per cent) with the area than with the accommodation itself (8.6 per cent). In this case the differential between tenures was rather less, however, with 8.8 per cent of owner-occupiers, 11.8 per cent of private tenants, 14.4 per cent of housing association tenants, and 15.2 per cent of local authority tenants dissatisfied with the area. In the case of the 1978 GHS, the environment was a subsidiary reason offered for overall satisfaction with accommodation (which may contribute to the somewhat greater dissatisfaction in the GHS responses shown in Table 5.24). 31 per cent of those who were dissatisfied with their accommodation mentioned reasons connected with the neighbours, the environment, or the neighbourhood as one of the causes of their dissatisfaction.

More recently, Hope and Hough (1988) have shown a link between satisfaction with people's area and the risk of crimes such as burglary and theft and 'incivilities' such as drunks on the street, litter lying around, or teenagers hanging around. Using data from the 1984 British Crime Survey, they showed that a greater proportion of people living in areas with 'low risk' of crime were 'very satisfied' with their area than the national average (46 per cent), while those in medium- or high-risk areas were less likely to be very satisfied, the proportion falling to 24 per cent for 'multi-racial areas' and the 'poorest council estates'.

Summary

In many ways, the picture presented in this section has been one of clear success, with an increasing stock of dwellings, fewer of which are unfit or lack amenities and with a lower density of occupation. Overall satisfaction levels changed little between the mid-1970s and mid-1980s, suggesting that the improvement in standards matched expectations increased by rising income. By and large the improvement has benefited all classifications of the community. In these respects, and to the extent that policy has been responsible for the improvements, housing policy must be regarded as a success. The tenure shifts since 1973 (and particularly since 1979) also mean that the policy aim of promoting owner-occupation has been substantially achieved.

None the less, there are clearly problems. Even if the stock is larger in relation to the number of households, many people still have problems in gaining access to it, as witnessed by the statistics for homelessness acceptances or the rising numbers in unsatisfactory temporary accommodation, not to mention the numbers sleeping rough. During the 1970s, the proportion of dwellings in serious disrepair increased, although the situation appears to have improved between 1981 and 1986. Not all groups have gained proportionately from improving conditions. In particular, it appears from the GHS that the housing conditions of those in the lowest income group may have fallen behind in various respects between 1979 and 1985, although this conflicts with English House Condition Survey findings for other aspects between 1981 and 1986. It also appears that while there has been substantial progress with physical conditions, there remain major problems in respect of wider aspects of housing conditions, such as the repair service received by local authority tenants or the environment in which people live.

IV. POLICY OUTCOMES: AT A PRICE WITHIN THEIR MEANS?

Determining what is meant by the 'price' of housing is not straightforward. The answer will depend on whether rents are taken gross or net of Housing Benefit receipts, and on whether rates and other items such as water charges and repair and maintenance costs are included. It will also depend on what are counted as the 'housing costs' of owner-occupiers. Should mortgage payments be used, and if so, what allowance should be made for the fact that those buying a house with a mortgage end up with an asset—the house—not just the ability to live in it for the period while they make the payments? Similarly, how should the capital gains from which owner-occupiers benefit be treated? This section therefore examines the evidence on how a number of possible indicators of the 'price' of housing in relation to incomes have changed since 1974.

Gross housing costs: owner-occupiers

The most straightforward indicator of the cost of housing is the price at which owner-occupied houses are bought and sold. The relationship between house prices and average earnings (mean earnings of full-time men on adult rates) since 1970, taking the ratio in that year as 100, is shown in Fig. 5.5. The house price index used is for all dwellings on which building society advances have been completed (DoE 1988*a*: table 10.8 and equivalents for earlier years). It is adjusted for changes in the mix of dwellings sold, removing problems of comparability otherwise caused by the fall in the building societies' share of lending on more expensive property after 1980.

The figure shows the well-known pattern of large fluctuations in house prices in relation to earnings. In 1973, a peak had been reached which was followed by five years during which nominal house prices increased much more slowly than either the general price level or average earnings.

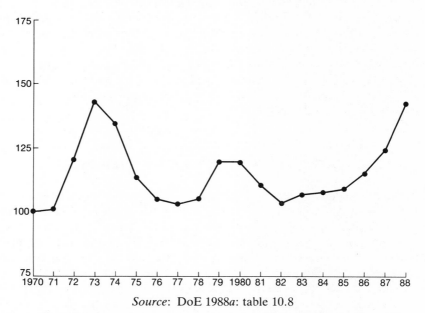

Source: DoE 1988*a*: table 10.8

FIG. 5.5. UK house price : earnings ratio (mix-adjusted price : earnings index; 1970 = 100)

A second but lower peak was reached in 1979, followed by a pronounced dip which bottomed out again in 1982. Since then the ratio has risen steadily, reaching a level in 1988 which was as high as in 1974. The variation of the cycle is quite startling—the 1974 peak being 50 per cent higher than the trough of 1982—but does not show any easily discernible trend.

For those buying houses, the price of the house they buy is only part of the equation which determines their monthly mortgage payments. These also depend on the proportion of the cost which is covered by the mortgage, the number of years over which repayment is made, and, of course, the interest rate (net of tax relief). Fig. 5.6 gives an impression of how these factors interacted, showing estimates of the mortgage out-goings (net of basic-rate tax relief) of first-time buyers, given their aver-age borrowing each year and the interest rates applying at the *end* of each year. The pattern differs in several ways from that shown in Fig. 5.5. In particular, it shows the effects of the coincidence of very high interest rates—15 per cent before tax relief at the end of 1979 and 12.75 per cent at the end of 1988—with the peaks in prices. It also shows the overall effect over the period of the extent to which owner-occupation has gone

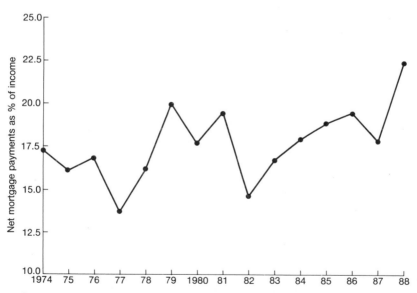

Source: DoE 1988*a*: tables 10.11, 10.16, and 10.25, and own calculations

Fig. 5.6. Mortgage payments of first-time buyers (building society advances, United Kingdom)

'down market': in 1974, the average income of first-time buyers (as reported to building societies and including that of a partner) was 30 per cent higher than average male earnings (in April of that year); by 1987, it was only 7 per cent higher. Allowing for all of this, the 1988 level actually put more strain on first-time buyers than that of 1974.

Gross housing costs: tenants

Fig. 5.7 shows a comparable picture for the variation in gross local authority and housing association fair rents as a proportion of the same measure of earnings. In comparing this with the costs of first-time buyers, one should, of course, bear in mind that housing outgoings *fall* over time for most owner-occupiers (and they acquire an asset), while this is not true for tenants. The main feature of the graph is the substantial jump in the ratio of rent to average earnings for local authority tenants between 1980 and 1982, which was followed by a decline until 1988, with rents only rising in line with prices rather than earnings (since then the 'guide-lines' for rent increases set by the DoE have been more rapid than inflation). By contrast, the fair rents set for housing association dwellings

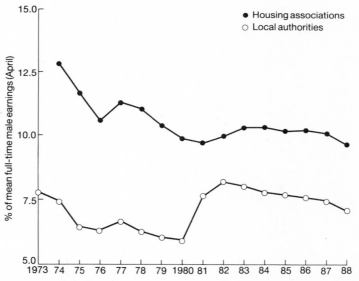

Sources: DoE 1988*a*: tables 11.1 and 11.15; Scottish Development Department 1987; DE 1989: table 5.6 and equivalents for other years

FIG. 5.7. Gross rents as percentage of average earnings, Great Britain

followed a much more stable path in relation to earnings (except in the first couple of years, when comparatively few rents were registered). The trends in relation to *average* earnings do not, of course, necessarily give a good guide to the relationship between rents and the incomes of those paying them, particularly in the period since 1979, when the dispersion of earnings has been widening. Table 5.25 gives some indication of the trends in relation to net incomes within each tenure.

Housing Benefit

The net amount which households—particularly tenants—have to pay for their housing depends not only on their gross costs, but also on the amount of help they receive from Housing Benefit. As discussed above, the cost of Housing Benefit to the government has increased rapidly since 1980. This has primarily been a result of rising rents, combined with the effects of increased unemployment and a larger pensioner population. It has not been because the benefit system has become inherently more generous.

Before April 1988, the amount of benefit to which those not receiving Supplementary Benefit (now Income Support) were entitled hinged around the level of their incomes in relation to a 'needs allowance' for a family of each particular type. If income equalled the needs allowance, a rent rebate (for council tenants) or rent allowance (for private tenants) would be given equalling 60 per cent of the gross rent. For those with lower incomes, this would be increased by an amount equal to the 'taper'—the means-test 'tax rate' on higher income—multiplied by the shortfall of gross income from the allowance. For those with incomes above the needs allowance, the rebate or allowance would equal 60 per cent of rent less a different taper multiplied by the excess.

The generosity of this system thus depended on two features: the level of the needs allowances and the steepness of the tapers (or marginal rates of benefit withdrawal as income rose). As Table 5.2 showed, the real value of the needs allowances stayed at much the same level throughout the period 1973/4–1987/8, apart from the three years 1974/5–1976/7, when they were rather more generous. In relation to *earnings* the allowances therefore became steadily less generous. Other things being equal, someone whose income and gross rent remained constant in relation to average earnings would have seen a fall in benefit over the period on this account.

The tapers remained constant until April 1983 at 25 per cent below the needs allowance and 17 per cent above it (as far as the rent element was concerned). At that point the system was reformed, one element of which was to give pensioners with incomes below the needs allowance a more generous taper of 50 per cent (so that benefit increased faster as income fell). However, this was at the cost of benefit recipients above the needs allowance, for whom the taper was increased to 21 per cent, so that benefit was withdrawn more rapidly as income rose. The taper was increased again in 1984 (twice), in 1986, and in 1987 until it had reached 33 per cent after April 1987.

After this the whole system was changed. The 1982/3 reforms had involved a shift in the administration of benefit for the housing costs of Supplementary Benefit recipients from the DHSS to the local authorities. This group was entitled to benefit in respect of 100 per cent of rent (and, until April 1988, 100 per cent of rates) and continued to receive 'certificated' benefit at this level after the change. There was no guarantee, however, that the income level at which the rebate system would give 100 per cent assistance would equal the income level at which the Supplementary Benefit system would do the same. The two systems did not mesh together. Before 1982/3 this led to what was known as the 'better-off problem', under which claimants like pensioners who could claim either rebates or Supplementary Benefit often chose the wrong one. After 1982/3, exacerbated by rising real rents, the same problem re-emerged in the form of an administrative horror known as Housing Benefit Supple-

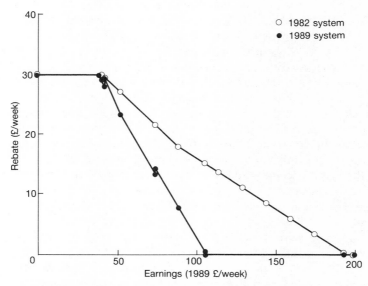

FIG. 5.8. Housing Benefit, 1981/2 and 1989/90 (single people over 25, rent £30)

ment, a top-up payment needed to stop some Housing Benefit recipients falling below the minimum income which Supplementary Benefit was supposed to guarantee.

Part of the April 1988 reform was to change the Housing Benefit formula so that it meshed in with the renamed Income Support system, payments being equal to 100 per cent of rent, less a new taper multiplied by the excess of a claimant's income over their Income Support rate. The new taper was based on *net* income (after allowing for tax, National Insurance contributions, and any other benefits received). The taper was raised to 65 per cent of net income in respect of the rent element of Housing Benefit (equivalent to roughly 43 per cent of gross income before tax for a basic-rate taxpayer).

The full effects of these changes between April 1982 and April 1989 are illustrated in Figs. 5.8 and 5.9. These compare the help given in respect of rent through the system as it was in April 1989 with the April 1982 system (on the assumption that the needs allowances in the earlier system would have been up-rated in line with earnings growth, i.e. by about 70 per cent).

Fig. 5.8 shows how large a rebate would be received by a single person aged 25 or over towards a rent of £30 per week under the two systems. At

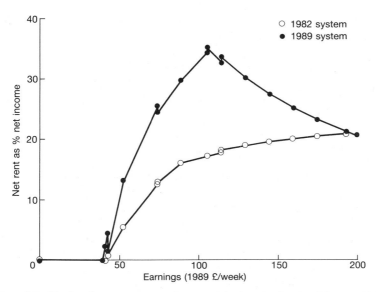

FIG. 5.9. Ratio of net rent to net income (single people over 25, rent £30)

the bottom, for this rent level, both systems would give 100 per cent assistance up to roughly the same earnings level. Thereafter, however, the tapers in the 1989 system are much steeper than those which applied in 1982, and benefit runs out much more rapidly. The picture would look somewhat different in respect of the levels of help given for different rents or different household types, but the overall direction of change would be the same.

One of the consequences of this shift is shown by Fig. 5.9. This shows the proportion which net rent (after Housing Benefit) would represent of net income (after tax and other benefits) at each income under the two systems. This ratio—a measure of the 'affordability' of rents after allowing for rebates—has entered the recent debate over rent levels for housing association tenants following the 1988 changes to the Housing Association Grant system. The difference between the two systems is dramatic. Under the up-rated 1982 system, those with a gross rent of £30 per week would have been protected from paying much more than 20 per cent of their net income in rent after allowing for benefit; under the 1989 system, the ratio can exceed 33 per cent.

In fact, what has happened since 1982 is the following. Before then, there was a system of rebates which gave significant amounts of help to those whose incomes were some way above Supplementary Benefit. Now the Housing Benefit system does little more than ensure that no one's income falls below the total of their Income Support rate and their housing costs. The combined taper for rent and rates—85 per cent on net income—is only marginally more generous than the 100 per cent taper which was embodied in the 'housing only' payments which were available under the Supplementary Benefit system until 1982. The old problem of which benefit would leave those with incomes just above their Supplementary Benefit scale rate 'better-off' (see Donnison 1982: 184–93) has been solved—through the effective abolition of the old rent rebate system.

Net housing costs in relation to income

It is, of course, the level of *net* housing costs after allowing for benefits which is of most importance in determining whether people have found housing 'at a price within their means'. Unfortunately, there is a major problem in the data sources concerning the treatment of the housing costs of those on Supplementary Benefit before and after the 1982/3 reforms to Housing Benefit which makes comparison over time very difficult. Before 1982, those on Supplementary Benefit paid their rents gross, but received extra income as part of their benefit with which to pay the rent. After 1982, they received 'certificated' Housing Benefit, meaning that they would receive a *net* rent demand, generally of zero (except for contributions to rent expected from 'non-dependants'), with no housing costs included in their income.

Thus in Table 5.25 the figures for 'net' housing costs as a percentage of gross income drawn from the 1974 and 1979 Family Expenditure Surveys actually show *gross* housing costs for those at the bottom of the income distribution and receiving Supplementary Benefit (and their incomes include the housing element of their Supplementary Benefit). Only for those on slightly higher incomes are the costs genuinely net of rebates. By contrast the 1985 figures are net of Housing Benefit for all cases. This gives a much better impression of the true position, but is difficult to compare with the earlier years.

The costs included in the table are rents, rates, mortgage payments, and repair and maintenance spending (but not allowing for owner-occupiers' imputed rents or capital gains in any way). Mortgage payments are shown net of basic-rate tax relief in 1974 and 1979 to give comparability with the payments net of relief through the MIRAS system in 1985.

The first clear message from the table is, unsurprisingly, that mortgagors make the greatest payments in respect of their income. Part of the benefit from this is, of course, that they become outright owners later on, with the lowest costs. Allowing for this, the group which is clearly in the worst position is that of furnished private tenants (many of whom are on low incomes). The relative balance between owners and tenants depends on how one allows for the asset purchase element of home buying.

Looking at the 1985 figures—which allow a fair comparison—for both mortgagors and council tenants it is those in the *second* income group, not the bottom one, who face the highest costs in relation to their incomes. For outright owners, the bottom group pays the most in relation to income, which is also true of private tenants, whose take-up of Housing Benefit is low.

Over the 1974–9 period there was some rise in the ratio of costs to income for mortgagors (associated with the rise in interest rates) but a small fall for local authority tenants (as rents declined in real terms). The 1985 ratios were higher again for mortgagors, as factors such as greater mortgages in relation to income and a lower basic rate of income tax on which relief was calculated offset the lower interest rate.

For local authority tenants, the rise in the overall ratio between 1979 and 1985—from 9.4 per cent to 10.6 per cent—looks at first sight less dramatic. But for tenants on Supplementary Benefit—a fifth of all council tenants in 1979—this is a comparison between gross costs in 1979 and net costs in 1985. A fairer guide to the trend for those not affected by the definitional problem is given by the ratio for the middle-income group rising from 9.0 per cent in 1979 to 11.8 per cent. Similar rises affected other tenants.

Whether the percentages of gross income absorbed by housing costs in

Table 5.25. *Net housing costs[a] as percentage of gross household incomes,[b]*
United Kingdom, 1974, 1979, and 1985

Income group	% of all households in group	Owners with mortgage[c]	Outright owners	Local authority tenants	Other unfurnished tenants	Furnished tenants
Family Expenditure Survey 1974						
Bottom	21	[40.0][d]	8.6	21.6	17.4	—[e]
2	20	19.8	7.7	12.8	11.1	—
3	18	17.2	6.2	10.1	8.4	—
4	19	14.5	5.2	8.3	8.3	—
Top	22	13.0	4.7	5.7	5.4	—
All	100	14.3	5.7	9.9	9.3	15.3
		11.2				
Family Expenditure Survey 1979						
Bottom	22	[44.9][d]	11.2	19.0	16.7	—
2	18	28.7	7.5	12.8	10.1	—
3	25	22.8	6.7	9.0	8.7	—
4	16	13.0	5.2	7.1	[7.0]	—
Top	19	13.3	4.1	4.8	5.1	—
All	100	15.7	6.1	9.4	9.4	15.1
		12.8				
Family Expenditure Survey 1985						
Bottom	22	[31.1][d]	10.6	8.7	16.3	—
2	19	34.3	9.8	12.7	14.8	—
3	19	22.9	6.4	11.8	11.4	—
4	24	19.4	7.4	9.1	[7.7]	—
Top	17	17.0	4.3	6.6	[4.6]	—
All	100	19.3	6.8	10.6	10.6	16.5
		15.9				

Note: The proportion of all households in each group in each year is as follows:

	1974	1979	1985
Owners with mortgage	28	32	38
Outright owners	22	21	22
Local authority tenants	32	33	30
Other unfurnished tenants	12	8	4
Furnished tenants	4	3	2
'Rent-free'	3	3	2

1985 are still 'within people's means' is a subjective judgement. What is clear is that costs rose substantially in relation to incomes for both mortgagors and tenants between 1979 and 1985. What is also clear is that, as the average ratios have risen, so a small, but increasing, number have been pushed to the point where, for one reason or another, they have ceased to be able to pay their mortgages or rents. In 1979, for instance, 2,000 households were accepted by local authorities in England as homeless principally as a result of mortgage default; by 1987 the number had risen to 10,500 (*Official Report*, 26 June 1988, WA, col. 146). Over the same period the number of building society loans which were more than six months in arrears rose from 8,420 at the end of 1979 to 60,000 at the end of 1987 (ibid.: cols. 149–50) and the number of properties taken into possession by building societies rose ninefold from 2,530 in 1979 to 22,630 in 1987, before falling back to 16,150 in 1988 (*Official Report*, 6 Mar. 1989, WA, col. 425). While these numbers may not be very large compared with the total number of mortgagors, it is clear that the numbers in difficulty have risen very rapidly indeed since 1979. Local authority rent arrears have also risen, but here the causes lie not only with changes in tenants' ability to pay increased rents, but also with local authority and Department of Social Security management competence, so it is not possible to say to what extent the higher arrears reflect a growing 'affordability' problem.

The balance between tenures: the economic cost of housing

One of the equity aims which has sometimes been stated for housing policy is that of 'neutrality' between tenures. The costs of housing to

---

(*Table notes cont.*)

[a] Net housing costs for owner-occupiers include mortgage interest after tax relief (through MIRAS in 1985, assumed to be at the basic rate in 1974 and 1979), net rates (after Housing Benefit), water charges, and repair costs. In 1974 and 1979 housing costs include the *gross* rates of those on Supplementary Benefit. Net housing costs for tenants include rents and rates (both after Housing Benefit), water charges, and repair costs incurred by tenants. In 1974 and 1979 housing costs include the *gross* rents and rates of those on Supplementary Benefit.

[b] Incomes are gross normal weekly incomes of households, not including mortgage interest relief through MIRAS in 1985 or at the basic rate in 1974 and 1979. Incomes in 1974 and 1979 include Supplementary Benefit payments in respect of rent and rates.

[c] All payments of interest and other payments for purchase and alteration of dwellings shown in the Family Expenditure Survey are assumed to be paid by mortgagors.

[d] Figures in square brackets are based on fewer than fifty households from sample.

[e] Dashes denote that numbers in sample are too small for meaningful results.

Source: Own calculations based on DE 1975, 1980, 1986.

owner-occupiers and tenants should in some way be equivalent. As discussed above, the cash outgoings of mortgagors and tenants are very different, but comparison requires some allowance for the asset purchase or saving aspect of owner-occupiers' costs.

One way of approaching the problem is to observe that owner-occupiers pay for the management and maintenance of their own dwellings in full and also face the full effects of any depreciation of their property or the cost of remedying it (apart from some repair grants). If these elements are also deducted from the rents paid by tenants, what remains—in effect, the charge they have to pay for the capital tied up in the dwellings they occupy—can be compared with the 'capital cost of housing services' to owner-occupiers (see below; see also King and Atkinson 1980).

This approach is illustrated in Fig. 5.10. This shows what rate of return on the capital value of the local authority stock was generated by gross rents (including rebates) in Great Britain between 1975/6 and 1986/7, using the data on rents and management and maintenance costs shown in Table 5.3. The top line shows gross rents as a percentage of the Central Statistical Office's estimate of the market value of the stock (as shown in CSO 1987*b*: table 11.8, for instance, but *without* adjustment to 'tenanted'

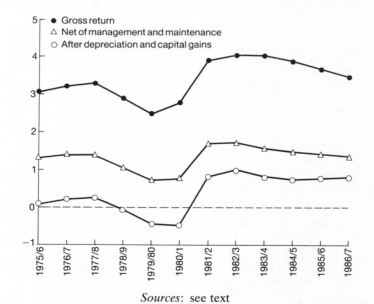

Sources: see text

Fig. 5.10. Rates of return on local authority housing, Great Britain (as percentages of current capital values)

market value as given in the published series; the estimates are derived from the relationship between Right to Buy valuations and characteristics of the stock). Over the period from 1975/6 to 1979/80 this fluctuated around 3 per cent. It then rose to about 4 per cent by 1981/2 as rents rose rapidly in real terms, but subsequently fell back somewhat as the capital value of housing rose more rapidly than rents.

The second line shows net rents after allowing for actual management and maintenance spending as a percentage of the stock's value. This was about 1.3 per cent between 1975/6 and 1977/8, fell to below 1 per cent, reached a maximum of 1.7 per cent in 1981/2, but has subsequently fallen back to 1.4 per cent again. This fall has resulted from the combination of the falling gross rents in relation to capital values and the rising real spending on management and maintenance noted earlier.

Depreciation is allowed for here as 1.2 per cent of the CSO's Blue Book estimates for each year of the value of the local authority stock at current replacement cost (i.e. excluding land values and giving dwellings a 'half-life' of fifty-seven years).

Deducting all of these costs gives the flow of net rents at any particular date as a percentage of current capital value. But if this net flow is expected to remain constant in relation to capital values, and those capital values are expected to rise in real terms as they have in the past, this net flow will also be expected to rise in real terms. A further adjustment is needed to allow for this rising rental stream to give the net return on capital which rents could be expected to be generating at each point. In effect this adjustment allows for the share of the expected real capital gain which will accrue to the landlord, given rents in relation to capital values (note that, with sub-economic rents, part of the capital gain effectively accrues to the tenant).

The final line of the figure shows the net return as a percentage of capital value after allowing for both depreciation and an assumption that net rents after allowing for other costs could be expected to rise at 1.5 per cent per year in real terms in perpetuity (a rate of growth somewhat slower than that of earnings, which seems reasonable). The figure thus shows a *prospective* return at each date, given this assumption, not one based on actual capital gains in any particular year. During the first part of the period this was about zero, but it has been close to 1 per cent since 1981/2.

Paying rents which represent a net real return on capital of 1 per cent—let alone zero—at a time when market real interest rates are 4 or 5 per cent or more might seem to imply a very favourable cost of housing to tenants. However, the net cost of capital to owner-occupiers is also very low, thanks to their favourable tax treatment. Apart from management and maintenance and depreciation costs, owner-occupiers either have to pay interest (net of tax relief) on their mortgage or forgo a cash return on their equity stake in the house. If the best alternative investment yielded interest subject to tax, the opportuniy cost of equity would equal the net interest rate, equal to the cost of the mortgage element after tax relief. The cost of capital tied up in a house would then be the same regardless of the owner's equity stake (in fact, there are better alternative investments than those giving fully taxable interest as a return, so the opportunity cost of the equity will be somewhat higher, but this simplifying assumption will be made in what follows).

In return for these costs, owners receive two kinds of return: the 'housing services' from living in their house, and the capital gain in its value. The capital cost of housing services to owner-occupiers is therefore given by the net interest rate *less* the return they might expect by way of capital gain (if the future resembles the past, which, of course, it may not). Note that this calculation would be rather different if mortgage interest relief were not given, or capital gains or imputed rents were taxable.

Over the 1979–88 period as a whole, interest rates net of basic-rate tax averaged 8.8 per cent (averaging the end-year interest rates). From mid-1979 to mid-1988 prices overall rose by 6.7 per cent per year. If one bases the long-run expected nominal capital gain on this figure plus the same 1.5 per cent long-run real capital gain per year, the expected annual gain comes to 8.2 per cent per year. The net cost of housing services to owner-occupiers would then be 0.6 per cent of capital value, just *below* the equivalent figure for local authority tenants shown in Fig. 5.10. The figure would be somewhat higher if the opportunity cost of equity in fact related to something giving a higher net return than fully taxable interest.

Now, these calculations are speculative and subject to very wide margins of error. What they do suggest none the less is that there may have been rough tenure neutrality in the period since 1979. There is certainly nothing to suggest that the net return on local authority housing generated by rents in recent years puts tenants in a much more favourable position than that of owner-occupiers.

Between mid-1974 and mid-1979 interest rates net of basic-rate tax averaged 7.3 per cent. However, prices rose by an average of 15.5 per cent each year. If this had been expected to be maintained in perpetuity, the same assumed 1.5 per cent annual real capital gain would then generate an expected nominal capital gain of 17 per cent and a cost of housing services to owner-occupiers of about *minus* 10 per cent, beside which the equivalent figure of zero for council tenants would look rather unfavourable! While it can be argued that inflation clearly was not expected to continue at this kind of rate, it would only have had to be expected to run at more than 5.8 per cent annually to generate a negative capital cost of housing services for owner-occupiers. Again, the calculation is speculative, but the evidence suggests that owners were in a more favourable position than tenants in the conditions of the late 1970s.

Summary

Putting all of this together, it is clear that housing has become significantly more expensive in relation to incomes in the period since 1979 compared with the period before. Gross rents and mortgage payments for first-time buyers have both averaged greater proportions of income. The assistance with such higher rents which would have been given through the Housing Benefit system has been substantially cut back. Net housing costs are clearly a higher proportion of incomes for both owners and tenants (although those incomes themselves are higher too). The net real return on capital generated by local authority rents is clearly higher than it was before 1979, while the equivalent capital cost of housing services for owner-occupiers has gone from being substantially negative to being marginally positive.

Whatever the bench-mark, the price of housing is clearly *less* within people's means than it was before. And around these increases in the average costs of housing, the rise has meant substantial increases since 1979 in the numbers so overstretched that they have defaulted on their mortgage payments or rents. For these people at least, the policy aim of housing within people's means has clearly failed.

V. IN BRIEF

● There was continuity in policy over the period 1974–89 in the general maintenance of tax concessions to owner-occupiers (with the major exception of the emerging effects of the cash limit on mortgages eligible for tax relief) and in the steady shift from public capital spending on new dwellings towards renovation of existing ones.
● The most striking policy differences before and after 1979 were the shift from general subsidies for public housing (towards higher rents and greater spending on Housing Benefit) and the Right to Buy, with local authorities' share of the housing stock falling since 1979.
● Net public spending on housing fell for most of the period, and dramatically so after 1979. But:
  * In real terms, cuts in current general subsidies were matched by increases in the cost of Housing Benefit.

* Despite the fall in *net* current spending, real management and maintenance spending per local authority unit rose by more than 4 per cent annually throughout the period. This was possible as the real burden of debt payments fell after 1979 and because the proportion of spending covered by rents increased as general subsidies fell.
* While *net* public capital spending fell by 90 per cent between 1976/7 and 1988/9, much of the recent fall represented an increase in capital receipts, not in *gross* spending. Allowing for changes in construction costs, the fall in the *volume* of gross capital spending was about 37 per cent between 1976/7 and 1987/8.
* Tax expenditures on owner-occupation increased steadily, the cost of mortgage interest tax relief more than doubling in real terms between 1973/4 and 1988/9.

● Promotion of owner-occupation has been a visible success, with its share of the stock in Great Britain rising from 52 per cent at the end of 1973 to 65 per cent at the end of 1988. This has been accompanied by a clear polarization between the tenures in terms of income.

● There were clear improvements in the overall number of dwellings in relation to households and their general physical standard:

* The shortfall between fit dwellings and households (including 'concealed' households) fell by over a million between 1971 and 1986, although the pace of improvement slowed after 1981.
* The proportion of people living at relatively high densities fell between 1974 and 1985, as did the proportion living without basic amenities or central heating. By and large, these improving conditions benefited all socio-economic and income groups.
* Overall satisfaction with housing changed little between the mid-1970s and the mid-1980s. Rising standards appear to have kept pace with expectations (although council tenants expressed significant dissatisfaction with their repair services in the mid-1980s).

● Meanwhile there has been an increase in acute problems of access to housing, with rapid rises in homelessness acceptances and numbers in temporary accommodation since the late 1970s, and the numbers of single people sleeping rough in city streets giving the most graphic evidence of failure to ensure a 'decent home for all'.

● General Household Survey evidence suggests that the improvement between 1979 and 1985 was not equally shared by the lowest income quintile, whose relative position deteriorated (although English House Condition Survey results suggest the opposite conclusion).

● Outgoings on housing have been substantially higher in relation to incomes for both owner-occupiers and tenants since the early 1980s compared with the mid-1970s. The rise in gross rents has been compounded by cuts in the relative generosity of the Housing Benefit system since 1982/3.

• The balance of advantages favoured owners compared with tenants (looking at their gross rents) throughout the period, but this advantage has been very much smaller since real interest rates became positive in the early 1980s.

Annexe

Table 5A.1. *Public spending on housing, United Kingdom (£ million at 1987/8 prices)*[a]

	1973/4	1974/5	1975/6	1976/7	1977/8	1978/9	1979/80	1980/1	1981/2	1982/3	1983/4	1984/5	1985/6	1986/7	1987/8	1988/9
Current Spending (GB)																
Exchequer subsidies[b]	1,553	2,239	2,374	2,796	2,627	2,772	2,996	2,803	1,729	1,047	640	687	695	778	657	679
Rate Fund Contributions[c]	373	625	605	465	425	536	709	770	726	717	764	657	593	521	524	438
Housing associations	18	26	35	41	39	43	46	44	55	58	31	23	29	32	37	41
Other current	75	121	105	307	155	185	228	219	194	191	223	218	234	253	284	257
Total current	2,022	3,011	3,117	3,605	3,245	3,536	3,981	3,834	2,704	2,014	1,659	1,586	1,552	1,584	1,502	1,415
Capital spending (GB)																
Gross spending																
Local authority[d]	6,404	8,511	7,079	7,222	5,795	5,345	5,344	4,080	3,223	3,771	4,767	4,399	3,679	3,717	3,894	4,018
Housing association[e]	430	684	944	1,307	1,284	1,170	1,174	1,154	1,063	1,350	1,240	1,128	1,063	1,054	1,057	1,029
Total gross capital	6,833	9,195	8,023	8,530	7,080	6,515	6,518	5,236	4,286	5,121	6,006	5,528	4,743	4,769	4,951	5,047
Capital receipts	969	548	1,117	786	973	1,181	912	1,010	1,630	2,696	2,764	2,456	2,264	2,548	2,855	3,733
Net capital spending	5,864	8,643	6,909	7,747	6,107	5,333	5,602	4,224	2,653	2,426	3,241	3,071	2,479	2,221	2,096	1,315
Housing Benefit (GB)[f]																
Local authority tenants	1,781	1,331	1,240	1,323	1,357	1,306	1,207	1,311	2,007	2,433	2,386	2,468	2,501	2,546	2,547	2,566
Other tenants	772	643	579	566	534	528	465	455	544	623	646	788	912	1,004	1,038	1,028
Total housing benefit	2,553	1,974	1,819	1,889	1,891	1,834	1,672	1,766	2,551	3,057	3,031	3,256	3,412	3,551	3,585	3,594
Northern Ireland																
Current and capital	189	246	240	457	389	378	372	354	316	348	360	385	376	353	337	315
Housing Benefit	204	158	145	151	151	147	134	141	204	245	155	248	263	283	321	335
Total Northern Ireland	393	404	385	608	540	525	506	495	520	592	516	633	640	636	658	651
United Kingdom																
Current and capital	8,075	11,901	10,266	11,809	9,741	9,246	9,954	8,412	5,672	4,786	5,260	5,041	4,408	4,158	3,935	3,047
Housing Benefit	2,757	2,132	1,964	2,040	2,042	1,980	1,806	1,907	2,755	3,301	3,187	3,503	3,676	3,834	3,906	3,929
Total UK public spending	10,831	14,033	12,230	13,849	11,783	11,227	11,760	10,319	8,427	8,087	8,447	8,545	8,084	7,992	7,841	6,976
Mortgage interest relief[g]	2,439	2,794	2,798	3,168	2,698	2,573	2,867	3,233	3,090	3,060	3,349	4,106	5,169	5,000	4,850	5,179
GDP (MP) deflator	22.8	27.2	34.2	38.7	44.0	48.7	57.0	67.5	74.1	79.4	83.0	87.2	91.9	95.0	100.0	106.2

[a] Adjusted by GDP (market prices) deflator.

[b] To local authorities, new towns, and Scottish Special Housing Association (SSHA).

[c] To local authority Housing Revenue Accounts.

[d] Local authorities, new towns, and SSHA, including support to private sector.

[e] Includes low-cost home ownership.

[f] Before 1983/4, figures show estimated rents of Supplementary Benefit recipients plus actual costs of rent rebates and allowances.

[g] Includes Option Mortgage Subsidy.

Sources: Current and capital spending numbers for Great Britain from 1976/7 derived as follows: for England from HM Treasury 1989: table 9.1 and equivalents for earlier years; for Wales from Welsh office 1987: table 63 and equivalents for earlier years, and total for 1986/7–1988/9 from HM Treasury 1989: table 17.1 with estimated breakdown between items; for Scotland from Scottish Development Department 1989 and equivalents for earlier years. GB figures for 1973/4–1975/6 estimated from survey price data in HM Treasury 1981: table 2.7 and earlier equivalents. Northern Ireland capital and current spending total since 1976/7 from HM Treasury 1989: table 18.1 and earlier equivalents. Northern Ireland totals for 1973/4–1975/6 estimated from HM Treasury 1981: table 2.17, adjusted for changes in definition.

Housing Benefit figures since 1983/4 from HM Treasury 1989: table 15.1. Figures for earlier years for Supplementary Benefit recipients derived from DHSS 1984: table 34.58 and earlier equivalents. Figures for rent rebates and allowances from DoE 1985: tables 11.1, 11.2, and 11.4, and from Scottish Development Department 1985: table 8 and earlier equivalents. Northern Ireland Housing Benefit figures since 1983/4 derived from UK total in HM Treasury 1989: table 21.1.7 and for earlier years estimated as 8 per cent of GB total.

Mortgage interest relief since 1978/9 from *Official Report*, 10 June 1988, WA, Cols. 702–4, and from HM Treasury 1989: table 21.1.25. Earlier figures from DoE 1977b: table V.1. Option Mortgage Subsidy from various Public Expenditure White Papers.

6

The Personal Social Services: 'Everyone's Poor Relation but Nobody's Baby'[1]

Maria Evandrou, Jane Falkingham, and Howard Glennerster

The public image of the personal social services (PSS) is usually that of a service composed almost exclusively of 'do-gooding' or altruistic social workers, their work or, more often, their inadequacies being highlighted by the media in times of crisis. The recurrent waves of concern about child sexual abuse are a good example. This is an unrealistic as well as an unfair image. The PSS extend far beyond those which social workers alone provide; and those provided by field-workers themselves are more complex than the narrow spectrum of activities highlighted by the popular press. The sector encapsulates a wide variety of services directed at a diverse range of client groups.

In this chapter we look at the effectiveness of the PSS in Britain since the early 1970s. We discuss the evolution of the PSS in relation to the goals and policies specified by both Labour and Conservative governments. We examine the trends in public expenditure in this area, looking at the resultant expansion and contraction of the different sectors and the impact on individuals using and in need of the PSS. We explore the consequent outcomes of these trends and discuss their policy implications. Finally, we conclude with a summary of the major points, tracking the development and effectiveness of the PSS in the context of political, economic, and demographic change.

I. GOALS AND POLICIES

The emergence of the personal social services

To understand the diverse nature of the PSS it is necessary to consider how such a disparate set of services came to be grouped together, dominated by a single department of local government. The very idea of a sector of statutory services called the 'Personal Social Services' dates back no further than the mid-1960s, though the idea of a single family service of a more restricted kind had been emerging for a decade before that. Up

---

[1] DHSS 1988c: p. iv, para. 9. This statement was made with regard to responsibility between government departments concerning community care but could equally have been made about the whole of the PSS.

to the formation of the Social Service Departments (SSDs) in England and Wales in 1971, services were provided by a wide variety of bodies. A disparate range of services had grown up over a century or more, supporting families and individuals who could not operate independently without help. Many of them, such as those services supporting individuals who were blind or disabled, or the elderly infirm, had begun as the work of voluntary organizations and gradually over time had become statutory responsibilities.

Separate from this group of supportive services for people living in the community was the provision for those who had ceased to be able to live without much more intensive residential care. In many cases, families could not provide such care themselves and were unable to buy it. In these instances responsibility for such people rested with the state. In the nineteenth century this function had been performed by the Poor Law authorities and had been inherited by local authority welfare departments.

Distinct yet again were the powers the state had taken at the end of the nineteenth century to safeguard the interests of children who had no parents or were neglected or cruelly treated by their parents—a function performed by Children's Departments up to 1971.

This is not the place to attempt to describe the interplay of professional, bureaucratic, and party politics which produced the new SSDs in England and Wales, and Social Work Departments in Scotland (see Hall 1976; Cooper 1983). Suffice to say that throughout the 1960s the social work profession had been fighting for recognition, while the medical profession had been pressing for the creation of comprehensive health-service agencies separate from local authorities. The reforms of the early 1970s gave to both a part of what they wanted. In England and Wales, following the Seebohm Report (Home Office 1968), the statutory social work agency became the SSD, and in Scotland, following the Kilbrandon Report (Scottish Home and Health Department 1964), Social Work Departments were established, which retained responsibility for the probation services. Under the reorganization, community health services were transferred to the National Health Service (NHS), under the new Health Authorities. The principle of professional demarcation is perhaps best illustrated by the medical social workers who practise in hospitals, working closely with medical teams. They were transferred to the *employment* of SSDs after 1974.

The main statutory changes which immediately precede our period of study and the broad functions of SSDs in 1974 are set out in Table 6.1. It is important to note that in Northern Ireland, health and social care services remain combined. Owing to the different nature of PSS in Northern Ireland, the differences in policies, and the difficulties in obtaining

Table 6.1. *The changing organizational structure for statutory personal social services, 1970–1974, England and Wales*

Field-work	Types of social services			Statutory authorities responsible		
	Residential care	Day care	Other services	Pre-1971: local authority committees	1971–4: local authority committee	April 1974 onwards: local authority committee
Preventive work with families	Reception centres for young offenders		Advice centres	Children's	Social Services	Social Services
Receiving children into care, supervising children in care, finding foster homes and supervising foster-parents, adoption work, work with offenders	Children's homes / Approved schools / Remand homes		Financial and material help to children coming into care or before a juvenile court			
Domiciliary care of the elderly, the physically handicapped, teachers of the blind, deaf, and dumb, work with problem families	Residential care for the elderly and disabled	Clubs for the elderly and handicapped	Meals on wheels, laundry service for the elderly, adaptations to houses for the aged and handicapped	Welfare		
Workers with mentally ill, social work with the after-care of people suffering illness, home helps	Hostels for the mentally ill and mentally handicapped	Day nurseries, junior and adult training centres for the mentally handicapped		Health		
Domiciliary care and education from health visitors, home nurses, midwives, occupational therapists, physiotherapists		Registering of child-minders. Clinics and infant welfare centres, health centres	Family Planning		National Health Service	National Health Service
Education welfare officers, social workers in schools	Boarding schools, especially for the handicapped	Special day schools for handicapped	Youth service, child guidance clinics	Education	Education	Education
	Medical social work in hospitals. Psychiatric social work in hospitals			National Health Service	National Health Service	Social services
Probation Officers	Probation Hostels			Home Office and Probation and After-Care Committees	Home Office and Probation and After-Care Committees	Home Office and Probation and After-Care Committees

Source: Glennerster 1975.

comparable disaggregated figures, Northern Ireland will not be explicitly discussed in this chapter. Expenditure from the province is, however, included in any UK figures presented. The structure of PSS in Scotland differs in turn from that obtaining in England and Wales, with the probation services being combined under the same authority as other juvenile services. Thus the latter two countries will provide the main focus for the chapter, although not exclusively.

Ultimate aims

As can be seen, the range of client groups served by the PSS is wide and objectives are necessarily varied. At one extreme there is the care and protection of children and work with the socially deviant, at the other the care of the elderly and the disabled. The potential values inherent in each are rather different. The PSS are in part concerned with *social control*. Indeed, the whole debate about the creation of the PSS began with concern about juvenile delinquency (Home Office 1959). It is thus extremely difficult to identify one overarching goal that unifies the aim of the sector.

On one level society could be said to be collectively concerned to protect its members from:

1. danger—from delinquents;
2. discomfort—mentally disordered behaviour we find embarrassing;
3. distress—seeing elderly people living in squalor.

John Stuart Mill argued that the state had a duty to protect minors (i.e. individuals in the making), who did not yet possess the capacity to look after themselves. Here, the state takes on the role of collective protector of children against 'cruel' parents. This is not a public good in the normal sense, but the state is the only agency normally vested with the power to take children away from their parents.

More centrally, it can be argued that the PSS are concerned to protect those unable to operate as 'full individuals' in an unprotected competitive environment—the mentally ill and handicapped, and frail, elderly people who have never had the opportunity to earn resources for themselves or have not been able to finance their care in old age. Then there are individuals with disabilities who can live 'normally', or near normally, with additional support in terms of physical help and care, as well as transport. We may summarize this goal as the pursuit of fostering greater *social integration* amongst individuals or groups in society who would otherwise be marginalized. More specifically, to maximize individual personal well-being in the face of a disabling condition. The dual aims of social control and social integration are summarized graphically in Fig. 6.1.

The pursuit of social integration for disabled groups in society involves fundamental issues of equity. Yet the PSS have largely been passed by in the debate on equality (though see Brown 1972). It is often assumed that the benefits of PSS provision go to the bottom end of the income distribution or to the lower social classes. This depends on how we calculate the costs of care and on whom they fall.

We examine to what extent these services are equally available in different parts of the country and to those from different income groups, and how far they have met the overarching aims of the PSS over time. How far the ultimate goals have been met by different governments is not independent of the specific policy goals of those administrations. Below we summarize central government policy objectives for the period since 1974 and distinguish those which have been common to both Labour and Conservative governments, and those on which the approach has differed.

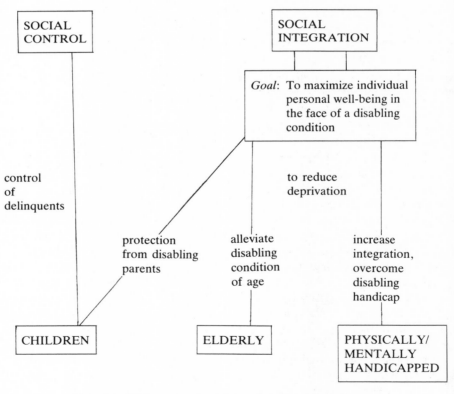

FIG. 6.1. Ultimate goals of the personal social services

Policy objectives

For most of the period since the Second World War, until Mrs Thatcher's administration, there has been cross-party support for all the major policy priorities pursued in the PSS. The reorganization itself was supported by both major parties in Parliament.

The most consistent and publicized aim throughout the last two decades has been that of fostering 'community care'. It has been a much-affirmed, if ill-defined, goal (Bulmer 1987; Walker 1982*b*) of both the last Labour government and successive Conservative administrations. However, its meaning has changed subtly over time. Initially the term meant, to many officials, no more than care outside NHS hospitals. The first Public Expenditure White Paper following the creation of the SSDs reflected that view: 'A major objective for local authority personal social services is to shift the balance of care from hospitals to the community where this is more appropriate' (HM Treasury 1971: 53).

In the wake of major political embarrassment at ill-treatment of patients in a number of long-stay institutions, governments of both parties issued policy statements setting out a time-scale for reducing places in such long-stay hospitals (DHSS 1971, 1975), for both the mentally handicapped and the mentally ill. Recently, the term has changed from meaning 'care *in* the community' to 'care *by* the community', and with this change has come a collapse in the consensus surrounding 'community care' as a policy aim. This is discussed further below, but for the time being let us continue with common policy aims.

Both governments have attempted to shift more health and PSS resources to the care of the priority groups, namely: frail, elderly people (over-75s); people mentally ill or handicapped; and individuals with physical handicaps. The objectives set out in the Labour government's *Priorities* document (DHSS 1976*c*) (see pp. 112–5 above) were largely repeated in the Conservative government's equivalent document, *Care in Action* (DHSS 1981*a*), except in vaguer, non-quantified terms. What differed between the two governments was the implementation of such policies, that is, the means rather than the ends.

A third policy objective common to both administrations was not the product of deliberate policy planning, but rather a by-product of public concern about child neglect, heightened by the treatment of the issue in the media. In November 1973 a child in the care of East Sussex Council died as the result of ill-treatment by her stepfather. The girl's name was Maria Collwell. This case was subjected to a public inquiry and the report became the focus of great public interest and criticism of the new SSDs. The Collwell case was merely the first in a series of highly publicized tragedies. The adverse publicity which SSDs and social workers received meant that the priority accorded to work with children increased, leaving less time, especially of skilled staff, for other groups (Parton 1985).

Under both governments the DHSS has continued to issue advice regarding child abuse, including the creation of 'at risk' registers, but the period ends with another even more widely publicized death—that of Jasmine Beckford (London Borough of Brent 1985).

Finally, both administrations have been concerned to reduce public expenditure in general, and local authority expenditure in particular. If we take the range of activities undertaken by the new SSDs, their predecessors had spent the equivalent of 0.2 per cent of Gross National Product (GNP) in the 1950s. In the 1960s expenditure on PSS roughly doubled in volume terms, while in the period 1970–5 real spending doubled again (Ferlie and Judge 1981; Webb and Wistow 1982; Glennerster 1985). Thus just over 1.0 per cent of the GNP was devoted to these services in 1974. This pace of expansion was to slow significantly, as we shall see.

If these themes were common (at least in principle) to both administrations, others were not. The Labour government had set guide-lines for social service provision and asked local authorities to submit plans for future development (DHSS 1976c, 1977b; Webb and Wistow 1986).

The Conservative government gave up any attempt to set guide-lines for local authority services (DHSS 1981a). Central direction and priority setting gave way to local choice, which was increasingly constrained by controls on local authority expenditure. These were exerted first through cash limits, then through a grant formula that penalized high spenders. Within that formula there was a grant-related expenditure figure, which was in effect a target figure for social service spending for each authority in the country. Finally, a rate-cap was introduced to put a limit on the capacity of high-spending local authorities to raise rates to finance their services.

The other major break in the policy continuity came after the 1979 election, when the new government began to give increasing encouragement to the non-statutory sector, with the implementation of the recommendations of the Wolfenden Committee (1978), and to extol the virtues of informal care by the family and neighbours. In *Growing Older* it is clearly stated that

the primary sources of support and care for elderly people are informal and voluntary. These spring from the personal ties of kinship, friendship and neighbourhood. They are irreplaceable. It is the role of public authorities to sustain, and, where necessary, develop—but never to displace—such support and care. Care *in* the community must increasingly mean care *by* the community. (DHSS 1981c: para. 1.9)

This statement reflects a move by the government to change the definition of community care. This philosophy was expounded more fully to the
Conference of Directors of Social Services at Buxton on 27 September
1984. Fowler (then Secretary of State for Social Services) rejected what
he called the monopolistic approach, under which local authorities provided all the services (a situation which had never existed). Instead, he
argued, drawing on the Seebohm Report, they should have 'an enabling
role'. For this government, moreover, the enabling role should be central. The same approach was endorsed by Sir Roy Griffiths in his report
on community care (DHSS 1988c). The response to Griffiths (*Official
Report*, 12 July 1989, cols. 975–9) again emphasized that government's
role should be seen as 'enabling' rather than 'providing'—an emphasis
which has been embodied in the recent White Paper *Caring for People:
Community Care in the Next Decade and Beyond* (DoH 1989b).

In summary, although there may have been common goals throughout
our period of investigation, the means employed to achieve them and the
final desired outcome have changed considerably. Throughout the period
there has been a steady shift away from a position where the policy focus
was on centrally defined need and equality, with an emphasis on priority
groups, targets, and planning, to one where the main concern is with
public expenditure restraint and a shift in the balance of care provision
between the state and the non-statutory sector. This change in emphasis
has been both explicit, enshrined in certain policy changes, and implicit
within the mechanisms used to achieve such aims.

To assess whether the different governments have been successful in
meeting such aims, both common and other, it is necessary to develop a
framework within which the effects of changes in policy over time can be
identified. The framework should enable us to look at changes in total
expenditure over time, as well as at shifts in the balance of resources
directed towards particular groups (such as children and the elderly) or
between types of care (such as residential or community). However,
given the overwhelming importance attached by recent government policy
to shifting resources and provision between sectors, it is also necessary to
be able to examine the changing balance of care between the informal,
statutory, and non-statutory sectors. To do this we need to examine the
'mixed economy of care' and the role of the state within that economy.

The 'mixed economy of care'

If a broader conception of what we mean by social care is adopted, the
traditional view that it is largely undertaken by statutory social care
agencies is misleading. Increasingly it has come to be recognized that
much of the care of the groups discussed is, in fact, provided by agencies

other than statutory ones; and by families, or more specifically close kin, usually women (Finch and Groves 1983), although also by men (Arber and Gilbert 1989). These agencies and informal carers may or may not receive help from public funds.

Non-statutory organizations have always played an important part in providing social care, children's homes and homes for the elderly being the obvious early examples. Both non-profit and for-profit organizations have continued to be major providers, but from the 1960s onwards, especially during the period under study, the range of work undertaken by such agencies has grown. The voluntary sector, which we here define as comprising non-statutory, non-profit, private organizations, was analysed in what became the influential Report of the Wolfenden Committee (1978). It charted the extent and changing nature of the sector and its important complementary role to both statutory services and families.

Throughout the post-war period organizations like Barnardo's, the National Children's Home, and the National Society for the Prevention of Cruelty to Children (NSPCC) have been diversifying their approach to provide more services supporting and advising families, rather than merely providing residential care. Other groups are also working for less favoured dependent people, such as the mentally ill and handicapped—MIND and MENCAP, for example. They campaign on behalf of those groups, but also provide less traditional services in sheltered staffed homes or work-places. Furthermore, they offer support to carers.

Moreover, a combination of factors has led housing associations to move increasingly into the business of providing care as well as dwellings. In the 1970s the NHS was being asked to provide more new non-hospital facilities for both the mentally ill and the handicapped (see pp. 112–5 above). Whilst local authorities faced constraints, housing associations had a more relaxed subsidy system (see p. 139 above), and the Hostel Deficit Grant supported the extra costs of care when such groups moved into specially designed housing association accommodation. Moreover, their residents could draw DHSS benefits, which they could not do in hospital. These incentives led the NHS to use housing associations as a source of new facilities for hospital residents.

These voluntary groups are not the only source of care outside the state sector. As Webb and Wistow (1987) observe, most people turn most often to their immediate family for help. Care and tending, as Roy Parker (1981) called it, is usually undertaken by spouses or parents, and usually by women for no financial reward (Finch and Groves 1980). Various benefits for the care of disabled dependants have been legislated in this period, such as the Invalid Care Allowance (surrounded by controversy even after its extension to married women carers in 1986). In a climate of public expenditure constraints the significance of such informal care has come to be more widely appreciated by politicians (Audit Commission 1986*b*). The more care that can be shifted from the public taxpayer to the private individual, the easier the pressures on the public spending total. This ideology tends to ignore private costs (financial, social, and health) met by the families concerned. We return to this theme below.

The private 'for-profit' sector has also been increasing in size and importance. The last twenty years have seen rising trends in privately funded residential care (and, to a lesser extent, domiciliary services) (Midwinter 1986). There has also been an increase in the number of local authority services 'contracted out' and supplied by non-statutory profit-making bodies.

Thus, *provision* can be summarized as coming from four sources: the state, non-statutory voluntary organizations, non-statutory 'for-profit' organizations, and the informal sector. Equally, *finance* or provision of *resources* for care (time, in the case of the informal sector) can be seen as coming from both statutory and non-statutory sources. The economy of social care can be conceptualized in terms of the framework in Fig. 6.2.

Conceptually, the involvement of the state in social care is complex. State activity ranges from the regulation and inspection of private provision, whether homes for the elderly or child-minder provision in people's own homes, through the direct provision of residential and day-care services, to payments for services provided in the private sector. Such payments may buy services of a formal kind, like a place in a home, or be cash payments to carers. Private funding may either take the form of charges levied by local authorities to help pay the costs of residential care or home helps, or it may constitute fees paid for the purchase of services from non-statutory sources. This could also be taken to extend to charitable donations.

By far the greatest proportion of care is provided by the informal sector, i.e. the bottom right-hand box (Bayley 1973; Moroney 1976; Walker 1982*b*; Finch and Groves 1983). This is also the most difficult cell to quantify in terms of finance, as the greater part of the input constitutes time rather than money. Government survey data show that 14 per cent of adults in Britain provide care to children and to adults who cannot look after themselves independently; that is, one in seven individuals. The policy implications of these 6 million carers are far-reaching and likely to gain greater urgency with future rises in the number of the frail elderly. Attempts to put figures to the costs of informal care raise fundamental theoretical issues, which we deal with later in the chapter (Nissel and Bonnerjea 1982; EOC 1980).

Different governments have put different emphases on the alternative elements in the matrix. In the following sections we use the framework developed here and attempt to establish the extent to which these differ-

	STATE ACTIVITY		PRIVATE SECTOR ACTIVITY			
	Regulation	Provision	Formal organization		Informal	
			Non-profit	Profit	Family	Neighbours etc.
STATE RESOURCES	regulation of private and voluntary homes, child-minders, nurseries, etc.	provision of services: residential homes, day care, meals on wheels, home helps	homes and hostels, clubs, visiting paid for out of DHSS, local authority, or DoE funds	residential homes, fees paid by DHSS or local authorities	attendance allowance from DHSS	payment to visitors, helpers, etc., by local authority
PRIVATE RESOURCES	fees paid for registration/ certification	charges paid by residents of homes, charges for home helps	homes fees paid by users or charitable donations	fees paid by or for users of homes or domestic services	opportunity cost of time spent caring, plus heating etc.	opportunity cost of travel, resources given etc.

FIG. 6.2. The mixed economy of social care

ing policies have resulted in changes in the balance of the mixed economy of social care over time, shifting resources and the responsibility of provision between cells.

To evaluate how successful different governments have been in meeting their different policy goals we need to look at changes in government provision to different client groups over time, different forms of care, and also the balance and substitutability between the statutory and non-statutory sectors. However, since the standard and availability of services is likely to be a function of the amount of resources devoted to them, we shall begin the next section by examining the trend over time in total government expenditure on the PSS. We examine expenditure in relation to changes in need as well as in policy.

II. EXPENDITURE TRENDS AND SERVICE OUTPUTS

The post-war period witnessed a dramatic increase in spending on what are now the PSS. In 1955 the equivalent of today's PSS accounted for just 0.2 per cent of GNP, but by the start of our period this had quintupled to about 1 per cent. The newly emergent social services experienced the fastest growth rate of all the social programmes throughout the 1950s and 1960s (Gould and Roweth 1980), although it must be noted that this was from a very low base. They expanded their share in total public expenditure from 0.6 per cent in 1955 to 1.9 per cent in 1975/6; and expenditure on the PSS grew at double the pace of growth for all social welfare expenditure. In the first four years after the establishment of the new SSDs in 1971, expenditure in constant prices increased by 74 per cent (Ferlie and Judge 1981). However, our period of study begins just as the 'golden age for spending' was about to come to an end. As we shall see, the adverse economic climate of the 1970s and a period of retrenchment in public expenditure put an end to differential growth.

Total expenditure

Table 6.2 shows total real expenditure on the PSS for the United King- dom from 1973/4 to 1987/8. Total expenditure on the PSS continued to increase throughout the 1970s and 1980s, although the pace at which it occurred was considerably slower than that experienced in the previous two decades. Expenditure, including capital expenditure, over the period up to 1987/8 grew by 55 per cent, an annualized rate of 3.2 per cent.

The growth has not, however, been consistent over the entire period. The Labour years (1973/4–1978/9) witnessed growth rates on average of 3.4 per cent per year whilst during the Conservative administrations (1978/9–1987/8) growth slowed to an average of 3.1 per cent per year. Most of the growth during the Labour government occurred in the first two years up to 1976, after which real expenditure actually fell. It did not return to the 1976/7 level until 1980/1. Again, during the first years of the Conservative governments there was a large injection of cash, following both the 1979 and 1983 elections. However, in the intervening years expenditure was largely stationary in real terms and actually fell slightly in 1981/2 and 1987/8. Fig. 6.3 looks at the components of this expenditure.

The PSS capital programme provides primarily for building new and improving existing residential accommodation and day facilities for the elderly, the physically or mentally handicapped and mentally ill, and children in care. Capital spending fell dramatically over the entire period. This was in part due to the shift of emphasis in planning away from residential care to care in the community. However, capital expenditure suffered disproportionately during a period of fiscal restraint, almost halving after 1976/7. It recovered slightly towards the end of the Labour administration, and positive rates of projected growth were included in the 1978 White Paper. These were scheduled for 1980/1. With the working through of these capital expenditure plans, capital spending rose in the early 1980s, only to fall again, as shown by Table 6.3 and Fig. 6.4.

Table 6.2. *Real government expenditure on the personal social services, United Kingdom*

	£m. (1987/8 prices)	As % of GDP	Index of real spending (1973/4 = 100)
1973/4	2,478	0.7	100
1974/5	2,875	0.9	116
1975/6	3,202	1.0	129
1976/7	3,266	1.0	132
1977/8	2,839	0.8	115
1978/9	2,922	0.8	118
1979/80	3,132	0.9	126
1980/1	3,304	0.9	133
1981/2	3,266	0.9	132
1982/3	3,300	0.9	133
1983/4	3,408	0.9	138
1984/5	3,460	0.9	140
1985/6	3,783	1.0	153
1986/7	3,974	1.0	160
1987/8	3,844	0.9	155

Note: Annualized growth rates: 1973/4–1978/9: 3.4%; 1978/9–1987/8: 3.1%; 1973/4–1987/8: 3.2%.

Sources: CSO 1985*b*, 1986*b*, 1988*c*, 1989*c*: table 3.4; GDP deflator from HM Treasury 1989.

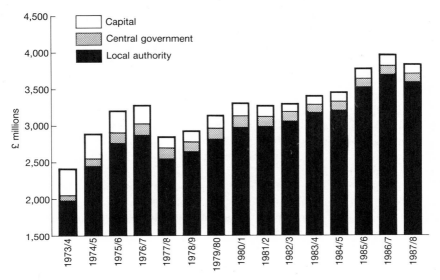

Sources: CSO 1985*b*, 1986*b*, 1988*c*, 1989*c*: table 3.4; GDP deflator from HM Treasury 1989

FIG. 6.3. Components of expenditure on personal social services, United Kingdom

Table 6.3. *Index of real government expenditure on the personal social services, United Kingdom* (1973/4 = 100)

	Local authority running expenses	Central government	Capital	Total
1973/4	100	100	100	100
1974/5	120	133	89	116
1975/6	136	172	82	129
1976/7	141	189	67	132
1977/8	125	188	38	115
1978/9	130	165	41	118
1979/80	138	189	45	126
1980/1	146	199	46	133
1981/2	147	160	40	132
1982/3	151	154	30	133
1983/4	156	146	31	138
1984/5	158	146	34	140
1985/6	174	145	37	153
1986/7	182	147	41	160
1987/8	177	150	35	155

Sources: CSO 1985*b*, 1986*b*, 1988*c*, 1989*c*: table 3.4; GDP deflator from HM Treasury 1989.

The current expenditure programme provides for the running costs of residential homes and day centres, for field social work, and for domiciliary support services, including aids and adaptations for physically handicapped people. In Scotland it also covers probation and after-care. Current expenditure by local authorities constitutes the major component of total expenditure, and has followed the trends for total spending outlined above. Current expenditure by central government is largely in the form of grants for specific projects, and constitutes a small proportion of total expenditure. Central government spending rose rapidly during the first part of the Labour years, then fell and recovered up to 1980/1, since when it has declined.

In terms of real expenditure, the different services under the umbrella of PSS have fared rather differently (Table 6.4). Spending within the miscellaneous category has increased dramatically (see end of Annexe to this chapter for key), but it constitutes a very small proportion of total expenditure. Of the major services, expenditure on day-care services increased the most rapidly over the period, and the growth rate of expenditure on community care exceeded that of residential care.

Total net local authority current expenditure on PSS within Great Britain grew rapidly at a rate of 7.6 per cent per year over the period

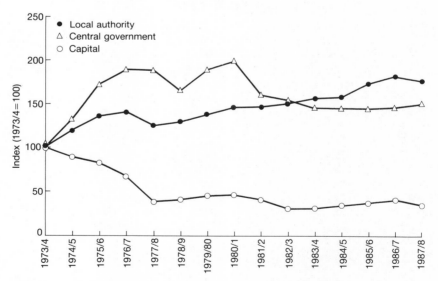

Sources: CSO 1985*b*, 1986*b*, 1988*c*, 1989*c*: table 3.4; GDP deflator from HM Treasury 1989

FIG. 6.4. Indices of components of expenditure on personal social services, United Kingdom

1973/4–1978/9. The rate of growth then fell to 2.4 per cent for the later period. These figures give a more differentiated view of growth between the two governments than that given by the growth rates presented at the bottom of Table 6.2. This is due to the exclusion of capital spending, which, as we have seen, fell dramatically in the seventies. In short, the period was one of rapid, then slower growth, although still positive.

Central government plans and local government spending

Public expenditure on PSS is almost wholly incurred by local authorities. It is financed by central government to the extent implied in the Rate Support Grant. Central government exercises control through cash limits on the total Rate Support Grant and on local authority capital spending, as well as through the Rate Support Grant formula and more recently rate-capping, but it cannot influence the mix of local authority spending. Thus, although total levels of expenditure allowed for by central govern-

Table 6.4. *Real net current expenditure by local authorities on the personal social services, by service sector,[a] Great Britain* (£ million at 1987/8 prices)

	Field-work	Residential care	Day care	Community care	Misc.	Total
1973/4	325	974	215	487	20	2,020
1974/5	435	1,090	263	594	48	2,429
1975/6	440	1,252	283	611	48	2,634
1976/7	466	1,416	288	643	52	2,865
1977/8	447	1,409	288	631	67	2,842
1978/9	449	1,438	305	661	67	2,920
1979/80	493	1,501	306	673	69	3,041
1980/1	530	1,571	332	686	76	3,195
1981/2	534	1,555	348	697	81	3,216
1982/3	542	1,572	370	732	84	3,300
1983/4	565	1,591	392	786	92	3,427
1984/5	579	1,559	406	800	98	3,442
1985/6	585	1,514	423	833	99	3,454
Real growth rates (% per year)						
1973/4–1978/9	6.7	8.1	7.2	6.3		7.6
1978/9–1985/6	3.9	0.7	4.8	3.3		2.4
1973/4–1985/6	5.0	3.7	5.8	4.6		4.6

[a] See key at end of Annexe to this chapter for allocation of expenditures to categories.

Sources: DHSS 1978: table 2.10 and equivalent for later years; Welsh Office 1979: table 2.10 and equivalent for later years; Scottish Office 1980: table 4.8 and equivalent for later years; GDP deflator from HM Treasury 1989.

ment were restrained by both political parties, decisions concerning the distribution and level of expenditure between individual services lie largely in hands of local authorities.

During the 1970s total spending by SSDs largely followed central government plans. In fact, from 1976/7 to 1978/9 local authorities underspent planned expenditure on PSS by between 0.5 per cent and 2 per cent (HM Treasury 1978, 1979a). Despite reductions in planned growth the PSS were largely protected from the cuts in expenditure experienced by other sectors during the 1970s, following the visit to the IMF. Although expenditure fell, the share of PSS in GDP was maintained at about 0.8 per cent. The cuts, as we have seen, were largely concentrated on capital rather than current expenditure. From Table 6.3 it can be seen that local authority spending on PSS in *real* terms fell in 1977/8, but recovered to its previous level within three years. In *volume* terms, however, even in 1977 local authority expenditure experienced a small increase (Ferlie and Judge 1981). This was due to a temporary negative relative price effect as a result of rigorous enforcement of an incomes policy in the public sector.

Thus, in the late 1970s both central government and local government were concerned to protect the relative position of PSS in the face of fiscal constraint. A low rate of growth of 2 per cent (in real terms), that is, that deemed necessary to maintain pace with changes in need, remained the target for growth in successive White Papers, with higher rates being envisaged in the future.

In the 1980s, however, policy changed. The Conservative government proposed radical reductions in PSS planned expenditure as part of an overall strategy to reduce total local authority spending. The Public Expenditure White Paper for 1980 indicated that current expenditure on PSS should be decreased by 6.7 per cent in volume terms in 1980/1. But during the fiscal restraint of the previous years many local authorities had already reduced their base as far as they were prepared to. Ferlie and Judge (1981) found that during this period SSDs reduced expenditure by only 2 per cent on average, overspending government targets by 4.7 per cent. However, there was variation between local authorities, with some pursuing government guide-lines more strictly than others, as is discussed further below.

The divergence between expenditure projections in successive White Papers and the actual spending levels of local authorities on PSS has increased. Throughout the Conservative government there have been continued calls for reductions in expenditure, yet total current expenditure has continued to grow, although at a reduced rate. In fact, 1981/2 was the first year (and the only one until 1987/8) that current expenditure on PSS fell in real terms. Local authority expenditure has been maintained in the face of centrally planned cuts.

In the early 1980s the Secretary of State, in evidence to the House of Commons Social Services Committee (1982), took the view that 'Local Authorities are "perfectly entitled" to spend more on PSS provided they keep within government overall expenditure targets.' He further stated, 'White Paper projections are indicative figures which were put in for the purpose of giving an indication, they are not planning figures, they are not a target in any sense which we would expect local authorities to follow.' In fact, increased expenditure was condoned as local authorities continued to 'protect the most vulnerable in society'. However, there was a growing planning paradox, with the Department of the Environment decreasing total levels of local authority spending, while the DHSS continued to issue directives for increased community care involving rises in social service provision, and thus in SSDs' expenditure. Continued increases in expenditure on PSS did lead to local authorities overspending, and in 1985 rate-capping for high-spending authorities was introduced, with the effect of damping growth and, as we shall see, reducing levels of service provision at the end of our research period. This had the perverse effect of penalizing local authorities which actively pursued the government aim of increasing community care.

Joint finance   The continued growth in expenditure on PSS was in part facilitated by the inclusion of joint finance projects in the figures. 'Joint finance has acted as an ever increasing source of inescapable growth in PSS revenue budgets' (Webb and Wistow 1986: 38). Health Service provision for joint finance schemes with local authorities to develop community care increased by about 60 per cent in real terms from nearly £35 million in 1978/9 to £105 million in 1985/6 (HM Treasury 1986: 215). The provision of such financing has allowed SSDs to expand provision in a period of increasing constraint on local authority budgets. However, there are problems involved with joint finance pick-up. Growth is needed in SSD budgets to continue to finance projects or provision once joint finance has expired, and this growth will be in addition to that necessary to keep pace with demographic and other changes. Thus, although joint finance has allowed growth of expenditure in the face of fiscal restraint, it also requires increased future growth to maintain present standards. It is not clear what the implications will be of community care schemes whose joint funding status runs out in the next five to ten years.

Charging   Another reason gross current spending on certain PSS has continued to rise is the increasing importance of charges during the 1980s. Cuts in central government finance and the need for income generation have meant that many local authorities have introduced charges or increased existing charges for domiciliary services. The Association of

Directors of Social Services (ADSS) reported to the House of Commons Social Services Committee in 1982 that 'local authorities who need to save money may well feel obliged to impose charges for services which were formerly free or to raise the level of those existing charges' (HC, Social Services Committee, 1982: p. xlvi). The income generated from such action has enabled some local authorities to prevent or avert cuts in services (Hedley and Norman 1982). This has resulted in an increase in the 'private funding of public provision'.

Statistics show that the number of metropolitan authorities and county councils which charged for the provision of home helps totalled ninety in 1984/5 (CIPFA 1985). The ADSS (1980) carried out a survey on the extent and effect of cuts/savings in expenditure on PSS. They found that most local authorities were cutting at least one domiciliary service, or that they were either introducing or increasing charges. The following year's ADSS survey found that the majority of local authorities had increased charges in line with, or above, the rate of inflation (HC, Social Services Committee, 1982).

Table 6.5 shows income from fees and charges as a percentage of PSS expenditure. No marked upward trend is visible in the total percentage, although the income from certain service areas has grown. However, the fact that the overall percentage has been fairly stable is worthy of note in itself. This has been despite the main income-generating service, i.e.

Table 6.5. *Fees as a percentage of personal social services expenditure, England*

Service area	1983/4	1984/5	1985/6	1986/7
Children in residential care	9.6	9.3	9.0	9.4
Residential care for the elderly, younger physically handicapped, blind, and deaf	36.2	35.6	41.7	39.5
Other residential care, including training and administration	10.4	10.4	11.3	11.1
Home helps	7.0	7.2	7.5	6.9
Meals in the home	36.1	38.5	38.1	38.3
Day care	5.4	4.9	4.8	4.6
Other	1.6	1.3	1.3	6.6
Total	13.8	13.5	14.9	15.3

Sources: HC, Social Services Committee, 1987, 1988.

residential care, constituting a declining proportion of total PSS. The fees and charges figures include charges to other local authorities, as well as income from users. It is interesting to note that it has been the services where *income from individual users* makes up a high proportion of the total income from fees and charges that have experienced the greatest rise: in particular, services for residential care of the elderly, where charges constituted 97 per cent of income generated in 1985/6; home helps 98 per cent; and meals 76 per cent (HC, Social Services Committee, 1988).

Regional variation Regional variation in charging is clear: recipients of the home-help service living in non-metropolitan districts in 1984/5 were more likely to be charged than users in London boroughs or metropolitan districts (CIPFA 1985). At the same time, expenditure in non-metropolitan districts was growing more rapidly than in metropolitan districts.

Despite real average growth in expenditure over our period, there have been wide variations around the mean between, and within, individual local authorities, both at one point in time and across time. Looking at Table 6.6, we see that growth in the earlier period (1977/8–1980/1) across types of local authority was more consistent. Variations in expenditure have increased over time. Furthermore, high levels of expenditure in a few local authorities can inflate aggregate growth measures, e.g. in the case of Inner London. Some overspending local authorities have been rate-capped since 1985/6, and this has reduced overall growth. Real growth for Southwark from 1982/3 to 1986/7 was 12.9 per cent, but the budgeted forecast for 1987/8 showed a reduction of more than 5 per cent on the previous year, as did the forecasts for Lambeth and Harrow (HC, Social Services Committee, 1988: 107). The impact of rate-capping indi-

Table 6.6. *Regional variation in growth of expenditure on personal social services, England* (real expenditure growth, %)

	1977/8–1980/1	1981/2–1985/6
Shire counties	9.0	8.8
Metropolitan districts	14.0	2.7
Inner London	14.0	8.0
Outer London	9.0	5.6
England	11.0	6.6

Source: HC, Social Services Committee, 1982, 1987.

vidual local áuthorities on overall growth rates has yet to work its way through, but it can only act to damp any upward trend.

So far we have only examined expenditure on public provision, be it from central or local government or from the private sector through charges. However, in considering changes in total government spending on the PSS, it is also important to take into account the shift of provision of services and resources to the private sector, as witnessed by the growth in Supplementary Benefit payments. Social security spending in 1985/6 on such services was equivalent to 10 per cent of the total sum spent on PSS (HC, Social Services Committee, 1986). Thus, it could be argued that overall growth in government spending in this sector has not been reduced, just redistributed between departments. One effect of this has been to reduce resources directed to local government and to increase Department of Social Security (DSS) resources, the latter of which is directly under central government control. We return to this theme when the changing 'balance of care' is discussed.

Expenditure and need

Although total real spending on the PSS has grown over the period, how has total government expenditure fared in relation to need? The DHSS in successive White Papers, as mentioned above, has argued that a growth rate of 2 per cent (in expenditure in real terms) is needed to meet demographic and other 'inescapable' increases in need. Tables 6.2 and 6.4 have shown that total expenditure has increased at a rate of 3.3 per cent per year over the entire period, and if capital expenditure is excluded, current spending on goods and services has increased at a rate of 4.6 per cent per year. In the light of this, growth in expenditure on the PSS appears not only to have kept pace with changes in need but to have exceeded them, which should result in improved services. However, these figures take no account of inflation within the sector. The 1985/6 Report of the House of Commons Select Committee on Social Services stated that over the five years 1980/1–1984/5 the PSS inflation rate exceeded the general inflation rate by 3.4 per cent. This is due to the higher than average labour intensity of PSS activities.

Volume expenditure   A consistent series for a service-specific volume deflator for the PSS over time is difficult to obtain. From 1982 onwards public expenditure plans were expressed in cash terms. Under the new cash-planning system no volume plans have been produced. However, Table 6.7 shows two series of indices of current expenditure oń the PSS at constant volume prices. The two series are drawn from different sources: Ferlie and Judge (1981), who use a deflator derived from CSO Blue

Books; and Robinson (1986), who used a deflator derived from the House of Commons reports. They cover different periods and so are not directly comparable. Nevertheless, they serve to illustrate actual levels of growth in the capacity to purchase increased levels of service provision in the PSS over time.

The annualized rates of growth in volume terms are, as we would expect, lower than the comparable rates of growth in constant prices for both periods obtained from Table 6.4. Irrespective of which deflator is used, the Conservative years clearly show a slower rate of growth. Most importantly, after 1979/80 the annualized growth rate in volume terms of 1.5 per cent falls below the 'target 2 per cent'. Thus, even if we accept the government allowance of 2 per cent growth in real expenditure as being adequate for meeting changes in need over time, it is questionable whether PSS have kept up, particularly since 1979/80.

It is not sufficient to look to expenditure alone. Expenditure measured in volume terms averages inflation across the sector, while the production of services is sensitive both to service-specific inflation, e.g. changes in the cost of residential care versus day care, and to local variations in these rates. Changes in expenditure may not be directly translated into changes in service outputs. Actual levels of service provision therefore need to be taken into account.

Service outputs   Table 6.8 shows selected activity statistics for the period 1977–87 drawn from the Public Expenditure White Papers. These figures provide us with an idea of what has been 'bought' by the growth in expenditure over that period. Given positive rates of growth in both current and volume expenditure across the period, one might expect this to be reflected in increases in service provision. However, there have

Table 6.7. *Indices of volume of current expenditure on the personal social services, at constant prices, 1974–1979 and 1979/80–1984/5*

Series 1		Series 2	
1974	100	1979/80	100
1975	115.4	1980/1	102.8
1976	119.6	1981/2	101.5
1977	119.8	1982/3	103.7
1978	127.3	1983/4	107.1
1979	131.9	1984/5	107.9

Note: Annualized rate of growth: series 1: 5.7%; series 2: 1.5%.

Sources: Series 1 derived from Ferlie and Judge 1981: table 2 (p. 313); series 2 from Robinson 1986: table 6 (p. 12).

Table 6.8. *Personal social services: Activity statistics,[a] England ('000)[b]*

	1977	1978	1979	1980	1981	1982	1983	1984	1985	1986	1987
Residential care (sponsored residents)											
Elderly	117.0	117.9	117.1	118.8	117.2	116.8	115.5	112.3	110.0	106.9	104.7
Younger physically handicapped	10.3	10.2	10.0	9.3	9.8	9.1	9.0	8.7	8.0	7.3	6.9
Mentally ill[c]	4.4	4.7	4.9	5.0	4.4	4.5	4.3	4.0	3.9	3.8	3.6
Mentally handicapped											
adults[c]	12.0	11.4	12.0	12.8	13.5	14.1	14.9	15.4	15.5	15.8	16.0
children[c]	n.a.	1.7	1.7	1.8	1.8	1.8	1.8	1.6	1.4	1.3	1.1
Children in residential care	36.0	34.4	32.8	32.5	29.7	26.4	22.1	18.2	16.1	15.1	14.3
Day care (places)											
Mixed clients	10.7	11.1	12.3	12.8	13.9	14.7	15.7	16.0	17.0	17.3	17.4
Elderly	15.3	17.5	18.9	20.0	20.7	21.5	21.1	21.5	21.8	21.6	21.9
Younger physically handicapped	10.3	10.4	10.2	9.8	9.6	9.4	9.1	9.4	8.7	9.1	9.0
Mentally ill	4.3	4.7	5.3	5.7	5.7	5.8	6.4	6.6	6.7	6.6	7.1
Mentally handicapped adult training centres	38.9	40.8	42.1	42.3	43.6	45.2	46.6	47.5	48.8	50.4	51.2
Children under 5 (day nurseries)	29.0	29.1	30.0	30.3	30.2	29.9	30.1	30.3	30.5	30.7	30.7

Support services

Boarded-out children	n.a.	33.1	34.3	35.2	35.7	36.9	36.5	36.1	34.8	35.1	34.6
Home helps (f.t.e.[d] staff)	42.1	44.7	44.7	46.1	46.6	47.3	49.3	50.6	52.0	53.7	56.5
Social workers (f.t.e.[d] staff)	n.a.	22.2	22.7	23.0	23.0	23.0	23.7	24.3	24.8	25.9	27.1
Main meals served	41,171	41,075	40,949	41,738	41,437	40,290	40,960	42,373	42,931	44,111	45,367

[a] Includes facilities and services made available to local authorities by voluntary organizations etc.

[b] The figures given are census-based and relate to 31 March, except for (i) staff numbers, which relate to 30 September; (ii) meals served, which are cumulative totals for the year ending 31 March.

[c] From 1981 the basis for counting supported residents was changed; figures for 1981 and subsequent years are not comparable with those for earlier years.

[d] Full-time-equivalent.

Source: HM Treasury 1981: table 2.11.3 and equivalents for subsequent years.

been reductions in absolute levels of activity in a number of categories, most notably residential care for the elderly and for children in care.

A number of alternative interpretations can be made when analysing the data in Table 6.8. On the surface the data could reflect the substitution of one mix of service provision for another, for example an increase in domiciliary support—home helps and meals—enabling more elderly people to remain in the community, and this being reflected in a decrease in the elderly in residential accommodation. Alternatively they may indicate a fall in the target group, such as the total number of children in care over time. However, the figures could also be interpreted to suggest that expenditure has failed to increase in line with rising unit costs, resulting in a fall in service output. Such activity statistics are limited in that they tell us about the *number* of people reached by the services, but not about *frequency* of use or *quality* of care.

Activity statistics alone tell us little about whether the provision of services allowed for by increasing real expenditure has kept pace with need and with changes in unit costs.

Changing levels of need—is 2 per cent enough?   It is far from clear that the target of 2 per cent real growth is itself an adequate level of growth. It has remained the target for growth in White Papers throughout the 1970s and 1980s, becoming institutionalized through successive planning years. This is despite the fact that over the last fifteen years there have been rapid demographic and socio-demographic changes, such as increases in the numbers of frail, elderly people and one-parent families. Furthermore, these changes have been occurring at an increasing rather than constant rate. In March 1986, the Parliamentary Panel for PSS suggested that a 2 per cent resource target was inadequate to meet the needs of the rapidly increasing number of people aged over 85, the increased number of carers, the planned growth in community care, the number of older children being taken into care, and rising unemployment levels (HC, Social Services Committee, 1986).

Table 6.9 shows changes in potential service client groups over time. Apart from a slight fall in the number of children under five in the population and the number of older children in care, there have been significant rises across the board. Most striking in an increase of nearly fivefold in the number of very severely handicapped people in the population, which are a key consumer group within the PSS.

Volume data take into account changes in unit costs, but do not allow for changes in need. As an alternative to volume expenditure data, Webb and Wistow (1986) employ a concept of constant level of service output (per head of the relevant population) as a useful analytical baseline or yardstick. Growth is needed in SSD revenue to avoid a reduction in existing levels of outputs.

Webb and Wistow (1986) conclude from their data analysis that a 2 per cent growth allowance has been insufficient to provide a constant level of service outputs over time, taking into account rises in unit costs, joint finance pick-up, and increases in need. A constant level of service outputs with respect to the elderly population has not been maintained, despite comparatively high levels of expenditure growth. Indeed, in some instances the level of service output has even fallen in absolute terms.

In our analysis we adopt this approach—of a constant level of service output—in order to assess the performance of PSS in relation to the needs of the elderly over the whole of the period of study (1974/5–1986/7). This extends work by both Webb and Wistow (1983) and the Family Policy Studies Centre (FPSC 1984, 1989). Table 6.10 shows selected service provision in absolute terms and per 1,000 elderly people, which we have taken to approximate to changes in need for this client group over time. The data source used here, CIPFA 'actuals', is different from that used to compile Table 6.8, and so the figures are not comparable. Coverage is for England and Wales, although it should be pointed out that the returns from local authorities are not always complete.

The percentage change in provision has been estimated over the whole period, as well as over the Labour and Conservative years. The clear

Table 6.9. *Growth in potential demand for personal social services, England* ('000 of people)

	1975	1981	1987
Very severely handicapped	15.6	59.1	76.1
	1975	1982	1986
Blind	99.3	111.7	120.5
	1975	1983	1986
Deaf	25.6	31.8	34.1
	1975	1981	1986
Aged 85 or over	451.9	511.3	603.3
Children aged under 5	3,227.9	2,833.4	3,004.2
Older (16+) children in care	19.0	22.7	17.8
Unemployed[a]	1,079.0	2,383.0	3,041.0

[a] 'Unemployed' defined as recipient of unemployment cash benefit.

Source: DHSS 1987*a* and earlier equivalents.

Table 6.10. *Elderly population and the personal social services: Indices, England and Wales*

	Number, 1974/5	Index (1974/5 = 100)													% change		
		1974/5	1975/6	1976/7	1977/8	1978/9	1979/80	1980/1	1981/2	1982/3	1983/4	1984/5	1985/6	1986/7	1986/7 on 1974/5	1978/9 on 1974/5	1986/7 on 1978/9
Total elderly pop. ('000)																	
aged 65+	6,929.2	100	101.5	102.7	104.1	105.6	106.9	108.3	108.9	108.9	108.2	107.9	110.2	111.9	+12	+6	+6
aged 75+	2,468.2	100	102.2	104.5	107.1	109.9	112.6	115.8	118.7	121.7	123.5	128.3	131.2	133.4	+33	+10	+23
Total elderly in residential care																	
('000)	107.2	100	102.4	107.4	108.7	110.0	109.3	110.8	109.1	109.1	107.8	104.8	102.6	99.6	0	+10	−10
per '000 pop. 65+	16.4	100	100.9	104.5	104.5	104.2	102.2	102.4	100.1	100.1	99.6	97.2	93.2	89.1	−11	+4	−15
per '000 pop. 75+	46.1	100	100.2	102.8	101.6	100.1	97.1	95.8	91.9	87.6	86.3	81.7	78.3	74.7	−25	0	−25
Home helps ('000 full-time-equivalents)	42.1	100	119.2	110.8	115.8	118.1	115.4	119.4	120.6	122.1	119.2	128.4	120.4	123.4[a]	+23	+18	+4
per '000 pop. 65+	6.1	100	117.4	107.8	111.2	111.8	107.9	110.3	110.7	112.1	110.1	119.1	109.3	110.3	+10	+12	−2
per '000 pop. 75+	17.0	100	116.6	106.1	108.1	107.5	102.5	103.2	101.6	100.3	96.5	100.1	91.8	92.4	−8	+8	−16
Meals ('000)	38,330	100	107.7	110.6	107.1	105.0	111.3	107.6	107.1	111.8	105.6	109.8	114.0	97.2[a]	−3	+5	−8
per '000 pop. 65+	5,532	100	106.1	107.6	102.8	99.5	104.1	99.4	98.4	102.6	97.6	101.8	103.5	86.9	−13	−1	−12
per '000 pop. 75+	15,529	100	105.3	105.8	100.0	95.6	98.8	93.0	90.3	91.8	85.5	85.6	86.9	72.8	−27	−4	−23

[a] CIPFA data local authority coverage was incomplete. This figure may therefore be an underestimate.

Sources: Residential care: DHSS 1987a and earlier equivalents; population figures: OPCS archives; all other data: CIPFA 1985 and earlier equivalents.

fall in per capita residential care between 1974/5 and 1986/7 is wholly accounted for by the post-1978/9 trends. The fall in provision is most marked in relation to the number of those aged over 75. Home-help provision increased by 23 per cent, 18 per cent of which was accounted for during the Labour period. When demographic change is taken into account, per capita provision fell, beginning in 1976/7—although the decrease was greater after 1978/9. Provision of meals fell, particularly in relation to the number of very elderly people. However, the meals figure for 1986/7 is not reliable and so should be interpreted with some degree of circumspection. What is evident from these statistics is that both residential and domiciliary services have failed to keep pace with increases in the level of potential demand. This is particularly clear during the Conservative years, with services experiencing negative growth which is compounded further when demographic changes in the target population are taken into account.

Thus, our expenditure (inputs) and service provision (outputs) figures would appear to have revealed trends which are not compatible with the strategy of community care and with the policy objective of 'protecting the most vulnerable'. Below we go on to examine these policy goals in more detail.

III. POLICY OUTCOMES

In this section we examine the extent to which policy aims and goals, other than general expenditure constraint, over our period of study have been met by the different governments. For the purposes of presentation the policies of targeting resources at the priority groups, the success or failure of the promotion of 'community care', and the extent to which changes in the balance of care within the 'mixed economy of welfare' have occurred are addressed separately. However, they are not the outcome of separate policy decisions, but rather are all interrelated. Indeed, the White Papers outlining policies for services for mentally ill and mentally handicapped people themselves proposed a shift in the pattern of service delivery from hospitals to community-based services and from health to social services.

Priority groups

It has been a major policy objective for many years to foster and develop community care for the main client groups—namely the elderly, mentally ill, mentally handicapped and disabled people as well as for the special and smaller groups such as alcoholics. (DHSS 1981*a*)

Two White Papers were published in the early seventies setting out policies for individual client groups: *Better Services for the Mentally Handicapped* in 1971, followed by *Better Services for the Mentally Ill* in 1975. However, *Priorities for Health and Personal Social Services in England* (DHSS 1976c) was the first document to establish 'rational and systematic priorities throughout the health and personal social services' (p. 1). It set the average rates of increase for current expenditure that would be necessary to fulfil the priorities proposed by the document. These were 2.2 per cent a year for services used by children and families with children; 3.2 per cent for services used by the elderly; 2.8 per cent for those directed at the mentally handicapped; and 1.8 per cent for those services used by the mentally ill. As stated in Chapter 4 above, the main emphasis was on community rather than hospital care, and thus increased services for these groups from the PSS. An overall growth rate of current expenditure for PSS of 2.9 per cent a year up to 1979/80 was proposed. This was to be made up of an annual increase in expenditure on residential care of about 2.6 per cent, on day care of about 5 per cent, and on the community support services such as home helps and meal services of 2 per cent.

The 1981 policy document *Care in Action* (DHSS 1981a) did not explicitly update these targets, but reiterated the general objectives of the earlier White Papers.

Table 6.11. *Index of real net public expenditure by local authorities on the personal social services, by service sector,[a] Great Britain* (1973/4 = 100)

	Field-work	Residential care	Day care	Community care	Misc.	Total
1973/4	100	100	100	100	100	100
1974/5	134	112	122	122	242	120
1975/6	136	128	132	126	243	130
1976/7	144	145	134	132	263	142
1977/8	138	145	134	130	340	141
1978/9	138	148	142	136	342	145
1979/80	152	154	142	138	351	151
1980/1	163	161	155	141	387	158
1981/2	165	160	162	143	410	159
1982/3	167	161	172	150	429	163
1983/4	174	163	183	162	470	170
1984/5	178	160	189	164	497	170
1985/6	180	155	197	171	502	171

[a] See key at end of Annexe to this chapter for allocation of expenditure to categories.

Sources: DHSS 1978: table 2.10 and equivalent for later years; Welsh Office 1979: table 2.10 and equivalent for later years; Scottish Office 1980: table 4.8 and equivalent for later years; GDP deflator from HM Treasury 1989.

Table 6.11 gives an index of real net expenditure by local authorities on PSS over the period. Expenditure on day care grew the most rapidly, although from a lower base than the other groups (see Table 6.4). The targets for growth over the period were met, and exceeded, up to 1979/80, and growth continued in later years, although at a reduced rate.

The client groups fared differently. Table 6.12 gives expenditure for England and Wales by client group as a whole. Expenditure on children increased by 22 per cent, on the elderly by 48 per cent, and on the 'other' category (includes younger physically disabled, mentally handicapped, and mentally ill) by 70 per cent. The majority of the increase in the latter group was accounted for by an increased number of residential places. Residential care expenditure on this group increased by 144 per cent from 1974/5 to 1984/5.

Although expenditure increased, we have seen that this is not necessarily translated into an increase in service provision. Below we examine each client group in turn in order to see if policy directives and/or targets concerning provision have been met.

Table 6.12. *Real net expenditure on the personal social services in England and Wales, by client group[a]* (£ million at 1987/8 prices)

	Children	Elderly	Other[b]
1974/5	557	801	256
1975/6	608	849	279
1976/7	613	1,018	292
1977/8	605	1,009	301
1978/9	618	1,042	320
1979/80	644	1,074	331
1980/1	683	1,099	346
1981/2	688	1,086	364
1982/3	695	1,122	388
1983/4	699	1,164	419
1984/5	680	1,189	435
Real growth rates (% per year)			
1974/5–1978/9	2.6	6.8	5.7
1978/9–1984/5	1.6	2.2	5.3
1974/5–1984/5	2.0	4.0	5.4

[a] Includes expenditure on administration where allocation possible, but excludes expenditure on field-work. See key at end of Annexe to this chapter for detailed allocation of expenditure to categories.

[b] 'Other' includes younger physically handicapped, mentally handicapped, and mentally ill.

Sources: DHSS 1978 and equivalent for later years; Welsh Office 1979 and equivalent for later years; GDP deflator from HM Treasury 1989.

Children 'Social Services Authorities are required to admit to care any child under 17 who is in need of care, where the Authority considers it necessary to do so in the child's interest' (Audit Commission 1986*a*). It is their duty to keep the child in care until 18 where his/her welfare requires it. The authority's major objective is the child's rehabilitation, and that the vast majority of children in care should eventually return to their own homes. The main policy objective is 'in developing forms of help which minimise the need to take the child away from the family' (DHSS 1976*c*: 64). This has remained the consistent goal throughout the period. The accepted view is that 'it is better not to disrupt a child's family relationship by taking him/her into care unless the family clearly cannot provide an acceptable level of parenting and there is no better alternative to local authority care' (Audit Commission 1986*a*: 17). Thus a preventive approach is of prime importance.

Government policy emphasizes the usefulness of preventive services. Social service authorities have a duty to provide preventive services such as pre-school play-groups, support for parents, self-help centres, mother-and-toddler groups, encouragement of child-minding, day nurseries, out-of-school supervision and activities, holiday schemes, and respite care to give parents a break.

Fig. 6.5 shows the trend in the numbers of children in the legal care of their local authority in England over time. There was a rise in the number of children taken into care through the 1970s, but there has been a

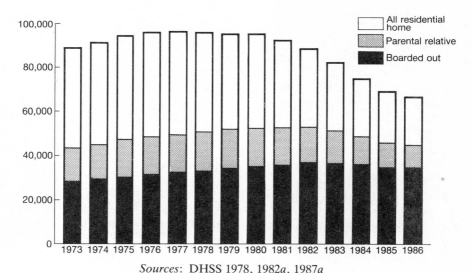

Sources: DHSS 1978, 1982*a*, 1987*a*

Fɪɢ. 6.5. Children in care, by manner of accommodation, England marked decline since 1980. It is difficult to interpret these figures, as it is not clear whether they reflect success or failure on the part of SSDs. The picture is further complicated in that demographic shifts have resulted in a decline in the number of children in the population as the 'baby-boomers' of the late 1950s and early 1960s moved into adulthood, along with a declining birth rate through the 1970s. Taking the number of children in care as a proportion of all children, the decline is much less steep.

The number of children entering into care owing to child abuse has been the subject of much publicity across the period. The DHSS does not, however, collect information specifically on child abuse, as children subject to abuse may come into care through a variety of legal routes and are thus not separately identifiable in the statistics collected. The NSPCC does collect figures from child abuse registers, but only in selected localities, and it is not possible to present a consistent time series.

It is possible to approach the question from the opposite direction and look at changes in the provision of preventive services directed at children over time. The number of day nursery places provided by local authorities for children under five has increased, although the rate of increase has slowed from 1979 onwards. This reflects the fall in the number of pre-school children within the population. But the number of children alone is not a good indicator of demand. There has been an increase in female labour-force participation across the period. The last fifteen years have also witnessed a rise in the number of lone mothers. Given these trends it would not be unrealistic to predict an increase in demand for nursery places for a given number of children under five.

Fig. 6.6 also shows the number of children registered at local authority nurseries over the same period. This figure has continued to rise over the period, and the ratio of children to places has increased dramatically over the 1980s as the rise in places has stagnated. There are more part-time attenders. The number of children placed with child-minders or attending privately run nurseries has increased over time, and in total there were nearly 200 places per 1,000 children aged under five in 1985 compared with about 140 in 1973 (Fig. 6.7).

Elderly There are currently just over 10 million people in the UK population aged 65 or over. Old people are the major users of most PSS, and those aged over 75 are the heaviest users. This group has increased in size dramatically over our period of study, from 2.8 million in 1974, to 3.1 million in 1979, to 3.7 million in 1986. The general aim of policy is to help elderly people maintain independent lives within the community, and thus the main emphasis of policy from both governments has been on the development of domiciliary services.

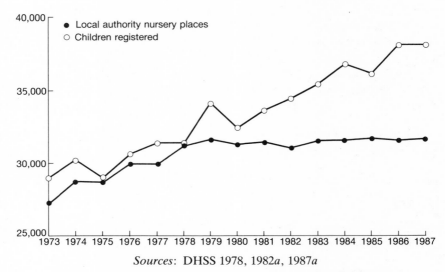

Sources: DHSS 1978, 1982*a*, 1987*a*

FIG. 6.6. Local authority day nurseries (part-time and full-time), England

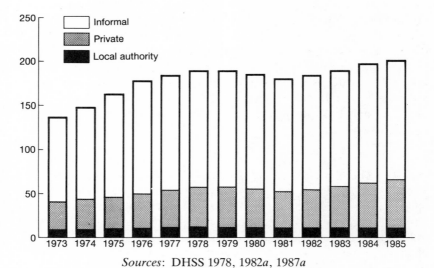

Sources: DHSS 1978, 1982*a*, 1987*a*

FIG. 6.7. Child-care places per 1,000 children aged under five, England

SSDs provide a wide range of services for the elderly. There are no requirements for the level of service provided. However, they are under statutory obligation to provide 'adequate' home-help services and services for mentally or physically handicapped or mentally ill people who may be elderly, and so to this extent there is some degree of regulation.

Priorities for the Health and Personal Social Services (DHSS 1976c) quoted targets and guide-lines for domiciliary service provision which were endorsed in 1977 in *The Way Forward* (DHSS 1977a): 12 home helps per 1,000 elderly population (aged 65 or over), and 200 meals provided per 1,000 elderly. In general, these were not met, and in fact, in 1981/2, the numbers of home helps and meals provided were lower than in 1975/6—when the guide-lines were first set (see Table 6.10). There is wide variation across local authorities: for example, in 1986 only 16 out of 109 authorities achieved the national guide-lines for home-help provision. In 1987, ten years after the targets were set, there were on average just under 7 full-time-equivalent home helps per 1,000 people aged 65 or over and about 100 meals provided for the same group, i.e. the level of provision has remained at approximately half of the target level. Domiciliary services for the elderly have failed to keep pace with the increasing number of people aged over 75 in the population, as Figs. 6.8 and 6.9 demonstrate.

Other services provided by local authorities for the elderly have also shown little increase over the period. From Table 6.8 it can be seen that the absolute level of SSD provision of residential care for the elderly (in local authority homes and sponsored places in private and voluntary homes) has fallen, despite an increase in the size of the 'target group'. This is examined in greater detail later. However, on a more optimistic note Table 6.8 also shows a marked increase in day-care places for elderly clients, rising from 15,300 in 1977 to 21,900 in 1987.

Mentally handicapped and mentally ill   About 0.3 per cent of the population are severely mentally handicapped. Many others have some degree of handicap that necessitates support from SSDs. The majority of mentally handicapped people live within the community: 90 per cent of children live at home, although the proportion falls with age, and 60 per cent of severely mentally handicapped adults receive institutional care (Audit Commission 1986a).

In 1971 the DHSS published a White Paper, *Better Services for the Mentally Handicapped*. This document identified a 'serious shortage of adult training centres and a great need for more trained staff'. It set targets for an increase in such training places to 74,500 and in residential care places to 29,800, these to be achieved over the next twenty years. Table 6.13 shows that there have been rapid increases both in the number

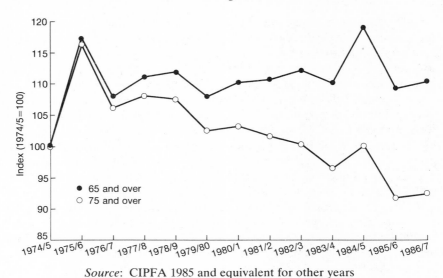

Source: CIPFA 1985 and equivalent for other years

FIG. 6.8. Full-time-equivalent home helps per 1,000 elderly people, England and Wales

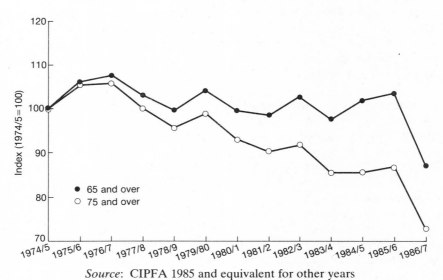

Source: CIPFA 1985 and equivalent for other years

FIG. 6.9. Meals provided per 1,000 elderly people, England and Wales

of adult day-care places and in residential care, although not as fast as planned. There have been differential growth rates across the period. The number of places in adult training centres increased by a third in the five years between 1974 and 1979. The rate of growth slowed down in the early 1980s and only increased by a further 20 per cent in the next seven years to 1986. Residential care places provided by local authorities increased by 76 per cent to 1979 (12 per cent per year). Again, the rate of increase then declined to 4.8 per cent per year.

This growth has not been sufficient to reach the targets set out in 1971. These figures do not include the impact of the rapidly expanding non-

Table 6.13. *Local authority residential and day-care places for the mentally ill, mentally handicapped, and younger people (under 65) with physical handicap, England*

	Mentally ill		Mentally handicapped		Physically handicapped	
	Res.[a]	Day-care	Res.[a]	Day-care[b]	Res.[c]	Day-care
1974	2,198	3,598	6,473	31,604	11,103	n.a.
1975	2,545	3,403	7,463	34,245	10,254	10,146
1976	2,738	3,681	8,703	35,811	10,652	n.a.
1977	3,092	3,914	9,751	38,682	10,331	10,277
1978	3,327	4,253	10,683	40,787	10,243	10,447
1979	3,592	4,622	11,381	42,061	10,008	10,475
1980	3,724	4,967	12,062	42,337	9,321	9,756
1981	3,981	4,907	12,712	43,627	9,703	9,647
1982	4,071	4,997	12,463	45,152	9,129	9,383
1983	4,173	5,159	13,735	46,558	9,024	9,120
1984	4,242	5,332	14,347	47,464	8,687	9,363
1985	4,363	5,414	15,152	48,824	8,046	8,729
1986	4,470	5,545	15,788	50,374	7,225	9,143
1987	n.a.	n.a.	n.a.	n.a.	6,704	9,095
Real growth rates (% per year)						
1974–9	10.3	5.1	11.9	5.9	−2.1	0.8[d]
1979–87[e]	3.2	2.6	4.8	2.6	−4.9	−1.8
1974–87[e]	6.1	3.7	7.7	4.0	−3.8	−0.9

[a] Homes and hostel places.
[b] Adult training centres.
[c] Residential places.
[d] 1975–9 growth rate.
[e] Or to 1986 if 1987 data are not available.

Sources: DHSS 1978, 1982*a*, 1988*d*: tables 7.1, 7.4, 7.5.

statutory residential care market (see Table 6.18 below), but nevertheless it is unlikely that targets will be met by 1991, despite the fact that provision to this group has been increasing at the fastest pace of all the priority groups.

The extent of mental illness nationally is unknown. In the 1975 White Paper *Better Services for the Mentally Ill* (DHSS 1975) it was estimated that 5 million people annually consulted GPs about mental health problems, and some 600,000 people receive specialist psychiatric care each year. More recent estimates do not exist nationally but it is reasonable to expect that these levels will have increased as awareness of mental illness in society in general rises. The Mental Health Act 1983 placed significant duties on SSDs for the appointment of social workers and for the provision of alternatives to psychiatric hospital care and the planning of post-hospital care.

The 1975 White Paper is still the basis of national policy. It pointed to serious deficiencies in existing local authority services for the mentally ill. The 1976 consultative document stressed the urgent need for more day care and set a target of an additional 1,200 day places a year. The need to develop a range of suitable residential accommodation was also dicussed, with a target of about 350 more places a year. Table 6.13 shows that local authority residential places increased rapidly during the 1970s, but once again the pace slowed in the 1980s. Day care expanded at a considerably slower pace, despite being singled out as the area of least adequate provision of all services to the mentally ill. The figures presented are for England, but development of this service has also been accorded a low priority in Scotland. In 1985 there was just one day centre for the mentally ill, with thirty-five places (Scottish Office 1987: 44).

Physically handicapped The OPCS Survey of Disability found that 14 per cent of all adults living in private households have at least one disability. Over 30 per cent of these were aged under 60 (Disability Alliance 1988). There has been no direct policy statement concerning targets or levels of service provision to this group as has been the case with the mentally handicapped and mentally ill. However, the 1986 Disabled Persons Act has given more positive responsibilities to local authorities for the care and welfare of handicapped people.

SSD services to this group include sheltered employment, day-care services, laundry and incontinence services, aids and adaptations, a range of domiciliary services, telephones and alarms systems, occupational therapy, and concessionary fares, as well as assistance to voluntary organizations. Services are also provided by a range of other bodies, such as the NHS, Training Commission, housing authorities (especially with regard to sheltered housing), and local education authorities.

Expenditure on local government services for the physically handicapped has increased in real terms, but not as rapidly as that for the mentally handicapped. However, owing to the diversity of services and providers it is difficult to make direct comparisons.

The 1976 *Priorities* document (DHSS 1976c) suggested that an additional 600 day places should be provided annually. This has not been the case. Table 6.13 shows that local authority day-care places remained roughly constant through the earlier part of the period and declined slightly in later years. The picture for publicly provided residential places has been one of continuous and increasing decline. In terms of the level of domiciliary service provision there has been an increase in aids and adaptations (see Table 6.15 below).

In summary, over the period as a whole the client groups which have benefited most from the growth in expenditure and service provision in PSS are the mentally handicapped and the mentally ill, in both absolute and relative terms. There has been a doubling of the number of residential care places for both the mentally ill and the mentally handicapped, while there has been a decrease of over 40 per cent in places for the younger physically handicapped, and stagnation in the level of local authority provision for the elderly. Furthermore, there have been an additional 19,000 day-care places for the mentally handicapped over the thirteen years 1974–1986. These two groups were singled out, in that separate White Papers were published laying out the priorities for service development.

To the extent that service provision to these groups grew disproportionately in relation to other groups, the targeting of resources to these 'priority groups' could be said to have been successful. However, even in the case of the mentally handicapped, *actual* targets for service expansion have not been attained. If the provision has been less than that required to meet need in the case of this 'privileged' group, then the shortfall for other groups is likely to have been even greater.

Community care

As we have seen, community care was an objective subscribed to by both Labour and Conservative governments from the early 1960s on. Initially it was most frequently interpreted as meaning non-hospital care. Alternatives to in-patient psychiatric treatment had become possible in the 1950s. Non-hospital care for the mentally handicapped was developed later. The pursuit of as normal a life as possible was advocated as a policy for both groups. As stated above, a White Paper set out targets for non-hospital care of the mentally handicapped in 1971 (DHSS 1971). It was paralleled by a composite statement of policy for the mentally ill in 1975 (DHSS

1975). It was also hoped to limit the use of hospital beds for the elderly and admissions to old people's homes by supporting the elderly in their own homes. To give local authorities a financial inducement to do this the NHS was given power to spend some of its resources funding local authority services that could keep people out of hospital finance. The local authority had to take over any long-term costs after an interim period. So-called day payments could also be made by the NHS to other organizations which took patients out of hospital.

The meaning of 'community care' has been refined over time and is now taken to be non-residential care as opposed to just non-hospital care. In *Making a Reality of Community Care* it was stated that community care involves

the bringing of health services out of hospital settings into more local, domestic settings; and a change in balance between the provision of residential care and the provision of day and domiciliary services. (Audit Commission 1986b: para. 10(b))

Thus it is necessary to look both at the balance between hospital and non-hospital care (i.e. between the health services and the social services) and also at the balance of care within the social services between residential care and day care and other support services. Furthermore, recently the aim of community care has increasingly been seen to mean care *by* the community (DHSS 1981c: para. 1.9). The balance of care between the statutory sector and the private/voluntary and informal sectors is examined later.

The balance between health and social services   As stated above, one of the main aims of community care has been the reduction of the number of people in long-stay hospital accommodation, particularly amongst the mentally handicapped and mentally ill. Implicit in this is a shift in responsibility between the health services and social services. Thus, although the focus of this chapter is on the PSS, we briefly look at the balance of spending between them and the health services.

The Audit Commission undertook a study to examine 'to what extent community care policies are being adopted in practice' (Audit Commission 1986b) and its report, as well as that of the National Audit Office (1987), has drawn attention to the relatively slow progress made towards these goals.

Table 6.14 shows the balance of expenditure between health and social services for specific groups. The change in the balance has not been as rapid as implied by the White Paper targets, despite the fact that 27 per cent of all joint finance between 1976/7 and 1980/1 was allocated to the mentally handicapped (Webb and Wistow 1986: 41). Nevertheless, there has been considerable movement between the two sectors.

If we look at the level of hospital provision for these groups, the average number of beds occupied daily in mental illness hospitals and units in the United Kingdom fell by 37 per cent from 1971 to 1986, while the number of out-patient attendances increased by 19 per cent. In 1976 there were 83,940 residents in psychiatric hospitals and units compared with 60,280 in 1986 (MIND, personal communication). A similar pattern occurred for mental handicap hospital and units. The average number of beds occupied daily fell by 35 per cent while out-patient attendances increased more than twofold (CSO 1988a). However, the decrease in hospital use has been uneven over time, with more than half the fall over the period occurring in the first five years and nearly three-quarters of it achieved by 1981.

It could be argued that these overall trends reflect moves towards keeping the mentally ill and handicapped living predominantly within the community, attending hospital when necessary rather than for long stays. Parallel to these decreases there has been an increase in the number of people living in local-authority-sponsored residential care for the mentally handicapped and mentally ill, as seen above. From 1974 to 1986 there were an additional 2,300 local-authority-funded residential places for the mentally ill and over 9,000 more places for the mentally handicapped. There is an obvious shortfall in the number of local authority places for the mentally ill when compared with the increase in discharge rate, and the Audit Commission has expressed concern about where these people have gone (1986b: 17–18). For the mentally handicapped, however, the

Table 6.14. *Balance of expenditure on mentally handicapped and mentally ill people, England (%)*

	1977	1985	Pattern implied by 1971/5 White Paper target
Mentally handicapped			
Health	73.8	64.5	44.2
Social services	26.2	35.5	55.8
Residential care	82.3	79.0	66.6
Community care	17.7	21.0	33.4
Mentally ill			
Health	97.0	95.5	87.0
Social services	3.0	4.5	13.0
Residential care	90.7	86.2	66.2
Community care	9.3	13.8	33.8

Source: Audit Commission 1986b.

build-up of local authority provision is ahead of the run-down of hospital places. But it is open to question whether one form of institutional care has just been substituted for another or whether there really has been an increase in those living in the community. We go on to look at the changing balance of care provided within the PSS themselves.

The balance between residential and community care within the PSS If local authority expenditure on the PSS is broken down by service (Table 6.4) it can be seen that spending on the community care services has grown at a faster rate than that on residential care, and that the growth in expenditure on day-care services has exceeded both of them. Table 6.14 shows that the balance of expenditure between residential and community care has shifted in favour of community care over the period 1977–85. Unsurprisingly, however, residential care still accounts for the greater part of non-field-work PSS expenditure.

The pattern of provision has changed over time. The activity statistics presented in Table 6.8, along with the other data shown in the priority groups section, further confirm that the trend within PSS has been one of increased day care and support service provision.

Figure 6.5 showed the number of children in care by manner of accommodation. There is a clear trend to reducing the proportion of children in care housed in residential homes, and increasing those boarded out. In 1986 over half of all children in local authority care were placed with foster-parents, compared with only a third in 1973. Local-authority-provided residential care has also fallen in absolute terms for the elderly and the younger physically handicapped. Table 6.15 gives an analysis of some of the services which local authority SSDs provide for the disabled. Such services are thought to allow disabled people to continue living in their own homes within the community instead of having to enter institutionalized care. Many voluntary organizations also provide similar services for the disabled or supplement those provided by the local authority.

It is clear that the provision of personal aids and adaptations to private properties has increased considerably over time. But the number of disabled people in the population has also risen: the number of very severely handicapped people in England rose from 15,600 in 1975 to 71,600 in 1984, whilst the number who are severely or appreciably handicapped increased from 59,600 to a startling 454,400 over the same period (DHSS 1987a: 123). This increase is mainly due to the rise in the number of elderly people. Fig. 6.10 illustrates how supply has failed to keep pace with rises in potential demand.

The growth in absolute terms of other services, such as assisted telephone rentals, has not been so marked, with the rate of growth slowing

Table 6.15. *Local authority services for disabled people, England* ('000)

	1974	1975	1976	1977	1978	1979	1980	1981	1982	1983	1984	1985	1986
Aids to households													
Telephone installation	21.8	22.0	14.8	11.4	14.0	16.9	12.9	8.9	9.4	11.7	14.5	14.4	14.5
Telephone attachments	1.1	1.6	1.6	1.2	2.1	1.6	1.4	1.4	1.6	2.1	2.9	3.2	3.7
Telephone rental	28.8	47.1	69.0	73.8	76.3	83.0	94.7	90.5	89.8	91.1	93.3	99.1	100.8
Television (supply)	2.5	2.2	1.6	1.3	1.2	1.1	0.7	0.5	0.3	0.4	0.4	0.5	0.7
Television licence	6.5	16.0	38.5	38.9	41.5	42.3	20.6	19.9	18.4	19.7	19.3	19.5	21.2
Radio (supply)	0.9	0.5	0.5	0.6	0.5	0.6	0.9	0.8	0.8	1.1	1.1	1.2	1.3
Other personal aids	142.5	159.4	191.2	199.4	219.3	237.4	245.9	262.1	278.6	305.9	345.6	385.8	394.8
Adaptations to property[a]	19.1	18.7	22.9	24.3	30.3	33.3	31.7	33.2	34.0	43.0	49.3	55.1	60.0
People receiving assistance with holidays	89.8	104.8	101.4	92.0	87.0	92.8	84.5	73.3	67.2	68.8	63.0	65.9	53.1

[a] Private dwellings only.

Sources: DHSS 1978: tables 7.10 and 7.11; DHSS 1982a, 1987a: table 7.8.

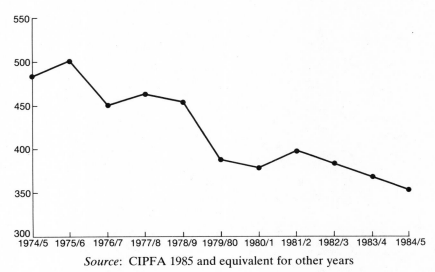

Source: CIPFA 1985 and equivalent for other years

FIG. 6.10. Aids and adaptations per 1,000 disabled people, England and Wales

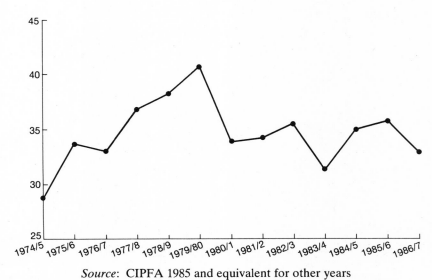

Source: CIPFA 1985 and equivalent for other years

FIG. 6.11. Telephones per 1,000 people aged 75 or over, England and Wales

considerably after 1980; indeed, provision of television licences showed an absolute decline from 1979. The number of people receiving assistance with holidays, which may provide the only respite from care for informal carers, has also declined over the period. Again, these trends have occurred during a period of rapidly changing needs (see Fig. 6.11).

Thus, although there have been marked improvements in the provision of domiciliary care and other support services, from Figs. 6.10 and 6.11 and Table 6.11 it can be seen that they have been struggling to keep pace with changes in need. It is far from clear that levels of services have been sufficient to keep people in their own homes and decrease the size of the residential sector. In fact, if the total real government expenditure on the residential care sector is examined, rather than just that from the PSS budget, there has been no decrease (Table 6.16).

Decreasing residential care?   Local authority and hospital residential care have been declining over the period. But this is ony a partial picture of the total residential sector. The total number of elderly people in residential accommodation in any sector between 1974 and 1986 in England increased by 41 per cent (the number of elderly people aged 75 and over rose by 33 per cent during this period). There was also an increase in the number of mentally handicapped and mentally ill people in residential accommodation, whilst there was a slight decline in overall places for the younger physically handicapped. Tables 6.17 and 6.18 map out this trend and distinguish the development of the private, local authority, and voluntary sectors.

What is striking when looking at the trends in the total number of

Table 6.16. *Public expenditure on the institutional care of the elderly*
(£ million at 1985 prices)

	1977/8	1980/1	1982/3[a]	1985/6
NHS geriatric beds	726	774	787	800
Local authority residential homes	569	617	608	630
Social security funding of private homes	11	25	116	500
Total	1,306	1,414	1,500	1,930
Social security funding as % of total	0.8	2.0	7.7	25.9

[a] Figures are as given in source, though slightly discrepant.
Source: Day and Klein 1987.

institutional places for elderly and disabled people is the marked growth in the private sector. The figures show that most of this rise is due to private-sector expansion in provision for the elderly; the proportion of elderly people accommodated in private homes increased from 13 per cent to 37 per cent during 1974–86. What is of particular interest is the accelerated growth from 1983 onwards in this sector (see Table 6.17, also Table 6A.2 in the Annexe to this chapter)—representing 58 per cent of total growth between 1974 and 1986. Between 1974 and 1979 the number of places in private residential homes for these individuals increased by a third, whereas the numbers more than doubled during the period 1979–86. The numbers in local authority homes, in contrast, show a moderate rise up to 1980, and begin to decline in 1983 (Table 6.17).

This trend of a gradual rise between 1974 and 1980 and then a fall after 1983 can also be detected within the voluntary sector for the elderly. The private and voluntary sectors cannot be distinguished for the mentally ill and mentally handicapped in Table 6.18. Government statistics combine private-sector figures (numbers or places) with those in the voluntary sector, which averages out differential rates of growth. However, growth

Table 6.17. *Number of elderly people in residential accommodation, by type of home, England ('000)*

	Local authority			Private	Voluntary	Total
	Total	Own[a]	V. & P.[b]			
1974	107.2	92.5	14.7	18.9	22.7	148.8
1975	109.7	95.1	14.6	18.8	22.5	151.0
1976	115.1	99.0	16.1	21.3	23.8	160.2
1977	116.6	101.7	14.9	22.7	24.5	163.8
1978	117.9	102.8	15.1	24.5	24.7	167.1
1979	117.2	102.1	15.1	26.0	24.8	168.0
1980	118.8	102.9	15.9	28.8	25.5	173.1
1981	116.9	103.1	13.8	31.8	26.0	174.7
1982	116.9	103.7	13.2	35.8	26.1	178.8
1983	115.5	103.6	11.9	42.1	26.5	184.1
1984	112.3	102.0	10.3	52.7	26.0	191.0
1985	110.0	101.5	8.5	66.1	25.8	201.9
1986	106.8	101.7	5.1	77.6	25.1	209.5
1987	104.6	100.6	4.0	n.a.	n.a.	n.a.

[a] Own = accommodation provided by local authority.
[b] V.& P. = accommodation provided on behalf of local authority in voluntary or private homes.

Source: DHSS 1978, 1982a, 1988d: tables 7.1, 7.2.

rates have not been nearly as rapid for these groups as for the elderly, and this partly reflects the relatively low limits for social security funding compared with the much higher costs these groups involve.

Some have termed this growth in the provision of private residential care to the elderly as 'creeping privatization' (Estrin and Perotin 1989); similar patterns have been found in France with respect to residential care. Levels of statutorily provided residential care have stayed roughly constant in the face of demographic change. This lack of growth has allowed the private sector to expand by soaking up the excess demand. This process is illustrated by the trends shown in Fig. 6.12.

In summary then, the goal of increased community care has not been met by either administration. Progress on reducing hospital places and increasing local authority residential and day-care places was more rapid during the 1970s than throughout the 1980s. Domiciliary and other support services have increased, although not at a sufficient rate. This is not the place to examine in detail the reasons behind the slow progress to community care. The Audit Commission report points to several underlying problems, including the deterrent effect of the Rate Support Grant

Table 6.18. *Numbers of people accommodated in local authority and private voluntary residential homes for the mentally ill, mentally handicapped, and younger people (under 65) with physical handicap, England*

	Mentally ill		Mentally handicapped		Physically handicapped	
	LA[a]	V. & P.[b]	LA	V. & P.	LA	V. & P.
1974	2,198	1,350	6,473	3,007	11,103	5,512
1975	2,545	1,366	7,463	2,885	10,254	5,469
1976	2,738	1,622	8,703	3,070	10,652	5,757
1977	3,092	1,864	9,751	3,266	10,331	5,879
1978	3,327	1,894	10,683	3,595	10,243	6,330
1979	3,592	2,015	11,381	3,773	10,008	6,639
1980	3,724	2,142	12,062	3,746	9,321	6,857
1981	3,981	n.a.	12,712	n.a.	9,703	7,776
1982	4,071	n.a.	12,463	n.a.	9,129	7,703
1983	4,173	2,367	13,735	5,046	9,024	8,368
1984	4,242	2,558	14,347	6,271	8,687	8,534
1985	4,363	3,171	15,152	7,096	8,046	8,462
1986	4,470	3,805	15,788	8,601	7,225	8,420

[a] LA = local authority.
[b] V.& P. = voluntary and private.

Sources: DHSS 1978, 1982*a*, 1988*d*: tables 7.1, 7.2, 7.3.

on local authorities, when increases in expenditure can result in loss of grant; inadequate joint finance and financial transfers; lack of bridging finance; organizational fragmentation and inadequate staffing arrangements, as well as the perverse effects of social security policies.

The 1980s have witnessed an increase in the total residential care sector. The Audit Commission (1986*b*) further notes that there appears to have been a shift from one pattern of residential care, based on hospitals, to an alternative, supported by Income Support payments—missing out community care altogether. How this has occurred and the implications for the balance of care provision between sectors are further examined below.

Changes in the mixed economy of welfare—increasing privatization

At the beginning of this chapter in Fig. 6.2 we distinguished between the provision of care and its finance. Increasingly, the Conservative administration has moved from a large reliance on services publicly financed and provided by SSDs to a pattern of services which remain largely publicly financed but are provided by a range of private bodies. The main vehicle for this change has been the social security system.

Social security and residential care—public finance of private provision
From 1948 on, the social security system had discretion to make limited contributions to the board and lodging costs of those living in residential and nursing homes. This discretion was sternly exercised and only small

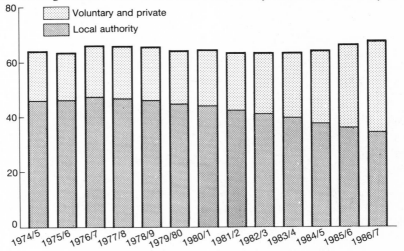

Source: DHSS 1978 and equivalents for subsequent years

FIG. 6.12. Residential places per 1,000 people aged over 75, England

sums were involved. As shown by Table 6.16, at the beginning of our study period DHSS payments for the care of elderly people in residential homes amounted only to about £10 million at 1985 prices. This figure began to creep up in the 1970s, but in 1980 the new social security regulations gave local DHSS offices scope to meet in full the charges made by private and voluntary homes. The relaxation led to a faster pace of public funding of private care. The regulations were tightened on subsequent occasions, but local authorities came to realize they could rely on the DHSS to finance old people's care rather than provide it themselves, and families began to realize that too. As local authority places became difficult to find, many families turned to the private sector as another option and relied on the DHSS to pay.

Thus the growth in the private residential sector has been stimulated by the changes within the social security system, which was largely unintended. It has resulted in the creation of perverse incentives, encouraging residential rather than community care.

It is important to point out that the local authorities' own provision of residential care has stayed roughly constant (although failing to expand to meet the increased demand due to demographic pressures). However, they have decreased the amount of residential care services bought in from the private and voluntary sectors (see Table 6A.3 in the Annexe to this chapter). There was no necessity to 'buy in' as they could rely upon the DHSS to pay the bill. This is somewhat counter to the government's overall strategy of promoting contracting out (Baldwin, Parker, and Walker 1989).

By mid-1985 the DHSS had introduced local ceilings set by local offices on the basis of reasonable average charges in their area. That gave an incentive for local homes to raise their average fees, and the publicity only added to the problem. The DHSS information system was such that it caught up late with this newly accelerating trend. When it did, it imposed absolute national ceilings on board and lodging payments related to the client groups and level of dependency. The damage, if that is what it was, had been done. The scale of DHSS involvement in the funding of private provision was now significant. Not only was the result costly, but it also funded institutional, not community, care. The perversity of this incentive and worry about the cost was discussed in a series of applied reports (Audit Commission 1986*b*; National Audit Office 1987; DHSS 1988*c*). By 1985/6 the original sum of £10 million spent by the DHSS on people in private homes for the elderly had risen to about £500 million (HC, Social Services Committee, 1986; Day and Klein 1987).

The scale of the public expenditure implications of this shift to an open-ended social security funding of residential care for the elderly worried the government. As a consequence Roy Griffiths was asked to find a way out of both this difficulty and the more general maze of community care responsibilities. His answer (DHSS 1988c) involved handing responsibility for financing the caring aspects of community care to local authorities; housing and basic benefits for living expenses remained with the DSS. This would effectively put a cap on central government's commitment to fund community care, but it would give local government more power and funds. Mrs Thatcher opposed this part of the package and stalled a decision to implement the Griffiths Report. By May 1989 social security expenditure for people in residential care and nursing homes had risen to £1,000 million (DoH 1989b). Such increases led to the principles of the Griffiths Report finally being embodied in the government White Paper *Caring for People* in November 1989 (DoH 1989b) and in the National Health Services and Community Care Bill 1990. Local authorities were made responsible for all aspects of community care, finance as well as provision.

Other public funding of private provision   A rather different example of the same trend can be seen in the policy of placing children in care with foster-parents rather than in residential accommodation. In 1973, 51 per cent of children in local authority care were housed in residential accommodation (children's homes), whilst 32 per cent were boarded out with foster-parents. By 1979 these percentages had changed to 45 and 36 respectively, while by 1986 the figures had reversed, with over 50 per cent of children fostered and only 33 per cent in local authority homes (Fig. 6.5).

This has also had the effect of increasing 'public' payments to the 'private' sector for provision of services. Concomitant with this is the trend of SSDs buying in services and contracting out—public funding of private provision. Table 6.19 shows the purchase of services by local authorities from the private and voluntary sectors. The buying in of residential care increased up to 1981/2, since when it has fallen sharply in real terms. This is due to the changes in social security noted above and the decreased incentive for local authorities to continue to sponsor residents in the private sector. More interestingly, the purchase of other services has also declined, perhaps highlighting a trend to leave private provision to the private sector.

The share of the private and voluntary sectors in both the funding and provision of certain services has risen over time. The private sector has met demand not met by statutory-sector provision. Nursery care and paid domiciliary services for the elderly are two examples of this.

Private resourcing of private provision   From Fig. 6.7 it can be seen that the number of nursery or child-care places provided by the private (registered nursery or registered child-minders) or informal (volunteer-run play-groups) sectors has increased over time. However, there is no specific information available on the level of expenditure on such services. Research on the extent of private domiciliary services is also limited. A small-scale report based on 150 carers, carried out by the Centre for Policy on Ageing (CPA), found the incidence to be very low (Midwinter 1986). This is confirmed by data from large national surveys—the General Household Surveys (GHS)—indicating the level to be 2 per cent of the elderly population (OPCS 1982). The CPA study found that most of the care which tended to be purchased was for help with domestic duties (80 per cent), although some paid for sitting-in services (16 per cent). The survey showed that the main sources of payment were the incomes of the carer and the dependant.

GHS data showed that elderly people living alone are more likely to purchase help for domestic tasks such as laundry-washing (7 per cent), cooking meals (6 per cent), and shopping (3 per cent), as well as walking outdoors (2 per cent) (OPCS 1982).

However, there is a variety of 'paid' care schemes and services, and these cover a range of client groups. Distinctions are made between paid care provided in the client's home and that provided in the carer's home; and also between substitute care (i.e. paid carer 'standing in') and supplementary care (Leat and Gay 1987). Paid care schemes within the voluntary sector have been noted to be rising by research at the Policy Studies Institute. Examples of these schemes include short-term respite paid care for the elderly, and paid fostering of 'normal' children as well as of those mentally and physically handicapped, and also of 'difficult adolescents'.

Table 6.19. *Purchase of services by local authorities from the private and voluntary sectors* (£ million at 1985/6 prices)

	Residential care		Other services		Total	
	Cash	Real	Cash	Real	Cash	Real
1979/80	99.2	160.6	19.2	31.0	118.4	191.6
1980/1	119.5	163.0	21.5	29.4	141.0	192.4
1981/2	135.3	168.1	25.2	31.4	160.5	199.4
1982/3	143.4	166.1	27.1	31.4	170.5	197.6
1983/4	149.0	164.9	22.6	24.9	171.6	189.9
1984/5	150.1	159.1	24.9	26.4	175.0	185.4
1985/6	119.8	119.8	26.9	26.9	146.7	146.7

Source: HC, Social Services Committee, 1987, 1988.

Charities and voluntary organizations   By far the largest amount of *formal* non-statutory provision (excluding residential care) and finance comes from the charitable and voluntary, i.e. non-profit, sectors.

Over the past two decades there has been a marked increase in the number, and income, of charities and voluntary organizations in Britain. In 1970 there were 76,000 registered charities, of which 65 per cent had an annual income of less than £100 (CSO 1976). By 1976 the number registered with the Charities Commission had risen to 123,000, and at the end of 1986 there were over 158,000 on the register, with an estimated total income of nearly £12.7 billion. A substantial proportion of these charities and voluntary organizations provide services and support that operate in parallel to the PSS.

In 1987/8, 33 per cent of the expenditure of the top 200 charities was directed to 'medicine and health' (with cancer research comprising about half of this, but services to blind, deaf, and physically disabled making up over a third) and 28 per cent to 'general welfare'. Thus it is estimated that about £400 million was expended on PSS-related activities in this sector. This is over 10 per cent of the total public-sector budget for PSS, and so constitutes a substantial contribution to the overall social services sector. Table 6.20 shows the expenditure of selected charities.

The highest expenditure is from those charities which support residential accommodation, such as the Salvation Army and Barnardo's, although their range of activities extends far beyond this. The non-statutory organizations have the freedom to develop more flexible approaches to care.

For example, the NSPCC provides immediate help for children in

Table 6.20. *Expenditure by selected charities* (£ million, cash)

Charity	1978/9	1985/6[a]
Salvation Army	13.1	38.7
Barnardo's	14.9	36.0
Spastics Society	13.9	35.7
Save the Children Fund	5.8	46.1
Royal National Institute for the Blind	10.6	20.5
Guide Dogs for the Blind Association	n.a.	9.9
National Society for the Prevention of Cruelty to Children	n.a.	14.7
Church of England Children's Society	n.a.	15.2
Help the Aged	5.8	11.5

[a] Or latest available year.
Source: CSO 1980, 1988*a*.

need, and since 1984 it has been establishing a 24-hour-a-day national network of 'Child Protection Schemes' which respond to calls from families and the general public as well as from professional workers. The Abbeyfield Society is a federation of local voluntary societies which set up and manage family-size houses. Each one can accommodate seven to nine elderly people who would otherwise be alone and at risk. By the end of 1986 it comprised 593 local societies managing aproximately 960 houses and caring for 7,500 residents.

As well as an increase in the range of provision from charities, during the 1970s a substantial network of voluntary advisory and counselling services developed. There has been a rise in the number of enquiries across the board. Two agencies in particular experienced marked increases. The number of calls received by the Samaritans rose from 87,000 in 1971 to 393,000 in 1986, whilst the number of 'clients' seen by Alcoholics Anonymous over the same period increased from 6,300 to 35,000 (CSO 1988a).

The last five years have also seen the emergence of the new phenomenon of charity appeals sponsored by television and radio, such as the 'Telethon'. The main aim of 'Telethon '88' was to raise money for work in five main categories: disability, training and employment, children, special need, and self-help and community groups. This event raised £22 million in 24 hours—more than some SSDs' annual budgets. The area of social services was also the target for the BBC 'Children in Need' appeal in 1987. Thus, it has become acceptable to supplement with self-help those services previously thought of as the preserve or, more centrally, the statutory requirement of public bodies—i.e. extending the ideology of the individual.

The White Paper *Growing Older* (DHSS 1981c) stressed the primary importance of informal care for the elderly and the importance of the 'personal ties of kinship and friendship'. There has been increased emphasis laid on the responsibility of the individual and a withdrawal from the idea of collective responsibility and provision. The informal care sector makes up by far the largest proportion of total care provision.

Costs of informal care　Most of the care and assistance provided to people with long-standing illnesses or disabilities, or to the elderly, comes from families, friends, and neighbours (Evandrou *et al.* 1986). This constitutes the informal part of the private resourcing of private provision section of Fig. 6.2. The scale of this informal care provision for incapacitated children and adults is significant. A recent government survey documented that one adult in seven provides such care (OPCS 1987).

The financial implications of informal care have been costed by academics and policy analysts (Nissel and Bonnerjea 1982; FPSC 1989). The

Family Policy Studies Centre estimates the 'value' of the current 6 million carers in Britain at between £15 and £24 billion per year. These figures are based on a calculation using the average hourly cost of providing local authority home helps in 1987, which was £4.09. The amount provided by the government for the whole of the PSS sector in 1987/8 (£3.8 billion) compares poorly with the cost of family support, at most constituting one-quarter. It is also important to note that this figure only deals with replacement costs of informal care, ignoring the opportunity costs of providing such support, which would require more complex analysis.

The financial disadvantages experienced by these carers, such as the earnings lost or forgone and additional expenses incurred, have been documented by a small number of studies (Nissel and Bonnerjea 1982; Glendinning 1987, 1988). However, the omission of these financial considerations of informal carers from the Griffiths Report (DHSS 1988c) is serious and can be seen as indicative of their invisibility in terms of their financial needs. The incomes of carers are not explicitly considered within community care policies or in social security policy-making. Few carers are eligible for Invalid Care Allowance (ICA) even after its extension to married women in 1986. The estimated number of carers receiving ICA for 1989/90 is 110,000 (HM Treasury 1989). This would constitute 2 per cent of carers nationally. The shortcomings and inadequacies of ICA, currently (1988/9) set at £26.20 per week, have been documented (McLaughlin 1988).

However, their contribution is certainly visible, and even relied upon in future statutory service provision planning: Griffiths proposes that local authorities should 'arrange the delivery of packages of care to individuals building *first* on the available contribution of informal carers and neighbourhood support, *then* the provision of domiciliary and day services' (DHSS 1988c: para. 1.3.3, p. 1, emphasis added).

Future directions   Levels of total local authority net current expenditure are expected to decrease by 1.1 per cent in real terms over the financial year 1988/9 and then remain constant up to 1991 (HC, Social Services Committee, 1988). However, as in previous expenditure White Papers, planned levels of local authority expenditure on the PSS, including allowance for demographic and other pressures, include incentives to accelerate community care. Real expenditure is expected to rise by about 2 per cent per year. It is questionable how local authorities will meet these targets when their total expenditure is to be cut. There is increasing emphasis on value for money from local authorities in the expenditure targets. It is assumed that SSDs will make 'efficiency savings' of about 0.5 per cent per year to 'finance other service developments' (HM Treasury 1987).

In the face of fiscal constraint, local authorities are also being called upon to implement the recommendations of Griffiths, as documented in the White Paper (DoH 1989*b*). The responsibility for community care has been firmly shifted to local authorities. The successful implementation of these policy changes depends not only on how local authorities deal with these additional responsibilities, but also on the adequacy of the level of funding from central government. The additional financial provision for local authorities will be distributed through the Revenue Support Grant. What will be critical is how this formula will be calculated. As our analysis has shown, it is open to question whether the 2 per cent increase built into expenditure plans, now cut to 1.5 per cent, has been adequate to meet current responsibilities.

IV. EQUITY AND FINAL OUTCOMES

Equity and distributional issues of the personal social services

The discussion so far has focused on central government policy and expenditure trends in relation to indicators of need, dealing more with the *macro* side of PSS. In this section, we confront issues of equity and analyse the distributional impact of PSS on individual users, examining the *micro* side too. Data from selected years (1974, 1979, and 1985) of the GHS were employed in order to unravel these issues.

The proportion of elderly people in receipt of domiciliary care provided by the state sector is generally small. The primary form of domiciliary care provided by local authority departments is home help. In Britain, 9 per cent of elderly people aged 65 and over were reported in 1985 to have received a home help in the previous month (Table 6.21). Even fewer (less than 3 per cent) received meals on wheels, and 5 per cent attended elderly day centres. These proportions vary with the age, household composition, social class, income, and degree of disability of the elderly person. For example, home-help utilization steadily rises with age, from 1 per cent of 65–9-year-olds to 36 per cent of those aged 85 or over, and is higher amongst elderly people living alone (19 per cent) than those living with their spouse only (4 per cent).

What is interesting to note is that there has been little change in these trends over time. Table 6.21 shows that between 1974 and 1979 the figure for home-help receipt rose by 2 per cent (from 6.6 to 8.8 per cent) and in the following six years leading up to 1985 the level rose by 0.4 percentage points (i.e. to 9.2 per cent). Other domiciliary care services, such as attending day centres, increased by similar magnitudes: 3.1 to 3.9 per cent in the first five years and then up to 5.0 per cent by 1985. Meals on wheels, lunch clubs, and community health services (e.g. health visitor,

Table 6.21. *Percentage of individuals aged 65 or over receiving selected personal social services, Great Britain*

	Home help	Meals on wheels	Day centre
1974	6.6	2.5	3.1
1979	8.8	2.1	3.9
1985	9.2	2.5	5.0

	Health visitor	District nurse	Chiropodist
1974	1.3	3.4	6.5
1979	1.5	4.8	10.2
1985	1.4	5.1	7.1

	Domiciliary[a]	Community health[b]	Any PSS[c]
1974	10.5	10.4	17.7
1979	12.6	14.7	22.4
1985	13.3	12.1	21.3

[a] Received at least one of the following services in the last month: home help, meals, day centre.

[b] Received at least one of the following services in the last month: health visitor, district nurse, chiropodist in surgery or at home.

[c] Received any one or more of the services listed in nn. *a* and *b*.

Source: Own calculation from GHS raw data files.

Table 6.22. *Percentage of individuals aged 65 or over receiving a service,[a] by socio-economic indicator, Great Britain*

(a) BY AGE					
	65–9	70–4	75–9	80–4	85 and over	All
1974	8.7	16.0	24.8	32.8	37.5	17.7
1979	11.1	19.2	28.7	40.2	57.9	22.4
1985	9.4	15.3	26.6	36.8	57.0	21.3

(b) BY SOCIAL CLASS			
	I & II	IIIN[b]	IIIM[b]	IV & V
1974	8.3	15.1	16.7	21.0
1979	15.1	20.8	19.5	25.5
1985	15.7	19.0	18.8	25.8

(*c*) BY INCOME QUINTILE

	Bottom	2	3	4	Top
Total population					
1974	21.2	20.8	10.9	8.7	4.6
1979	24.0	26.5	13.4	13.8	9.6
1985	26.0	23.6	14.6	13.5	7.3
Pensioner population only					
1974	17.9	23.4	24.4	11.7	7.6
1979	22.8	27.0	27.9	20.6	12.8
1985	24.3	29.8	22.1	18.4	10.1

(*d*) BY REGION[c]

	North	South	Wales	Scotland
1974	18.0	17.0	16.6	19.0
1979	23.3	19.8	29.2	26.6
1985	22.2	19.9	20.2	25.1

(*e*) BY TENURE

	Owner-occupier	Local authority	Other
1974	13.8	24.0	17.2
1979	17.9	27.1	24.7
1985	16.5	27.8	23.7

[a] Received at least one of the following services in the last month: home help, meals, centre, health visitor, district nurse, chiropodist in surgery or at home.
[b] 'N' denotes 'non-manual', 'M' denotes 'manual'.
[c] 'North' includes: North, Yorkshire and Humberside, North-West, East Midlands, and West Midlands. 'South' is rest of England.
Source: Own calculations from GHS raw data files.

district nurse) provided similar levels of service over this period. However, receipt of chiropody services, in surgery or at home, rose from 6.5 to 10.2 per cent in the first five years and then fell to 7.1 per cent by 1985 (see Table 6.21).

Receipt of home help across social class was examined using a five-category classification based on socio-economic group. This indicated that in 1985 a higher proportion of elderly people from classes IV and V (i.e. skilled, semi-skilled and unskilled manual) used the home-help service (11.3 per cent) than those from classes I and II (i.e. professional and managerial) (6.2 per cent). Mapping these trends over time, the

Table 6.23. *Percentage of individuals aged 65 or over receiving home help,*
Great Britain

(*a*) BY AGE

	65–9	70–4	75–9	80–4	85 and over	All
1974	2.0	5.4	10.8	14.3	16.3	6.6
1979	2.3	6.3	11.2	21.9	31.3	8.8
1985	1.3	5.4	10.9	21.1	35.4	9.2

(*b*) BY SOCIAL CLASS

	I & II	IIIN[a]	IIIM[a]	IV & V
1974	3.3	6.5	5.5	7.4
1979	5.2	7.0	8.3	10.1
1985	6.2	8.0	8.2	11.3

(*c*) BY INCOME QUINTILE

	Bottom	2	3	4	Top
Total population					
1974	7.5	8.9	3.1	1.1	1.3
1979	8.6	12.2	3.0	3.8	2.5
1985	13.1	10.0	4.5	4.4	4.0
Pensioner population only					
1974	5.3	9.1	10.4	4.2	1.3
1979	7.6	11.2	13.2	8.5	3.1
1985	12.2	15.6	7.3	7.1	3.4

(*d*) BY REGION[b]

	North	South	Wales	Scotland
1974	7.1	6.3	7.5	4.5
1979	9.7	7.6	11.0	8.9
1985	9.8	8.5	9.0	9.0

(*e*) BY TENURE

	Owner-occupier	Local authority	Other
1974	4.1	10.2	7.2
1979	5.3	12.7	10.0
1985	6.2	13.5	9.7

percentage-point increase between 1979 and 1985 was slightly lower within social classes I and II than in classes IV and V (see Table 6.23), i.e. a rise of 1.0 percentage point compared with 1.2 percentage points respectively.

Using a measure of equivalized income of the elderly person, we examined the proportion in receipt of a home help (in the last month) by income quintiles. As Table 6.23 shows, in 1974 and 1979 elderly people in the second-from-bottom income quintile were more likely to be in receipt of a home help than elderly individuals in the other quintile groups, including the bottom group. However, in 1985 it was the elderly in the bottom quintile group of the income distribution for the whole population who were more likely to report home-help receipt—13 per cent, compared with 4 per cent of those in the top quintile group (i.e. in the richest 20 per cent of the whole population, and hence a 'very well-off' proportion of elderly individuals).

When we look at these figures over time, we find that the proportion of elderly people in receipt of a home-help service rises between 1974 and 1979, and also between 1979 and 1985 across most of the quintile groups, the two exceptions being quintile group 2 in the later period and group 3 in the earlier one. The proportionate change in home-help visits was greater for elderly people categorized in the top quintile than for those in the bottom, i.e. proportionate changes of 92 per cent between 1974 and 1979 and 60 per cent between 1979 and 1985, compared with 14 per cent and 51 per cent respectively.

These figures are based on the relative position of the elderly person's income (in quintile groups) within the income distribution for the population as a whole. However, we also provide these trends using the elderly person's position within the income distribution for just the elderly population. This was felt to be of importance as the majority of elderly people fall within the bottom two quintiles of the general income distribution. Looking at the relative position solely within the elderly population allows a more focused approach.

This has produced varied results; some trends are intensified and others are reversed. For example, the elderly in income quintile groups 2 and 3 were more likely to report home-help receipt than those in any other quintile groups, including the bottom group (within each year). Furthermore, although the percentage of elderly people in receipt of a home help

---

(*Table notes cont.*)

[a] 'N' denotes 'non-manual', 'M' denotes 'manual'.
[b] 'North' includes: North, Yorkshire and Humberside, North-West, East Midlands, and West Midlands. 'South' is rest of England.
Source: Own calculations from GHS raw data files.

increased within each income quintile group of the elderly between 1974 and 1979, this was not the case in the following six years. For example, the percentage of elderly people in receipt in the third quintile group rose in the first period (10 to 13 per cent), and then fell to 7 per cent in the period between 1979 and 1985. A similar rise and then a fall occurred in the third group over the same period. However, it is worth noting that the proportionate rise in receipt between 1979 and 1985 was far greater for the elderly in the bottom group (60 per cent) than for those in the top group (10 per cent).

In short, elderly people at the lower end of the income distribution (although not necessarily at the bottom) are more likely to be in receipt of a home help than those at the top end. This trend occurs even after standardizing on the age of the elderly person, which takes into account a proxy for need. This reflects evidence of targeting at the lower end of the income distribution.

Final outcomes in relation to ultimate aims

There is a difficulty in defining measures of outcome for the PSS. One possible way is to look at consumer satisfaction and whether 'the political market' has met rising expectations. However, to date the British Social Attitudes Survey has contained no questions on attitudes to, or satisfaction with, social services provision.

Another possible measure of outcome would be in relation to the ultimate aims of PSS: namely, to what extent have the PSS been successful in increasing social integration or, alternatively, reducing social isolation? Further, how successful have SSDs been in exercising their role as agents of social control? The latter would be very difficult to measure.

A broad indicator reflecting the general level of social control in society is the level of crime. Government data show a twofold increase in the total number of notifiable offences recorded by the police in England and Wales over the period 1971–86 (a rise from 1.6 million to 3.8 million). Another indicator proposed to measure the extent of social control is the number of children taken into local authority care. The number of children in care fell by a quarter between 1977 and 1985 (CSO 1988a).

There is the question of how one would interpret a change in these statistics. A decrease in the number of older children in care could be a sign that delinquency is decreasing and thus that social control has increased. However, the rise in crime statistics would indicate an opposing trend. Changes in the number of children in care could alternatively be taken to indicate that the social services are not being effective in reaching those children in need of care, and indicate decreasing social control. Similarly, rising recorded offences could indicate improved detection and thus greater social control.

Social integration may be defined in terms of 'contrasting those who have many community and family ties with those who are isolated' (Stark 1987). The reported frequency of social contact is only *one* indicator of social integration/isolation. It does not take account of the subjective feelings of the individual, no matter how frequent the level of contact. The Health and Lifestyle Survey found that perceptions of a lack of social support appear to be more important than objective indicators of social contact, especially amongst women (Stark 1987). However, we feel it is still a useful measure, and it is also employed by others (Willmott 1986) in their research.

These measures are examined using the GHS data. Fifteen per cent of elderly people in the GHS survey saw relatives and friends less often than once a week, or not at all, in both 1980 and 1985 (OPCS 1982, 1985). Lack of contact rises with age: in 1985, 13 per cent of 65–9-year-olds saw friends or relatives less often than once a week (but at least sometimes), compared with 20 per cent of those aged 85 or over. Both proportions had increased over the five-year period; however, for the age groups in the middle, the percentages fell (see Table 6.24). The percentage of elderly reporting that visits to relatives and friends were less frequent than once in the last week (but did visit in the last month) fell from 33 per cent (1980) to 28 per cent (1985) (Table 6.24). These proportions are lower for those individuals who drove and had access to a car (i.e. they tend to see people more often), and higher among those who are house-bound.

The use of public transport and private cars is also indicative of the level of social isolation experienced by individuals in society. One's ability to get around generally is related to access to transport, as well as to one's ability to get around on foot (OPCS 1987). We examine the level of public transport use over time and look at the reasons for not using it. The percentage of elderly people reported to have used public transport fell from 69 to 62 per cent in the five-year period between 1980 and 1985 (OPCS 1982, 1987). The level of use is related to age and gender, with younger elderly people and elderly women being more likely to be users than their respective counterparts (Table 6.25).

Use of public transport by the elderly is related to access to private transport and to their own health and personal locomotive ability. In fact, these were the two main reasons reported for not using public transport. To what extent has the importance of these reasons changed over time? The GHS shows that the proportion of elderly reporting access to a household or other car as the main reason for not using public transport increased from 16 to 25 per cent between 1980 and 1985. Similarly, the percentage stating ill-health or disability as the reason rose from 10 to 14 per cent over the same period (Table 6.25). The influence of ill-health rises sharply with age: in 1985 only 5 per cent of those aged 65–9 gave this reason, compared with 45 per cent of those aged 85 and over. What is of interest, however, is that the proportion of elderly people living in households with a car increased from 35 to 40 per cent over the five-year period.

Table 6.24. *Indicators of social isolation: Frequency of social contacts in 1980 and 1985, Great Britain* (%)

	1980		1985	
Frequency of *seeing* relatives and friends:				
Every day	32 ⎫		33 ⎫	
2–3 times a week	29 ⎬	85	29 ⎬	84
Once a week	25 ⎭		22 ⎭	
Less often, but did last month	10 ⎫		9 ⎫	
Not last month	2 ⎬	15	4 ⎬	15
Not at all nowadays	3 ⎭		2 ⎭	
Seeing relatives and friends in the last month, but not in the last week:				
65–9	10		13	
70–4	12		11	
75–9	14		13	
80–4	19		16	
85 and over	16		20	
All elderly	12		13	
Visits to relatives and friends in the last month, but not in the last week:				
All elderly	33		28	
Visits from relatives and friends in the last month, but not in the last week:				
All elderly	28		26	

Source: OPCS 1982, 1987.

Table 6.25. *Indicators of social isolation: Use of public transport in 1980 and 1985, Great Britain* (%)

	1980	1985
USE OF PUBLIC TRANSPORT		
All elderly		
Using PT[a]		
65–74	75	69
75 and over	58	52
All	69	62
Not using PT	31	38
Elderly living alone		
Using PT		
65–74	85	80
75 and over	60	57
All	73	68
Not using PT	27	32
Using PT		
Men (65 and over)	67	59
Women (65 and over)	70	65
REASONS FOR NOT USING PUBLIC TRANSPORT		
All elderly		
Uses household car	13	18
Uses other car	3	7
Ill-health/disability	10	14
PT inconvenient	2	4
PT too expensive	1	1
Other	3	1
Elderly aged 85 and over		
Uses household car	9	9
Uses other car	11	14
Ill-health/disability	38	45
PT inconvenient	1	7
PT too expensive	0	1
Other	9	4

[a] PT = 'public transport'.
Source: OPCS 1982, 1987.

V. IN BRIEF

• The two major trends in the PSS since the early 1970s have been expenditure constraint and the growth of private provision. Both of these were under way before 1979 but both intensified thereafter (Webb and Wistow 1986: 199).

• The policies and practices which were shared by both Conservative and Labour governments during this period were: first, a reactive approach to child abuse cases; secondly, the tightening of public expenditure directed to the PSS; and thirdly, the shift to community/non-institutional care. The last two commonalities represented the result of planned policies and deliberate action. The divergence in these policies between the two parties is clearly demarcated in the tools employed to implement them: under the Conservative government, primary emphasis was placed on the means to achieve policy objectives rather than on the ends, shifting towards privatization and changing the role of Social Service Departments from that of 'provider' to that of 'regulator'.

• A policy of community care has been fostered by both Labour and Conservative governments over the last two decades. However, the meaning attributed to it has changed: initially it meant shifting the balance of care from hospitals to the community, but more recently, it has been used in a way which reasserts family responsibility.

• Total UK real expenditure on PSS increased throughout the 1970s and 1980s, although at a slower rate than in the previous two decades. During the years 1973/4–1978/9 real expenditure growth averaged 3.4 per cent per year, but slowed down to 3.1 per cent per year during the period 1978/9–1987/8.

• Current expenditure (GB) figures, in both real (adjusted by GDP deflator) and volume terms, show that the annualized rate of growth was far slower during the Conservative period than during the Labour years:

    * Between 1973/4 and 1978/9 real expenditure grew by 7.6 per cent, but by 2.4 per cent between 1978/9 and 1985/6.

    * Growth in volume terms over the same periods was 5.7 per cent and 1.5 per cent, respectively.

• Thus the 2 per cent level of growth deemed necessary by the DHSS to meet demographic changes in need was only just achieved during the Conservative period, although if the figures are taken in volume terms, expenditure has not kept pace at 1.5 per cent per year.

• Current expenditure on PSS was generally maintained (except in 1981/2, when it fell in real terms) irrespective of the Conservative government's planned local authority expenditure cuts and greater constraints through cash limits and rate-capping. Joint finance and implementation of or increases in charges were important here.

● Growth in expenditure and PSS service provision was greater for some client groups (the mentally handicapped and mentally ill) than for the other groups, in both absolute and relative terms:

    * There has been a doubling of the number of residential care places for the mentally ill and mentally handicapped.

    * There has been a 40 per cent fall in the number of places for younger physically handicapped individuals.

    * There has been stagnation in the level of local authority provision for the elderly.

Even though resource targeting in the direction of the mentally handicapped and the mentally ill was achieved, service expansion targets in order to meet need were not attained.

● There have been marked improvements in the provison of local authority domiciliary services between 1974 and 1985. However, they have struggled to keep pace with need. It is far from clear whether the level of provision has been sufficient to enable people to remain in their own homes and live 'independently in the community'.

● Domiciliary and other support services increased, but not at a sufficient rate to meet need, during both Labour and Conservative periods.

● Total residential care provision has increased over the period under study. State-provided residential care remained constant in the face of demographic change. This made way for the rapid expansion in the private residential care sector, which 'mopped up' excess demand. The marked growth in the private sector has been stimulated by changes in the social security system.

● The balance of care shifted from public provision and funding to private provision and funding. The 1980s witnessed an increasing importance of the private (for-profit) sector, especially in residential care.

● The informal care sector constitutes the largest in the provision of care for incapacitated adults and children.

    * One adult in seven provides such assistance (14 per cent), constituting 6 million carers in Britain.

● In financial cost terms alone, the locus of social care provision by different sectors is clear:

    * Expenditure by charities constituted £400 million.

    * Social security expenditure on private (for-profit) residential care in 1985 was £500 million.

    * Statutory PSS support cost £3,800 million in 1987/8.

    * Informal care provides support to the estimated value of £24,000 million (1986).

Annexe

Table 6A.1. *Real government expenditure on the personal social services,*
United Kingdom (£ million at 1987/8 prices)

	Local authority running expenses	Central government	Capital	Total
1973/4	2,031	83	364	2,478
1974/5	2,441	110	324	2,875
1975/6	2,760	143	298	3,202
1976/7	2,866	158	243	3,266
1977/8	2,543	157	139	2,839
1978/9	2,637	138	148	2,922
1979/80	2,809	158	165	3,132
1980/1	2,969	166	169	3,304
1981/2	2,985	134	147	3,266
1982/3	3,062	128	110	3,300
1983/4	3,175	122	112	3,408
1984/5	3,213	122	125	3,460
1985/6	3,529	121	134	3,783
1986/7	3,703	122	148	3,974
1987/8	3,593	125	126	3,844

Sources: CSO 1985*b*,1986*b*, 1988*c*, 1989*c*: table 3.4; GDP deflator from HM Treasury 1989.

Table 6A.2. *Elderly people in residential accommodation, by type of home,*
England (%)

	All local authority	Private	Voluntary
1974	72.0	12.7	15.3
1975	72.6	12.5	14.9
1976	71.8	13.3	14.9
1977	71.2	13.9	14.9
1978	70.6	14.7	14.8
1979	69.8	15.5	14.8
1980	68.6	16.6	14.7
1981	66.9	18.2	14.9
1982	65.4	20.0	14.6
1983	62.7	22.9	14.4
1984	58.8	27.6	13.6
1985	54.5	32.7	12.8
1986	51.0	37.0	12.0

Sources: DHSS 1978, 1982*a*, 1988*d*: tables 7.1, 7.2.

Table 6A.3. *Residential accommodation for elderly people: Contribution of private and voluntary sectors to total local authority provision; England (%)*

	Own[a]	V. & P.[b]		Own[a]	V. & P.[b]
1974	86.3	13.7	1981	88.2	11.8
1975	86.7	13.3	1982	88.7	11.3
1976	86.0	14.0	1983	89.7	10.3
1977	87.2	12.8	1984	90.8	9.2
1978	87.2	12.8	1985	92.3	7.7
1979	87.1	12.9	1986	95.2	4.8
1980	86.6	13.4	1987	96.2	3.8

[a] Own = accommodation provided by local authority.
[b] V. & P. = accommodation provided on behalf of local authority in voluntary or private homes.

Sources: DHSS 1978, 1982*a*, 1988*d*: table 7.1.

Key to Public Expenditure in Tables 6.4 and 6.11

Expenditure on personal social services in Great Britain by service group:

FIELD-WORK

Scotland: administration; case-work.
England and Wales: social work, staff, and related expenses; administration for field-work.

RESIDENTIAL CARE

Scotland: residential care of children; residential care of the elderly.
England and Wales: community homes for children (further broken down into local authority, assisted, and controlled community homes for Wales up to 1984/5); registered voluntary homes outside the community home system (Wales up to 1984/5 only); other children's accommodation; accommodation for mothers and babies;[1] accommodation for mentally handicapped children; youth treatment centres (Wales up to 1981/2 only); accommodation for the elderly; accommodation for younger physically handicapped; accommodation for mentally handicapped adults; accommodation for mentally ill; temporary accommodation; other accommodation; administration for residential care.

DAY CARE

Scotland: day nurseries; day centres for the mentally disordered.
England and Wales: day-care centres for children; intermediate treatment centres

---

[1] Included as a separate item up to 1981/2 in Wales.

for children; day nurseries; pre-school play-groups; child-minding;[2] day centres and clubs for the elderly (excluding meals); meals in centres and clubs; day centres, occupational centres, and clubs; adult training centres.

COMMUNITY CARE

Scotland: home-help services; children's panels.

England and Wales: home helps; laundry; boarded-out children in foster-homes; preventive and supportive services for families; meals in the home; adaptations to homes; aids; telephones; contributions to wardens' salaries; holidays; other community care; administration for all support services (i.e. community care, day care, and other miscellaneous support services).

MISCELLANEOUS

Scotland: other services.

England and Wales: miscellaneous support services; training[3]; research and development.

Key to Public Expenditure in Table 6.12

Expenditure on personal social services in England and Wales by client group:

CHILDREN AND FAMILIES

Residential care: community homes for children (further broken down into local authority, assisted, and controlled community homes for Wales up to 1984/5); registered voluntary home outside the community home system (Wales up to 1984/5 only); other children's accommodation; accom.nodation for mothers and babies;[4] temporary accommodation; accommodation for mentally handicapped children; youth treatment centres (Wales up to 1981/2 only).

Day care: day-care centres for children; intermediate treatment centres for children; day nurseries; pre-school play-groups; child-minding.[5]

Community care: boarded-out children in foster-homes; preventive and supportive services for families; percentage share of the following community-care services: 10% home helps, 20% telephones, 5% holidays and recreation; percentage share of 'other community care';[6] percentage share of miscellaneous support services.[6]

---

[2] Included as a separate item in local authority returns in England from 1982/3.

[3] Included as a separate item in local authority returns in both England and Wales from 1977/8.

[4] Included as a separate item up to 1981/2 in Wales.

[5] Included as a separate item in local authority returns in England from 1982/3.

[6] Proportion allocated to each client group was calculated from the distribution of all other community-care services (home help, laundry, boarded-out children, boarded-out others, preventive and supportive services, meals, aids, adaptations, telephone, contributions to wardens' salaries and holidays) between client groups, and was assigned in the same proportion as the latter.

ELDERLY

Residential care: accommodation for the elderly.

Day care: day centres and clubs for the elderly (excluding meals); meals in centres and clubs.

Community care: laundry; meals in the home; contributions to wardens' salaries (i.e. sheltered housing); percentage share of the following community-care services: 80% home helps, 60% adaptations to homes, 60% aids, 60% telephones, 70% holidays and recreation; percentage share of 'other community care;[7] percentage share of miscellaneous support services.[7]

OTHER ADULTS[8]

Residential care: accommodation for younger physically handicapped; accommodation for mentally handicapped adults; accommodation for mentally ill; other accommodation.

Day care: day centres, occupational centres, and clubs; adult training centres.

Community care: boarded-out (other than children in care); percentage share of the following community care services: 10% home helps, 40% adaptations to homes, 40% aids, 20% telephones, 25% holidays and recreation; percentage share of 'other community care';[9] percentage share of miscellaneous support services.[9]

---

[7] See previous footnote.
[8] Including mentally and physically handicapped (non-elderly) adults.
[9] See n.6 above.

7

Social Security: Solution or Problem?

Nicholas Barr and Fiona Coulter

The mid-1970s saw major reform: some cash benefits were substantially increased (the basic retirement pension), new benefits were introduced (Child Benefit and the State Earnings-Related Pension), and contributions became almost wholly income-related. To oversimplify somewhat, cash benefits were the solution; the only problem was how to pay for them. By the mid-1980s, high replacement rates[1] were regarded as a major problem, in that high benefits discouraged people from joining or rejoining the labour force and, by requiring higher taxation to pay for them, were also a labour-supply disincentive for people in work. One of the major themes of this chapter is how the emphasis, at least in the sense of stated policy goals, changed from equity objectives relating to living standards and the reduction of inequality to efficiency goals concerned with incentives.

I. GOALS AND POLICIES

This section establishes the ultimate goals of the cash benefit system, discusses their incorporation into the stated policy aims of different governments, and briefly surveys actual policies in the periods 1974–9 and 1979–88.

Ultimate goals

In a fundamental sense the ultimate objectives of cash benefits, as in any other area of economic policy, are efficiency, equity, and administrative feasibility. Efficiency, according to the Meade Report (Meade 1978: 269), requires that 'The design of benefits, and of the taxes necessary to finance them, should be such as to minimise any adverse effects on the incentive to work and save.'

Equity has many aspects: the following is a minimum summary, and we return to the various issues shortly in some detail. First, 'The system should aim at guaranteeing an adequate minimum income for everyone' (ibid.); it is open to discussion (below) whether that minimum should be

---

[1] The replacement rate is defined as the ratio of income when unemployed to income (after tax and transfers) when in work.

at subsistence or whether it should be higher, and if so by how much. These benefits 'should be provided with dignity, so that the recipient perceives no loss of social esteem' (ibid.). A third, and to some extent conflicting, equity aim is to seek to pay benefit only to those who 'need' it; this is the issue of whether or not benefits should be 'targeted'. Fourth, the system should be redistributive towards the less well-off.

Administrative feasibility has two aspects. 'The whole system should be as simple, as easy to understand and as cheap to administer as possible' and 'The benefits from the system should be as little open to abuse as possible' (ibid.).

These goals, however, are very general, so that analysis is more usefully conducted in terms of three strategic goals round which the chapter is organized: income support, the reduction of inequality, and social integration.

Income support has different aspects. The first is *poverty relief*, whereby no individual or family/household should fall below some minimum, which can be set at subsistence or higher. A scheme with that objective is Income Support. The effectiveness of any scheme in relieving poverty (however defined) is measured by statistics relating to how many people there are in poverty (so-called 'head-count' measures) or to how much they fall below the poverty line (so-called 'poverty gap' measures).

A second, and separate, aspect is the *protection of accustomed living standards,* so that no one has to face an unexpected and unacceptably large drop in their standard of living. A scheme with this objective is unemployment benefit. This aspect of cash benefits is measured by the replacement ratio, which shows a person's income when receiving benefit in comparison with their income (net of taxes and benefits) when working.

The third aspect of income support is to *smooth out income over the life-cycle.* This can take the form, at least notionally, of the individual redistributing from him/herself at one stage in the life-cycle to him/herself at another; an example is the National Insurance Retirement Pension. Alternatively, there can be provision out of general taxation (i.e. with no pretence of individual contributions) to groups whose stage in the life-cycle suggests that they are likely to be financially constrained, an example being Child Benefit. Assessment of the success of cash benefits in smoothing out income has to rely on comparing the incomes of different groups (e.g. families with young children, or the elderly) with some bench-mark level of income.

Turning to the second strategic goal, the reduction of inequality implies redistribution towards individuals/families with lower incomes. All means-tested benefits contribute to a greater or lesser extent to this aim, and so do non-means-tested benefits whose recipients disproportionately have lower incomes, e.g. the National Insurance Retirement Pension. One way of assessing the success or failure of this aspect of cash benefits is by inspection over time of aggregate inequality measures such as the Gini coefficient or Atkinson measure.[2] However, it should always be remembered that the distributional impact of the cash benefit system is complex, and that summary statistics should therefore be regarded with caution.

In addition to matters of vertical equity, reductions in inequality might also seek to ensure that all groups receive equal access to different benefits, irrespective of such factors as race and gender.

Social integration, the third ultimate goal, is broadly the same aim as for the personal social services (Chapter 6). Two aspects will be discussed. Benefits should not be stigmatizing or socially divisive, but should foster social solidarity. One approach is to condition benefits on criteria unrelated to socio-economic status (e.g. age or having children) rather than on an income test. Second, writers such as Townsend (1979: chs. 1 and 6) and Mack and Lansley (1985: ch. 2) argue that benefits should be sufficiently high to enable recipients to participate fully in the life of the society in which they live.

Specific policy aims of different governments

The distinction between social security[3] as a solution or as a problem emerges clearly in the contrast between stated policy objectives in the mid-1970s and the mid-1980s. Aims of the mid-1970s were established in a Labour White Paper setting out the framework for the 1975 Social Security Pensions Act. The proposals (DHSS 1974: pp. iii–iv) fulfilled the government's pledge 'to end the massive dependence on means-tested supplementary benefit'. The new scheme would 'bring security at the end of working life'. It would also 'provide earnings-related pensions . . . fully protected against inflation'. The proposals were designed 'to help particularly the lower paid', i.e. would be redistributive. A further claim was that the scheme would provide equality for women.

The cost of the proposals was 'very carefully considered in relation to the capacity of the country to support it'. The proposal implied 'a growing cost to be met by the rest of the community . . . The Government are confident that the country will be ready to pay that cost.'

---

[2] The Gini coefficient is a measure of overall inequality which varies from zero (implying complete equality) to one (implying complete inequality). The Atkinson measure is another such statistic. For further discussion, see Atkinson (1983: ch. 3) or Barr (1987: ch. 6).

[3] Social security is defined as all publicly organized cash benefits. This standard British usage differs from the narrower US definition of social security as retirement benefits, and the broader EC definition, which includes health services. Throughout the chapter the term is used in its British sense.

The aims, in short, were to avoid means-testing; to pay indexed benefits; to pay earnings-related benefits which, nevertheless, were redistributive; and to offer equality for women. The belief was that the economy could support a substantial commitment of this sort, a belief based, *inter alia*, on a continued adherence to the 1944 White Paper (Ministry of Reconstruction, 1944) committing government to the maintenance of a 'high and stable level of employment'.

The contrast with a decade later is sharp. Aims of the mid-1980s derive from two sources: the 1985 Employment White Paper (DE 1985) and the Green and White Papers on Social Security (DHSS 1985*a*, *e*). The Green Paper announced 'the most fundamental examination of our social security system since the Second World War' (DHSS 1985*a*: preface). It set out three broad objectives: 'the social security system must be capable of meeting genuine need' (DHSS 1985*a*: para. 1.12), an aim related to the ultimate objective of income support; 'the social security system must be consistent with the Government's overall objectives for the economy' (ibid.). One way of looking at this objective is as part of the aim of efficiency; another is to say that it is not an *aim* of the cash benefit system, but a *constraint* (see the next paragraph for support of the latter view). Third, 'The social security system must be simple to understand and easier to administer' (ibid.).

These aims need to be seen against the backdrop of the 1985 Employment White Paper, which cites the following employment policies: 'bringing inflation under control ...; restraining public expenditure ...; breaking up monopolies ...; providing a surer and better-balanced framework of law for responsible and constructive industrial relations' (DE 1985: para 4.4). Its echo in the Social Security Green Paper (published three months later) is the statement that

While it is one of the functions of the social security system to help those who are unemployed, it is self-defeating if it creates barriers to the creation of jobs, to job mobility or to people rejoining the labour force. Clearly such obstacles exist if people believe themselves better off out of work than in work. (DHSS 1985*a*: para 1.12)

Two policies are implied by these objectives. First, the replacement rate should be reduced, thus giving those out of work a greater incentive to rejoin the labour force. Second, more benefits should be means-tested, the resulting 'targeting' of benefits reducing the cost of the benefit system, thus reducing taxation and improving incentives for those in work.

Policy 1974–1979

The major developments in the welfare state up to 1974 were set out in Chapter 2. The system of cash benefits in 1974 was recognizably that of

1948: individuals still paid a weekly stamp and benefits remained flat-rate. There were only two major exceptions: an additional, earning-related contribution was levied from 1961, which entitled individuals (other than the lowest-paid) to a graduated pension; and the 1966 Social Security Act introduced earnings-related supplements for Unemployment and Sickness Benefits. However, the system was increasingly criticized and was about to change substantially. Three major Acts were passed or took effect in 1975 which, notwithstanding later changes, were to have lasting effects on the social security landscape.

The Social Security Act 1975   Beveridge's contributory scheme was modelled on actuarial insurance. The only changes from private arrangements were that insurance was compulsory, and that everyone was to be in the same pool. The insurance premium was therefore based on the average risk, with two effects: flat-rate benefits implied flat-rate contributions; and since many workers were poor, flat-rate contributions had to be kept low, and so, in consequence, had benefits. Though egalitarian in one sense, the arrangement was repeatedly attacked for being regressive and because benefits were thought to be too low.

The 1975 Social Security Act completely changed the basis of contributions for employees. The weekly stamp was abolished and replaced by a Class 1 social security contribution which was fully earnings-related. When it was first introduced in April 1975, employees earning £11 per week or more contributed $5\frac{1}{2}$ per cent of their earnings up to £69 per week. Self-employed individuals continued to make a weekly flat-rate payment (the Class 2 contribution), and those with profits above a certain level were required in addition to pay an earnings-related contribution.

The main change after 1975 was the increase in the contribution rate: it rose from $5\frac{1}{2}$ per cent of the relevant earnings in 1975/6 to $6\frac{1}{2}$ per cent in 1979/80; thereafter the rise was sharp, from $7\frac{3}{4}$ per cent from April 1981, to $8\frac{3}{4}$ per cent a year later, to 9 per cent from April 1983. Later discussion examines the extent to which rising contributions were the result of larger numbers of beneficiaries (e.g. unemployed people) and how much was due to rising real benefits, such increases being possible because earnings-related contributions broke the actuarial link between contributions and benefits.

The Social Security Pensions Act 1975   Increasingly over the 1950s it was argued that the National Insurance pension was too low. During the later 1960s and early 1970s there was much political wrangling over a series of pension proposals, including Labour's Crossman Plan and a Conservative scheme by Sir Keith Joseph. Neither scheme was implemented. The 1975 Act was in certain respects a blend of the two sets of proposals. In a wide-ranging overhaul it considerably extended earnings-related pensions and, for the first time, gave a statutory basis for the indexation of benefits (for a contemporary analysis, see Barr 1975).

The major features of the Act were the following:

1. A state earnings-related pension scheme (SERPS) was superimposed on the basic (i.e. flat-rate) pension.

2. The basic pension was indexed to changes in earnings or in prices, whichever was the larger (giving rise to the 'ratchet effect' discussed shortly); the earnings-related component was indexed to changes in prices. Pensioners were thus formally protected against inflation.

3. The position of people taking time out of the labour force to look after young children or the disabled was protected in two ways: *home responsibility protection* credited such individuals with a minimum level of contribution so that years spent at home would count towards pension entitlement; and *earnings-related benefit* was calculated on the basis of the individual's twenty best years, thus protecting individuals with fluctuating or steadily rising earnings.

4. The scheme was, for the most part, gender-free, in that the formula was symmetric between spouses.

5. The formula by which the pension was calculated was redistributive from rich to poor.

Though the scheme did not *per se* increase pension expenditure at the time, since entitlement to the earnings-related component was to be built up only gradually, it had major long-term expenditure implications (Barr 1987: ch. 9; Falkingham 1989*b*; Hemming and Kay 1982), to which we return.

The basic pension was increased in July 1974 to £10/£14 per week for a single person/married couple to fulfil an election pledge. Pensions rose sharply in several years in the later 1970s because of the 'ratchet'. The indexation rule tied the basic pension to changes in average earnings, unless prices rose faster. A rule of this sort, if implemented on a strict year-by-year basis, gives an upward bias to the real pension in any year in which prices rise faster than earnings, thereby causing an unintended increase in expenditure.[4]

The Child Benefit Act 1975   The post-1948 system of family support had two strands. *Child Tax Allowances* (£240 for a child not over 11 in 1974/5)

---

[4] Suppose that pensions are £100 in period 0; that in period 1 earnings rise by 100 per cent, with no increase in prices; and that in period 2 prices rise by 100 per cent, with no increase in earnings. Over the whole period real earnings remain unchanged; but pensions have been increased to £200 in period 1, and to £400 in period 2. Pensions, unintentionally, have doubled in real terms while real earnings are unchanged.

were normally payable to the father and, like all tax allowances, were worth more to higher-income families. *Family Allowances* were normally payable to the mother at a weekly rate of 90p in 1974/5. Family allowances were paid only for the second and subsequent children and were taxed as earned income; from the late 1960s they were also subject to 'claw-back', whereby the Child Tax Allowance was reduced by £52 per year for any child for whom Family Allowance was claimed. The combined effect of the two tax rules was to make Family Allowance worth less the higher a family's income and, for the highest earners, to make it worth while not to claim it at all.

Child Tax Allowances were thus worth more to higher-income families, and Family Allowance worth less; and the tax allowances went normally to the father, Family Allowance to the mother. The system, in short, was a mess. The Child Benefit Act 1975 abolished both institutions and replaced them with Child Benefit, a weekly, flat-rate, tax-free cash payment for each child in the family, together with an additional payment to single parents. The system was phased in over three years, and was fully in place by April 1979.

A number of trends may be perceived in these developments. First, in a move which departed sharply from the original Beveridge proposals, there was a major shift towards making both contributions and the major benefits earnings-related. Second, earnings-related contributions, by breaking the link between contributions and benefits, made it possible to increase benefits. In becoming more flexible and redistributive, cash benefits were becoming less and less like actuarial insurance, and increasingly like a tax-transfer scheme.

Policy 1979–1988

It is helpful to look separately at Unemployment Benefit, cash benefits for people with short-term health problems, and Supplementary Benefit and Housing Benefit.

Unemployment Benefit   There were many changes in both the level of benefit and in eligibility conditions, of which the following were the most important. The earnings-related supplement for Unemployment and Sickness Benefits was abolished, with full effect from June 1982. Second, from July 1982, Unemployment Benefit and Supplementary Benefit paid to unemployed people (with the exceptions of additions for children) became taxable.

The indexation of National Insurance benefits was changed in a number of ways, including the suspension for three years of the requirement to up-rate short-term benefits in line with inflation. In this way a real benefit cut was implemented in 1980 and not restored until 1983, by which time benefit had become taxable. A number of other changes were technical: the linked spell rule was tightened in September 1980, and administration was made more stringent, including a major project into social security abuse in 1984.

The overall effect of these piecemeal changes, many of them individually small, was cumulatively to bring about a major reduction in support for the unemployed (for detailed analysis and an account of the many changes, see Atkinson and Micklewright 1989).

Statutory Sick Pay Until 1983 compensation for short-term sickness was treated in the same way as unemployment. In 1983 the Social Security and Housing Benefit Act 1982 transferred to employers the administration of short-term sickness benefits. Under the Act, employees are eligible for Statutory Sick Pay for up to eight weeks (subsequently extended to twenty-eight weeks) in a tax year, which covers the vast majority of health-related absences. Benefits are partially earnings-related and are subject to income tax and National Insurance contributions. Various groups are excluded, notably those below the lower earnings limit, the self-employed, and people over pensionable age. In addition, benefit is not payable in respect of the first three days of absence from work. A medical certificate is required only where sickness lasts more than seven days.

Statutory Sick Payments are made by employers, who simply deduct such disbursements from their monthly return of National Insurance contributions. The original intention had been fully to privatize sick pay, but the suggestion raised a storm of protest, notably from the insurance industry, which was reluctant to insure anyone except white-collar, salaried employees (for an account of the pitfalls of attempts at reform, see Prest 1983). As a result, far from privatizing sick pay, the benefit is, in effect, paid from the National Insurance Fund.[5] The main effects of the changes were the transfer of administration from the Department of Health and Social Security (as it then was) to employers, and also the greater administrative ease of subjecting such benefit to tax and National Insurance contributions. From an economic viewpoint, compensation for sickness remains firmly in the public sector.

---

[5] Formally, Statutory Sick Pay disbursements by employers appear as a negative item in the *revenue* of the National Insurance Fund. The only advantage of such an accounting fiction is the apparent reduction in public spending. A similar effect is caused by tax expenditures, i.e. public expenditure implicit in the granting of tax relief to certain activities, such as approved private pension contributions or mortgage interest payments. See Barr (1986).

Supplementary Benefit and Housing Benefit   The Supplementary Benefits Commission was established in 1966 with wide-ranging discretionary powers. These arrangements remained in force until November 1980, when the Commission was wound up and its discretionary powers replaced by legally binding regulations. In addition, the administration of Supplementary Benefit (SB) was tightened during the first half of the 1980s (Atkinson and Micklewright 1989).

Housing Benefit was introduced in 1983 under the Social Security and Housing Benefit Act 1982 to replace earlier arrangements whereby people on SB received their housing assistance as part of SB, and other claimants received Rate Rebates and Rent Rebates or allowances as separate benefits. We simply note the introduction of Housing Benefit, which is discussed in detail in Chapter 5.

The social security review   The 1985 review discussed earlier was published as a Green Paper, together with three accompanying technical volumes (DHSS 1985*a*, *b*, *c*, *d*), and a subsequent White Paper (DHSS 1985*e*). The reform was intended to deal with what the government regarded as the major problems of the system, namely that the social security system was 'too complex', failed to 'give effective support to many of those in greatest need', left 'too many people trapped in poverty or unemployment', could 'stand in the way of individual . . . choice', and failed 'to take account of the very substantial financial debt [being handed] down to future generations' (DHSS 1985*e*: para. 1.1).

The Green Paper was greeted with considerable hostility, particularly in respect of its proposal to abolish SERPS. The latter proposal was almost universally opposed, not least by the private pensions industry: as with sick pay, insurance companies were concerned at the prospect of having to provide pensions not just for salaried professionals, but also for those with patchier job prospects. The White Paper was rather more circumspect in its proposals. In particular, it retained SERPS but announced that benefits in the medium-term future would be less generous than specified in the 1975 Social Security Pensions Act.

The other major reform was a deliberate move towards more means-testing. For instance, Family Income Supplement (a means-tested benefit for supplementing the incomes of working families with children) was replaced by the rather more generous Family Credit, but at the same time Child Benefit was frozen, thus tilting the balance from (non-means-tested) Child Benefit towards Family Credit, for which only families with low incomes were eligible. This change, along with others, was introduced in 1988 and caused considerable controversy (see Dilnot and Webb 1989).

Though affected by the economic crisis, the 1970s may not unfairly be characterized as a time of innovation and expansion of the cash benefit system. The 1980s, in contrast, were a period less of novelty than of consolidation. There was a deliberate attempt to reduce the replacement rate for those groups for whom labour-supply incentives are relevant, a move to reintroduce substantial means-testing, and, more generally, an attempt to arrest the rate of increase in expenditure on benefits.

II. EXPENDITURE TRENDS

After brief discussion of data sources, this section looks at expenditure by type of benefit, and then by type of recipient.

The data

The expenditure data, for the most part, are drawn from the Public Expenditure White Paper (PEWP) and relate to Great Britain. The raw data were adjusted in four ways.

First, the PEWP for the initial two years of the period published figures only in volume terms; later years were in cash terms. It was therefore necessary for the first two years to inflate the volume data into cash figures using the Retail Price Index. Since the PEWP publishes both cash and volume figures for the following three years, we were able to confirm that the Retail Price Index was the appropriate index for the adjustment.

The cash series were adjusted in two ways. Applying the Gross Domestic Product (GDP) deflator gives a measure of real spending in terms of resources forgone, i.e. it sheds light on macro-economic resource allocation. Deflating by the Retail Price Index gives a volume series, showing the 'output' of cash benefits, which represents more clearly the effects on recipients of changes in benefit levels.

The second major adjustment was the inclusion of Statutory Sick Pay, which appears in the public-sector accounts as an item of negative revenue in the National Insurance Fund (see n. 5 above). But Statutory Sick Pay is as much a cash benefit as is Sickness Benefit *per se*, and so, in the expenditure tables, spending on Statutory Sick Pay is added to the figures in the PEWP.

Third, it is necessary to separate spending on Supplementary Benefit from that on Housing Benefit. Housing Benefit is included in the body of the expenditure tables but, to avoid double counting with Chapter 5, is not included in the figure for total social security spending.

Finally, it is necessary to take some account of tax expenditures since, parallel to the system of cash benefits, the tax system provides financial support to some groups in the form of tax relief. Such support takes two forms. First, there are additional personal allowances such as the Age Allowance, the Additional Personal Allowance for a single parent, the Blind Person's Allowance, and the Widow's Bereavement Allowance. Their value in recent years has been small except for the first two, the cost of which had grown by 1987/8 to £450 million and £170 million, respectively.

The second type of tax expenditure arises because some social security benefits are tax-free. There are few data for the 1970s, and Inland Revenue estimates for the 1980s are very rough, so the main expenditure tables have not been adjusted to take account of these exemptions. Their value can be quite large: the exemption for Unemployment Benefit in 1981/2 cost £400 million, nearly 10 per cent of all benefit spending on the unemployed. The total value of such exemptions fell substantially from just over £1 billion in cash terms in 1981/2 to £485 million two years later, as benefits in respect of unemployment and ill-health became taxable.

The combined cost of the additional tax allowances and the exemption from tax of some cash benefits fell over the period from about 4 per cent of all social security spending in 1978/9 to about 1.3 per cent in 1982. For further discussion, see Willis and Hardwick (1978); data on various tax expenditures are also shown each year in *Inland Revenue Statistics*.

Allowances and exemptions like these are not usually considered part of the social security system, and in the main we follow that convention. However, one tax expenditure, the Child Tax Allowances (which reached nearly £1 billion before the introduction of Child Benefit), is so large that its omission would distort the picture. To present a consistent series, the value of Child Tax Allowances has been added to the PEWP figures for Family Allowance in the expenditure tables.

Public expenditure by type of benefit

Real benefit spending in the United Kingdom (at 1987/8 prices adjusted by GDP deflator) rose from £26.5 billion in 1973/4 to £43.2 billion in 1988/9 (Table 7.1), an increase of nearly two-thirds, from 18.9 per cent of total public spending to 24.5 per cent, and from 8.1 to 9.7 per cent of GDP (down from a peak of over 11 per cent in the mid-1980s). Real spending over the whole period rose by 3.3 per cent per year on average, falling from 4.6 per cent per year for the period 1973/4–1978/9 to about 2.7 per cent thereafter. Over the same period, GDP rose on average by 2.1 per cent per year, and over the two sub-periods by 1.6 and 2.2 per cent per year, respectively.

Insurance benefits Real expenditure rose in the mid-1970s, mainly because of the pensions increase promised before the February 1974 elec-

Table 7.1. *Summary of benefit expenditure* (£ billion, real, at 1987/8 prices)

	Insurance benefits (GB)	Non-contributory non-means-tested (GB)	Means-tested (GB)	Administrative costs (GB)	Other (Inc. Northern Ireland)	Total social security spending (UK)
	(1)	(2)	(3)	(4)	(5)	(6)
1973/4	17.1	5.5	1.7	1.1	1.1	26.5
1974/5	18.2	5.3	1.9	1.3	1.1	27.8
1975/6	19.7	5.6	2.3	1.6	1.0	30.2
1976/7	20.8	5.7	2.7	1.5	0.9	31.6
1977/8	21.3	5.3	2.8	1.4	1.2	32.0
1978/9	21.8	6.2	2.8	1.4	1.0	33.2
1979/80	21.2	7.3	2.5	1.4	1.2	33.6
1980/1	21.8	5.9	3.0	1.5	1.3	33.5
1981/2	23.1	6.2	4.2	1.7	1.2	36.4
1982/3	23.3	6.5	5.3	1.7	1.2	38.0
1983/4	24.2	6.8	6.9	1.7	1.5	41.1
1984/5	24.2	7.1	7.6	1.8	1.4	42.1
1985/6	24.8	7.2	8.2	1.8	1.5	43.5
1986/7	25.8	7.4	8.6	1.9	1.4	45.1
1987/8	25.5	7.5	8.1	2.0	1.5	44.6
1988/9	24.8	7.1	7.8	2.0	1.5	43.2

Notes and Sources: See Table 7A.1 in Annexe to this chapter.

tion, thereafter remaining at about £21 billion over the later 1970s. The sharp increase from 1980/1 onwards has several strands (see Table 7A.1). Spending on pensions rose as real benefits and the number of recipients both increased; and real spending on Invalidity Benefit rose as recipients increased. There was a sharp increase in real spending on contributory Unemployment Benefit, which doubled in the two years after 1979/80. Thereafter, real spending remained about £1.8 billion over the mid-1980s, new entrants to unemployment being roughly offset by those rejoining the labour force and (considerably more numerous) those moving entirely on to SB, having exhausted their insurance entitlement.

Non-means-tested non-contributory benefits Real spending rose from £5.5 billion in 1973/4 to £7.1 billion in 1988/9, partly because of increased expenditure on the Attendance Allowance and the introduction of new benefits such as the Invalidity Pension/Severe Disablement Allowance and the Mobility Allowance.

Some benefits did not survive, or came close to being abolished. Real spending on the Maternity Grant and Death Grant (Table 7A.1) totalled £123 million in 1973/4. Neither benefit was up-rated in line with inflation, and so real spending had fallen to £34 million by 1986/7. In the 1985 benefit review (DHSS 1985a, e) they were abolished as universal benefits and replaced by higher benefits payable only on the basis of a means test.

Child Benefit was not abolished but, if newspaper reports at the time are to be believed, came close to it when the benefit reviews were in a formative stage before the publication of the Green Paper (DHSS 1985a). In April 1988 and again in April 1989 the benefit was not up-rated in line with inflation, as part of the deliberate attempt, described earlier, to move towards means-tested benefits. At the time of writing it is far from clear what the future of Child Benefit will be.

Means-tested benefits Real spending rose sharply from £1.7 billion in 1973/4 to £7.8 billion in 1988/9, the main driving force being the huge increase in Supplementary Allowance expenditure, the great bulk of it because of rising unemployment.

The overall picture shows up clearly in Fig. 7.1, which incorporates all cash benefits, *including* Housing Benefit. As discussed earlier, one of the aims of the 1974–9 Labour governments was to reduce dependence on means-tested benefits; and Fig. 7.1 shows how increased real expenditure was mainly on the National Insurance and non-means-tested benefits. Since 1980 there has been increased emphasis on 'targeting', which, together with rising dependence by the unemployed on SB, explains the sharp increase in spending on means-tested benefits, which shows up clearly in Fig. 7.1. In fact, the targeting is even more precise. Fig. 7.2

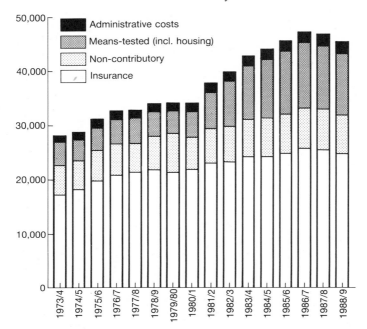

FIG. 7.1. Social security spending, Great Britain (£ million, real, at 1987/8 prices)

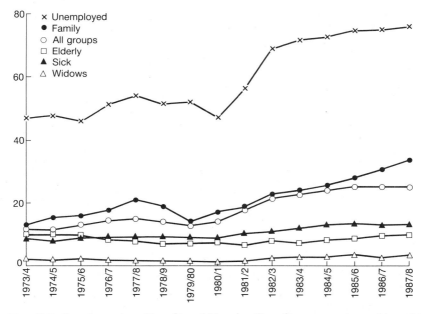

FIG. 7.2. Supplementary Benefit and Housing Benefit as percentage of benefit
payments, by client group

Nicholas Barr and Fiona Coulter

Table 7.2. *State benefits[a] by client group, Great Britain*

	Elderly[b]	Sick[c]	Unemployed	Widows	Family[d]	Total	Total assuming constant population[e]
	(1)	(2)	(3)	(4)	(5)	(6)	(7)

Real expenditure (£ bn at 1987/8 prices)

1973/4	13.7	4.0	1.4	1.5	5.3	26.0	26.0
1974/5	14.8	4.2	1.5	1.6	5.1	27.1	26.6
1975/6	15.4	4.3	2.4	1.5	5.5	29.1	26.8
1976/7	16.2	4.6	3.0	1.5	5.8	31.0	27.9
1977/8	16.8	4.9	3.1	1.4	5.4	31.6	27.8
1978/9	17.9	5.1	2.8	1.4	6.2	33.5	29.6
1979/80	17.8	4.9	2.6	1.3	7.2	33.7	30.0
1980/1	18.0	4.7	3.7	1.3	5.8	33.5	28.3
1981/2	19.3	5.0	5.4	1.3	6.2	37.2	29.9
1982/3	20.3	5.2	6.3	1.3	6.6	39.7	31.3
1983/4	21.3	5.9	6.9	1.3	7.0	42.4	32.6
1984/5	21.6	6.3	7.3	1.2	7.3	43.7	33.0
1985/6	22.3	6.7	7.6	1.2	7.5	45.3	33.9
1986/7	23.1	7.4	7.7	1.2	7.7	47.0	34.4
1987/8	23.1	7.9	6.9	1.1	7.7	46.6	34.2

As percentage of total benefits

1973/4	53	15	6	6	21		
1974/5	54	15	6	6	19		
1975/6	53	15	8	5	19		
1976/7	52	15	10	5	19		
1977/8	53	15	10	5	17		
1978/9	54	15	8	4	19		
1979/80	53	14	8	4	21		
1980/1	54	14	11	4	17		
1981/2	52	13	15	3	17		
1982/3	51	13	16	3	17		
1983/4	50	14	16	3	17		
1984/5	49	14	17	3	17		
1985/6	49	15	17	3	17		
1986/7	49	16	16	3	16		
1987/8	50	17	15	2	16		

[a] The figures include the housing cost element of Supplementary Benefit and Rent and Rate Rebates/Allowances before the introduction of Housing Benefit in 1982/3, and Housing Benefit thereafter. Rate Rebates are not part of public expenditure. A small amount of Housing Benefit paid to people in work is excluded. Expenditure is classified according to the underlying grounds of entitlement to a benefit, so that, for example, Child Benefit paid

shows payments of SB and Housing Benefit, the two major means-tested benefits, as a percentage of total benefits paid for different groups. The bottom three lines show that payments of these means-tested benefits remained roughly constant as a proportion of benefit spending for the elderly, the sick, and widows. For families, however, and particularly for the unemployed, there was a sharp increase in reliance on means-tested benefits.

Public expenditure by type of beneficiary

It is important to break down changes in real spending into (*a*) increased benefit per recipient, and (*b*) rising numbers of recipients. The first represents active government policy and shows the system becoming, in some sense, more generous; the second is a response to demographic, social, and economic change and represents more of a passive response to increased demand or increased need. Table 7.2 looks at total spending (i.e. at the combined effects of (*a*) and (*b*)); Table 7.3 shows average weekly spending per beneficiary (adjusted for inflation) and hence measures changes in the generosity of support for individuals.

The tables are in no way definitive, for at least two reasons. There are different ways of measuring the number of recipients (e.g. does one include individuals who are unemployed or retired but who, for whatever reason, are not receiving benefit?). Second, the average payment per recipient is not entirely the result of government policy, particularly for the unemployed, since it also depends on the duration of unemployment.

Spending on different groups   Real spending on the elderly rose from £13.7 billion in 1973/4 to £23.1 billion in 1987/8 (Table 7.2). The number of recipients rose from 7.7 million to 9.9 million. In addition, the real pension rose, both because the basic pension increased from £35.90 (1987 prices) in July 1974 to £39.50 in July 1987, and latterly also because

---

(*Table notes cont.*)

to an unemployed person is allocated to the family group, and Attendance Allowance paid to a retirement pensioner appears under the sick and disabled category.

   [b] Includes Supplementary Benefit paid to men under retirement age but over 60.

   [c] Includes specific benefits for disabled people, in addition to Sickness Benefit, Invalidity Benefit, Supplementary Allowance, and Housing Benefit. From 1983 onwards the figures also include Statutory Sick Pay.

   [d] Includes Child Benefit, One-Parent Benefit, Family Income Supplement, Maternity Benefit, and Supplementary Allowance paid to one-parent families and to people looking after elderly parents. The figures also include the estimated cost of Child Tax Allowances.

   [e] The constant population figures assume that the numbers of pensioners, unemployed people, etc. remained unchanged at their 1973/4 levels. The figures are calculated by dividing real spending on each benefit each year by the average number of recipients of that benefit in that year, and then multiplying the resulting per capita benefit by the 1973/4 numbers of recipients.

Source: HM Treasury 1989 and equivalents for earlier years.

SERPS became payable. As a result, the average spending per elderly recipient (Table 7.3) rose from £32 per week in 1973/4 to £44.8 per week in 1987/8.

Total real expenditure on unemployed people rose from £1.4 billion to £6.9 billion (Table 7.2). Spending on insurance benefits rose from £0.8 billion to a peak of £2.2 billion in 1981/2, thereafter declining to about £1.8 billion (Table 7A.1); in addition, there was a vast increase in the number of unemployed people, their insurance entitlement exhausted, dependent on SB. Total numbers receiving one or both benefits rose over the period from 509,000 to 3 million. Total support per unemployed person (Table 7.3), when adjusted for changes in the Retail Price Index, rose very slightly from £49.3 to £50.9 per week. As we shall see later, however, this result is misleading: it ignores the possibility that people on lower incomes might face higher than average rates of inflation; nor does it take account of the fact that after 1982, compensation for the unemployed became taxable.

Real spending on family benefits rose (Table 7.2) from £5.3 billion to £7.7 billion, in part because Child Benefit, unlike Family Allowance, was payable to the first child in the family. As a result, the number of recipients almost doubled in April 1978. Separately, real benefits per child (Table 7.3) rose substantially.

The figures on the sick and disabled in Table 7.2 are adjusted to include Statutory Sick Pay. Real spending on existing benefits rose as the number of recipients increased, and new benefits were introduced, so that total spending increased from £4.0 billion to £7.9 billion.

The overall picture   The pattern in Fig. 7.3 shows increasing real expenditure on the elderly and on families. Much the largest proportionate increase is expenditure on the unemployed. In consequence (see the lower half of Table 7.2), though absolute spending on pensions rose, its share fell from 53 per cent of total benefit expenditure to 50 per cent, adding weight to Falkingham's (1989*b*) argument against the crude gerontic dependency ratio as a measure of the burden of supporting the elderly.

The effect of rising numbers of recipients is shown in Table 7.2. Col. (6) shows that total real spending on cash benefits rose over the period by about £20 billion, from £26.0 billion to £46.6 billion; had the numbers of recipients of the different benefits remained at their 1973/4 levels (col. (7)), spending would have increased only by £8.2 billion, to £34.2 billion. Of the total increase, therefore, £8.2 billion (about one-third) represented increased generosity (though subject to caveats, in that some benefits became taxable), and the remaining £12.4 billion was a response to increased numbers of recipients and was therefore, in some sense, a response to increased need or increased demand.

The relative importance of the two factors changed over time. Of the total increase in real spending between 1973/4 and 1979/80, £4 billion (over half) was due to increased spending per recipient, the remaining £3.7 billion being caused by increased numbers. Over the 1980s, the greater proportion of increased spending (almost inevitably, given the

Table 7.3. *Social security spending per recipient,[a] Great Britain*
(£ per week, volume, at 1987/8 prices)

	Elderly (1)	Sick (2)	Unemployed (3)	Widows (4)	Family (5)
1973/4	32.0	65.8	49.3	44.3	6.5
1974/5	33.3	69.2	50.4	51.8	6.3
1975/6	33.7	64.3	47.1	53.1	6.8
1976/7	33.6	65.1	49.9	53.1	7.1
1977/8	33.9	65.8	49.4	52.3	6.7
1978/9	36.6	65.9	49.2	53.8	8.0
1979/80	36.8	64.9	47.4	51.8	9.5
1980/1	37.4	66.1	44.4	51.4	7.9
1981/2	39.1	65.6	44.9	53.2	8.5
1982/3	40.1	68.0	48.5	54.0	9.2
1983/4	41.7		49.3	54.8	10.0
1984/5	41.5		50.0	55.5	10.5
1985/6	42.9		51.8	56.4	10.9
1986/7	43.8		50.2	56.5	11.3
1987/8	44.8		50.9	56.4	11.4

[a] The figures are obtained by dividing aggregate spending on each benefit by the average number of recipients. Aggregate spending is the cash figure in the Public Expenditure White Paper deflated by the relevant price index: spending on the elderly was deflated using the Pensioner Price Index, and other benefits were deflated using the Retail Price Index.

[b] The figures for the numbers of recipients are as follows:

  (i) Elderly: average numbers receiving retirement pension at any time, plus pensioners receiving supplementary pension only, including, for 1982/3 and after, those men aged over 60 who do not have to register for work.

  (ii) Sick: those receiving Sickness or Invalidity Benefit, Non-Contributory Invalidity Pension, or Severe Disablement Allowance, plus those receiving Supplementary Benefit only who are classified as short- or long-term sick. This series only goes up to 1982/3, since no figures are available for those receiving Statutory Sick Pay.

  (iii) Unemployed: all those receiving Unemployment Benefit or Supplementary Benefit as an unemployed person.

  (iv) Widows: those receiving widow's benefits.

  (v) Family: the population aged under 18.

Sources: Data on total spending: HM Treasury 1989 and earlier equivalents; numbers of recipients: for elderly, sick, unemployed, and widows, Public Expenditure White Paper where possible (mainly later years); otherwise DHSS 1987g and earlier equivalents, except for the numbers of children under 18, which are OPCS figures.

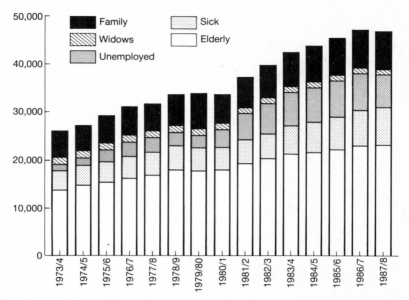

FIG. 7.3. State benefits by client group, Great Britain (real, 1987/8 = 100)

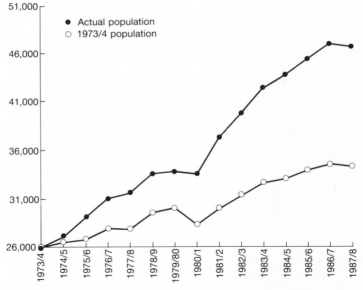

FIG. 7.4. Real benefit expenditure, Great Britain (£ million, 1987/8 = 100)

large rise in unemployment) was the result of increased numbers of recipients.

The most important demographic, social, and economic changes affecting expenditure were the increased number of elderly and, above all, the huge increase in the number of unemployed people. Col. (3) of Table 7.2 shows that real spending on the unemployed rose by £5 billion between 1979/80 and 1985/6, the *increase* alone representing some 15 per cent of *total* spending on cash benefits. The last two columns of Table 7.2 are shown in Fig. 7.4: the lower line shows the effect on real spending of rising benefits per recipient, and the difference between the lower and the upper lines the effect of increased numbers of beneficiaries.

The public private mix

The private sector is relevant, even in principle, only to the insurance benefits. Unemployment, for technical reasons, is not an insurable risk, and so cannot be covered by private companies (see Barr 1987: chs. 5 and 8; 1988). Sickness and disability, in contrast, are insurable, and such policies are offered by insurance companies. But the aggregate amounts involved are small and there is no source of data on their precise magnitude.

The one area in which the private sector plays a major role is pensions. Table 7.4 shows total pensions originating from the state (col. (1)) and the private sector (col. (2)). In the years after 1973/4 the state pension rose from 45.8 per cent of the total to over 52 per cent in 1978/9. The growing importance of private pensions thereafter had two sources. Real state pension spending grew more slowly after 1980 because the state pension was indexed to changes in prices rather than average earnings. Separately, private pension disbursements grew because each individual occupational pensioner was receiving more, and also because the number of occupational pensioners was rising. Data on the latter are given in Table 7.5, which shows that the proportion of elderly people with occupational pensions rose from 29 per cent in 1975 to 37 per cent ten years later, with broadly similar increases for men and women separately. For further discussion see Hannah (1986) and Falkingham (1989a).

A complete picture of the cash benefit system thus includes both private and publicly organized cash benefits; the latter include (a) direct expenditures (e.g. Child Benefit), (b) tax expenditures (e.g. Child Tax Allowances), and (c) public-sector benefits some of whose administration has been hived off to the private sector (e.g. Statutory Sick Pay). Table 7.1, 7.2, 7A.1 contain (a) from the PEWP, adjusted from other sources to include (b) and (c); they do not, however, include private-sector benefits, such as occupational pensions, or the tax relief on private insurance premiums.

III. OUTPUTS

This section returns to the specific policy aims set out in section I, and briefly considers the extent to which they were achieved.

Table 7.4. *State and private pension payments, United Kingdom* (£ billion, cash)

	State pensions[a] (1)	Private pensions (2)	Total (3)	State/ total (%) (4)
1973/4	2.9	3.4	6.3	45.8
1974/5	3.7	4.0	7.7	47.9
1975/6	4.9	4.7	9.7	51.1
1976/7	5.9	5.3	11.2	52.4
1977/8	6.9	6.1	13.0	53.1
1978/9	7.9	7.1	15.0	52.5
1979/80	9.2	8.5	17.7	51.8
1980/1	10.9	10.7	21.7	50.5
1981/2	12.6	13.4	26.0	48.6
1982/3	14.1	15.3	29.4	48.0
1983/4	15.4	17.3	32.7	47.0
1984/5	16.2	19.3	35.5	45.6
1985/6	17.6	21.8	39.5	44.7
1986/7	19.0	25.0	44.0	43.2

[a] Contributory Retirement Pensions, Non-Contributory Pension, and Supplementary Pension.

Sources: State pension: Table 7A.1; private pensions: CSO 1988*b*: table 4.9.

Table 7.5. *Percentage of elderly people in receipt of income from occupational pensions*

	Men	Women	Total
1975	51	15	29
1980	56	19	33
1985	58	23	37

Notes: Estimates, based on General Household Survey.
Source: Falkingham 1989*a*.

Achieving policy objectives

Policies in the mid-1970s The prime aim was to move away from means-testing by raising various benefits to a level above that of SB. There was a sharp increase in the basic pension in 1974, and the 1975 Social Security Pensions Act introduced SERPS, though the effect of the latter was only gradual. Separately, the introduction of Child Benefit sharply increased family support, mainly because benefit was extended to the first child in each family. From Table 7.1, real spending on insurance and other non-means-tested benefits rose by 25 per cent between 1973/4 and 1979/80, a result which shows up clearly in Fig. 7.1.

A second major aim was to pay benefits which would not be eroded by inflation. The 1975 Social Security Act introduced statutory indexation, which was also incorporated in the Social Security Pensions Act of the same year. In many ways, however, this merely gave statutory force to established custom, since benefits up to 1975 had been indexed *de facto* to average earnings even in the absence of any legal requirement (Barr 1981).

The third aim was to extend earnings-related benefits, mainly through the introduction of SERPS. In addition, the new pension arrangements contributed to a fourth aim, that of increased equality for women in the context of cash benefits. For similar reasons, Child Benefit, like Family Allowance, was normally payable to the mother.

A final aim of the mid-1970s was to devote more resources to cash benefits. From Table 7.1, real spending rose from £26.5 billion in 1973/4 to £31.6 billion three years later, an increase of nearly one-fifth.

Policy in the 1980s There were two overriding objectives: incentives and targeting. On the former, it was argued that the replacement rate was too high, so that the financial gain from resuming work after a spell of unemployment was too small to encourage people to rejoin the labour force. As a matter of deliberate policy, therefore, Unemployment Benefit was cut. First, the earnings-related supplement to Unemployment Benefit was abolished with effect from 1982. Second, by parsimonious indexation, the flat-rate benefit fell relative to average earnings (see Fig. 7.5). Third, Unemployment Benefit became taxable with effect from 1982. Fourth, eligibility conditions were tightened in a number of ways. The overall result was a decline in overall support to unemployed individuals in comparison with what they could earn if employed, a topic to which we return in section iv.

Targeting, too, had a major effect on the landscape. As discussed earlier, the 1970s policy of reduced reliance on non-means-tested benefits was explicitly reversed. Fig. 7.1 shows the rising proportion of means-tested benefits throughout the 1980s, partly the result of large numbers of unemployed people on SB, having exhausted their insurance entitlement, but partly also because non-means-tested benefits were up-rated only in line with the Retail Price Index rather than with average earnings.

A third aim was to reduce the proportion of national resources devoted to cash benefits, hence less generous indexation, the move towards means-testing, and the reduction in the generosity of SERPS after the turn of the century announced in the Fowler review (DHSS 1985*e*). Had unemployment remained constant, that aim would largely have been achieved; but, mainly because of the large rise in unemployment, real spending increased by about one-third between 1979/80 and 1986/7 (Table 7.1), and from 9.2 to 11.1 per cent of GDP.

Take-up

In both periods a stated aim of policy was to improve take-up. Yet throughout the period many people with apparent entitlement to benefit failed to claim it.

There are two main measures of take-up: the *case-load* take-up rate refers to the proportion of eligible *claimants* who receive benefit; the *entitlement* measure relates to the percentage of total *benefit* claimed. Take-up is typically higher according to the entitlement measure—for

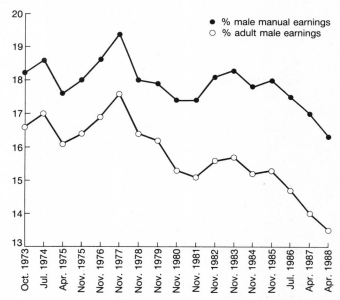

FIG. 7.5. Unemployment Benefit, standard rate, as percentage of average male earnings

example, DHSS estimates for 1981 found an overall case-load take-up rate of 71 per cent for SB, but found that the proportion of benefit claimed was considerably higher at 85 per cent (DHSS 1986a). This reflects the fact that individuals are more likely to claim the larger the entitlement, and, therefore, that non-claimants will be predominantly those with small entitlements. In fact, one of the drawbacks of using a case-load measure of take-up is that it is sensitive to the inclusion or exclusion of groups with small entitlements, for reasons that are discussed below.

It should be stressed, however, that the average amounts unclaimed (£5 per week for a pensioner, and £18 per week for a non-pensioner in 1981) are not trivial for a person with an income near the SB level. Moreover, since on average a non-claiming non-pensioner appeared to be prepared to give up £18 per week rather than claim benefit, these figures represent the average money cost (for non-claimants) of claiming benefits in 1981. If these costs are similar for claimants and non-claimants (though this is probably not the case) then we should deduct these amounts from any measure of the money income of SB recipients, to take account of the effect on individual welfare of the cost of claiming benefit. The nature of these costs, and hence the reasons why individuals may fail to claim benefits to which they are entitled, is discussed below.

Problems of definition and measurement   Much of the empirical evidence relates to case-load take-up, and so it is on this that we concentrate. Table 7.6 summarizes some of the evidence.

The take-up rate is defined as the number receiving a benefit divided by the number receiving it plus those estimated to be entitled to but not actually receiving that benefit. Both the definition of take-up and its measurement raise considerable problems (most of which also apply to entitlement measures), so that estimates must be interpreted with caution.

First, not all those receiving a benefit at any one time may actually be entitled; if they were excluded, estimated take-up would be lower (see Dilnot, Kay, and Morris 1984).

A further problem arises where different benefits overlap. Individuals may be eligible for more than one benefit, and their entitlement may depend on which benefit they decide to claim. Some may claim the 'wrong' benefit (which gives them a lower entitlement) or may claim neither. If so, there is ambiguity in the definition of take-up for an individual benefit.

Once the definition of take-up has been decided, empirical estimates generally have to be derived from sample survey, usually the Family Expenditure Survey (FES). The FES suffers from non-response (about 70 per cent of people respond), and so may not accurately reflect the

Table 7.6. *Estimates of the case-load take-up of social security benefits* (%)

(a) SUPPLEMENTARY BENEFIT

	Pensioners	Non-pensioners	Males over 65	All
DHSS estimates				71[b]
1973	74[a]	70[a]		75[b]
1974	76[a]	72[a]		77[b]
1975	74[a]	75[a]		77[b]
1976	74[a]	79[a]		74[b]
1977 (orig.)	73[a]	76[a]		75[c]
1977 (revd.)	72[c]	79[c]		70[d]
1979	65[d]	78[d]		71[d]
1981	67[d]	75[d]		n.a.
1981[e]	72[d]	n.a.		76[f]
1983	67[f]	83[f]		
Altmann[g]				
1973			59.2	
1974			58.2	
1975			59.6	
1976			48.9	
1977			58.4	
Fry and Stark[h]				
1984	66	78		74
Blundell, Fry, and Walker[i] 1984				76[j]

(b) ONE-PARENT BENEFIT

	DHSS estimates	OPCS estimates[k]
1979		70
1980	66[l]	77
1981	70[m]	78
1982		83
1983		89
1984		93

(c) FAMILY INCOME SUPPLEMENT[n]

	DHSS estimates	Dilnot, Kay, and Morris[o]
Oct. 1978–Sept. 1979	51[p]	
1981		48
Jan. 1981–Dec. 1982	50[q]	
1983/4	54[r]	

numbers of low-income families in the population. Moreover, income may be recorded inaccurately, a problem which may be particularly important for individuals with income near the level which entitles them to benefit, since small errors in reported income may affect their benefit entitlement. Hence any bias in recording income may have large effects on estimated take-up, particularly case-load-based estimates. The problem is particularly important for pensioners, large numbers of whom have incomes near the SB level.

The FES does not contain all the information required for establishing entitlement, such as data on capital assets and on cohabitation. For benefits with small numbers of recipients the estimates may be subject to considerable sampling error.

All these points need to be borne in mind when interpreting the figures

---

(Table notes cont.)

Note: In part (*a*) of the table, all estimates for the take-up of Supplementary Benefit quoted use the Family Expenditure Survey (FES) to estimate those entitled to but not receiving SB, the DHSS uses its own statistics to estimate those receiving, while the other studies quoted here used the FES. Take-up is defined in n. 8 below.

[a] Supplementary Benefits Commission 1979.

[b] *Official Report*, 28 Oct., 1980, WA, col. 268.

[c] *Official Report*, 5 Apr. 1982, WA, cols. 247–50. The main difference between the original and revised estimates for 1977 is in the assumed eligibility of a residual group, originally classified as being 'unoccupied', whose entitlement to benefit was in doubt. Two-thirds of these were excluded from the revised estimates, and the remaining third reclassified to the 'sick and disabled' group.

[d] *Official Report*, 30 Nov. 1983, WA, cols. 533–6.

[e] Before 1981 the estimates exclude entitlement to heating additions, which leads to an overstatement of take-up. By 1981 entitlement to heating additions for those over 70 had become automatic and were therefore taken into account. For comparative purposes, the estimate excluding heating additions is shown for 1981.

[f] Social Security Advisory Committee 1988.

[g] Altmann 1981. The figures are not strictly comparable with the DHSS figures, since the DHSS analysis excludes those people who would have been better-off claiming housing rebates from its estimates of those entitled. However, the major reason for the much lower take-up is probably the exclusion of single females, who tend to have higher take-up rates.

[h] Fry and Stark 1987. The figures are comparable with DHSS estimates.

[i] Blundell, Fry, and Walker 1988.

[j] Authors' calculation intended to produce an estimate consistent with DHSS estimates.

[k] HM Treasury 1988.

[l] Social Security Advisory Committee 1982.

[m] Social Security Advisory Committee 1983.

[n] The figures for the take-up of Family Income Supplement are derived from the FES, which gives a very small sample; about fifty people are recorded as being in receipt, with a further fifty or so calculated as being entitled but not receiving.

[o] Dilnot, Kay, and Morris 1984.

[p] Social Security Advisory Committee 1983.

[q] DHSS 1986*a*.

[r] The source is Social Advisory Committee 1988. The figures are derived from data from the FES pooled for the years 1983 and 1984. The standard errors for the estimate are about 10%.

discussed shortly. For further discussion of estimation problems, see Supplementary Benefits Commission (1978), Altmann (1981), Atkinson (1983), Dilnot, Kay, and Morris (1984), Fry and Stark (1987), and Blundell, Fry, and Walker (1988).

Reasons for incomplete take-up   Little is known about why people do not claim benefits. The theories most often put forward can be grouped under the headings of 'ignorance', 'inconvenience', and 'stigma'. Most people are ignorant about the workings of the benefit system (see Spicker 1986). This is not surprising, in view of its complication. It appears that even those who administer the system are themselves often ignorant, given the non-trivial number of incorrect payments discussed shortly.

Ignorance alone, however, is implausible as a complete explanation. Campaigns to improve take-up through publicity campaigns have only limited effect (Spicker 1986). Many people, even if fully informed, might prefer not to claim. According to the Social Security Advisory Committee (1983), 'DHSS-funded research on take-up of supplementary pensions found that of a group of 92 pensioners who would have been eligible for Supplementary Pension only 10 bothered to claim it, even when told exactly what to do and what their probable entitlement was.'

Inconvenience may be a second cause of incomplete take-up. Claiming benefits imposes costs on the claimant, including the time spent filling in long and complicated forms and the need to answer potentially embarrassing questions on income and family circumstances. An important example is the cohabitation rule, whereby unmarried couples living together as husband and wife are treated as a single income unit for benefit purposes. In order to determine whether they are cohabiting, claimants may have to provide detailed and very personal information. According to the Child Poverty Action Group guide to the benefit system,

DHSS officers are instructed *not* to ask the claimant questions about the existence of a sexual relationship, so they will only have the information you volunteer. This means that if you do not have a sexual relationship, you should tell the officer yourself—and perhaps offer to show him/her the separate sleeping arrangements.... It used to be common for a woman to have her benefit withdrawn if she slept with a man on, say, three consecutive nights, even though the couple might feel none of the long-term commitments generally associated with marriage. Such cases are now less common. But the pendulum has swung, and, as a result, couples with no sexual relationship who live together (e.g., as landlady/lodger, tenant/housekeeper, or as flatsharers) are in danger of falling foul of the rule. (CPAG 1988: 123)

'Stigma' may arise if individuals feel that if they claim certain benefits they will be labelled as belonging to a socially rejected group, such as the 'poor', or 'unemployed'. Hence there is a psychological cost to claiming benefit, in addition to those imposed by the process of claiming itself. One consequence is that take-up may vary according to the number of potential recipients. For example, if unemployment rises, unemployed people may be more likely to claim benefits if there is a widespread feeling that it is 'not their fault' (see Cowell 1986). This may be the explanation for the considerably higher estimates for take-up of SB for non-pensioners in 1983 compared with 1981 (though this explanation should be treated with caution, since there is only one observation for the period after 1981/2, when the large rise in unemployment occurred).

Estimates of take-up

There has been little research on the take-up of non-means-tested benefits. Take-up of the Retirement Pension and Child Benefit is close to 100 per cent (DHSS 1986*a*: 273). Lower take-up is possible, however, for obscure benefits such as Guardian's Allowance, for which ignorance may be a problem. For many non-means-tested benefits there may be substantial costs of claiming. In the case of Disability Benefit, for example, people have to undergo a lengthy and possibly humiliating test to determine the extent of disability. To claim Unemployment Benefit, individuals must complete a questionnaire to determine availability for work. After six months they will be called for an interview at the local Job Centre, and they may be recalled at any time for interview by a 'claimant adviser'.

Moreover, there is some evidence that unemployed people may be deterred from claiming benefit, at least in the early weeks of unemployment. The DHSS Cohort Study of Unemployed Men, conducted in the autumn of 1978, found that on average the men in the sample had spent two weeks in the previous year in unregistered unemployment. The average masks wide variation: while the majority (73 per cent) had registered immediately, 17 per cent had spent up to four weeks in unregistered unemployment, while 5 per cent had spent four to eight weeks, and 3 per cent had spent nine to sixteen weeks (Moylan, Millar, and Davies 1984: table 3.3). Since 1978 the administration of the 'availability for work' test has become stricter, suggesting that unemployed people are more likely to be deterred from registering. Working in the opposite direction, however, unemployment has increased, so that people who become unemployed may be less optimistic about finding another job quickly, thus increasing the incentive to claim benefit.

Take-up is a problem for One-Parent Benefit (Table 7.6(*b*)). In this case, it may be that potential claimants find being labelled a single parent stigmatizing and, since it is counted as a resource for Supplementary

Benefit/Income Support, those receiving SB/IS have no incentive to claim.

Has the situation improved since 1973? From Table 7.6(*a*), take-up of SB appears to have increased for non-pensioners from 70 per cent in 1973 to 83 per cent ten years later; for pensioners take-up has declined from three-quarters in 1973 to two-thirds in 1983. In both cases, however, the estimates for different years are not strictly comparable and should therefore be treated with caution. Also, the estimates for pensioners are very sensitive to small variations in the relationship of the long-term SB scale rate to the standard rate of Retirement Pension. A small relative rise in the SB scale rate may make a large number of pensioners eligible for small amounts of SB which few will claim, thus reducing take-up.

However, the situation among non-pensioners does appear to have improved. This may be a response to higher levels of unemployment reducing the stigma associated with claiming benefits. However, if non-take-up is more serious for means-tested than for non-means-tested benefits, the greater reliance on means-tested benefits for the unemployed, discussed earlier, suggests that the problem is still serious.

Administration

Considerable effort has been devoted to computerization and the stream-lining of procedures. Total administrative expenditure is shown in Table 7A.1, and further detail in Table 7A.2. Administrative cost was low for long-term benefits (1.3 per cent of expenditure on the Retirement Pensions and 2.2 per cent of that on Child Benefit in 1986/7), but higher at over 10 per cent for Unemployment Benefit and SB. A different question is whether benefit payments are correct. The pattern broadly parallels that for administrative costs, namely that incorrect amounts are paid in about 1 per cent of long-term benefit cases such as Child Benefit; however, error rates are much higher, at over 10 per cent, for more complex benefits such as SB (figures on error rates are given in recent Public Expenditure White Papers). There is no evidence of *systematic* malad-ministration (DHSS 1982*b*), though the system has been accused of being cumbersome (Dilnot, Kay, and Morris 1984). The 1988 reforms sought to address the latter fault, though the discretionary Social Fund was heavily criticized, not least for being hard to administer.

IV. OUTCOMES

It can be argued that governments in the 1970s and 1980s were able at least to bend the system towards their specific policy objectives. To what extent, over the two periods, did benefits contribute to the ultimate goals discussed at the start of the chapter, namely income support, the reduction of inequality, and social integration?

Income Support 1: Analytical aspects of poverty relief

Are benefits sufficiently high to relieve poverty? There are two overarching questions so far as individuals and families are concerned: are benefits high enough, assuming everyone receives all the benefit to which in theory they are entitled; and to what extent do people receive their theoretical entitlement? The first topic concerns the definition of poverty, the latter brings us back to discussion of take-up. A third strategic question is what has happened to the number of individuals/families in poverty.

Problems of definition Both the definition and the measurement of poverty are controversial and the literature is huge. No attempt is made to survey the subject here. Morris and Preston (1986a) summarize various empirical studies, and discuss different measures; Piachaud (1987) discusses different approaches to establishing a poverty line. The large number of technical problems involved in measuring income, and hence poverty, are summarized by Atkinson (1983) and Barr (1987: ch. 6).

The major conceptual difficulty is that defining a poverty line involves judgements about the minimum acceptable level of resources which individuals (or families or households) should have. Different methods of establishing a poverty line, such as using the SB scale rates, or by public opinion poll, as attempted in the Breadline Britain survey (Mack and Lansley 1985), involve different methods of making this judgement. Since judgements of value rather than of fact are involved, it is unlikely that there will ever be agreement.

A key issue is whether poverty is regarded as 'absolute' or 'relative'. If it is absolute, we measure the numbers in poverty in relation to a fixed subsistence level up-rated only in line with price inflation, the idea being that poverty is defined as the inability to afford a fixed bundle of goods. Relative poverty, in contrast, is defined in terms of the living standards of the population as a whole, through being up-rated broadly in line with earnings or income.

There is a case for regarding the SB level as the 'official' poverty line (see Barr 1981), i.e. the officially defined level of income below which the social security system should ensure that no one falls. As we shall see, however, the cash benefit system cannot ensure that no one falls below this level. There are a number of other drawbacks to using the SB level as a yardstick: it is essentially arbitrary, being chosen for political convenience rather than being based on any explicit attempt to measure living standards; and it suffers from the major drawback that, if the real SB level rises, so does the number of 'poor' people. Nevertheless, most studies use the SB level or some multiple as the poverty line, and so there is some justification for our doing the same.

Measurement problems Three issues require discussion: how many people are poor (i.e. a 'head-count' measure), by how much they fall below the poverty line (i.e. a 'poverty gap' measure), and for how long they are poor (i.e. life-cycle and inter-generational matters). We start with the first.

It is helpful to begin with some illustrative numbers. Suppose that in the baseline period (*a*) the level of SB for a hypothetical individual/family is £50, (*b*) there are 1,000 recipients, (*c*) the take-up rate is 75 per cent, (*d*) the Retail Price Index (RPI) is 100, and (*e*) mean weekly earnings (pre-tax) are £150. Finally, suppose that in period 2 the level of SB is £100.

In analysing what has happened, it is necessary to ask four key questions, the first two relating to the circumstances of the individual household in receipt of SB, the other two to number of households receiving benefit.

Question 1: What has happened to the real level of SB? The question is important for two reasons. First, if real SB has risen, that fact alone will increase the number of people counted as poor. Second, the answer tells us about the absolute living standard of a household on SB.

In terms of the illustrative numbers, therefore, if the RPI in period 2 is less than 200, then the poverty line has risen relative to the RPI. Thus, on the face of it, (*a*), there is an upward bias in the number of people counted as poor, and (*b*) the living standard of an individual on SB has risen.

This line of argument, however, contains an important implicit assumption, namely that the RPI is an accurate measure of the rate of inflation faced by the poor. If in reality they face a higher than average rate of inflation, then, even if SB has risen by more than the RPI, the living standard of each individual on SB may have fallen, resulting in *more poverty*.

Question 2: What has happened to SB relative to mean/median earnings? The question is important in that the answer tells us how each individual/family on SB has fared in comparison with the country as a whole. In terms of the illustrative example, if average earnings are now greater than £300 (i.e. exceed the 3:1 relativity in the baseline period) then SB has failed to keep pace with average earnings; though the consumption of the poor family may have risen, the difference between its standard of living and that of the average family has increased. The relative living standard of the poor, in other words, has fallen, and in that sense there is *more poverty*.

Question 3: What has happened to the number of individuals/families on SB? The answer gives an indication of how widespread poverty is. If the number of recipients has risen above the 1,000 in the baseline period, say to 1,200, then in some sense the number of poor people has risen. But it is important to interpret the outcome correctly.

One potential cause is the SB level itself. If it has risen faster than the RPI *and* if the RPI accurately measures the inflation experienced by the poor, then the larger number of people counted as poor is (at least in part) a statistical artefact. However, if the level of SB has been exactly indexed to the appropriate rate of inflation, it is then correct to interpret 1,200 people on SB as showing that *poverty has increased*. The cause, in the latter case, is such factors as increased long-term unemployment, or rising numbers of pensioners with National Insurance entitlement below the SB level.

Question 4: What has happened to take-up? If the number of recipients has remained at 1,000, but take-up has fallen to 60 per cent, then the number of poor people has increased, but this fact is not apparent merely by scrutiny of the SB case-load. Thus falling take-up reinforces rising numbers of recipients as showing that *poverty has increased*; similarly, rising take-up offsets, partly or wholly, any increase in the number of recipients.

To sum up, if the SB level has risen from £100 to £200, the consequences need to be interpreted in the light of four key factors:
* the rate of inflation faced by the poor (of which the RPI may or may not be an accurate indicator);
* the increase in average (mean or median) earnings;
* the number of recipients of SB;
* take-up rates.

Income Support 2: Interpreting empirical results

What has happened to the real level of SB?   In December 1974 the single householder scale rate for SB was £8.40; for most of 1985 it was £28.05. Converted into December 1974 prices using the RPI (excluding housing costs), the 1985 SB level was £9.15; thus SB rose by 9 per cent after adjusting for inflation. Taken at face value, real SB, and hence the living standard of poor families, has risen, as shown in Fig. 7.6.

This conclusion, however, rests on the assumption that the poor face the same (average) rate of inflation as other income groups. This might not be so for a number of reasons, of which arguably the most important is the shift in 1979/80 towards indirect taxation. This change will bear

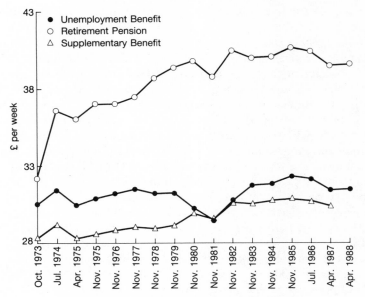

FIG. 7.6. Standard rates of benefit at April 1987 prices

more heavily on people with lower incomes (*a*) to the extent that they spend a larger proportion of their income than better-off people, and (*b*) to the extent that a larger proportion of their expenditure is on goods which attract higher rates of indirect tax. It is argued by some commentators that both have happened, and that in consequence the sharp increase in indirect taxation in 1979/80 has borne disproportionately upon individuals/families with lower incomes. In consequence, the RPI (which includes the indirect taxes of the *average* individual/family) understates inflation for those with lower incomes.

Estimates which take account of the differential burden of indirect tax suggest that the living standards of the bottom 20 per cent of incomes fell by up to 8 per cent between 1979 and 1986.[6] Since SB has risen only

---

[6] We are grateful to John Hills for giving us his estimates in greater detail than those reported in 'Moore's New Poor Lore', *The Observer*, 14 May 1989, p. 15. His method takes data on changes in real per capita disposable income to measure the increase in the *average* standard of living, and uses data on changes in the share of each quintile group in income after all taxes and benefits (from CSO 1988*d*) to show the *dispersion* about that average. He argues that though average living standards rose by 10 per cent between 1979 and 1986, the share of the bottom quintile fell sufficiently to more than offset this increase. This finding contrasts with government claims in the late 1980s that the living standards of the bottom quintile had risen—a claim based on deflating incomes by the RPI, which implicitly assumes that the burden of indirect tax is invariant across income groups. Though the Hills procedure is undoubtedly superior to simple use of the RPI, it should be remembered that the resulting estimates are only as good as the data on which they are based.

slightly over the 1980s when deflated by the RPI (see Fig. 7.6), the differential impact of indirect taxes suggests that real SB has risen even less; it may even be that the living standard of families on SB has fallen.

What has happened to SB relative to mean/median earnings?   Alternatively, we can consider the effect on the poverty line of indexing the December 1974 SB scale to changes in average earnings. Fig. 7.7 shows that the SB scale rate fell from about 16 per cent of adult male earnings in the mid-1970s to below 14 per cent in 1987, so that *relative poverty increased*.

These conclusions are supported by Morris and Preston (1986*a*, *b*). They compare various poverty measures for 1968, 1977, and 1983, using as a poverty line the 1983 SB scale backdated in line with (*a*) the RPI, and (*b*) average earnings. The results are shown in Table 7.7. Relative to an absolute yardstick, the proportion of the population in absolute poverty remained fairly constant between 1968 and 1977, and then *fell* between 1977 and 1983 from 11.6 to 9.9 per cent of the population (though this result takes no account of the extra indirect tax burden on the poor). Relative to mean earnings, the proportion in poverty *rose* both between 1968 and 1977 and between 1977 and 1983.

A similar approach by Piachaud (1988) argues that the poverty line should be a fixed percentage of per capita disposable income, giving a 'constant relative poverty line'. This definition has the advantage that it

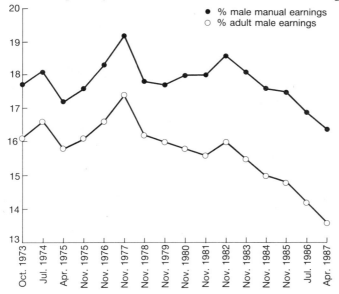

FIG. 7.7. Supplementary Benefit, standard rate, as percentage of average male earnings

makes possible an unambiguous comparison of the numbers in relative poverty over time. The disadvantage is that the percentage chosen is to some extent arbitrary.

Table 7.8, which is based on this approach, shows that the proportion of pensioners in relative poverty rose between 1975 and 1979 from 36 per cent to 52 per cent, fell again between 1979 and 1983, before rising slightly to 47 per cent in 1985. The SB level and the state Retirement Pension rate have always been very close, and most pensioners have incomes around this level. Hence the proportion of pensioners in poverty is highly sensitive to the relationship between the SB level and per capita disposable income. The changes for non-pensioner families are even sharper. In 1975, slightly over 5 per cent of families were poor according to this definition; the proportion rose to nearly 10 per cent by 1979 and to 17 per cent by 1983; it was still at that level in 1985.

Table 7.9 gives a breakdown by family type and shows the large variations in the likelihood of being poor. Two groups are at highest risk: the proportion of single parents in poverty rose from 47 per cent in 1979 to 53 per cent in 1983, and to 64 per cent in 1985 (col. (3)); for single pensioners the proportion fell from 60 per cent in 1979 to 52 per cent in

Table 7.7. *Percentage of individuals in poverty,[a] 1968–1983*

	Absolute poverty[b]	Relative poverty[c]
1968	11.4	4.1
1977	11.6	7.7
1983	9.9	9.9

[a] The income measure is annualized income net of housing costs.
[b] 1983 SB level deflated by Retail Price Index.
[c] 1983 SB level deflated by average earnings.
Source: Morris and Preston 1986*b*.

Table 7.8. *Percentage of families in constant relative poverty*

	Pensioners	Non-pensioners	All
1975	36.3	5.4	14.2
1979	52.1	9.6	20.1
1983	44.0	17.0	23.4
1985	47.3	17.3	24.0

Source: Derived from Piachaud 1988.

1983, rising to 56 per cent in 1985. The group least likely to be poor are married couples without children.

What has happened to the number of individuals/families on SB? Numbers in poverty relative to SB have risen substantially since 1974, from about 3.4 million families with incomes on or below SB levels in 1974 (2.2 million pensioner plus 1.2 non-pensioner families) to 5.7 million in 1985

Table 7.9. *Families in poverty, by family type, at constant relative poverty line,*
1979–1985

		Poverty line as % of SB	Nos. in poverty ('000)	As % of all such families
		(1)	(2)	(3)
1979				
Pensioner	single	1.14	2,499	59.6
	married	1.15	840	37.8
Non-pensioner with children	single	1.23	396	46.6
	married	1.26	484	7.7
Non-pensioner without children	single	1.16	838	11.1
	married	1.20	160	3.3
1983				
Pensioner	single	1.07	2,248	52.3
	married	1.07	664	28.6
Non-pensioner with children	single	1.13	503	52.9
	married	1.18	802	13.3
Non-pensioner without children	single	1.09	1,960	20.7
	married	1.12	347	7.2
1985	single	1.13	2,404	55.6
Pensioner	married	1.13	757	32.1
Non-pensioner with children	single	1.22	582	63.9
	married	1.24	854	14.4
Non-pensioner without children	single	1.15	1,977	19.1
	married	1.18	380	8.0

Source: Piachaud 1988.

(Table 7.10(a), col. (7)). The number of individuals rose from 5.1 million in 1974 to 9.4 million in 1985 (Table 7.10(d), col. (7)).

What are the causes of such an increase? Table 7.10(c) gives a breakdown of low-income families by economic status. An obviously important factor has been the large rise in unemployment from 290,000 on SB in 1975 to 1.5 million in 1985 (col. (2)); in addition the number of non-recipient unemployed families with income below the SB level rose over the same period from 60,000 to 320,000. There has also been a substantial increase in the 'others' category of non-recipients, i.e. single parents, full-time students, full-time workers temporarily away from work for reasons other than sickness, persons looking after sick relatives, and any others under pension age not working and not seeking work. The numbers on SB in this category (col. (4)) rose from 290,000 in 1975 to 730,000 ten years later; the numbers below the SB level rose slightly from 210,000 to 230,000. In addition (Table 7.10(a), col. (2)), the number of pensioner families below the SB level rose from 440,000 in 1975 to 770,000 in 1985.

How should these numbers be interpreted? In many ways these are conservative estimates. First, since the SB scale rate over the 1980s hardly rose in real terms, and on some measures has fallen, there is no upward bias on that account in the number of people counted as poor. Thus the level of SB is not itself a primary cause of rising numbers of recipients. Second, the SB poverty line is a parsimonious definition of poverty—with a poverty line of 140 per cent of the SB level, there would be 9 million poor families containing well over 15 million poor individuals. Third, these are the numbers of poor relative to an absolute poverty line; with a relative definition of poverty the number of poor would have grown yet more rapidly.

What has happened to take-up? Take-up was discussed in section III. It is necessary at this stage to quantify the holes in the safety net, and to focus on individuals with income within selected ranges of the SB level who do not receive SB. Such estimates have been presented since 1974 in the Low Income Families statistics. Some of this information is reproduced in Table 7.10(a) for families, and in Table 7.10(d) for individuals within those families.

In Table 7.10(a) and (d), col. (1) shows the number of families on SB and col. (2) the number of families not on SB whose income is below the SB level. Col. (3) is the sum of cols. (1) and (2). It needs to be interpreted with care: since some families on SB may have total income greater than the SB level because of disregarded earnings,[7] the total in col. (3) is not a

---

[7] The SB disregard is the amount of earnings or other income which is disregarded (i.e. ignored) in calculating the benefit to which an individual or family is entitled.

Table 7.10. *Numbers of families and individuals with low incomes*

(a) PENSIONER AND NON-PENSIONER FAMILIES ('000)

| | Pensioner families | | | Non-pensioner families | | | |
	On SB (1)	Below SB (2)	Total (3) (=1+2)	On SB (4)	Below SB (5)	Total (6) (=4+5)	Total (7) (=3+6)
1974[a]	1,800	440	2,240	720	470	1,190	3,430
1975[b]	1,640	590	2,230	780	500	1,280	3,510
1977[c]	1,700	620	2,320	950	640	1,590	3,910
1979[d]	1,680	850	2,530	910	550	1,460	3,990
1981[e]	1,670	740	2,410	1,350	870	2,220	4,630
1983[e]	1,600	870	2,470	2,040	1,010	3,050	5,520
1985[e]	1,620	770	2,390	2,490	830	3,320	5,710

(b) PERCENTAGE OF LOW-INCOME NON-PENSIONER FAMILIES ENTITLED TO SB

| | On SB | Not on SB | |
		Entitled to benefit	Not entitled to benefit
1974	60.5	23.5	16.0
1975	60.9	20.3	18.8
1977	59.8	15.9	24.4
1979	62.3	17.6	20.1
1981	60.8	20.3	18.9
1983	66.9	13.7	19.4

Table 7.10. (cont.)

(c) NON-PENSIONER FAMILIES BY ECONOMIC STATUS ('000)

	Numbers of families					As % of total					
	Sick	Unemp.	In work	Others	Total	Sick	Unemp.	In work	Others	Total
	(1)	(2)	(3)	(4)	(5)	(6)	(7)	(8)	(9)	(10)
Families on SB										
1975[b]	190	290	—	290	780	24	37	—	37	100
1977[c]	180	420	—	350	950	19	44	—	37	100
1979[d]	170	380	—	360	910	19	42	—	40	100
1981[e]	170	780	—	400	1,350	13	58	—	30	100
1983[e]	170	1,290	—	580	2,040	8	63	—	28	100
1985[e]	220	1,540	—	730	2,490	9	62	—	29	100
Families not on SB										
1975[b]	20	60	210	210	500	4	12	42	42	100
1977[c]	40	150	230	220	640	6	23	36	34	100
1979[d]	40	100	180	220	550	7	18	33	40	100
1981[e]	50	280	230	310	870	6	32	26	36	100
1983[e]	50	370	290	300	1,010	5	37	29	30	100
1985[e]	50	320	240	230	830	6	39	29	28	100

(d) INDIVIDUALS IN LOW-INCOME FAMILIES ('000)

	Pensioners			Non-pensioners			Total
	On SB (1)	Below SB (2)	Total (3) (=1+2)	On SB (4)	Below SB (5)	Total (6) (=4+5)	(7) (=3+6)
1974[a]	2,130	550	2,680	1,600	860	2,460	5,140
1975[b]	1,930	740	2,670	1,780	1,100	2,880	5,550
1977[c]	2,000	760	2,760	2,160	1,270	3,430	6,190
1979[d]	1,990	1,110	3,100	1,990	980	2,970	6,070
1981[e]	1,960	950	2,910	2,880	1,660	4,540	7,450
1983[e]	1,880	1,080	2,960	4,250	1,700	5,950	8,910
1985[e]	1,880	960	2,840	5,080	1,460	6,540	9,380

Notes: The figures for the numbers of SB recipients are derived from the DHSS annual and quarterly statistical enquiry, which uses a sample of its own administrative records. The figures for those not receiving SB are derived from the DHSS analysis of the Family Expenditure Survey. The figures up to and including 1977 are for December of the relevant year; thereafter they are annual averages, so the figures are not comparable over time. Since the annual up-rating was in November, the pre-1979 figures are peaks for that year. Income is net of housing costs and estimated work expenses. For a more detailed discussion of the methodology, see DHSS 1988b.

[a] CSO 1976: 124.
[b] DHSS 1976b: 220–1.
[c] DHSS 1981b: 250–1.
[d] DHSS 1986b.
[e] DHSS 1988a.

precise estimate of the number of families with income at or below the SB level.

Some families have income below the SB level because they fail to claim benefit. Others, however, despite having income below the SB level, are not eligible: they include people in full-time work or full-time education; people whose savings are large enough to disqualify them from benefit; or unemployed people who fail the 'availability for work' test. It is therefore necessary to split cols. (2) and (5) into those who are not entitled to benefit and those who are entitled but do not receive any benefit, and who therefore fall through the safety net.

The results of dividing families into these two categories are shown in Table 7.10(b) for non-pensioners.[8] They suggest that in 1974, 23.5 per cent of the 1,190,000 non-pensioner SB families, i.e. about 280,000 families in all, fell through the SB safety net although entitled to assistance. By 1983, though the proportion of non-recipients had declined to 13.7 per cent, their absolute number had risen by half to 420,000 families—a large hole, indeed.

The conclusions are fairly straightforward. The numbers in poverty and changes over time depend on the poverty line used. With an absolute definition, the living standards of the poor may have risen slightly over time, but this conclusion is questionable over the 1980s, when indirect tax increases have fallen disproportionately on the poor. Relative to average income, the living standards of the poor have decreased, especially for non-pensioner families. Whatever the poverty line used, the number of poor individuals and families has risen very substantially over the period for all groups. The number of individuals in poor households rose from 5.1 million to 6.1 million between 1974 and 1979, and to 9.4 million in 1985 (Table 7.10(d), col. (7)). Nor is this result a statistical artefact caused by increases in the poverty line itself.

---

[8] Using the estimates of take-up rates for SB in Table 7.12, it is possible to estimate the numbers who fall through the SB safety net. By definition:

$$\text{take-up rate} = \frac{\text{nos. on SB}}{\text{nos. on SB} + \text{nos. eligible but not claiming}} \quad \text{(A1)}$$

Thus,

$$\text{eligible non-claimants} = \text{nos. on SB} \times (1/(\text{take-up}) - 1). \quad \text{(A2)}$$

Equation (A2) gives an estimate of the numbers entitled to SB but not claiming; subtracting this estimate from the numbers of families with income below the SB level, the residual is an estimate of the number who are not entitled. This is likely to be an underestimate, since this method assumes that all non-claimants have incomes below the SB level, though this is not necessarily the case, since some income is disregarded in the assessment for SB. The results for non-pensioners are shown in Table 7.10(b) as a proportion of all those on SB or with income below the SB level.

Income Support 3: Other aspects

The previous two sections discussed how many poor people there are. This section briefly considers by how much people fall below the poverty line and, very roughly, for how long.

Poverty gap measures By how much do the incomes of poor individuals/ families fall short of some sensibly defined poverty line? Data are scant. Beckerman (1979) found that cash benefits in 1975 reduced the income gap (i.e. the aggregate shortfall of incomes below the poverty line) from £5.9 billion per year to £0.25 billion. Morris and Preston (1986*b*: table 2) estimate that in terms of an absolute poverty line, the income shortfall per poor person was 2.9 per cent of the SB level in 1968, i.e. that in 1968, averaged across all poor people, only £97.10 of SB was distributed out of every £100 which would have been distributed assuming complete take-up. By 1977, the shortfall was 3.2 per cent of the SB level, falling to 2.5 per cent in 1983. For a poverty line defined relative to average earnings, they found that the income shortfall rose sharply, from 1.3 per cent in 1968, to 2.2 per cent in 1977, and to 2.5 per cent in 1983.

In broad terms, this suggests that until 1983 the poverty gap remained roughly constant relative to changes in the RPI (i.e. ignoring the possibility that the poor face a higher than average rate of inflation). Compared with average earnings, the poverty gap rose unambiguously.

The protection of accustomed living standards One way of measuring the extent to which cash benefits preserve a family's living standard is the replacement rate, i.e. the ratio of income when unemployed to net income when working. It became explicit government policy over the 1980s to reduce the replacement rate, out of a belief that high replacement rates created an 'unemployment trap', and that a lower replacement rate would encourage people to rejoin the labour force.[9]

Social Security Statistics (DHSS 1986*a*: table 46.13) publishes data for a worker on average male earnings by family type. The figures show that the replacement rate relative to average earnings for a single person rose from 22.3 per cent in 1973 to 24 per cent in the later 1970s, thereafter falling, especially after 1985, to 18.9 per cent in 1988. The figures for couples with different numbers of children show a similar pattern.

These results suggest that governments since 1979 have achieved their policy objective. The figures, however, need to be treated with caution

---

[9] The unemployment trap arises where, with a high replacement rate, individuals may be not much better-off in work than unemployed; this, it is argued, is a cause of unemployment.

for two reasons: it is open to question whether reducing the replacement rate is a desirable aim; and replacement rates as conventionally measured may be a misleading guide as to what has actually happened. These objections require separate discussion.

First, a reduction in the replacement rate is not necessarily desirable. The argument that higher replacement rates lead to increased unemployment is, to put it no more strongly, not proven (see the survey by Atkinson (1987: sect. 5.3) and, for specific studies, Nickell 1979*a*, *b*, 1984; Atkinson *et al.* 1984; and Minford *et al.* 1985). Nor, in equity terms, is reducing the relative living standard of unemployed individuals and their dependants, and possibly also their absolute standard of living, a policy with which everyone would agree.

Quite separately, calculations of this type may be misleading. They are relevant only for the individuals concerned, i.e. those receiving average earnings, paying National Insurance contributions at the not-contracted-out rate, and receiving Unemployment Benefit at the standard rate. Such calculation fails to capture the variety of individual circumstances. So far as income when unemployed is concerned, an individual may not be eligible for full benefit; in contrast, up to its abolition in 1982, some unemployed individuals were eligible for the earnings-related supplement to Unemployment Benefit. The relationship between income in and out of work will be affected also by variations in housing costs, which affect entitlement to Housing Benefit. If the individual receives not Unemployment Benefit but Supplementary Benefit/Income Support instead, entitlement may be affected by the existence of savings. Nor do the calculations take account of the existence of tax refunds for the unemployed, which were particularly relevant before benefits for the unemployed became taxable in 1982.

Income when in work will vary according to earnings and also, if earnings are low, according to whether the family claims Family Income Supplement/Family Credit (the take-up rate for which (Table 7.6(*c*)) is about 50 per cent). Net income will also depend on whether the individual is contracted in or out of SERPS, on work expenses, and on the existence of other sources of income, such as the earnings of a spouse.

In order to get an accurate picture of changes over time it is necessary to take account of variations in individual circumstances. The best way to do so is through data on a sample of individuals, such as the FES. This is the approach adopted by Dilnot and Morris (1984). Though their method was very different from that in *Social Security Statistics*, their results confirm a substantial fall in replacement rates between 1980 and 1983; and since earnings have risen substantially since then, whilst Unemployment Benefit has (barely) kept pace with inflation, the replacement rate has undoubtedly fallen further since 1983. In addition, they find a substantial fall in the proportion with replacement rates of over 90 per cent, from 21 per cent of the employed population in 1978 to under 3 per cent in 1983.

Redistribution over the life-cycle   Earnings tend to rise over the working life of the main earner and to fall sharply on retirement. 'Need' also varies over the life-cycle with family size. The distribution of earnings over the life-cycle will not generally reflect the distribution of need; earnings reach their peak near retirement, while most families have children at a younger age. Under reasonable assumptions, such as diminishing marginal utility of income, people prefer a steady consumption stream. With perfect capital markets, individuals could borrow early in life, repay when their earnings were high, and save for retirement, thus bringing about their own redistribution. Since capital markets are not perfect, the benefit system has to assist this function.

Two stages in the life-cycle are particularly relevant: families with young children, and pensioners. There has been no significant improvement for either group. As Table 7.10(*d*), col. (3), shows, 2.7 million pensioners in 1974 were on SB or had income below the SB level; in 1985 the figure was 2.8 million. Table 7.9 defines poverty relative to per capita disposable income. On this definition, the proportion of poor pensioners fell slightly from just over half to just under half between 1979 and 1985. Single-parent families also are disproportionately poor. Given the definition of poverty in Table 7.9, nearly two-thirds of them were poor in 1985, up from 47 per cent in 1979. For two-parent families, 8 per cent were poor in 1979, rising to 14 per cent in 1985. The disproportionate incidence of poverty on the elderly and single-parent families is nothing new; it was found *inter alia* by Layard *et al.* (1987) and Mack and Lansley (1985).

A more detailed picture can be derived from the *Economic Trends* analysis of the FES, which shows the effects of taxes and benefits on household incomes. One of the tables shows benefits by household type, and these data were used to construct an income profile over the 'life-cycle'. We assumed that a family consists initially of a single adult, then two adults, then two adults plus children, then two retired adults, and finally one retired adult.

A number of limitations should be noted from the start: first, family composition in practice shows great diversity, so that this is a 'stylized' life-cycle; second, the data are only averages for each family type, thus concealing considerable diversity (e.g. of income) *within* each group; third, since we cannot follow specific families over time this is a life-cycle only in the sense that we focus on different *types* (e.g. pensioners, families with children), but all the data relate to a single point in time. Fourth, the analysis assumes that if cash benefits were abolished, the life-cycle distribution of original income would remain unchanged; this is

Table 7.11. *Effects of benefits on household income over the life-cycle, 1971–1986* (£ per year)

	Unadjusted income		Scale	Equivalent income	
	Original income	Original income + benefits		Original income	Original income + benefits
	(1)	(2)		(3)	(4)
1971					
Single adult	1,101	1,216	1.0	1,101	1,216
Couple	2,060	2,171	1.6	1,280	1,348
Couple plus 1–4 children	2,053	2,152	2.5	824	864
Retired, couple	434	953	1.6	270	592
Retired, single	256	600	1.0	256	600
Average over 'life-cycle'	1,181	1,418		746	924
Coefficient of variation	0.651	0.449		0.564	0.337
Gini coefficient	0.354	0.245		0.309	0.184
1976					
Single adult	2,609	2,865	1.0	2,609	2,865
Couple	4,511	4,792	1.6	2,802	2,976
Couple plus 1–4 children	4,491	4,693	2.5	1,804	1,885
Retired, couple	949	2,218	1.6	589	1,378
Retired, single	428	1,265	1.0	428	1,265
Average over 'life-cycle'	2,598	3,167		1,646	2,074
Coefficient of variation	0.659	0.437		0.601	0.349
Gini coefficient	0.361	0.241		0.329	0.189
1979					
Single adult	3,590	3,949	1.0	3,590	3,949
Couple	6,500	6,936	1.61	4,037	4,308
Couple plus 1 child	5,874	6,339	2.05	2,865	3,092
Couple plus 2 children	6,795	7,324	2.49	2,729	2,941
Couple plus 3 or				2,042	2,374
more children	5,983	6,956	2.93	657	1,856
Retired, couple	1,058	2,988	1.61	484	1,770
Retired, single	484	1,770	1.0		
Average over 'life-cycle'	4,326	5,180		2,344	2,899
Coefficient of variation	0.566	0.400		0.541	0.313
Gini coefficient	0.304	0.217		0.302	0.176

	Unadjusted income		Scale	Equivalent income	
	Original income	Original income + benefits		Original income	Original income + benefits
	(1)	(2)		(3)	(4)
1986					
Single adult	6,743	7,653	1.0	6,743	7,653
Couple	13,126	14,106	1.61	8,153	8,761
Couple plus 1 child	12,233	13,401	2.05	5,967	6,537
Couple plus 2 children	12,800	14,109	2.49	5,141	5,666
Couple plus 3 or more children	10,330	12,688	2.93	3,526	4,330
Retired, couple	3,521	7,282	1.61	2,187	4,523
Retired, single	1,258	3,754	1.0	1,258	3,754
Average over 'life-cycle'	8,573	10,428		4,711	5,889
Coefficient of variation	0.517	0.368		0.491	0.292
Gini coefficient	0.284	0.198		0.279	0.164

Source: Calculated from CSO 1988*d* and earlier equivalents.

clearly unrealistic, but no other assumption is possible. Finally, the results presented in Table 7.11 show how original income (i.e. income from employment, self-employment, investment income, and occupational pensions) and gross income (original income plus cash benefits) vary by family type; this procedure leaves out the effects of the tax system.

Difficulties arise with comparisons before and after 1979: the breakdown by household type and by type of benefit varies between years; there is also the problem of the switch from Child Tax Allowances (which were not counted as a cash benefit) to Child Benefit (which is). There were changes in 1979 in the underlying methodology, e.g. a change in the treatment of Rent Rebates and Allowances from a housing subsidy to a cash benefit. Comparisons between 1979 and earlier years must therefore be made with caution.

From Table 7.11 a typical single adult in 1971 received £1,101 annually in original income, plus £215 in cash benefits, making a total of £1,216 in gross income (cols. (1) and (2)). For a family of two adults plus children the comparable figures are £2,053 and £2,152. Note the very low original income of retired families. Table 7.11 also gives two measures of inequality over family type, the coefficient of variation and the Gini coefficient,[10] both of which show the substantial equalizing effect of the benefit system.

[10] The Gini coefficient was defined in n. 2 above.

Table 7.12. *Effects of different benefits on household equivalent income over the life-cycle, 1971–1986* (£ per year)

	Original income plus:			
	Retirement pension	Family allowances	Unemp. and sick	Other pensions
1971				
Single adult	1,101	1,101	1,120	1,180
Couple	1,280	1,280	1,293	1,329
Couple plus 1–4 children	824	843	834	829
Retired, couple	538	270	270	280
Retired, single	508	256	256	274
Average over life-cycle	850	750	754	778
Coefficient of variation	0.358	0.562	0.567	0.566
Gini coefficient	0.198	0.307	0.310	0.309
1976				
Single adult	2,609	2,609	2,635	2,795
Couple	2,802	2,802	2,829	2,934
Couple plus 1–4 children	1,804	1,832	1,825	1,817
Retired, couple	1,265	589	589	658
Retired, single	1,099	428	428	455
Average over life-cycle	1,916	1,652	1,661	1,732
Coefficient of variation	0.359	0.599	0.602	0.598
Gini coefficient	0.198	0.328	0.330	0.328
	Age-related	Child-related	Income-related	Other
1979				
Single adult	3,800	3,590	3,682	3,646
Couple	4,193	4,039	4,080	4,107
Couple plus 1 child	2,885	2,985	2,915	2,903
Couple plus 2 children	2,733	2,888	2,754	2,753
Couple plus 3 or more children	2,044	2,265	2,118	2,073
Retired, couple	1,669	657	745	756
Retired, single	1,502	484	710	526
Average over life-cycle	2,689	2,415	2,429	2,395
Coefficient of variation	0.356	0.529	0.505	0.527
Gini coefficient	0.200	0.292	0.282	0.296

	Original income plus:			
	Retirement pension	Family allowances	Unemp. and sick	Other pensions
1986				
Single adult	6,861	6,743	7,190	7,089
Couple	8,355	8,157	8,322	8,387
Couple plus 1 child	5,979	6,150	6,216	6,095
Couple plus 2 children	5,141	5,433	5,300	5,214
Couple plus 3 or more children	3,526	3,933	3,831	3,617
Retired, couple	4,061	2,191	2,358	2,473
Retired, single	3,213	1,258	1,633	1,424
Average over life-cycle	5,305	4,838	4,979	4,900
Coefficient of variation	0.329	0.478	0.462	0.476
Gini coefficient	0.185	0.270	0.263	0.272

The right-hand part of Table 7.11 shows the effect of cash benefits when income is adjusted for family size. This adjustment reduces inequality in original income, suggesting that the pattern of earnings over the life-cycle, at least to some extent, reflects differences in needs. Table 7.12 shows that Retirement Pensions have much the greatest impact on life-cycle inequality, reducing the Gini coefficient from 0.309 for original equivalent income in 1971 to 0.198 when the Retirement Pension is included.

Comparing original and gross income in Table 7.11 between 1971 and 1976, inequality grew slightly for original income, but fell for (unadjusted) gross income, suggesting that the benefit system had become more redistributive. However, inequality in equivalent gross incomes grew slightly. Again, the reduction in inequality was largely due to the Retirement Pension.

The relative position of pensioners improved between 1979 and 1986, resulting in a fall in inequality in both original and gross income—in 1979 a single pensioner received (on average) 21 per cent of average equivalent income (28 per cent for a pensioner couple); by 1986 these proportions had increased to 27 per cent and 46 per cent respectively. If these results seem difficult to reconcile with our results on the relative poverty of pensioners discussed earlier, it should be remembered that these averages do not take account of the considerable inequality *among* pensioners. The bottom 20 per cent of pensioner couples received only £30 per year in original income in 1986; the top 20 per cent received on average £11,704 (CSO 1988*d*: table 4).

Equivalent income amongst non-retired couples shows a strong tendency to fall with family size; equivalent income for a three-child family is half or less that of couple with no children. Table 7.11 shows clearly the relative affluence of childless couples. As a result, we would expect child-related benefits to reduce inequality in equivalent incomes, which, from Table 7.12, they do. Both income-related and other benefits appear to reduce inequality, but age-related benefits have by far the most dramatic effect on life-cycle inequality.

The reduction of inequality

Horizontal equity To what extent is there equal access to cash benefits? A central theme of the Beveridge Report was that National Insurance should be comprehensive, unified, and compulsory, and should be buttressed by a system of family support and by residual income-tested benefits. This aim has been achieved in the sense that there is no evidence of discrimination in the payment of benefit, or of substantial maladministration. That said, horizontal equity can be violated in at least three ways: groups can be treated differently depending on the cause of their poverty; women do not always receive symmetrical treatment; and not all individuals receive all the benefits to which they are entitled.

Not all groups are treated equally generously for benefit purposes. Fifty years ago most single-parent families arose out of widowhood, which received extensive cover. It is argued that this group (which today comprises only one in six single-parent families in Britain) is treated generously relative to families separated by causes such as divorce. The difficulty (and the prominence of the latter group among the poor) arises largely because the insurance benefits are conditioned on cause (e.g. widowhood) rather than outcome (i.e. being a single parent).

Disability benefits have also been criticized. Again, individuals with similar disabilities do not necessarily receive the same benefit. Under plausible assumptions a single man will receive twice as much if 100 per cent disabled in an industrial accident as with identical injuries from a non-industrial cause (Hemming 1984: 119; see also Disability Alliance 1975, Disablement Income Group 1979).

Pensioners, too, figure disproportionately among the poor, mainly because the Beveridge policy that all the main insurance benefits should be at or above the SB level was never put into effect.

The second problem area is the relative treatment of men and women. The 1975 Social Security Pensions Act went a long way towards making the pensions regime gender-free, though it left in place the glaring anomaly that the normal retirement age is 65 for men, 60 for women; nor is the pensions treatment of widows and widowers yet symmetrical.

The third issue is take-up. As discussed earlier, this varies from close to 100 per cent for the major insurance benefits and Child Benefit, to about 50 per cent for Family Income Supplement (Table 7.6). Take-up of SB by pensioners fell from 74 per cent to 67 per cent between 1973 and 1983; for non-pensioners it rose from 70 per cent to 83 per cent.

Vertical equity The formula by which contributions and benefits are organized implies redistribution from rich to poor. Contributions, for the most part, rise proportionately with earnings, whilst insurance benefits are either flat-rate or rise less than proportionately with earnings. Means-tested benefits, financed out of general taxation, to an even greater extent go to people on lower incomes.

Other factors, however, work in the opposite direction. There is differential mortality, in that the better-off have a greater life expectancy (and hence collect their pensions longer) and, a related phenomenon, tend to stay in education longer (and hence start to pay contributions later). In addition, it is disproportionately the better-off who contract out of the state scheme and this, too, reduces its redistributive impact. The effects these factors can have in different areas of social spending are analysed by Woolley and Le Grand (1990).

The overall redistributive effect is therefore complex. Table 7.13, which shows the effect of the tax and benefit system on income inequality as measured by the Gini coefficient, illustrates the point. We set to one side the conceptual and measurement problems of the Gini coefficient (see Barr 1987; ch. 6) and concentrate on the interpretation of the results. Taken at face value, taxes and benefits in 1975 reduced the Gini coefficient from 43 per cent to 31 per cent, i.e. by 12 per cent; in 1986 they reduced it from 52 to 36 per cent, i.e. by 16 per cent. The tax and benefit system, it seems, was one-third more redistributive in 1986 than in 1975. The explanation, however, is not that, other things being equal, the

Table 7.13. *Gini coefficients for the distribution of income (%)*

	1975	1979	1983	1986
Original income	43	45	49	52
Gross income	35	35	36	40
Disposable income	32	33	33	36
Income after all taxes and cash benefits	33	35	36	40
Final income	31	32	33	36

Source: CSO 1988*d*.

Table 7.14. *Percentage shares of original income and benefits, by quintile group, 1971–1986*

	Bottom	2	3	4	Top
1971					
Original income	1.6	10.9	18.6	25.4	43.4
Child Benefit	5.8	19.4	26.2	27.7	20.9
Pensions	55.7	22.6	8.7	6.9	6.0
Unemployment/Sickness/ Injury	25.3	32.4	17.8	12.4	12.0
Other benefits	62.6	19.4	7.4	6.5	4.2
All benefits	47.6	23.0	11.5	9.8	8.1
Original income plus benefits	5.9	12.1	18.0	24.0	40.1
1976					
Original income	1.2	9.7	18.7	26.5	44.0
Child Benefit	6.5	15.4	27.6	28.0	22.5
Pensions	49.9	31.3	8.8	5.3	4.7
Unemployment/Sickness/ Injury	13.2	34.7	22.1	16.8	13.2
Other benefits	63.9	16.4	9.5	4.7	5.5
All benefits	45.9	28.3	11.3	7.7	6.8
Original income plus benefits	6.1	11.7	17.9	24.4	39.9
1979					
Original income	0.5	8.7	18.8	27.1	44.9
Contributory benefits	45.8	32.3	9.4	6.1	6.4
Non-contributory benefits	10.4	17.1	26.6	24.9	21.0
Means-tested benefits	68.8	20.2	5.0	3.0	3.0
Child Benefit	5.6	14.5	28.8	27.1	24.0
Retirement Pension	53.5	31.1	6.4	4.2	4.8
Unemployment/Sickness/ Injury	8.7	34.2	22.3	17.7	17.1
All benefits	41.1	27.4	12.6	9.8	9.2
Original income plus benefits	6.0	11.3	17.9	24.7	40.0
1986					
Original income	0.3	5.7	16.4	26.9	50.7
Contributory benefits	34.9	37.5	14.7	7.6	5.3
Non-contributory benefits	20.0	19.5	20.6	21.7	18.2
Means-tested benefits	62.7	24.6	6.0	3.6	3.1
Child Benefit	13.5	13.8	22.5	26.8	23.4

	Bottom	2	3	4	Top
Retirement Pension	39.9	38.3	12.5	5.6	3.7
Unemployment/Sickness/					
Injury	10.1	25.8	26.3	20.1	17.7
All benefits	38.3	31.0	13.9	9.5	7.3
Original income plus benefits	6.1	9.5	16.0	24.3	44.0
Lorenz curves					
Original income 1971	1.6	12.5	31.1	56.6	100.0
Income plus benefits 1971	5.9	18.0	36.0	59.9	100.0
Original income 1976	1.2	10.8	29.5	56.0	100.0
Income plus benefits 1976	6.1	17.8	35.7	60.1	100.0
Original income 1979	0.5	9.3	28.1	55.1	100.0
Income plus benefits 1979	6.0	17.3	35.2	60.0	100.0
Original income 1986	0.3	6.0	22.4	49.3	100.0
Income plus benefits 1986	6.1	15.6	31.7	56.0	100.0

Source: CSO 1988*d* and earlier equivalents.

cash benefit system has become more redistributive, but that other things have not remained equal. In particular, unemployment rose considerably; more individuals received benefit and, in consequence, more resources were transferred from taxpayers to the (now more numerous) poor, as shown in Table 7.2, col. (3).

Table 7.14 looks at the effect of benefits in more detail. It shows, for various years, the percentages of original income (i.e. income before taxes and benefits) and of cash benefits received by each quintile group of households, where the households are ranked by original income. In 1971, the original income of the bottom 20 per cent of households was only 1.6 per cent of total income; but since they received 47.6 per cent of all benefits, their share of income after benefits rose to 5.9 per cent of the total. Similarly, benefits increased the share of the second quintile from 10.9 to 12.1 per cent of the total. The effect of cash benefits was to reduce the shares of gross income of third, fourth, and top quintiles.

A number of points emerge clearly. The National Insurance pension goes disproportionately to the bottom quintile, who received about 50 per cent of all pension payments in 1971, 1976, and 1979; in 1986 they received only 40 per cent. The main reason for the decline is not that pensioners were less well treated in 1986, but that they were less dominant a proportion of the bottom quintile than in earlier years, their place being taken by the unemployed.

Contributory benefits as a whole go disproportionately to the bottom and second quintiles. They appear to be much less redistributive in 1986 than in 1979; in part, however, this is a statistical artefact, in that many of the poorest households in 1986 were unemployed people who had run out of entitlement to insurance benefit and were wholly dependent on means-tested benefits. The latter, almost by definition, are highly concentrated on the bottom quintile.

Non-contributory, non-means-tested benefits (mainly Family Allowance/Child Benefit) go disproportionately to the third and fourth quintiles, because families with children (unless lone-parent households) are typically not among the least well-off. It is open to argument whether this is a desirable outcome. Governments in the 1980s argued that Child Benefit, because it is not restricted to the least well-off, is poorly targeted; this, however, overlooks other important goals of cash benefits, most particularly life-cycle redistribution.

The final part of Table 7.14 shows the cumulative shares in total income of each quintile (i.e. the figures underlying the Lorenz curves for each year.) The share in original income of the bottom, second, and third quintiles has declined steadily since 1971. However, the cumulative post-benefit shares remained very steady over the 1970s, the Lorenz curve for 1979 being almost identical to those for 1971 and 1976. Between 1979 and 1986, the share of the bottom quintile was protected, but the shares of gross income of the second and third quintiles fell. Therefore, it appears that the benefit system was able to prevent an increase in inequality in gross income during the 1970s by becoming increasingly redistributive, but that the system became less redistributive between 1979 and 1986, allowing the share of the top quintile to rise from 40 to 44 per cent of gross income.

The conclusion that the share of the bottom quintile was protected should be qualified with a note of caution. The data refer to households, not individuals. It is quite possible for the share in original income plus benefits to fall for the bottom quintile group of individuals, while the share for the bottom quintile group of households stays constant, if the average household size becomes disproportionately larger for the bottom group. There are grounds for supposing that this did indeed happen between 1979 and 1986, as the rise in unemployment of the early 1980s did produce a change in the composition of the quintile groups. In 1979, 80 per cent of the bottom quintile group of households in the FES were retired, while by 1986 retired households comprised only 64 per cent of the group (see CSO 1981, 1988*d*: tables 7, 9). The proportion of retired households rose for both the middle 40 per cent of households (from 16 per cent to 29 per cent) and for the top 40 per cent (from under 1 per cent to 2.5 per cent). Since non-retired households are generally larger than retired ones, this does suggest that the relative number of individuals in the bottom quintile grew, suggesting in turn that the shares of gross income of *individuals* in the bottom quintile may have fallen between 1979 and 1986.

However, our figures should be interpreted with caution, when used to compare the distribution of gross income over time. Our quintile groups are always ranked by original income, hence the last row for each year shows the shares of original income plus benefits received by each quintile group of original income. Our tables are intended to show which groups receive which benefits, and the extent to which different benefits are received by low-income groups. It is possible, however, that some households who are in the bottom quintile group when ranked by original income may no longer be, when ranked by gross income. Therefore these figures may overstate the relative share of gross income of the bottom quintile group when ranked by gross income. Therefore, in order to make accurate comparisons of inequality in the distribution of gross income over time, the quintile groups should really be re-ranked.

Nevertheless, the evidence does suggest that there has been an increase in inequality in both original and gross income since the 1970s. Moreover, this is not an artefact of the particular data source or methods used. Jenkins (1989) examines the evidence on UK income inequality, and concludes that the evidence that inequality has increased between the mid-1970s and the mid-1980s is strong.

Social integration

Cash benefits should not themselves be socially divisive or stigmatizing. This is not an aim whose achievement can be measured quantitatively. But take-up can be used as a rough-and-ready guide. We know that take-up for the major insurance benefits is close to 100 per cent, as it is also for Child Benefit. This is no accident: first, the procedures for establishing entitlement to Child Benefit and the Retirement Pension are non-stigmatizing; second, both benefits are conditioned on criteria (age, having children) which are largely unrelated to socio-economic status.

Unemployment Benefit meets neither criterion, so that it should not be surprising, as discussed in section III, that the 1978 Cohort Study of Unemployed Men found that only 73 per cent of the sample had registered as unemployed immediately, whilst 8 per cent had remained unregistered for four weeks or longer.

Means-tested benefits, as we have seen, score even less well. The procedure for establishing entitlement is complex and the main criterion for awarding benefit—poverty—is itself demeaning.

A second aspect of social integration is that benefits should be high enough to allow recipients to participate fully in the life of the society in which they live. There is controversy as to whether social integration in this sense should be an aim of policy and, separately, whether benefits are in fact sufficiently high to achieve the aim. For support of the objective and the claim that government policy over the 1980s has failed to achieve it, see Mack and Lansley (1985: ch. 10). Government in the later 1980s, in contrast, has claimed that the standard of living of the poor is rising, an issue we discussed earlier.

Incentive issues

The ultimate goals of cash benefits are redistributive; but the system also has efficiency goals in that the benefits themselves, and also the taxes which finance them, should minimize adverse incentives to work and save. The US debate has centred on the argument that the welfare system has produced an 'underclass'; Murray (1984), who follows discussion in the 1960s of the so-called 'welfare subculture', presents just such a case. The UK debate has concentrated more on the narrower economic effects of cash benefits, a key ingredient being the incentive effect of the cash benefit system through the poverty and unemployment traps.[11]

The poverty trap: facts In analysing who receives cash benefits, two questions are relevant: do benefits go to those who need them; and do benefits go *only* to those who need them? The first is the issue of poverty relief and the associated issue of take-up. The second raises two new questions: how high are implicit tax rates[12] (i.e. are they high enough to cause a poverty-trap-type problem); and how many people face them? For any given family the effect on benefits of an increase in earnings depends on several factors: the size and composition of the family; the precise formula for each benefit; the mix of benefits the family is receiving; and the way the scheme works in practice, which may differ substantially from the scheme on paper.

Having answered that very complex question, there is a second set of complications. To assess the impact of the poverty trap, we need also to know *how many* families face poverty-trap-type rates of withdrawal. This requires knowledge of how many families of different sizes and types there are at each income level; which benefits they actually receive (the

---

[11] The poverty trap arises when individuals or families who earn an extra £1 lose £1 or more in income-tested benefits, and hence make themselves absolutely worse-off. The unemployment trap was defined in n. 9 above.

[12] An implicit tax arises when a family in receipt of a means-tested benefit earns extra income, and as a consequence loses benefit. If benefit is lost pound for pound with earnings, the implicit tax rate is 100 per cent.

take-up question); and which margin we are discussing—that for the main earner or a secondary earner. Exactly similar issues arise in assessing the effects of replacement rates in the context of the unemployment trap.

According to Atkinson (see HC, Treasury and Civil Service Committee 1983: table 15), in 1980 600,000 tax units faced a marginal tax rate of over 50 per cent, of whom 120,000 faced marginal rates of 70 per cent and over. It was estimated (*Official Report*, 25 Nov. 1987, WA, cols. 243–4) that after the Fowler reforms, introduced in April 1988, the number of tax units facing marginal rates of over 70 per cent had risen to 530,000. The increase was partly because of the larger number of families receiving means-tested benefits; in addition, the reforms systematically kept tax rates below 100 per cent, but in so doing increased the number of people facing high rates below 100 per cent.

It is worth investigating in more detail the effect of the Fowler reforms which took full effect in 1988. One of their major objectives was to reduce the severity of the poverty trap. Under the old system a person claiming Family Income Supplement (FIS) and Housing Benefit could, in extreme cases, be made absolutely worse off by an earnings increase. In March 1988 a person receiving FIS and Housing Benefit who earned an extra pound could lose 27p in income tax payments, 9p in National Insurance Contributions, 50p in FIS, and 23p in Rent and Rate Rebates, giving a total marginal tax rate of 109 per cent.

The 1988 reforms sought to avoid this problem by basing entitlement on income *net* of income tax, National Insurance contributions, and most cash benefits. This arrangement, though it does not guarantee that no one will face marginal tax rates in excess of 100 per cent, makes that outcome considerably less likely.[13] However, the rate of withdrawal remains high—for Family Credit it is 70 per cent, while for Housing Benefit and Rent and Rate Rebates it is 65 and 20 per cent respectively (for further discussion, see Dilnot and Webb 1989).

We used the LSE tax and benefit model TAXMOD, based on data from the FES, to simulate the effects of the 1988 reforms on the poverty trap.[14] We took as our basis the October 1989 (i.e. post-Fowler) tax and benefit system, and simulated the effects of reintroducing the pre-

[13] It is still possible for marginal tax rates to exceed 100 per cent—e.g. where a family only just qualifies for Housing Benefit. Since there is a minimum payment of 50p, earning an extra pound may reduce net income by more than a pound. Also, since eligibility for means-tested benefits such as Family Credit leads to entitlement to other 'passport' benefits such as free school meals, losing entitlement to a means-tested benefit through a small increase in earnings may lead to a substantial fall in the value of total benefits received. However, these problems affect only a very small number of families.

[14] For a full description of TAXMOD see Atkinson and Sutherland (1988).

Fowler Housing Benefit, FIS, and SB schemes, with benefit rates up-rated in line with inflation.

The results are summarized in Table 7.15. Parts (*a*) and (*b*) show the distribution of marginal tax rates on a pound of additional earnings for working household heads for the post- and pre-Fowler benefit structures, respectively. Parts (*c*) and (*d*) do the same thing for working wives.

The numbers facing marginal tax rates of over 70 per cent are nearly

Table 7.15. *Marginal tax rates before and after the 1988 reforms*[a]

Marginal tax rate (upper end)	Numbers ('000)	Percentage	Cumulative numbers ('000)	Cumulative percentage
(a) *Household heads: reformed system*				
0–10%	555	3.09	555	3.09
10–30%	3,159	17.58	3,714	20.67
30–40%	12,667	70.49	16,382	91.96
40–70%	1,129	6.28	17,508	97.43
Over 70%	462	2.57	17,970	100.00
(b) *Household heads: old system*				
0–10%	559	3.11	559	3.11
10–30%	3,125	17.21	3,682	20.49
30–40%	12,676	70.54	16,360	91.04
40–70%	1,369	7.62	17,728	98.65
Over 70%	243	1.35	17,970	100.00
(c) *Working wives: reformed system*				
0–10%	1,994	32.35	1,994	32.35
10–30%	1,022	16.58	3,016	48.93
30–40%	2,765	44.86	5,781	93.79
40–70%	223	3.62	6,004	97.41
Over 70%	160	2.59	6,164	100.00
(d) *Working wives: old system*				
0–10%	1,908	30.96	1,908	30.96
10–30%	1,071	17.38	2,980	.48.34
30–40%	2,786	45.20	5,765	93.53
40–70%	312	5.06	6,077	98.59
Over 70%	87	1.41	6,164	100.00

[a] Based on October 1989 tax and benefit system.

Source: TAXMOD, the LSE tax and benefit model; see Atkinson and Sutherland 1988.

twice as high in the reformed scheme, both for household heads and for working wives. While few people now face marginal rates of over 100 per cent, the 1988 reforms did little to alleviate the poverty trap. It should be noted, however, that though the poverty trap is a severe problem for the individuals directly affected, the actual number of such individuals is relatively small. Under both systems, over 97 per cent of household heads in work and working wives face marginal rates of under 50 per cent.

The poverty trap: interpretation   Where implicit tax rates, as imposed by the *de facto* operation of the benefit system, are high and are faced by substantial numbers, the problem of the poverty trap with its inequities and disincentives becomes important. Where implicit tax rates are low, the issue arises of benefits paid to those who do not 'need' them. This is the issue of what governments in the 1980s called 'poorly targeted' benefits, which is one of the main reasons why Child Benefit was under threat in the late 1980s.

The targeting of benefits was investigated by Dilnot, Kay, and Morris (1984: table 2.4) for 1981. Their conclusion—that almost 100 per cent of SB expenditure went to people below the poverty line—is almost tautological given that (*a*) poverty is defined in terms of the SB level, and that (*b*) SB incorporates a 100 per cent rate of withdrawal of benefit for each pound of net earnings. For FIS and Rent and Rate Rebates (the precursor of Housing Benefit) the corresponding figure was 35.5 per cent, i.e. 64.5 per cent of these benefits went to families with pre-transfer incomes *above* the SB level, or were payments in excess of those necessary to bring incomes to that level. For cash benefits as a whole, 54 per cent of payments went to families whose post-transfer income did not exceed the SB level.

It is not clear how these figures should be interpreted. Dilnot *et al.* take them to imply that the system is 'wasteful' in that benefits 'leak out' to the non-poor. But to the extent that the harsher aspects of the poverty trap are thereby ameliorated, the leakages may have benefits in incentive as well as in equity terms, if one remembers that families with incomes just above the SB level can hardly be regarded as comfortably off. In addition, though 'targeting' arguably contributes to the aim of poverty relief, it conflicts with other aims, such as protecting accustomed living standards and redistributing over the life-cycle.

V. IN BRIEF

● The main conclusion is the success of governments in both periods in achieving their stated aims, namely, in the 1974–9 period:

* More resources to cash benefits;
* Reduced reliance on means-tested benefits; and
* Improved take-up;

and in the period after 1979:

* Fewer resources to cash benefits relative to GDP;
* Lower replacement rates; and
* Increased targeting.

● Resources for cash benefits grew more rapidly in the earlier period, when GDP was growing more slowly. Table 7.2 and Fig. 7.4 divide the increase into that due to increased generosity per recipient (which was more pronounced in the 1970s) and that due to increased numbers of recipients. The latter, particularly the large increase in unemployment, dominated expenditure in the 1980s. With a constant number of recipients, spending would have fallen as a proportion of GDP. Spending rose relative to need, particularly for families and for the retired; and real spending per head rose more slowly in the period when GDP was rising more rapidly.

● Reliance on means testing. Fig. 7.1 shows the diversion of resources in the earlier period towards National Insurance and non-means-tested benefits. After 1980, there was increased emphasis on targeting, together with rising dependence by the unemployed on SB; the two trends jointly explain the sharp increase in spending on means-tested benefits.

● Take-up. Most estimates relate to SB. From Table 7.10(b), only about three-quarters of potentially eligible non-pensioner families in 1974 received SB. Thus about 280,000 families potentially entitled to benefit did not receive it. By 1983 take-up had increased to just over 83 per cent; but because there were so many more poor people, about 420,000 potentially eligible non-pensioner families were not receiving any SB.

● The unemployment trap. From 1979 it was increasingly argued that the replacement rate was too high, creating labour-supply disincentives. Benefit was therefore deliberately reduced relative to earnings:

* The earnings-related supplement was abolished from 1982.
* Indexation was parsimonious so that benefits fell relative to average earnings (see Fig. 7.5).
* Unemployment Benefit became taxable from 1982.
* Eligibility conditions were tightened.

The targeting was very precise. Fig. 7.2 shows that reliance on SB and Housing Benefit remained roughly constant for the elderly, the sick, and widows. For families, however, and particularly for the unemployed, there was a sharp increase in reliance on means-tested benefits in the 1980s.

● The poverty trap. In 1980 about 120,000 families faced marginal tax rates of 70 per cent or more. By the late 1980s, when the 1988 reforms were in place, it was estimated that the number had increased to 530,000 families, in part because of the increased number of recipients of means-tested benefits, but also as a direct consequence of the reforms.

● Gainers and losers. After adjusting for inflation, benefits per recipient (Table 7.3) rose for the elderly, for widows, for families, and for the sick. When account is taken of the counter-measures to the unemployment trap, it is clear that unemployed people were among the losers in the 1980s, as a deliberate policy to reduce the replacement rate.

● The living standards of poor people:

  * Relative to the Retail Price Index, the living standards of the poor rose slightly over the 1970s, and more slowly over the 1980s. The latter conclusion, however, is questionable, since indirect tax increases in the 1980s fell disproportionately on the poor.

  * Relative to average income, the living standards of the poor have decreased, especially for non-pensioner families.

  * Whatever the poverty line used, the number of poor individuals and families rose substantially for all groups. The number of individuals in poor households rose from 5.1 million to 6.1 million between 1974 and 1979, and to 9.4 million in 1985 (Table 7.10(*d*), col. (7)). This result is not a statistical artefact caused by increases in the poverty line itself.

  * Consistent with other studies, the likelihood of poverty was greatest for single pensioners and single-parent families (Table 7.9).

● The overall conclusion is that, although social security was regarded more as a solution in the 1970s and more as a problem in the 1980s, the changes, in reality, though genuinely meeting some of the stated objectives of policy, did not come close to matching the rhetoric. The exception was the position of unemployed people, which was deliberately worsened relative to earnings in the 1980s. The unemployed apart, there was less discontinuity between the two periods than is often supposed. Whether that outcome is desirable has less to do with economic efficiency than with readers' ideological tastes.

Table 7A.1. *Benefit expenditure (£ million, real, at 1987/8 prices)*

	1973/4	1974/5	1975/6	1976/7	1977/8	1978/9	1979/80	1980/1	1981/2	1982/3	1983/4	1984/5	1985/6	1986/7	1987/8	1988/9
Contributory benefits (GB)																
Retirement Pension	12,083	13,048	13,930	14,630	15,030	15,507	15,467	15,594	16,364	17,064	17,606	17,509	18,046	18,706	18,648	18,155
Widow's Benefits	1,075	1,140	1,149	1,121	1,059	1,037	988	945	935	913	929	900	871	868	839	855
Unemployment Benefit	763	787	1,327	1,444	1,430	1,298	1,146	1,896	2,297	1,889	1,804	1,810	1,729	1,825	1,468	1,076
Sickness Benefit[a]	1,491	1,397	1,357	1,401	1,470	1,429	1,149	969	918	698	907	857	928	856	1,027	1,009
Invalidity Benefit	1,061	1,169	1,304	1,460	1,600	1,725	1,746	1,704	1,849	2,006	2,255	2,456	2,556	2,814	2,968	3,211
Death Grant	57	51	44	39	34	33	28	24	23	21	20	19	20	19	3	—
Industrial Disablement Benefit	382	404	424	432	434	444	428	418	425	432	445	437	443	463	453	428
Industrial Death Benefit	57	63	67	67	66	66	63	62	63	64	65	63	63	64	56	54
Maternity Allowance	118	118	117	171	173	216	219	221	213	191	170	185	178	177	51	25
Other contributory benefits	18	18	18	16	16	14	12	10	9	9	8	8	7	6	5	5
Total contributory	17,105	18,195	19,737	20,780	21,311	21,768	21,246	21,843	23,097	23,288	24,210	24,244	24,840	25,799	25,518	24,819
Non-contributory, non-means-tested (GB)																
Retirement Pension	122	112	99	93	82	76	63	56	53	50	49	45	45	47	37	34
War Pension	719	750	754	731	705	698	658	628	646	635	631	624	632	620	599	568
Attendance Allowance	158	228	281	295	325	345	353	385	445	508	596	661	746	820	897	981
Invalid Care Allowance	—	—	—	5	7	8	7	8	8	10	12	13	14	109	184	151
Invalid Pension/SD Allowance	—	—	35	88	100	142	149	160	175	194	219	271	289	300	295	290
Mobility Allowance	—	—	—	21	45	97	139	185	233	297	366	408	459	541	690	629
Child Benefit[b]	4,412	4,118	4,383	4,478	3,966	4,710	5,793	4,373	4,563	4,622	4,805	4,904	4,862	4,751	4,598	4,258
One-Parent Benefit	—	—	—	—	14	45	75	90	103	115	129	138	146	156	163	164
Maternity Grant	66	55	44	39	34	33	28	24	22	20	20	21	18	15	—	—
Total non-contributory, non-means-tested	5,477	5,263	5,596	5,749	5,277	6,154	7,265	5,910	6,248	6,451	6,829	7,083	7,212	7,359	7,463	7,074

Means-tested (GB)

Supplementary Pension^c	368	404	409	488	539	554	547	566	621	645	855	1,021	1,098	1,240	1,321	}7,358
Supplementary Allowance^c	1,276	1,438	1,877	2,163	2,245	2,150	1,905	2,394	3,467	4,567	5,881	6,400	7,004	7,146	6,635	
Family Income Supplement	53	44	35	47	57	49	47	62	89	118	148	144	141	169	180	397
Housing Benefit—rents^d	2,553	1,974	1,819	1,889	1,891	1,834	1,672	1,766	2,551	3,057	3,031	3,256	3,412	3,551	3,585	3,594
Total means-tested (excl. Housing Benefit)	1,697	1,886	2,322	2,698	2,841	2,754	2,500	3,022	4,177	5,330	6,884	7,565	8,244	8,556	8,136	7,755
Pensioners' Christmas Bonus	350	338	—	—	223	207	177	153	144	136	131	127	122	121	116	109
Total benefits (excl. housing)	24,630	25,681	27,654	29,227	29,652	30,883	31,188	30,927	33,667	35,205	38,054	39,019	40,418	41,835	41,233	39,758
Administrative costs (GB)	1,138	1,338	1,638	1,475	1,425	1,448	1,412	1,532	1,661	1,651	1,737	1,818	1,771	1,856	2,028	2,041
Social security spending (GB)	25,768	27,020	29,292	30,703	31,077	32,331	32,600	32,459	35,328	36,856	39,792	40,837	42,189	43,691	43,261	41,799
Social security spending (NI^e)	736	815	867	920	934	994	1,000	1,000	1,080	1,151	1,299	1,278	1,322	1,388	1,385	1,388
SOCIAL SECURITY SPENDING (UK)	26,504	27,835	30,159	31,623	32,011	33,325	33,600	33,459	36,407	38,008	41,090	42,115	43,512	45,078	44,646	43,187
Total public expenditure	140,351	157,721	157,310	154,005	146,136	154,004	158,421	161,481	163,293	167,632	170,602	175,229	175,082	177,789	177,000	176,083
Gross Domestic Product	328,070	327,574	323,977	334,367	342,727	355,441	364,211	350,519	350,742	358,438	371,807	379,014	392,927	406,000	424,500	443,503
GDP deflator	22.8	27.2	34.2	38.7	44.0	48.7	57.0	67.5	74.1	79.4	83.0	87.2	91.9	95.0	100.0	106.2

^a Includes the cost of Statutory Sick Pay. The source before 1987/8 is the National Insurance Fund Account. The source for 1987/8 is DSS (unpublished) and is a UK figure, since GB was unavailable. The figure for 1988/9 is an estimate.

^b Includes the estimated Exchequer cost of Child Tax Allowances (Cmnd. 7841).

^c The pre-1983/4 figures are estimates, based on data from *Social Security Statistics*, of the expenditure on Supplementary Benefit excluding the housing costs now met by the Housing Benefit scheme.

^d See text. The figures for Housing Benefit are not included in the totals in this table.

^e Estimates.

Source: HM Treasury 1989 and earlier equivalents.

Table 7A.2. *Administrative costs, 1982/3–1986/7, Great Britain*
(real, at 1987/8 prices)

	1982/3	1983/4	1984/5	1985/6	1986/7
Real (£ million)					
Retirement Pension	258	248	344	254	247
Widow's Benefits	28	27	32	26	22
Unemployment Benefit	166	159	153	174	188
Sickness and Invalidity	186	177	127	120	131
Maternity Allowance	15	17	14	13	14
War Pension	20	19	18	20	20
Attendance Allowance	21	23	24	26	28
Invalid Pension/Severe					
Disablement Allowance	9	12	13	13	16
Mobility Allowance	8	10	11	13	16
Supplementary Benefit	747	790	847	913	978
Child and One-Parent Benefit	122	123	130	97	107
Family Income Supplement	6	7	6	5	9
As percentage of benefit expenditure					
Retirement Pension	1.5	1.4	2.0	1.4	1.3
Widow's Benefits	3.0	2.9	3.6	3.0	2.5
Unemployment Benefit	8.8	8.8	8.4	10.1	10.3
Sickness and Invalidity	6.9	6.9	4.6	4.2	4.3
Maternity Allowance	7.9	9.9	7.5	7.3	7.7
War Pension	3.2	3.1	2.9	3.1	3.2
Attendance Allowance	4.2	3.8	3.6	3.5	3.5
Invalid Pension/Severe					
Disablement Allowance	4.5	5.5	4.7	4.5	5.3
Mobility Allowance	2.8	2.6	2.7	2.8	2.9
Supplementary Benefit	9.5	11.7	11.4	11.3	11.7
Child and One-Parent Benefit	2.6	2.5	2.6	1.9	2.2
Family Income Supplement	4.8	4.5	4.4	3.8	5.6
Real administrative costs per claim (£)					
Retirement Pension	397	376	425	295	325
Widow's Benefits	396	379	459	373	368
Unemployment Benefit	32	31	29	32	36
Sickness and Invalidity	29	111	90	81	133
Maternity Allowance	23	25	21	18	22
War Pension	2,015	1,928	2,294	2,448	2,500
Attendance Allowance	113	100	109	104	95
Invalid Pension/Severe					
Disablement Allowance					
Mobility Allowance	82	88	84	87	93

	1982/3	1983/4	1984/5	1985/6	1986/7
Supplementary Benefit	125	131	137	155	180
Child and One-Parent Benefit	163	171	196	136	149
Family Income Supplement	17	18	16	14	23

Source: HM Treasury 1989.

8

The State of Welfare

Julian Le Grand

As mentioned in the Introduction, some people may have come to this work expecting to find a chronicle of decline. Nor would such an expectation have been unreasonable. It would have been plausible to suppose that a combination of the economic difficulties encountered by the Labour government in the 1970s and the ideological hostility to welfare of the Conservative government in the 1980s had led to a sharp diminution of the welfare state and, in consequence, to an increasing marginalization of public welfare. Yet more seriously, this would have been accompanied by damaging changes in welfare 'outcomes', including falls in the average levels of key indicators of welfare and perhaps also increasing inequalities in those indicators.

There are indeed important parts of the welfare state which show the expected pattern of decline. But the overall picture is rather different. This chapter tries to demonstrate this by bringing together material from previous chapters into a coherent whole. It also considers possible explanations for what happened to the welfare state over the period—in particular, why expectations of its demise were unfulfilled. The chapter concludes with some speculations, informed by that analysis, about the future.

I. THE STATE OF WELFARE: PAST AND PRESENT

The previous five chapters have analysed recent trends in specific areas of public welfare in some detail. Here we concentrate on perhaps the two most salient: trends in public welfare spending and in welfare outcomes.

Public expenditure trends

Fig. 8.1 and Table 8.1, based on Table 8A.1 in the Annexe to this chapter, give an indication of the importance of public spending on welfare for the United Kingdom from 1973/4 to 1987/8. Public welfare spending is defined as the sum of public expenditures on education, health, housing, personal social services, and social security. Fig. 8.1 shows the trend in real terms of total welfare expenditure for each year, compared with the trend in real terms of general (all) government expenditure and of Gross Domestic Product (GDP): the real value in each

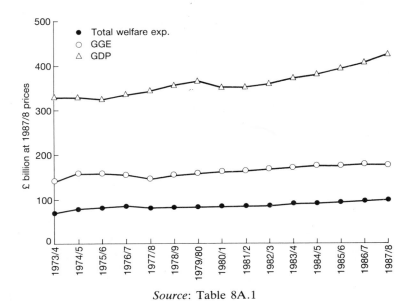

Source: Table 8A.1

FIG. 8.1. Public welfare expenditure, United Kingdom

Table 8.1. *Public expenditure on the welfare state: Overall trends,*
United Kingdom (1987/8 prices)

	Year-on-year change (%)	% of general government expenditure	% of GDP
1973/4	—	50.5	21.6
1974/5	13.3	51.0	24.5
1975/6	2.5	52.2	25.4
1976/7	3.7	55.4	25.5
1977/8	−4.7	55.7	23.7
1978/9	1.5	53.6	23.2
1979/80	1.1	52.6	22.9
1980/1	1.0	52.1	24.0
1981/2	1.1	52.1	24.3
1982/3	1.9	51.7	24.2
1983/4	4.9	53.3	24.5
1984/5	1.2	52.5	24.3
1985/6	1.4	53.3	23.7
1986/7	4.4	54.7	24.0
1987/8	1.0	55.6	23.2

Source: Table 8A.1.

case is obtained by adjusting expenditures in current prices by the GDP deflator. Table 8.1 gives the year-on-year changes in welfare expenditure and the proportion it takes up of general government expenditure and of GDP.

Total welfare spending in real terms increased slowly over the period, with an increase overall of approximately 37 per cent. Nearly half of this increase was after the first year of the Labour government, when welfare expenditures increased by over 13 per cent. In the next two years there were further increases of 2.5 and 3.7 per cent respectively; but then came the IMF visit and the year following (1977/8) saw a sharp drop of nearly 5 per cent. During the Conservative period, the year-on-year changes were less dramatic (increases mostly about 1 per cent), with the significant exceptions of increases of nearly 5 per cent in 1983/4 and of over 4 per cent in 1986/7, both around election years. In absolute terms, therefore, so far from there being a decline, there was a rise—indeed, at over a third, a significant one.

However, an increase in absolute terms is not very surprising, since GDP and general government expenditure were also rising over the period. But even relative to these there were no signs of a sharp fall. As a percentage of total government spending, welfare expenditures rose from 50.5 per cent in 1973/4 to a high of 55.7 per cent in 1977/8. By the beginning of the Conservative administration, it had fallen to about 52 per cent, where it remained until 1984/5, since when it has increased, reaching 55.6 per cent in 1987/8. As a percentage of GDP, welfare spending increased from 21.6 per cent in 1973/4 to 25.5 per cent by 1976/7; it then fell back to 23.7 per cent the following year and remained between 23 and 24.5 per cent for the whole of the rest of our period. Again, there is no evidence here to support a story of serious decline.

It should be noted, however, that this does represent a significant change in the *rate of growth* of the welfare state. As shown in Chapter 2, from the end of the Second World War until the early 1970s welfare expenditures not only grew enormously in real terms, but also increased substantially as a proportion of GDP. From a date that roughly coincides with the IMF visit in 1976, however, although some growth in real terms continued, it was broadly in line both with general government expenditure and with GDP. In that sense, therefore, the increase in the importance of the welfare state relative to other areas in the economy stopped in the mid-1970s.

The picture of relative stability since 1976, moreover, masks some significant shifts in the make-up of public welfare. The proportions of total welfare expenditures taken up by the various services are illustrated in Fig. 8.2 (based on Table 8A.2). It is apparent that here there have been some major changes, with personal social services (PSS) as the only stable category at between 3 and 4 per cent of the total. Education has fallen as a proportion of overall spending, from 26.3 per cent in 1973/4 to 20.4 per cent in 1985/6; since then it has risen slightly to nearly 22 per cent in 1987/8. Over the same period expenditures on the National Health Service (NHS) have steadily risen, from 17.6 per cent to nearly 21 per cent.

But the big changes have occurred in social security and housing. From 1974/5 there was an increase in the proportion taken up by social security from 34.7 per cent to about 40 per cent in the early 1980s. From 1981/2 it continued to increase until it reached 46.6 per cent in 1985/6; it then slightly declined to 45.4 per cent in 1987/8. These changes were in large part due to the huge increase in unemployment over the period and to its subsequent slight decline. Public expenditure on housing (taken here to include Housing Benefit and its predecessors, but not mortgage interest tax relief), on the other hand, fell from 17.4 per cent in 1974/5 to about 14 per cent in the late 1970s, and continued to fall throughout the Conservative period to a low of 8 per cent in 1987/8.

There have also been substantial changes in the relative proportions devoted to transfers (social security expenditure, Housing Benefit, and grants to students), current expenditures on goods and services and on capital spending. These are illustrated in Fig. 8.3. In real terms, transfers

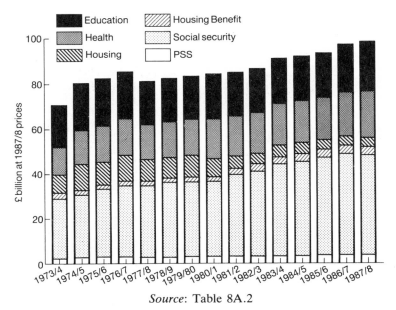

Source: Table 8A.2

FIG. 8.2. Public welfare expenditure by function, United Kingdom

have increased by two-thirds and current expenditures by half. However, by 1987/8 the real value of capital spending had fallen to less than half its value in the mid-1970s. In relative terms, the change is even more dramatic, with capital spending falling from nearly 15 per cent of total welfare expenditure in 1973/4 to 4.7 per cent in 1987/8.

How does this pattern of expenditures for welfare services compare with trends in the 'needs' for them? 'Need' is a notoriously difficult concept to define in the context of welfare policy, and we shall not debate the topic here. Instead, we shall follow the preceding chapters and, where possible, use simple demographic changes as the best (indeed often the only) indicator of changes in needs.

In education, the indicators used were the numbers of people in the relevant age bands for the different sectors. Expenditure per unit of need on this basis showed, over most of the period, an increase for primary education, approximate stability for secondary, further, and adult education, and a fall for polytechnic and university education. The principal indicator of need used for the NHS was a composite demographic indicator constructed by the Department of Health and Social Security; under both administrations, this rose more slowly than the rise in expenditure, although much less so under the Conservatives than Labour. Also, per

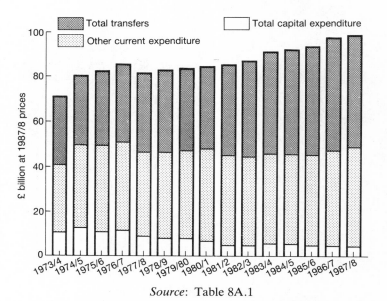

Source: Table 8A.1

FIG. 8.3. Public welfare expenditure by economic category, United Kingdom

capita estimates of the cost of care per elderly person showed an overall rise over the period, although it seems to have peaked in 1984/5.

A simple demographic indicator of the need for public housing subsidies is more difficult to find, and in consequence no estimates of expenditure per unit of need are available. Such need indicators as there are tend to be contradictory. The ratio of fit dwellings to number of households is a possible indicator of the overall need for housing; this has fallen, suggesting a drop in need. However, since the bulk of housing is provided through private expenditures, the need for housing overall is not the same as the need for publicly subsidized housing. With the exception of mortgage interest tax relief, perhaps more appropriate indicators (although far from unproblematic themselves) of the need for public housing subsidies are the numbers of homeless and the numbers in bed-and-breakfast accommodation; both of these rose after 1978, unlike the total of the relevant public expenditures, which fell. An indicator of the 'need' for mortgage interest tax relief is the number of owner-occupiers; this also rose over the period, but in this case not as fast as the value of mortgage interest tax relief (especially since 1978/9), leading to a rise in the value per owner-occupier.

Indicators of the 'need' for personal social services are also extremely difficult to find. A government estimate is of a growth in need of 2 per cent per year. If this is accepted, then it appears that there was an increase in expenditure over the whole period relative to need if the former is measured in real terms; but, if measured in volume terms, the growth in expenditure after 1979 fell below that of need. Measures of service provision for the elderly, such as residential care places, meals on wheels, and home helps per elderly person, also show a fall, particularly after 1979.

For social security, demographic indicators on need are easier to obtain. There was a rise in the numbers of elderly people, but a faster rise in the total expenditure on pensions, leading to an increase in the value of the average weekly payment in real terms. The numbers of children fell; so did expenditures on family benefits, but not as fast, leading again to an increase in the real value of the average weekly payment. The average weekly payment to the sick, widows, and the unemployed remained fairly constant. In the case of unemployment, however, this masked changes in the definition of the unemployed that occurred under the Conservative government. If the pre-1979 definitions were used, the numbers of unemployed would have been much larger in the 1980s, and hence the weekly payment per person unemployed smaller. Also, Unemployment Benefit and Supplementary Benefit for the unemployed became taxable, thus further reducing the value of the weekly payment.

The pattern concerning the distribution of these expenditures is both incomplete and rather more mixed. We have information on the distribution of expenditures for education by region, and for the NHS by region and by socio-economic group. For personal social services there is information on the distribution of domiciliary care services by region, income group, and tenure. In education, there was a widening of the disparities in expenditure per pupil across local education authorities. On the other hand, there has been an equalization of hospital resources relative to need across regions. There also appears to have been an equalization of utilization relative to self-reported morbidity by socio-economic group, with an elimination of the previously pro-rich distribution, although this appears to have been due more to an increase in self-reported morbidity by the higher social groups than to any change in the pattern of utilization. There was also some equalization of domiciliary care services in the opposite direction, with the top groups catching up (although not overtaking) use by the bottom groups, at least until 1979.

Overall, therefore, we see a picture where, on the whole, trends in expenditures seem to have followed trends in needs, at least as expressed by demographic indicators, but not always at the same rate. How can this picture be explained?

Following the discussion by Glennerster and Low in Chapter 3, we can identify three types of explanation for patterns of welfare spending in times of perceived stringency (whether economically or ideologically induced). The first is that, in this situation, the political and bureaucratic process would operate essentially in the 'public interest'. The perceived need to cut spending would break the pattern of incremental spending that dominates periods of relative resource abundance; instead, there would be a systematic reappraisal of welfare needs, leading to selective treatment of areas depending on their pattern of needs. On this hypothesis, we might expect to see changes in the volume of spending in different areas that reflected changes in (departmental perceptions of) needs in those areas.

The second theory is that a combination of bureaucratic inertia and self-protection would create strong resistance to cuts in budgets. In consequence, welfare spending overall might be maintained (perhaps even increased), and the pattern of service spending would be dominated by incrementalism (a broadly equal increase in percentage terms across all services). If the pressures for cuts became irresistible, it would be replaced by 'decrementalism': an equal proportional decline in all services on the principle of equal pain for all. On this hypothesis, budget shares would remain stable regardless of changes in needs.

The third possible explanation, derived from public choice theory, is that politicians will seek to minimize vote loss by treating less favourably those services with lowest demand or need; but that this pressure will be differentially applied, depending on the political power of the groups affected. A version of this which has been extensively explored by the present author and others emphasizes the importance of the middle classes as a pressure group affecting welfare expenditures (Le Grand and Winter 1987; Goodin and Le Grand 1987). Here the extent to which the middle classes used or were employed by the service in question would be crucial in determining its fate. On this hypothesis, we might expect expenditures to follow changes in needs, as in the public interest theory; but that the response to need would be different, depending on whether the service concerned had middle-class support or not.

As is so often the way in social science, all three theories can take some comfort from the evidence—at least, that presented in the preceding chapters. But this is not to say that each is equally satisfactory, or indeed, that any is wholly satisfactory. Perhaps the least successful is the incrementalism/decrementalism hypothesis. Welfare spending overall was maintained, and indeed increased. However, contrary to the predictions of the theory, as we have seen, there were substantial changes in budget shares for the major areas over the period. It is true that *within* two of the areas, education and the NHS, there was broad stability in budget shares between the principal sectors; but this was not true for the remaining three, housing, personal social services, and social security.

The public interest hypothesis does rather better. There was a fall in the share of education expenditure (although the absolute amount in volume terms remained constant); and there was a fall in the numbers in some of the relevant age groups—perhaps the best indicator of need—during the period. Both the absolute amount and the share of health spending rose; and this reflected a rise in the relevant demographic indicators. If the ratio of fit dwellings to households is a good indicator of the need for housing, then the fall in that, according to the public interest model, should have been accompanied by a fall in the volume of direct public housing spending—and indeed it was. (On the other hand, possibly superior indicators of public housing need, such as the number of homeless or in bed-and-breakfast accommodation, moved in the opposite direction.) There was an increase in most areas of need for the personal social services and an increase in expenditure as well. The rise in unemployment and numbers of elderly persons over most of the period should have led to a rise in the real value of social security spending—indeed it did.

However, there are problems for this explanation too. Although in most cases spending followed need, it did not always do so at the same rate. In only a few cases did expenditure change at the same rate as need: secondary education, further and adult education, sick pay, and Widow's Benefit. In several cases it changed faster, thus leading to a rise in expenditure relative to need, at least as measured by demographic indicators: primary education, health care, pensions, family benefits, and mortgage interest tax relief. There were yet others where expenditure fell relative to need: polytechnic and university education, personal social services (since 1979), benefits to the unemployed, and public housing subsidies. How can this be explained?

A possible explanation is offered by the version of the third hypothesis that emphasizes the influence of the middle classes. As the distributional analyses of the preceding chapters demonstrates, all the services which grew at the same rate as or faster than need are those which benefit the middle classes (professionals, employers, and managers, and their families) at least as much as, if not more than, the less well-off; all those which fell relative to need, except for higher education, are those in which the middle classes have little or no stake, either as users or as employees of the service concerned.

Le Grand and Winter (1987) tested this proposition more systematically, using data on changes in public expenditures and needs across a wide variety of welfare and non-welfare services to estimate the relationship between them and indicators of middle-class benefit over the Labour period and over the first term of the Thatcher government. The results for Labour were unsatisfactory, probably because the econometric techniques used were not able adequately to capture the shifts in policy that occurred after 1976. However, those for the Conservative government were much more robust, showing that services extensively *used* by the middle classes (although not necessarily those with a high proportion of middle-class employees) fared substantially better relative to need than those used primarily by the less well-off.

However, not all the evidence supports this view. Few institutions are more middle-class in both staff and clientele than polytechnics and universities; yet the data presented in Chapter 3 indicated a drop in expenditure relative to need. Part of the explanation may lie in the definition of need in this case as the numbers in the age range 18–24; these showed a very substantial rise over the period, to which it may have been difficult to respond speedily. In fact, given the scale of the demographic fluctuations for all sectors of education, it is possible that *within* education a better explanation for the observed pattern than the middle-class hypothesis is the incrementalism/decrementalism view, with budgets remaining broadly stable independently of changes in needs.

Nor is the middle-class theory quite consistent with the equalization that appears to have occurred in health, particularly in hospital resources across the regions; in this case the principal losers were the more middle-class health authorities and the principal gainers the poorer ones. However, the policy was a controversial one, and the principal agent of that equalization, the Resource Allocation Working Party (RAWP), has just been abolished. Also, the increase in self-reported morbidity by the middle classes between 1972 and 1985 (apparently the principal cause of the equalization in utilization across social classes) may be one of the factors that has contributed to the strong support the NHS enjoyed over the period. It should be noted that the equalization that seems to have occurred in domiciliary care, particularly between 1974 and 1979, with the higher socio-economic groups 'catching up' the lower groups, *is* consistent with the middle-class hypothesis (although 'catching up' is less evident when analysis is by income).

There is also an apparent inconsistency between the middle-class theory and the phenomenon to which the housing and social security chapters drew attention: the move under the Conservative government away from 'universal' benefits towards more targeted means-tested ones. Means-tested benefits by design do not benefit the better-off; hence any move towards a greater reliance on them appears to be in contradiction to the hypothesis.

However, in this case the contradiction is more apparent than real. In the most important example of this, the replacement of the general subsidies to council housing by Housing Benefit, the 'universal' subsidy being replaced is one in which the middle class had little interest. Moreover, in many cases, some better-off 'losers' from the policy shift are benefiting from other major areas of public housing subsidy: the sale of council housing at a discount, and the subsequent receipt of tax subsidies for owner-occupation. The other significant example—the increasing amount of the unemployed on long-term means-tested Income Support, instead of on Unemployment Benefit—also involves a 'universal' benefit in which the middle class have little stake. Moreover, the switch here does not arise from a conscious policy decision; rather, it is the unintended consequence of a combination of the growth of long-term unemployment and of a structural feature of the system: namely, that eligibility for Unemployment Benefit ceases after a fixed period.

Overall, therefore, there is no one simple explanation for the trends in public spending on welfare. However, it does appear that, with the possible exception of education, both changes in needs and middle-class interests were important influences on the overall pattern, with the latter particularly so in the Conservative period.

Outcomes

As has been emphasized at several points throughout this book, there is no simple relationship between the resources devoted to public welfare and welfare outcomes. The latter are also influenced by private expenditures on welfare services (heavily so in areas as housing) and by factors that lie quite outside welfare services as the latter are conventionally defined (such as nutrition levels in the case of health). However, it is unlikely that there is *no* link between the activities of the welfare state and welfare outcomes; and therefore any assessment of the former would be incomplete without an examination of the latter.

Again perhaps contrary to initial perceptions, here too there has been a steady improvement, at least in the average levels of key welfare indicators. In education, there was a dramatic increase in the skills of the labour force, at least as measured by the spread of educational qualifications. The proportion of the population with degrees trebled between 1974 and 1985. Over the same period the proportion of those with A-level or post-A-level qualifications increased by two-thirds, those with O-level or post-O-level qualifications by nearly half. This may be in part attributable to an improvement in the examination performance of average and below average children also observed over the period, an improvement that was achieved mostly in the comprehensive schools.

In health, there does appear to have been an increase in self-reported morbidity, although there is evidence that this does not represent an increase in illness that limits activities. However, mortality indicators— probably a better indicator of the overall health of the population than self-reported morbidity—show a steady improvement over the period, with the (age-standardized) mean age at death for both men and women increasing by over a year.

In housing, there has been rapid progress in reducing the number of dwellings lacking standard amenities. Other, previously 'non-standard', amenities have become standard: in 1974 most people lacked central heating, for example, but by 1985 only a quarter did so. The number of dwellings in serious disrepair did increase over the period, but the proportion of dwellings unsatisfactory in one or more respects (unfit, lacking amenities, or in serious disrepair) more than halved.

Indicators of outcomes for personal social services are even more difficult to find than for the other services. Perhaps the least unsatisfactory is the extent of social isolation, as measured by frequency of social contact. For most people this did not change very much between the only two years for which data are available (1980 and 1985); exceptions are the 'young' elderly (65–9) and the 'very old' elderly (85 and over), for both of whom social contact fell. Another indicator, the use of public transport by the elderly, fell over the same period, but this in part appears to be due to an increase in access to private cars.

As well as improvements in average levels of most welfare outcomes, there were reductions in inequalities in those outcomes—at least for some of them. There are a variety of kinds of inequality on which we have some information, of which the principal ones are inequality between individuals (population inequality), inequality between social classes or socio-economic groups, and inequality between income groups.

There was a fall in inequality over the population in years of post-school education, suggesting some equalization of skill levels. Further, there was an improvement in the highest level of educational qualification achieved by children from the families of semi- and unskilled manual workers relative to those from professional and managerial backgrounds.

So far as health is concerned, there may have been a rise in the difference in standardized mortality ratios for males aged 15–64 between the top and bottom social classes from 1971 to 1981, but the small numbers of deaths in this group make this information difficult to interpret. In contrast, the gap between the classes for self-reported morbidity seems to have narrowed from 1974 to 1985, but again there are doubts about the usefulness of the data. What we do know with reasonable certainty is that over the same period there were falls in inequality in the (standardized) age at death over the whole population; hence there was a reduction in individual inequality, if not in 'social' inequality.

In housing, the picture is slightly more mixed. There are no measures of population inequality; but the proportional differentials in housing conditions between social classes and income groups either declined or remained constant (depending on the data source). An exception to this may be the experience of the poorest income quintile between 1979 and 1985, since, according to the General Household Survey, their position with respect to basic amenities, central heating, and overcrowding worsened relative to that of the population as a whole. There are also growing signs of problems of access to housing at the margins of society, with increases in the numbers of homeless and in bed-and-breakfast accommodation. However, the English House Conditions Survey shows a different picture, with improvements in living conditions from 1981 to 1986 being *concentrated* in the lowest 25 per cent.

The social security system has two major roles: to help smooth income over the life-cycle for each individual and to redistribute income between individuals so as to reduce inequality and poverty. So far as the first is concerned, our evidence suggests that throughout the period it was very successful: there were substantial reductions in the variation of individuals' lifetime incomes.

It was also increasingly successful with respect to redistribution, with a greater fall in the gap between 'original' (i.e. market) incomes and 'gross' incomes (original income plus cash benefits) in 1986 than in 1975. However, this is in part because it has had more to do with a marked widening in original income, especially since 1979, a widening that it has only partially been able to ameliorate. Also, the numbers in poverty rose (at least up to 1985), whether poverty was measured relative to the Supplementary Benefit level or to a fixed percentage of per capita disposable income.

This brings us to a wider point, first made by Glennerster (1988), concerning the welfare state as a whole. Glennerster points to the increase in the redistributive power of the welfare state over the period, and argues that perhaps the single greatest achievement of the welfare state at this time was to modify what would otherwise have been a disastrous impact on income distribution of the economic crises of the 1970s and 1980s. It is striking (and was much remarked upon at the time) how little social discord or political upheaval occurred during this period, despite mass unemployment of a kind not seen for nearly fifty years. In Glennerster's view, much of the credit for this is due to the welfare system, which not only permitted the economy to weather the storms without too much social distress, but also permitted it to make the subsequent economic adjustments. If the economic gains of the Thatcher government are real, then they were possible because there was a welfare safety net.

Overall, what all this shows is that the welfare state, and indeed welfare itself, is very robust. Over the thirteen years from 1974 to 1987, welfare policy successfully weathered an economic hurricane in the mid-1970s and an ideological blizzard in the 1980s. The resources going to public welfare were maintained; welfare indicators continued to show a steady improvement (although the fact that the welfare state is not the only, or perhaps even the major, factor determining welfare outcomes cannot be emphasized too strongly). Even more significantly, the welfare system acted with increasing effectiveness as a safety net over a period of economic crisis and restructuring. The most important 'outcome' of the welfare state in the period may have been the economic gains of the 1980s.

II. THE STATE OF WELFARE: FUTURE

It seems reasonable to describe the welfare state over the period 1973–87 as a success. It survived; key parts even thrived. Welfare outcomes rose; some inequalities diminished, and others were far less than they would have been had there been no welfare state. But what are its prospects? Despite its successes, will a combination of private prosperity and a weakening of community spirit result in it withering away during the 1990s, as some have predicted? What is the likely impact of the post-1987 reforms in key areas of welfare policy? In short, does the welfare state have a future and, if so, in what form? It is obviously impossible to provide definitive answers to these questions; but here we offer some speculations concerning them that may be of interest.

1988: The year of quasi-markets

One of the striking features of the first eight years of Mrs Thatcher's government was how little it affected the welfare state. With the major exception of public housing, dramatically affected by council house sales and rising rents, the welfare system in 1987 was much the same as in 1979. Moreover, not only was the structure of the system unchanged, but, as we have seen, the overall resources going into welfare had not altered significantly—again with the major exception of housing.

All this apparently altered in 1988, a year that may come to be seen as the one when the dog finally barked. That year saw the passage of the Education Reform Act, with provisions for a National Curriculum, for open enrolment, and for schools to opt out of local authority control. It saw a White Paper proposing the introduction of loans for students in higher education (DES 1988b). It saw the setting up of a review into the NHS leading to the publication of another White Paper in January 1989 (DoH 1989a). The Housing Act of that year provided for other landlords to bid to take over local authority housing; together with the 1989 Housing and Local Government Act, it also established a variety of provisions designed to ensure that rent levels in all sectors more closely approximated market rents. The Griffiths Report into community care was published, with its provisions being finally accepted by the government in a White Paper published in November 1989 (DoH 1989b). Even in social security, 1988 saw the final introduction of the Fowler social security reforms, with an increasing role for the private sector in pension provision.

Not only did all these changes occur in the same year, but most display strong similarities. In particular, the proposed reforms in primary and secondary education, health, housing, and social services all involve the introduction of what might be termed 'quasi-markets': the separation of state finance from state provision and the introduction of competition for provision from independent agencies. If these reforms are carried through to their logical conclusion, the welfare state in the 1990s will be one where local authorities will not own and operate schools, houses, and residential homes, and where health authorities will not own and operate hospitals. Instead local authorities and, increasingly, central government will be financing a growing number of private and voluntary institutions, all competing for custom: opted-out and other independent schools, housing associations, private landlords, trust hospitals, private and voluntary residential homes. This shift from the state as funder *and* provider to the state primarily as funder with perhaps only a residual role as provider will undoubtedly create enormous changes in the way services are delivered and employees treated.

But will these quasi-market proposals make a significant difference to the numbers of the kind that we have been exploring in this book? Will there be a substantial fall in the public proportion of resources going into welfare? And will there be major changes in measures of welfare outcomes?

The evidence accumulated in this book suggests that the answer to these questions is firmly in the negative. Over the past two decades, despite major economic upheavals, despite major ideological shifts in government, despite the alleged break-up of the welfare consensus, the resources going into welfare have increased. Public funding of welfare, in particular, has remained constant as a share of Gross Domestic Product. Also, virtually all areas of welfare outcomes have shown an improvement. There seems no reason to suppose that the decade to come will be significantly different.

Indeed, there are two reasons for believing that the position of the key areas of the welfare state may even be strengthened. First, there is likely to be an increase in demand for many welfare services, partly because of the ageing of the population and partly because of social and economic changes, some of which are already in progress. Second, there will also be strong pressure to retain public finance of those services, if not public provision. Let us examine these in more detail.

The ageing of the population

Thompson (1987) has a useful description of the demographic changes expected in the next decades. She divides the population into three broad age bands: the first age, 0–15, the second age, 16–59, and the third age, 60 and over. It is easiest to start with the third age. Contrary to much popular belief, the numbers of people over age 60 will remain fairly constant until the turn of the century. However, this conceals sharp changes in the numbers of 'young' elderly people (in their sixties) and the numbers of 'old' elderly people (80 and over). The young elderly people will actually decline in numbers until 2001; but the numbers of old elderly people will increase dramatically, from 1.8 million in 1985 to 2.4 million in 2001 and to 2.6 million by 2011. Old elderly people need substantially more care than young elderly people; one estimate puts the care needs of an 80-year-old as between five and ten times that of a 60-year-old (Craig 1983). Even if some improvement in the overall health of 80-year-olds is allowed for, there is likely to be a substantial rise in the demands for health and social care from this group and hence from the third age overall. There may also be implications for the demand for housing, if the trend for old people to live on their own continues to increase.

The second age will remain almost static between 1985 and 2011.

However, this again conceals a compositional shift. There is an immediate and precipitate decline in the numbers at the younger end of the age band (16–29); by 2001, the number will have fallen by 2.5 million. At the same time the numbers at the other end of the age band (30–59) will soon begin to rise, with an increase of over 3 million by 2001.

The fall in the numbers in the 16–29 age band will lead to a fall in the formation of new households and therefore in their demand for housing. Perhaps more significantly, it will reduce substantially the numbers of potential entrants for further and higher education and for other sorts of training. However, it is far from clear that this will reduce overall demand for education and training from the second age. The ageing of the labour force may lead to a need for people to change jobs or shift careers in their later lives, shifts that may well require retraining.

On another front, the rise in the numbers of elderly will lead to an increase in the 'gerontic' dependency ratio (the ratio of the numbers of elderly people to the numbers in the labour force)—although, owing in part to the likely increase in female participation in the labour force, not by as much as is often feared (Falkingham 1989*a*). This will cause an increased demand for the 'labour' of the second age and therefore is likely to lead to a reduction in unemployment and hence in the demand for Unemployment Benefit. It may also lead to a pressure to raise the retirement age, creating a reduced demand for pensions.

Predictions concerning the first age (0–15) are more speculative than those concerning the other ages, for they depend on predictions concerning fertility rates, a notoriously difficult exercise. On the assumption that the average number of children per woman remains at its current level of two, the numbers of births will rise until the mid-1990s, owing to the previous peak in the 1960s, followed by a fall to 1975 levels by 2005. In consequence the earlier half of the decade may see a rise in the demand for maternity and infant children's services; the later half may see a fall in that demand, but, as the children born in the early 1990s grow older, there will be a corresponding rise in demand for primary-school places.

Social and economic shifts

As well as demographic changes, there are likely to be a number of social and economic shifts over the next decade that will impact on the demand for welfare. First, there is likely to be a continued growth in personal incomes, leading to an increase in demand for welfare services that are income-elastic, including education and health care. Accompanying this, there may be structural changes in the economy that require new forms of training.

General prosperity should lead to a reduced demand for income support, particularly for 'young' elderly people, in so far as they have shared in the recent growth. However, a growing average level of prosperity may be accompanied by growing inequality, as in the 1980s. The pattern is likely to be rather different in the 1990s, however, since for the reasons already discussed this period is unlikely to be characterized by high unemployment. Instead, if inequality does continue to grow, it will probably be driven by a widening earnings gap. This may lead to an increase in demand for income support from those in low-paid employment. Another, more certain, need for income support will arise from the apparently inexorable rise in single-parent families.

The increase in the demand for income support from single-parent families is also likely to lead to pressure for the parent to return to the labour force. This will contribute to an increased demand for nursery schooling and for more general child-care facilities, a demand already fuelled by the overall increase of female participation in the labour force.

Overall, therefore, what are we likely to see so far as the demand for welfare is concerned in the 1990s? An increase in the demand for nursery schooling and for other child-care facilities. A rise in the demand for primary schooling in the latter half of the decade. Perhaps a fall in the demand for secondary and further education and training, but not by as much as simple observation of the demographics would suggest. A short-term rise in the demand for maternity services and for infant children's health care, followed by a fall; but this will be more than offset by an increase in demand for both health and social care driven partly by the ageing of the population and partly by its getting richer. Probably, an overall fall in the demand for housing. A fall in the demand for pensions due to the raising of the retirement age, and a fall in unemployment benefit due to a fall in unemployment; and a fall in the demand for income support in so far as that is driven by loss of income due to old age and unemployment. But there will be a definite increase in demand for income support arising from the growth in single-parent households. And there may be an increase in demand for income support for the low-paid.

Public support for the welfare state

Changes in demand for key welfare services of the kind just discussed are not the same as changes in demand for the welfare state: that is, for welfare that is publicly financed and/or publicly provided. Welfare services are provided by, and financed from, many sources in addition to the state: the family, friends, private and voluntary agencies, and employers. Is there any reason to expect that a continued demand, or indeed an increased demand, for welfare services will be met by state finance and state provision at a similar, or even increased, level?

There are two reasons why this might be a reasonable expectation, at least for state *finance*. First, there is broad—and growing—support among the population as a whole for the public finance of welfare. In the annual British Social Attitudes Survey, respondents were asked if they wanted the government (*a*) to reduce taxes and public spending on health, education, and social benefits, (*b*) to keep them as they are now, or (*c*) to increase both taxes and spending. In 1983, 54 per cent plumped for stability, 32 per cent for increases, and only 9 per cent for reductions. By 1987, the proportion opting for reductions had fallen to just 3 per cent; 42 per cent wanted stability and 50 per cent now wanted increases. Moreover, and of particular interest given the apparent importance of the middle classes, in 1985, 59 per cent of Conservative voters wanted stability and 33 per cent wanted increases; by 1987, the latter figure had risen to 35 per cent (Bosanquet 1986, 1988).

Second, there are economic arguments for maintaining public finance in key areas of welfare. Many economists have argued that there is an *efficiency* case for state subsidy of key welfare services (recent examples include Heald 1983; Le Grand and Robinson 1984; Barr 1987), even if some have been sceptical of the *equity* case for such subsidy (Le Grand 1982). Although economists of this persuasion have not been noticeable among the Conservative government's advisers, it appears that many of the relevant arguments have been accepted.

As evidence for this, and/or for the government's sensitivity to public opinion in this area at least, it should be noted that the 1988/9 quasi-market proposals are all about changes in the system of state *provision*—not about changes in the level of state *finance*. There are exceptions to this: tax relief for private health insurance for elderly people, student loans, and the continued pressure to switch the system of housing sub-sidies from general subsidies to means-tested ones (although, as argued in Chapter 5, even this is more about changes in the method of funding than about levels). Otherwise the Education and Housing Acts, the NHS Review, the Griffiths Report all have little to say about state finance in the area concerned—unless they explicitly endorse its continuation, as, for instance, the Prime Minister does in her foreword to the White Paper on the NHS (DoH 1989*a*).

But will this support continue? It is possible to construct a scenario of 'privatization by stealth', which could lead to an erosion of support for publicly funded services, particularly by powerful groups such as the middle classes. This would involve a steady running down of public services, creating dissatisfaction and an eventual 'exit' to the private sector by those able to afford it. Once the powerful groups no longer used the relevant services, they could be further cut back and perhaps even-tually privatized completely with relative electoral impunity.

Indeed, it could be argued that elements of this strategy may have been pursued already, consciously or unconsciously. The decline in capital spending documented above, and the failure of even current spending to keep up with expectations in areas such as health care and education, could all be viewed as part of an attempt to persuade the better-off that they would be better served in the private sector.

However, if this is the case, the strategy seems relatively ineffective; for, as the previous chapters have demonstrated, although there has been some increase in privately financed education and health care, neither here nor in most other areas of welfare has there been a massive flight by the better-off into the private sector. Nor is this very surprising. Users of declining services are likely to protest before they 'exit'. Hence running services down while remaining politically responsible for them is likely to have damaging electoral consequences. In this context, it is significant that, as noted earlier, the biggest increases in public welfare spending under the Conservatives occurred around election years.

Moreover, an interest feature of several of the quasi-market reforms is that they are intended to improve publicly financed services in precisely the areas where the private sector is supposed to be superior. Thus the NHS reforms are intended, among other things, to reduce waiting lists and to improve the quality of the 'hotel' care provided; the education reforms are supposed to improve state schools' responsiveness to parents' views. If the reforms succeed, they will *reduce* the incentive for the better-off to exit, hence increasing rather than diminishing public support for state finance.

The effects of quasi-markets

Thus the changes likely to dominate welfare policy in the 1990s will be concerned more with reducing state provision than with state finance. Does this imply that they will have no effect on the kinds of indicators we have been exploring in this book? Not quite. There are three possible consequences to which we should draw attention.

The first concerns the effects on costs. The switch from public monopoly to competitive private providers is often defended on the grounds of reducing the costs of service delivery. Public providers, it is argued, partly because they are public and hence not driven by the profit motive, and partly because they face no competition, are inherently wasteful and inefficient. As a result, costs of service delivery are higher than they need be; and a given budget will deliver less service. The switch to competitive provision will, on this argument, reduce costs and thus release resources for more services (or reduce the burden on the taxpayer).

However, the privatization of provision may also create an upward pressure on costs. This is for at least four reasons. First, for markets to operate efficiently, activities must be accurately costed and their purchasers billed. Both costing and billing procedures are themselves costly; competing institutions also devote resources to sales efforts and marketing devices.

This is not to imply that these extra resources are necessarily wasted. Spending on advertising may make for better-informed consumers. Costing activities properly can improve efficiency through improving decisions about resource allocation. However, it is important to note that the procedures necessary to reap these particular efficiency gains are themselves costly; and the eventual cost savings may be outweighed by the costs of these procedures.

Second, the switch from monopolistic providers to competitive ones may bring about a rise in labour and in other input costs. Staff in many areas of welfare provision are organized in trade unions or in powerful professional associations (such as the British Medical Association in health) which in key respects operate very much like trade unions. Economic theory suggests that the power of these labour 'monopolies' can be offset if there is also a monopoly purchaser of that labour. However, if there is competition for labour, then the competitors, bidding against one another, will drive up wages. This in turn will put considerable pressure on budgets, leading either to strong political representations for an increase in the budget limit or, if those fail, to a reduction in service quality or 'output'—which then can be used as ammunition for a further attempt to raise the budget.

Again, this is not to imply that if wages do rise it is automatically undesirable. Monopolies of any kind can be exploitative. Rising wages can lead to increases in morale and increases in productivity. But these may have to be large if they are fully to offset the impact on unit costs of higher wages.

Third, the difficulty in assessing quality in many areas of the social services leads to a temptation to believe that higher price means higher quality. The higher-priced school or hospital is seen not as being inefficient, but as offering higher quality. This offers a further incentive to drive up prices and therefore costs. It is also possible that private monopolies may develop in key areas of service delivery, again driving up prices and therefore costs.

Finally, costs may rise in the short term owing to political pressures. In many cases the providers of welfare services are hostile to the proposed changes, partly from conservatism, partly because the changes, although providing new opportunities, also create threats to their job security, and partly because they have a genuine fear that the changes will harm the people they serve. Faced with such hostility, the government may try to defuse it by increasing salaries.

In other words, what we may see by the switch away from state provision is not a bonanza of resources released by services delivered with increasing efficiency, but an upward pressure on costs, leading either to reduced service for a given budget or to pressures for an increase in that budget. If the latter is acceded to, then we shall indeed see more financial resources going into welfare, but with the increase going into administration and higher wages and/or profits, rather than into more and better services.

A second possible effect of the quasi-market reforms concerns the poor. A major justification for most of the changes is that they are intended to make the welfare system more responsive to the needs and wants of its users. This is a laudable intention and, if fulfilled, will undoubtedly constitute a major improvement over the status quo. However, markets are more responsive to the wants of those with more resources and quasi-markets are no exception. In the quasi-market proposals, direct purchasing power is generally equalized, usually through some kind of per capita resource allocation formula. But other kinds of resources are not: transport, articulacy, and information. Those poorly endowed with any of these—the poor, the diffident, the less educated—will be disadvantaged when operating in a quasi-market environment, relative to those who are not.

Against this it has to be said that the poor are not noted for their ability to deal with monolithic bureaucratic providers, either. Indeed if the introduction of competition actually offers alternatives to the poorer consumers, they may benefit through being less at the mercy of, for instance, the recalcitrant housing clerk or the insensitive teacher. However, the middle classes will also be able to take advantage of the potential for competition and perhaps do it better; if this does occur, then although everyone's lot may improve, inequalities may widen.

A third problem concerns 'high-risk' clients (a group that may overlap with, but is not the same as, the poor). Cost-minimizing organizations are reluctant to accept as clients anyone who may require substantial resources devoted to them. Thus self-governing hospitals are likely to shy away from the chronically sick; private residential homes from the confused, incontinent elderly; opted-out schools from those with learning difficulties. Those who need the most by the way of welfare services might, under some forms of quasi-markets, be those who get the least.

In short, the quasi-market reforms may create incentives for cost-cutting and for increased responsiveness to users' wants. But there is also a real risk that the overall consequence will be higher costs and less service for the poor and other high-risk users than under the present system. The proof of the pudding will be in the eating.

Welfare outcomes

Finally, a brief word on the future of welfare outcomes. Throughout this book we have emphasized that public welfare 'inputs' are only one of the factors that contribute to welfare outcomes. Hence any predictions about the former will not necessarily carry over to the latter. However, in the absence of any catastrophe such as a major economic depression, it is difficult to see the gradually improving trends in most welfare outcomes that have characterized the last two decades being reversed.

However, again we must sound a note of caution with respect to those at the margins of society. We have seen that the plight of the poor has not improved in the 1980s, either in terms of income, access to housing, or (more controversially) in health. The quasi-market reforms may, as we have indicated, make access to welfare services more difficult for the poor and, in so far as use of these services affects welfare outcomes, the consequence may be a further worsening of the poor's situation. A major task of the welfare state since its inception has been the protection of the poor; the 1990s may see an increase in the magnitude of that task, simultaneously with a decrease in the ability of the welfare state to perform it.

III. IN BRIEF

• Perhaps contrary to expectations, from 1973/4 to 1987/8 public expenditure on welfare increased by over a third in absolute terms. However, it remained a fairly constant proportion of general government expenditure (just over half), and as a proportion of GDP (nearly a quarter). So the growth in the relative importance of the welfare state that was such a salient feature of the post-war years stopped in the mid-1970s.

• As a proportion of total public welfare expenditure, only spending on personal social services remained stable, at between 3 and 4 per cent. Expenditure on the National Health Service increased from 18 to 21 per cent. Driven by the large increase in unemployment, expenditure on social security increased from 35 per cent in 1974/5 to 47 per cent in 1985/6; it then fell back slightly to 45 per cent by 1987/8, again probably reflecting trends in unemployment. Education fell from 26 per cent in 1973/4 to 20 per cent in 1985/6; it then recovered slightly. Housing fell from 17 per cent in 1974/5 to 8 per cent in 1987/8.

• Total welfare expenditures on transfers rose by two-thirds in real terms over the period, and on other current expenditure by a half. But total capital spending on welfare fell by more than half in real terms; as a proportion of total spending it fell from 15 per cent to 5 per cent.

• For most services, expenditures and needs moved in the same direction, supporting the view that the political process determining these expenditures has responded, at least in part, to the public interest. However, expenditures on most 'middle-class' services rose relative to need, suggesting that there was also a powerful middle-class influence on the political process. Against this view was a fall in expenditure relative to need for higher education and an apparent equalization of some health care in relation to need.

• There was a general improvement in the mean level of welfare outcomes, and a reduction in inequality in most—though not all.

• Perhaps the greatest achievement of the welfare state over the period was to alleviate the otherwise disastrous impact of the economic restructuring of the 1980s on income distribution and thereby on social stability. If there are real economic gains from this process, they were made possible by the welfare state.

• Owing in part to public support, the future of state *finance* for welfare is relatively secure. However, monopoly state *provision* of services is being replaced by a number of 'quasi-markets' where independent agents compete for state-funded consumers. This may lead to improved efficiency and to a greater responsiveness to clients' wants. But there are aspects of the quasi-market reforms that may lead to an overall increase rather than a decrease in costs; they may also worsen access for the poor and for those with special needs.

• Welfare outcomes are likely to continue to improve for the bulk of the population. But again there may be problems for the poorest sections of society. What many people believe to be the principal role of the welfare state—the protection of the poor—may be harder to perform during the 1990s than it has been in the 1970s and 1980s.

Annexe

Table 8A.1. *Public expenditure on the welfare state, United Kingdom* (£bn. at 1987/8 prices)

	Transfers	Other current expenditure	Total capital expenditure	Total welfare expenditure	General government expenditure	GDP
1973/4	30.0	30.4	10.5	70.9	140.5	328.1
1974/5	30.7	36.8	12.8	80.3	157.6	327.6
1975/6	33.0	38.5	10.9	82.3	157.5	324.0
1976/7	34.5	39.4	11.4	85.4	154.1	334.4
1977/8	34.9	37.5	8.9	81.3	146.1	342.7
1978/9	36.2	38.4	7.9	82.5	153.8	355.4
1979/80	36.3	38.9	8.1	83.4	158.6	364.2
1980/1	36.3	41.1	6.8	84.2	161.5	350.5
1981/2	40.1	40.0	5.0	85.1	163.3	350.7
1982/3	42.3	39.7	4.7	86.7	167.6	358.4
1983/4	45.3	40.1	5.6	90.9	170.5	371.8
1984/5	46.6	40.0	5.4	92.0	175.2	379.0
1985/6	48.1	40.4	4.8	93.3	175.0	392.9
1986/7	50.1	42.6	4.7	97.4	177.9	406.0
1987/8	49.8	44.1	4.6	98.4	177.0	424.5

Sources: Equivalent tables in preceding chapters; HM Treasury 1989: table 21.4.1.

Table 8A.2. Composition of public expenditure on the welfare state, United Kingdom (% of total welfare expenditure)

	Education	Health	Housing[a]	PSS	Social security
1973/4	26.3	17.6	15.3	3.4	37.4
1974/5	25.5	18.8	17.4	3.6	34.7
1975/6	25.2	19.4	14.9	3.9	36.7
1976/7	24.0	18.9	16.2	3.8	37.1
1977/8	23.4	19.3	14.5	3.5	39.4
1978/9	22.9	19.5	13.6	3.5	40.4
1979/80	22.5	19.4	14.1	3.8	40.3
1980/1	23.1	21.0	12.3	3.9	39.7
1981/2	22.4	21.0	9.9	3.8	42.8
1982/3	22.1	20.9	9.3	3.8	43.9
1983/4	21.4	20.4	9.3	3.8	45.2
1984/5	20.9	20.3	9.3	3.8	45.8
1985/6	20.4	20.2	8.7	4.1	46.6
1986/7	21.3	20.2	8.2	4.1	46.3
1987/8	21.8	20.9	8.0	3.9	45.4

[a] Includes Housing Benefit (or equivalent).

Sources: Equivalent tables in preceding chapters; HM Treasury 1989: table 21.4.1

Bibliography

ABEL-SMITH, B. (1958), 'Whose Welfare State?', in N. MacKenzie (ed.), *Conviction*, London: MacGibbon and Kee.
—— (1983), 'Assessing the Balance Sheet', in H. Glennerster (ed.), *The Future of the Welfare State*, London: Heinemann.
—— and TOWNSEND, P. (1965), *The Poor and the Poorest* (Occasional Paper in Social Administration), London: Bell.
ADSS [Association of Directors of Social Services] (1980), *Report of the Second Survey of the Extent and Effect of Cuts/Savings in Expenditure on the Personal Social Services*, Newcastle upon Tyne: ADSS.
ALLEN, I., WICKS, M., FINCH, J., and LEAT, D. (1987), *Informal Care Tomorrow* (Policy Studies Institute Occasional Paper), London: PSI.
ALLSOP, J. (1984), *Health Policy and the National Health Service*, London: Longman.
ALTMANN, R. M. (1981), 'Take-up of Supplementary Benefit by Male Pensioners' (ESRC Programme on Taxation, Incentives and the Distribution of Income, Discussion Paper No. 25), London: London School of Economics.
APU [Assessment of Performance Unit] (1988), *Science at Age 15*, London: DES.
ARBER, S., and GILBERT, G. N. (1989), 'Men: The Forgotten Carers', *Sociology*, 23 no. 1: 111–18.
ATKINSON, A. B. (1983), *The Economics of Inequality* (2nd edn.), Oxford: University Press.
—— (1984), 'Take-up of Social Security Benefits' (ESRC Programme on Taxation, Incentives and the Distribution of Income, Discussion Paper No. 65), London: London School of Economics.
—— (1987), 'Income Maintenance and Social Insurance', in A. J. Auerbach and M. S. Feldstein (eds.), *Handbook of Public Economics*, ii, Amsterdam: North Holland.
—— and MICKLEWRIGHT, J. (1989), 'Turning the Screw: Benefits for the Unemployed 1979–1988, in A. W. Dilnot and I. Walker (eds.), *The Economics of Social Security*, Oxford: University Press.
—— and SUTHERLAND, H. (1988), *Tax-Benefit Models* (STICERD Occasional Paper No. 10), London: London School of Economics.
—— Hills, J., and LE GRAND, J. (1987), 'The Welfare State', in R. Dornbusch and R. Layard (eds.), *The Performance of the British Economy*, Oxford: University Press.
—— *et al.* (1984), 'Unemployment Benefit, Duration and Incentives in Britain: How Robust is the Evidence?', *Journal of Public Economics*, 23 no. 1/2: 3–26.
AUDIT COMMISSION (1986a), *Performance Review in Local Government: A Handbook for Auditors and Local Authorities (Social Services)*, London: HMSO.
—— (1986b), *Making a Reality of Community Care*, London: HMSO.
—— (1989), *Housing the Homeless: The Local Authority Role*, London: HMSO.
BACON, R., and ELTIS, W. (1976), *Britain's Economic Problem: Too Few Producers*, London: Macmillan.

BALDWIN, S., PARKER, G., and WALKER, R. (eds.) (1989), *Social Security and Community Care*, Avebury: Gower.

BARCLAY, P. (1982), *Social Workers: Their Role and Tasks*, London: Bedford Square Press.

BARNES, J., and BARR, N. A. (1988), *Strategies for Higher Education*, Aberdeen: University Press.

BARR, N. A. (1975), 'Labour's Pension Plan—A Lost Opportunity?', *British Tax Review*, no. 2: 107–13, and no. 3: 155–74.

—— (1981), 'Empirical Definitions of the Poverty Line', *Policy and Politics*, 9 no. 1: 1–21.

—— (1986), 'Revenue, Expenditure and the Government Accounts', *British Tax Review*, no. 6: 340–6.

—— (1987), *The Economics of the Welfare State*, London: Weidenfeld and Nicolson.

—— (1988), 'The Mirage of Private Unemployment Insurance' (Welfare State Programme, Discussion Paper No. 34), London: London School of Economics.

—— GLENNERSTER, H., and LE GRAND, J. (1988), 'Reform and the National Health Service' (Welfare State Programme, Discussion Paper No. 32), London: London School of Economics.

BAYLEY, M. (1973), *Mental Handicap and Community Care*, London: Routledge.

BECKER, G. S. (1964), *Human Capital: A Theoretical and Empirical Analysis with Special Reference to Education*, Princeton: University Press.

BECKERMAN, W. (1979), 'The Impact of Income Maintenance Payments on Poverty: 1975', *Economic Journal*, 89: 261–79.

BEER, S. (1982), *Britain Against Itself*, London: Faber.

BERTHOUD, R. (1989), 'Social Security and the Economics of Housing' in A. Dilnot and I. Walker (eds.), *The Economics of Social Security*, Oxford: University Press.

BEVERIDGE REPORT (1942), *Social Insurance and Allied Services*, Cmd. 6404, London: HMSO.

BIRCH, B., and MAYNARD, A. (1986), 'The RAWP Review: RAWPing Primary Care: RAWPing the United Kingdom' (Centre for Health Economics, Discussion Paper No. 19), York: University of York.

BLACK, D. (1980), *Inequalities in Health: Report of a Research Working Group* (Black Report), London: DHSS.

BLAUG, M. (1970), *An Introduction to the Economics of Education*, Harmondsworth: Penguin Books.

—— (1976), 'Human Capital Theory: A Slightly Jaundiced Survey', *Journal of Economic Literature* (Sept.), 827–55.

BLUNDELL, R., FRY, V., and WALKER, I. (1988), 'Modelling the Take-up of Means-Tested Benefits: The Case of Housing Benefits in the United Kingdom', *Economic Journal*, Conference Papers, 98 no. 390: 58–74.

BOARD OF EDUCATION (1943), *Educational Reconstruction*, Cmd. 6458, London: HMSO.

BOSANQUET, N. (1986), 'Interim Report: Public Spending and the Welfare State', ch. 7 in R. Jowell, S. Witherspoon, and L. Brook (eds.), *British Social Attitudes: The 1986 Report*, Aldershot: Gower.

——(1988), 'An Ailing State of National Health', ch. 6 in R. Jowell, S. Wither-spoon, and L. Brook (eds.), *British Social Attitudes: The 5th Report*, London: Gower.

——and TOWNSEND, P. (1972), *Labour and Inequality*, London: Fabian Society.

BOSWORTH, D., and FORD, J. (1985), 'Income Expectations and the Decision to Enter Higher Education', *Studies in Higher Education*, 10 no. 1: 257–67.

BRADSHAW, J., and DEACON, A. (1986), 'Social Security', in P. Wilding (ed.), *In Defence of the Welfare State*, Manchester: University Press.

BRETON, H. (1974), *The Economic Theory of Representative Government*, London: Macmillan.

BROWN, M. (1972), 'Inequality and the Personal Social Services', in P. Townsend and N. Bosanquet (eds.), *Labour and Inequality*, London: Fabian Society.

BULL, D. (1980), *What Price Free Education?* (Poverty Pamphlet No. 48), London: Child Poverty Action Group.

BULMER, M. (1987), *The Social Basis of Community Care*, London: Allen and Unwin.

BUXTON, M. S., and KLEIN, R. E. (1978), *Allocating Health Resources* (Royal Commission on the NHS, Research Paper No. 3), London: HMSO.

CANTER, D., DRAKE, M., LITTLER, T., MOORE, J., STOCKLEY, D., and BALL, J. (1989), *The Faces of Homelessness in London*, Guildford: University of Surrey, Department of Psychology.

CENTRE FOR CONTEMPORARY CULTURAL STUDIES (1981), *Unpopular Education: Schooling and Social Democracy in England Since 1944*, London: Hutchinson.

CHALLIS, L., *et al.* (1988), *Joint Approaches to Social Policy: Rationality and Practice*, Cambridge: University Press.

CHR [Centre for Housing Research] (1989), *The Nature and Effectiveness of Housing Management in England*, London: HMSO.

CIPFA [Chartered Institute of Public Finance and Accountancy] (1985), *Personal Social Services Statistics 1984/5 (Actuals)*, London: CIPFA.

——(1988*a*), *Education Statistics 1985–86 Actuals,* London: CIPFA.

——(1988*b*), *Handbook of Education Unit Costs 1986–87*, London: CIPFA.

CLARK, A., and TARSH, J. (1987), 'How Much is a Degree Worth?', in *Education and Training UK 1987*, London: Policy Journals.

CLARKER, L. (1984), *Domiciliary Services for the Elderly*, London: Croom Helm.

COLE, D., and UTTING, J. (1962), *The Economic Circumstances of Old People* (Occasional Papers in Social Administration No. 4), Welwyn: Codicote Press.

CONGRESSIONAL BUDGET OFFICE (1987), *Educational Achievement: Explorations and Implications of Recent Trends*, Washington, DC: Congress of the United States.

COONS, J., and SUGARMAN, S. (1978), *Education by Choice: The Case for Family Control*, Berkeley: University of California Press.

COOPER, J. (1983), *The Creation of the Personal Social Services 1962–1974*, London: Heinemann.

COWELL, F. A. (1986), 'Welfare Benefits and the Economics of Take Up' (ESRC Programme on Taxation, Incentives and the Distribution of Income, Discussion Paper No. 89), London: London School of Economics.

Cox, C. B., and Dyson, A. E. (eds.) (1969), *Fight for Education: A Black Paper*, London: Critical Quarterly Society.

CPAG [Child Poverty Action Group] (1987), *Charges for School Activities: A Consultation Document—CPAG's Response*, London: CPAG.

——(1988), *National Welfare Benefits Handbook* (18th edn.), London: CPAG.

CPRS [Central Policy Review Staff] (1975), *A Joint Framework for Social Policies*, London: HMSO.

——(1977), *Population and the Social Services*, London: HMSO.

Craig, J. (1983), 'The Growth of the Elderly Population', *Population Trends*, no. 32: 28–33.

Cresswell, M., and Gubb, J. (1987), *The Second International Mathematics Study in England and Wales*, Windsor: NFER–Nelson.

Crosland, C. A. R. (1956), *The Future of Socialism*, London: Cape.

CSO [Central Statistical Office] (1974), 'The Incidence of Taxes and Social Service Benefits in 1973', *Economic Trends* (Dec.), London: HMSO.

——(1976), *Social Trends 1976*, London: HMSO.

——(1977), *National Income and Expenditure 1966–76*, London: HMSO.

——(1978), 'The Effects of Taxes and Benefits on Household Income, 1976', *Economic Trends*, no. 292, London: HMSO.

——(1979), *Annual Abstract of Statistics 1979 Edition*, London: HMSO.

——(1980), *Social Trends 1980*, London: HMSO.

——(1981), 'The Effects of Taxes and Benefits on Household Income, 1979', *Economic Trends*, no. 327, London: HMSO.

——(1982), *Annual Abstract of Statistics 1982 Edition*, London: HMSO.

——(1983), *United Kingdom National Accounts 1983*, London: HMSO.

——(1985a), *United Kingdom National Accounts: Sources and Methods* (3rd edn.), London: HMSO.

——(1985b), *Annual Abstract of Statistics 1985 Edition*, London: HMSO.

——(1986a), *Social Trends 1986*, London: HMSO.

——(1986b), *Annual Abstract of Statistics 1986 Edition*, London: HMSO.

——(1987a), *Social Trends 1987*, London: HMSO.

——(1987b), *United Kingdom National Accounts 1987*, London: HMSO.

——(1988a), *Social Trends 1988*, London: HMSO.

——(1988b), *United Kingdom National Accounts 1988*, London: HMSO.

——(1988c), *Annual Abstract of Statistics 1988 Edition*, London: HMSO.

——(1988d), 'The Effects of Taxes and Benefits on Household Income, 1986', *Economic Trends*, no. 422, London: HMSO.

——(1989a), *Social Trends 1989*, London: HMSO.

——(1989b), *Economic Trends Annual Supplement 1989 Edition*, London: HMSO.

——(1989c), *Annual Abstract of Statistics 1989 Edition*, London: HMSO.

Cullis, J., and Jones, P. (1986), 'Rationing by Waiting Lists: An Implication', *American Economic Review*, 76: 250–6.

Davies, B. (1968), *Social Needs and Resources in Local Services*, London: Michael Joseph.

Day, P., and Klein, R. (1987), 'Residential Care for the Elderly: A Billion Pound Experiment in Policy Making', *Public Money*, 6 no. 4: 19–24.

DE [Department of Employment] (1975), *Family Expenditure Survey 1974*, London: HMSO.

—— (1980), *Family Expenditure Survey 1979*, London: HMSO.

—— (1985), *Employment: The Challenge for the Nation*, Cmnd. 9474, London: HMSO.

—— (1986), *Family Expenditure Survey 1985*, London: HMSO.

—— (1988), *Family Expenditure Survey 1986 (Revised)*, London: HMSO.

—— (1989), *Employment Gazette* (Apr.), London: HMSO.

DEAKIN, N. (1989), 'In Search of Post-War consensus', *LSE Quarterly*, 3 no. 1: 65–83.

DEARLOVE, J. (1979), *The Reorganisation of British Local Government*, Cambridge: University Press.

DES [Department of Education and Science] (1963), *Higher Education* (Robbins Report), Cmnd. 2154, London: HMSO.

—— (1966), *Progress in Reading 1948–1964* (Education Pamphlet No. 50), London: HMSO.

—— (1967), *Children and their Primary Schools* (Plowden Report), London: HMSO.

—— (1972), *Education: A Framework for Expansion*, Cmnd. 5174, London: HMSO.

—— (1974), *Educational Disadvantage and the Educational Needs of Immigrants*, Cmnd. 5720, London: HMSO.

—— (1975), *A Language for Life* (Bullock Report), London: HMSO.

—— (1977*a*), *Education in Schools*, Cmnd. 6069, London: HMSO.

—— (1977*b*), *A Study of School Building*, London: HMSO.

—— (1977*c*), *Statistics of Education*, vols. 1, 3, 5, and 6, London: HMSO.

—— (1978), *Primary Education in England: A Survey by HM Inspectors of Schools*, London: HMSO.

—— (1979), *Aspects of Secondary Education in England: A Survey by HM Inspectors of Schools*, London: HMSO.

—— (1982), *Mathematics Counts* (Cockcroft Report), London: HMSO.

—— (1983), 'School Standards and Spending: Statistical Analysis', *Statistical Bulletin*, 16/83, London: DES.

—— (1984*a*), *Report on Education*, no. 100 (Statistical Methodology Paper), London: DES.

—— (1984*b*) 'School Standards and Spending: Statistical Analysis: A Further Appreciation', *Statistical Bulletin*, 13/84, London: DES.

—— (1985*a*), *Better Schools*, Cmnd. 9469, London: HMSO.

—— (1985*b*), *The Development of Higher Education in the 1990s*, Cmnd. 9624, London: HMSO.

—— (1985*c*), *Education for All: Report of a Committee of Enquiry into the Education of Children from Ethnic Minority Groups* (Swann Report), Cmnd. 9453, London: DES.

—— (1985*d*), *The Curriculum from 5–16* (HMI Curriculum Matters Series No. 2), London: HMSO.

—— (1987*a*), *The National Curriculum 5–16: A Consultation Document*, London: DES.

DES (1987*b*), *Statistical Bulletin*, 14/87, London: DES.

—— (1987*c*), *Statistics of Education: Finance*, London: DES.

—— (1988*a*), *Mathematics for Ages 5–16*, London: DES.

—— (1988*b*), *Top-up Loans for Students*, Cm. 520, London: HMSO.

—— (1988*c*), *Statistics of Education: Schools*, London: DES.

—— (1989), *Statistical Bulletin*, 1/89, London: DES.

DHSS [Department of Health and Social Security] (1971), *Better Services for the Mentally Handicapped*, Cmnd. 4683, London: HMSO.

—— (1974), *Better Pensions: Fully Protected Against Inflation*, Cmnd. 5713, London: HMSO.

—— (1975), *Better Services for the Mentally Ill*, London: HMSO.

—— (1976*a*), *Sharing Resources for Health in England: Report of the Resource Allocation Working Party*, London: HMSO.

—— (1976*b*), *Social Security Statistics 1976*, London: HMSO.

—— (1976*c*), *Priorities for the Health and Personal Social Services in England: A Consultative Document*, London: HMSO.

—— (1977*a*), *Priorities in Health and Personal Social Services: The Way Forward*, London: HMSO.

—— (1977*b*), *Forward Planning of Local Authority Social Services*, Circular 2ASSL (77/13), London: DHSS.

—— (1978), *Health and Personal Social Services Statistics for England*, London: HMSO.

—— (1981*a*), *Care in Action: A Handbook of Policies and Priorities for the Health and Personal Social Services in England*, London: HMSO.

—— (1981*b*), *Social Security Statistics 1981*, London: HMSO.

—— (1981*c*), *Growing Older*, Cmnd. 8173, London: HMSO.

—— (1982*a*), *Health and Personal Social Services Statistics for England*, London: HMSO.

—— (1982*b*), *Social Security Operational Strategy*, London: HMSO.

—— (1984), *Social Security Statistics 1984*, London: HMSO.

—— (1985*a*), *Reform of Social Security*, Cmnd. 9517, London: HMSO.

—— (1985*b*), *Reform of Social Security: Programme for Change*, Cmnd. 9518, London: HMSO.

—— (1985*c*), *Reform of Social Security: Background Papers*, Cmnd. 9519, London: HMSO.

—— (1985*d*), *Housing Benefit Review: Report of the Review Team*, Cmnd. 9520, London: HMSO.

—— (1985*e*), *Reform of Social Security: Programme for Action*, Cmnd. 9691, London: HMSO.

—— (1986*a*), *Social Security Statistics 1986*, London: HMSO.

—— (1986*b*), *Low Income Families—1983*, London: DHSS.

—— (1986*c*), *Health and Personal Social Services Statistics for England*, London: HMSO.

—— (1987*a*), *Health and Personal Social Services Statistics for England*, London: HMSO.

—— (1987*b*), *Social Security Statistics 1987*, London: HMSO.

——(1988*a*), *Low Income Families—1985*, London: DHSS.

——(1988*b*), *Low Income Statistics—Report of a Technical Review*, London: DHSS.

——(1988*c*), *Community Care: Agenda for Action* (Griffiths Report), London: HMSO.

——(1988*d*), *Health and Personal Social Services Statistics for England*, London: HMSO.

DIGBY, A. (1989), *British Welfare Policy: Workhouse to Workfare*, London: Faber.

DILNOT, A. W., and MORRIS, C. N. (1984), 'Private Costs and Benefits of Unemployment: Measuring Replacement Rates', in C. A. Greenhalgh, P. R. G. Layard, and A. J. Oswald (eds.), *The Causes of Unemployment*, Oxford: University Press.

——and WALKER, I. (eds.) (1989), *The Economics of Social Security*, Oxford: University Press.

——and WEBB, S. (1989), 'The 1988 Social Security Reforms', *Fiscal Studies*, 9 no. 3: 26–53 (also in Dilnot and Walker 1989).

——KAY, J. A., and MORRIS, C. N. (1984), *The Reform of Social Security*, Oxford: University Press.

DISABILITY ALLIANCE (1975), *Poverty and Disability: The Case for a Comprehensive Scheme for Disabled People*, London: Disability Alliance.

——(1988), 'Briefing on the First Report from the OPCS Surveys of Disability: "The Prevalence of Disability Among Adults"', London: DA.

DISABLEMENT INCOME GROUP (1979), *Disablement Income Group's National Disability Income*, London: Disablement Income Group.

DoE [Department of the Environment] (1971), *Fair Deal for Housing*, Cmnd. 4728, London: HMSO.

——(1973), *Better Homes: The Next Priorities*, Cmnd. 5339, London: HMSO.

——(1977*a*), *Housing Policy: A Consultative Document*, Cmnd. 6851, London: HMSO.

——(1977*b*), *Housing Policy Technical Volume*, London: HMSO.

——(1978), *National Dwelling and Housing Survey*, London: HMSO.

——(1982), *English House Condition Survey 1981*, Part 1. *Report of the Physical Condition Survey*, London: HMSO.

——(1983), *English House Condition Survey 1981*, Part 2. *Report of the Interview and Local Authority Survey*, London: HMSO.

——(1985), *Housing and Construction Statistics 1974–1984*, London: HMSO.

——(1987), *Housing: The Government's Proposals*, Cm. 214, London: HMSO.

——(1988*a*), *Housing and Construction Statistics 1977–1987*, London: HMSO.

——(1988*b*), *New Financial Regime for Local Authority Housing in England and Wales: A Consultation Paper*, London: DoE.

——(1988*c*), *English House Condition Survey 1986*, London: HMSO.

——(1989*a*), *Housing and Construction Statistics March Quarter 1989*, pt. 1, London: HMSO.

——(1989*b*), *Housing and Construction Statistics December Quarter 1988*, pt. 2, London: HMSO.

DoE (1989c), *Local Authorities' Action under the Homelessness Provisions of the 1985 Housing Act: England. Results for First Quarter of 1989. Supplementary Tables*, London: DoE.

DoH [Department of Health] (1989a), *Working for Patients*, Cm. 555, London: HMSO.

——(1989b), *Caring for People: Community Care in the Next Decade and Beyond*, Cm. 849, London: HMSO.

DONNISON, D. (1982), *The Politics of Poverty*, Oxford: Martin Robertson.

DORNBUSCH, R., and LAYARD, R. (1987), *The Performance of the British Economy*, Oxford: University Press.

DSS [Department of Social Security] (1988), *Social Security Statistics 1988*, London: HMSO.

ECKSTEIN, H. (1959), *The English Health Service*, Oxford: University Press.

EOC [Equal Opportunities Commission] (1980), *The Experience of Caring for Elderly and Handicapped Parents*, London: EOC.

ESTRIN, S., and PEROTIN, V. (1989), 'Creeping Privatisation: Old Age Homes in Britain and France', London: London School of Economics (mimeo).

EVANDROU, M., ARBER, S., DALE, A., and GILBERT, G. N. (1986), 'Who Cares for the Elderly?: Family Care Provision and Receipt of Statutory Services', in C. Phillipson, M. Bernard, and P. Strang (eds.), *Dependency and Interdependency in Old Age—Theoretical Perspectives and Policy Alternatives*, London: Croom Helm.

FALKINGHAM, J. (1989a), 'Changes in the Income of the Elderly Population: Increasing Polarisation?', paper presented at the 1989 Conference of the British Society of Gerontology (mimeo).

——(1989b), 'Dependency and Ageing in Britain: A Re-Examination of the Evidence', *Journal of Social Policy*, 18 no. 2: 211–33.

FERLIE, E., and JUDGE, K. (1981), 'Detrenchment and Rationality in Personal Social Services', *Policy and Politics*, 9 no. 3: 313–14.

FINCH, J., and GROVES, D. (1980), 'Community Care and the Family: A Case for Equal Opportunities', *Journal of Social Policy*, 9 no. 4: 487–511.

——(eds.) (1983), *A Labour of Love: Women, Work and Caring*, London: Routledge and Kegan Paul.

FLOUD, J. E., HALSEY, A. H., and MARTIN, F. M. (1956), *Social Class and Educational Mobility*, London: Heinemann.

FOOT, M. (1975), *Aneurin Bevan 1945–1960*, London: Paladin.

FOSTER, C. D., JACKMAN, R., and PERLMAN, M. (1980), *Local Government Finance in a Unitary State*, London: Allen and Unwin.

FPSC [Family Policy Studies Centre] (1984), *The Forgotten Army: Family Care and Elderly People* (Briefing Paper), London: FPSC.

——(1989), *Family Policy Bulletin*, no. 6 (Winter 1989), London: FPSC.

FRY, V., and STARK, G. (1987), 'The Take-up of Supplementary Benefit: Gaps in the "Safety Net"?', *Fiscal Studies*, 8 no. 4: 1–14 (also in Dilnot and Walker 1989).

GARDEN, R. A. (1987), 'The Second IEA Mathematics Study', *Comparative Education Review*, 31 no. 1: 47–68.

GEORGE, V., and WILDING, P. (1984), *The Impact of Social Policy*, London: Routledge.

GLENDINNING, C. (1987), *The Financial circumstances of Informal Carers: Interim Report*, York: Social Policy Research Unit.

—— (1988), *Sources of Control and Allocation of Financial Resources in Households of Informal Carers: The Impact on Carer's Overall Living Standards* (Discussion Paper), York: Social Policy Research Unit.

GLENNERSTER, H. (1972), 'Education and Inequality', in N. Bosanquet and P. Townsend (eds.), *Labour and Inequality*, London: Fabian Society.

—— (1975), 'Social Services in Great Britain', in O. Thursz, and J. L. Vigilante (eds.), *Meeting Human Needs*, London: Sage.

—— (1980), 'Prime Cuts: Public Expenditure and Social Service Planning in a Hostile Environment', *Policy and Politics*, 8 no. 4: 367–82.

—— (1981), 'The Role of the State in Financing Recurrent Education: Lessons from European Experiences', *Public Choice*, 36/3: 551–71.

—— (1983), *Planning for Priority Groups*, Oxford: Robertson.

—— (1985), *Paying for Welfare*, Oxford: Blackwell.

—— (1987), 'Goodbye Mr. Chips', *New Society*, 9 Oct.

—— (1988), 'What Commitment to Welfare?' (The Richard Titmuss Memorial Lecture), Jerusalem: School of Social Work, Hebrew University.

—— and WILSON, G. (1970), *Paying for Private Schools*, Harmondsworth: Allen Lane.

—— POWER, A., and TRAVERS, T. (1989), 'A New Era for Social Policy: A New Enlightenment or a New Leviathan?' (Welfare State Programme, Discussion Paper no. 39), London: London School of Economics.

GLYNN, S., and OXBORROW, J. (1976), *Interwar Britain: A Social and Economic History*, London: Allen and Unwin.

GOODIN, R., and LE GRAND, J. (1987), *Not Only the Poor: The Middle Classes and the Welfare State*, London: Allen and Unwin.

GORDON, C. (1988), 'The Welfare State: Sources of Data on Government Expenditure' (Welfare State Programme, Research Note No. 14), London: London School of Economics.

GOSDEN, P. H. J. H. (1976), *Education in the Second World War*, London: Methuen.

GOUGH, I. (1979), *The Political Economy of the Welfare State*, London: Macmillan.

GOULD, F., and ROWETH, B. (1980), 'Public Spending and Social Policy: The United Kingdom 1950–1977', *Journal of Social Policy*, 9 pt. 3: 337–57.

GRAY, J., JESSON, D., and JONES, B. (1984), 'Predicting Differences in Examination Results between LEAs: Does School Organization Matter?', *Oxford Review of Education*, 10 no. 1: 45–61.

—— McPHERSON, A. F., and RAFFE, D. (1983), *Reconstruction and Secondary Education: Theory, Myth and Practice since the War*, London: Routledge and Kegan Paul.

GRIFFITH, J. A. G. (1965), *Central Departments and Local Authorities*, London: Allen and Unwin.

GUDEX, C., and KIND, P. (1988), 'The QALY Toolkit' (Centre for Health Economics, Discussion Paper No. 38), York: University of York.

HAGENBUCH, W. (1953), 'The Rationale of the Social Services', *Lloyds Bank Review* (July), 1–16.

HALL, P. (1976), *Reforming the Welfare*, London: Heinemann.

HALSEY, A. H., HEATH, A. F., and RIDGE, J. (1980), *Origins and Destinations*, Oxford: Clarendon Press.

HANNAH, L. (1986), *Inventing Retirement*, Cambridge: University Press.

HARRIS, J. (1977), *William Beveridge: A Biography*, Oxford: University Press.

HC [House of Commons] (Education, Science and Arts Committee) (1989), *Educational Provision for the Under Fives*, First Report, Session 1988/9, HC 30-I, London: HMSO.

—— (Social Services Committee) (1982), *Public Expenditure on the Social Services, Session 1981/2*, HC 306i–v, London: HMSO.

—— (Social Services Committee) (1984), *Public Expenditure on the Social Services, Session 1983/4*, HC 395, London: HMSO.

—— (Social Services Committee) (1986), *Public Expenditure on the Social Services, Session 1985/6*, HC 387, London: HMSO.

—— (Social Services Committee) (1987), *Public Expenditure on the Social Services, Session 1986/7*, HC 413, London: HMSO.

—— (Social Services Committee) (1988), *Public Expenditure on the Social Services, Session 1987/8*, HC 548, London: HMSO.

—— (Treasury and Civil Service Committee) (1983), *The Structure of Personal Income Taxation and Income Support*, Third Special Report, Session 1982/3, HC 386, London: HMSO.

HEALD, D. (1983), *Public Expenditure: Its Defence and Reform*, Oxford: Martin Robertson.

HEALTH SERVICES BOARD (1980), *Report, 1979*, London: HMSO.

HEATH, A. (1984), 'In Defense of Comprehensive Schools', *Oxford Review of Education*, 10 no. 1: 115–23.

HECLO, H., and WILDAVSKY, A. (1974), *The Private Government of Public Money*, London: Macmillan.

HEDLEY, R., and NORMAN, A. (1982), *Home Help: Key Issues in Service Provision*, London: Centre for Policy on Ageing.

HEMMING, R. (1984), *Poverty and Incentives*, Oxford: University Press.

—— and KAY, J. A. (1982), 'The Costs of the State Earnings-Related Pension Scheme', *Economic Journal*, 92 no. 366: 300–19.

HENWOOD, M., and WICKS, M. (1985), 'Community Care, Family Trends and Social Change', *Quarterly Journal of Social Affairs*, 1 no. 4: 357–71.

HIGGINS, J. (1989), 'Defining Community Care: Realities and Myths', *Social Policy and Administration*, 23 no. 1: 3–16.

HILLS, J. (1989), 'Distributional Effects of Housing Subsidies in the United Kingdom' (Welfare State Programme, Discussion Paper No. 44), London: London School of Economics.

HININGS, C. R., GREENWOOD, R., RANSON, S., and WALSH, K. (1980), 'The Organizational Consequences of Financial Restraint', in M. Wright (ed.), *Public Spending Decisions: Growth and Restraint in the 1970s*, London: Allen and

Unwin.

HM TREASURY (1971), *Public Expenditure to 1975–76*, Cmnd. 4829, London: HMSO.

——(1978), *The Government's Expenditure Plans 1978–79 to 1981–82*, Cmnd. 7049, London: HMSO.

——(1979*a*), *The Government's Expenditure Plans 1979–80 to 1982–83*, Cmnd. 7437, London: HMSO.

——(1979*b*), *The Government's Expenditure Plans 1980–81*, Cmnd. 7746, London: HMSO.

——(1980), *The Government's Expenditure Plans 1980–81 to 1983–84*, Cmnd. 7841, London: HMSO.

——(1981), *The Government's Expenditure Plans 1981–82 to 1983–84*, Cmnd. 8175, London: HMSO.

——(1984), *The Government's Expenditure Plans 1984–85 to 1986–87*, Cmnd. 9143, London: HMSO.

——(1985), *The Government's Expenditure Plans 1985–86 to 1987–88*, Cmnd. 9428, London: HMSO.

——(1986), *The Government's Expenditure Plans 1986–87 to 1988–89*, Cmnd. 9702, London: HMSO.

——(1987), *The Government's Expenditure Plans 1987–88 to 1989–90*, Cm. 56, London: HMSO.

——(1988), *The Government's Expenditure Plans 1988–89 to 1990–91*, Cm. 288, London: HMSO.

——(1989), *The Government's Expenditure Plans 1989–90 to 1991–92*, Cm. 601–621, London: HMSO.

HOME OFFICE (1959), *Committee on Children and Young Persons*, Cmnd. 1191, London: HMSO.

——(1968), *Local Authority and Allied Personal Social Services* (Seebohm Report), Cmnd. 3703, London: HMSO.

HOOD, C., and WRIGHT, M. (eds.) (1981), *By Government in Hard Times*, Oxford: Robertson.

HOPE, T., and HOUGH, M. (1988), 'Area, Crime and Incivilities: A Profile from the British Crime Survey', in T. Hope and M. Shaw (eds.), *Communities and Crime Reduction*, London: HMSO.

HOUSING CORPORATION (1988), *Tenants Guarantee: Guidance on Housing Management Practice for Registered Housing Associations*, London: Housing Corporation.

ILEA [Inner London Education Authority] (1981), *Black British Literacy: A Study of Reading Attainment of London Black Children from 8 to 15 Years* (Research and Statistics Report 776/81), London: ILEA.

——(1987), *Ethnic Background and Examination Results 1985 and 1986*, London: ILEA.

ILLSLEY, R., and LE GRAND, J. (1987), 'The Measurement of Inequality in Health', in A. Williams (ed.), *Health and Economics*, London: Macmillan.

ISIS [Independent Schools Information Service] (1986*a*), *Annual Census*, London: ISIS.

——(1986*b*), *Basic Facts about Independent Schools*, London: ISIS.

JENCKS, C. (1972), *Inequality: A Reassessment of the Effect of Family and School-ing in America*, New York: Basic Books.

JENKINS, S. P. (1989), 'Recent Trends in UK Income Inequality', paper presented at the 1989 Conference of the Social Policy Association (mimeo).

JOWELL, R., and AIREY, C. (1984), *British Social Attitudes: The 1984 Report*, Aldershot: Gower.

—— WITHERSPOON, S., and BROOK, L. (eds.) (1986), *British Social Attitudes: The 1986 Report*, Aldershot: Gower.

JUDGE, K. (1982), 'The Rise and Decline of Social Expenditure', in A. Walker (ed.), *Public Expenditure and Social Policy*, London: Heinemann.

KING, M. A., and ATKINSON, A. B. (1980), 'Housing Policy, Taxation and Reform', *Midland Bank Review* (Spring), 7–15.

KINGS FUND INSTITUTE (1989), *Efficiency and the NHS* (Occasional Paper No. 2), London: Kings Fund Institute.

KLEIN, R. (1983), *The Politics of the National Health Service*, London: Longman.

—— (1985), 'Health Policy, 1979 to 1983: The Retreat from Ideology', in P. Jackson (ed.), *Implementing Government Policy Initiatives: The Thatcher Admi-nistration 1979–1983*, London: Gower.

—— and O'HIGGINS, M. (eds.) (1985), *The Future of Welfare*, Oxford: Blackwell.

KLEINMAN, M. P. (1988), 'Where Did it Hurt Most? Uneven Decline in the Availability of Council Housing in England', *Policy and Politics*, 16 no. 4: 221–33.

KOGAN, M. (1978), *The Politics of Educational Change*, London: Fontana.

LAMBERT, R. (1964), *Nutrition in Britain 1950–60* (Occasional Paper in Social Administration No. 6), London: Bell.

LANSLEY, S. (1979), *Housing and Public Policy*, London: Croom Helm.

LAYARD, R., and PSACHAROPOULOS, G. (1974), 'The Screening Hypothesis and Returns to Education', *Journal of Political Economy*, 82 no. 5: 985–98.

—— (1979), 'Human Capital and Earnings', *Review of Economic Studies*, 46 (3), no. 144: 485–504.

—— et al. (1978), *The Causes of Poverty* (Royal Commission on the Distribution of Income and Wealth, Background Paper No. 5), London: HMSO.

LE GRAND, J. (1978), 'The Distribution of Public Expenditure: The Case of Health Care', *Economica*, 54: 125–42.

—— (1982), *The Strategy of Equality: Redistribution and the Social Services*, London: Allen and Unwin.

—— (1985), 'Inequalities in Health: The Human Capital Approach' (Welfare State Programme, Discussion Paper No. 1), London: London School of Econo-mics.

—— (1987), 'Three Essays on Equity' (Welfare State Programme, Discussion Paper No. 23), London: London School of Economics.

—— and RABIN, M. (1987), 'Trends in British Health Inequality', in A. Culyer and B. Jonsson (eds.), *Public and Private Health Services*, Oxford: Basil Black-well.

—— and ROBINSON, R. (1984), *The Economics of Social Problems: The Market Versus the State* (2nd edn.), London: Macmillan.

—— and WINTER, D. (1987), 'The Middle Classes and the Welfare State under

Conservative and Labour Governments', *Journal of Public Policy*, 6: 399–430.

—— (1989), 'Bureaucracies and Distribution', paper presented to the conference of the European Economic Association, Augsburg (mimeo).

LEAT, D., and GAY, P. (1987), *Paying for Care: A Study of Policy and Practice in Paid Care Schemes* (PSI Research Report No. 661), London: PSI

Leather, P. (1983), 'Housing (Dis?) Investment Programmes', Policy and Politics, 11 no. 2: 215–29.

LEVITT, M. S., and JOYCE, M. A. S. (1987), *The Growth and Efficiency of Public Spending*, Cambridge: University Press.

LONDON BOROUGH OF BRENT (1985), *Committee of Enquiry into the Death of Jasmine Beckford*, Brent: LB Brent.

MACK, J., and LANSLEY, S. (1985), *Poor Britain*, London: Allen and Unwin.

McKEOWN, T. (1976), *The Role of Medicine*, London: Nuffield Provincial Hospitals Trust.

McLAUGHLIN, E. (1988), *The Invalid Care Allowance: Problems and Perspectives* (Discussion Paper), York: Social Policy Research Unit.

MACLEOD, I., and POWELL, E. (1952), *The Social Services: Needs and Means*, London: The Conservative Political Centre.

MALPASS, P. (1989), 'The Road from Clay Cross', *Roof* (Jan.–Feb.), 38–40.

MARKS, J., COX, C., and POMIAN-SRZEDNICKI, M. (1983), *Standards in English Schools: An Analysis of the Examination Results of Secondary Schools in England for 1981*, London: National Council for Educational Standards.

MARMOT, M., and McDOWALL, M. (1986), 'Mortality Decline and Widening Social Inequalities', *The Lancet* (2 Aug.), 274–6.

MARQUAND, D. (1988), *The Unprincipled Society*, London: Cape.

MAYS, N., and BEVAN, G. (1987), *Resource Allocation in the Health Service*, London: Bedford Square Press.

MEADE, J. E. (1978), *The Structure and Reform of Direct Taxation*, London: Allen and Unwin.

MHLG [Ministry of Housing and Local Government] (1953), *Houses: The Next Step*, Cmd. 8996, London: HMSO.

—— (1957), *Local Government Finance*, Cmnd. 209, London: HMSO.

—— (1968), *Old Houses into New Homes*, Cmnd. 3602, London: HMSO.

MICKLEWRIGHT, J., PEARSON, M., and SMITH, S. (1989) 'Has Britain an Early School-Leaving Problem?', *Fiscal Studies*, 10 no. 1: 1–16.

MIDWINTER, E. (1986), *Caring For Cash: The Issue of Private Domiciliary Care*, London: Centre For Policy on Ageing.

MINFORD, P., ASHTON, P., PEEL, M., DAVIES, D., and SPRAGUE, A. (1985), *Unemployment: Cause and Cure* (2nd edn.), Oxford: Basil Blackwell.

MINISTRY OF RECONSTRUCTION (1944), *Employment Policy*, Cmd. 6527, London: HMSO.

MINISTRY OF SOCIAL SECURITY (1954), *Report of the Committee on the Economic and Financial Problems of the Provision for Old Age* (Phillips Committee), Cmd. 9333, London: HMSO.

MoH [Ministry of Health] (1944), *A National Health Service*, Cmd. 6502, London: HMSO.

—— (1956), *Report of the Committee of Enquiry into the Cost of the National*

Health Service (Guillebaud Committee), Cmd. 9663, London: HMSO.

MORONEY, R. (1976), *The Family and the State: Considerations for Social Policy*, London: Longman.

MORRIS, N., and PRESTON, I. (1986*a*), 'Inequality, Poverty and the Redistribution of Income', *Bulletin of Economic Research*, 38 no. 4: 275–344.

—— (1986*b*), 'Taxes, Benefits and the Distribution of Income', *Fiscal Studies*, 7 no. 4: 18–27.

MOYLAN, S., MILLAR, J., and DAVIES, R. (1984), *For Richer, for Poorer? DHSS Cohort Study of Unemployed Men* (DHSS Research Report No. 11), London: HMSO.

MSC [Manpower Services Commission] (1984), *Annual Report 1983/4*, Sheffield: MSC.

MURPHY, M. J. (1989), 'Housing the People: From Shortage to Surplus?', in H. Joshi (ed.), *The Changing Population of Britain*, Oxford: Blackwell.

MURRAY, C. (1984), *Losing Ground: American Social Policy 1950–1980*, New York: Basic Books.

NATIONAL AUDIT OFFICE (1987), *Community Care Developments*, London: HMSO.

NEWHOUSE, J. P. (1987), 'Cross-National Differences in Health Spending; What Do They Mean?', *Journal of Health Economics*, 6: 159–62.

NEWTON, K., and KARRAN, T. (1985), *The Politics of Local Expenditure*, London: Macmillan.

NHS [National Health Service] Management Inquiry (1983), *Report* (Griffiths Report), London: DHSS.

NICKELL, S. J. (1979*a*), 'The Effect of Unemployment and Related Benefits on the Duration of Unemployment', *Economic Journal*, 89 no. 353: 34–49.

—— (1979*b*), 'Estimating the Probability of Leaving Unemployment', *Econometrica*, 47 no. 5: 1249–66.

—— (1979*c*), 'Education and Life Time Patterns of Unemployment', *Journal of Political Economy*, 87 no. 5/2: pp. S117–S132.

—— (1984), 'A Review of *Unemployment: Cause and Cure*, by Patrick Minford with David Davies, Michael Peel and Alison Sprague', *Economic Journal*, 94 no. 376: 946–53.

NINER, P. (1989), *Homelessness in Nine Local Authorities: Case Studies of Policy and Practice*, London: HMSO.

NISBET, J., WATT, J., and WELSH, M. (1972), *Reading Standards in Aberdeen 1967–72*, Aberdeen: University Press.

NISKANEN, W. (1971), *Bureaucracy and Representative Government*, Chicago: Aldene Atherton.

NISSELL, M., and BONNERJEA, L. (1982), *Family Care of the Handicapped Elderly: Who Pays?*, London: Policy Studies Institute.

O'CONNOR, J. (1973), *The Fiscal Crisis of the State*, London: St James Press.

O'DONNELL, O., and PROPPER, C. (1989), 'The Distribution of Public Expenditure on Health Care' (Welfare State Programme, Discussion Paper No. 45), London: London School of Economics.

OECD [Organization for Economic Co-operation and Development] (1985), *Social Expenditure 1960–1990: Problems of Growth and Control*, Paris: OECD.

OFFICE OF HEALTH ECONOMICS (1987), *Compendium of Health Statistics* (6th edn.), Luton: White Crescent Press Ltd.

OPCS [Office of Population Censuses and Surveys] (1977), *General Household Survey 1974*, London: HMSO.

—— (1980), *General Household Survey 1978*, London: HMSO.

—— (1981), *General Household Survey 1979*, London: HMSO.

—— (1982), *General Household Survey 1980*, London: HMSO.

—— (1984), *Mortality Statistics 1985: England and Wales*, ser. DH1 no. 17, London: HMSO.

—— (1986), *Occupational Mortality 1979–80, 1982–83*, ser. DS no. 6, London: HMSO.

—— (1987), *General Household Survey 1985*, London: HMSO.

—— (1989), *Hospital In-Patient Enquiry*, ser. MB4 no. 29, London: HMSO.

ORROS, G. C. (1988), *The Potential Role of Private Health Insurance*, London: Institute of Health Service Managers.

PAPADAKIS, E., and TAYLOR-GOOBY, P. (1987), *The Private Provision of Public Welfare: State, Market and Community*, Brighton: Wheatsheaf.

PARKER, G. (1989), *A Study of Non-Elderly Spouse Carers: Summary of Final Report* (Discussion Paper), York: Social Policy Research Unit.

PARKER, R. (1981), 'Tending and Social Policy', in E. M. Goldberg, and S. Hatch (eds.), *A New Look at the Personal Social Services*, London: Policy Studies Institute.

PARKIN, D., McGUIRE, A., and YULE, B. (1987), 'Aggregate Health Care Expenditures and National Income: Is Health a Luxury Good?', *Journal of Health Economics*, 6: 109–27.

PARTON, N. (1985), *The Politics of Child Abuse*, London: Macmillan.

PATERSON, K. (1981), 'The Black Report and Causality', *The Lancet* (6 June).

PEACOCK, A., and WISEMAN, J. (1961), *The Growth of Public Expenditure in the United Kingdom*, London: Allen and Unwin.

PEARSON, M., SMITH, S., and WATSON, S. (1988), 'Research on Medium Term Influences on Public Expenditure on Education', paper presented to ESRC Public Expenditure Seminar, 15/16 Dec. (mimeo).

PESTON, M. (1982), 'Public Expenditure on Education', in A. Walker (ed.), *Public Expenditure and Social Policy*, London: Heinemann.

PHILLIPS COMMITTEE (1954), *Report of the Committee on the Economic and Financial Problems of Old Age*, Cmd. 9333, London: HMSO.

PIACHAUD, D. (1987), 'Problems in the Definition and Measurement of Poverty', *Journal of Social Policy*, 16 no. 2: 147–64.

—— (1988), 'Poverty in Britain', *Journal of Social Policy*, 17 no. 3: 335–49.

PIDGEON, D. A. (1967), *Achievement in Mathematics*, Windsor: NFER.

PIRIE, M. (1988), *Privatization*, Aldershot: Wildwood House Limited.

PISSARIDES, C. (1982), 'From School to University: The Demand for Post Compulsory Education in Britain', *Economic Journal*, 92 no. 367: 654–67.

POSNETT, J., and CHASE, J. (1985), 'Independent Schools in England and Wales', *Charity Statistics*, Tonbridge: Charities Aid Foundation.

PRAIS, S. J. (1981), 'Vocational Qualifications of the Labour Force in Britain and Germany', *National Institute Economic Review*, no. 98 (Nov.), 47–59.

Prais, S. J. (1987), 'Educating for Productivity: Comparisons of Japanese and English Schooling and Vocational Preparation', *National Institute Economic Review*, no. 119 (Feb.), 40–56.

—— and Steedman, H. (1986), 'Vocational Training in France and Britain: The Building Trades', *National Institute Economic Review*, no. 116 (May), 45–55.

—— and Wagner, K. (1983), 'Some Practical Aspects of Human Capital Investment: Training Standards in Five Occupations in Britain and Germany', *National Institute Economic Review*, no. 105 (Aug.), 46–65.

—————— (1985), 'Schooling Standards in England and Germany: Some Summary Comparisons Bearing on Economic Performance', *National Institute Economic Review*, no. 112 (May), 53–76.

—————— (1988), 'Productivity and Management: The Training of Foremen in Britain and Germany', *National Institute Economic Review*, no. 123 (Feb.), 34–47.

Prest, A. R. (1983), 'The Social Security Reform Minefield', *British Tax Review*, no. 1: 44–53.

Propper, C. (1989a), 'Working for Patients: The Implications of the NHS White Paper for the Private Sector' (NHS White Paper Occasional Paper Series No. 6), York: Centre for Health Economics, University of York.

—— (1989b), 'An Econometric Analysis of the Demand for Private Health Insurance in England and Wales', *Applied Economics*, 21: 777–92.

—— (1990), 'Contingent Valuation of Time Spent on NHS Waiting Lists', *Economic Journal* (Conference Supplement), 100 no. 400: 193–200.

Psacharopoulos, G. (1973), *Returns to Education: An International Comparison*, Amsterdam: Elsevier.

Public Schools Commission (1970), *Second Report*, London: HMSO.

Radical Statistics Health Group (1987), *Facing the Figures: What Really is Happening to the National Health Service?* London: Radical Statistics.

Riley, J. G. (1979), 'Testing the Educational Screening Hypothesis', *Journal of Political Economy*, 87 no. 5/2 (Oct.), 5227–52.

Robinson, R. (1986), 'Restructuring the Welfare State: An Analysis of Public Expenditure, 1979/80–1984/85', *Journal of Social Policy*, 15 no. 1: 1–21.

—— and Judge, K. (1987), *Public Expenditure and the NHS: Trends and Prospects* (Briefing Paper No. 2), London: Kings Fund Institute.

Robitaille, D. F., and Garden, R. A. (1989), *The IEA Study of Mathematics*, ii. *Contexts and Outcomes of School Mathematics*, Oxford: Pergamon.

Robson, M. H., and Walford, G. (1989), 'Independent Schools and Tax Policy under Mrs. Thatcher', *Journal of Education Policy*, 4 no. 2: 149–62.

Royal Commission on the National Health Service (1979), *Report*, Cmnd. 7615, London: HMSO.

Rutter, M., *et al.* (1979), *Fifteen Thousand Hours: Schools and their Effects on Children*, London: Open Books.

Ryan, M., and Birch, S. (1989), 'Estimating the Effects of Health Service Charges: Evidence on the Utilisation of Prescriptions' (Centre for Health Economics, Discussion Paper No. 37), York: University of York.

St. John Brooks, C. (1983), *Who Controls Training? The Rise of the MSC*, London: Fabian Society.

Scott, M. (1980), 'Net Investment in Education in the U.K. 1951–71', *Oxford Review of Education*, 1 no. 6: 21–30.

Scottish Development Department (1985), *Scottish Housing Statistics 1984*, Edinburgh: HMSO.

—— (1987), *Scottish Housing Statistics 1986*, Edinburgh: HMSO.

—— (1989), *Commentary on Scottish Programme to 1991/2*, Edinburgh: SDD.

Scottish Home and Health Department (1964), *Children and Young Persons* (Kilbrandon Report), Cmnd. 2306, Edinburgh: HMSO.

Scottish Office (1980), *Scottish Abstract of Statistics*, no. 9, Edinburgh: HMSO.

—— (1987), *Scottish Abstract of Statistics*, no. 16, Edinburgh: HMSO.

Shah, A. (1985), 'Does Education Act as a Screening Device for Certain British Occupations?', *Oxford Economic Papers*, 37 no. 1: 118–24.

Smith, D. J., and Tomlinson, S. (1989), *The School Effects of Multi-Racial Comprehensives*, London: Policy Studies Institute.

Smith, R. (1987), *Unemployment and Health*, Oxford: University Press.

Social Security Advisory Committee (1982), *First Report*, London: HMSO.

—— (1983), *Second Report*, London: HMSO.

—— (1988), *Sixth Report*, London: HMSO.

Spicker, P. (1986), 'The Case for Supplementary Benefit', *Fiscal Studies*, 7 no. 4: 28–44.

Stark, J. (1987), 'Health and Social Contacts', in Health Promotion Research Trust, *The Health and Lifestyle Survey*, London: HPRT.

Start, K. B., and Wells, B. K. (1972), *The Trend of Reading Standards 1970–71*, Slough: NFER.

Supplementary Benefits Commission (1978), *Take-up of Supplementary Benefits* (Supplementary Benefits Administration Papers No. 7), London: HMSO.

—— (1979), *Annual Report*, London: HMSO.

Tapper, T., and Salter, B. (1986), 'The Assisted Places Scheme: A Policy Evaluation', *Journal of Education Policy*, 6: 315–30.

Taubman, P., and Wales, T. (1974), *Higher Education and Earnings: College as an Investment and a Screening Device* (Report prepared for the Carnegie Commission on Higher Education and the National Bureau of Economic Research, General Series, 101), London: McGraw-Hill.

Tawney, R. H. (1931), *Equality*, London: Allen and Unwin.

Thompson, J. (1987), 'Ageing of the Population: Contemporary Trends and Issues', *Population Trends*, no. 50: 18–22.

Titmuss, R. M. (1950), *The Problems of Social Policy*, London: HMSO.

—— (1958), *Essays on 'the Welfare State'*, London: Allen and Unwin.

—— (1968), *Commitment to Welfare*, London: Allen and Unwin.

Townsend, P. (1957), *Family Life of Old People*, London: Routledge and Kegan Paul.

—— (1979), *Poverty in the United Kingdom*, London: Penguin.

—— and Davidson, N. (1982), *Inequalities in Health: The Black Report*, Harmondsworth: Penguin.

—— Walker, R., and Lawson, R. (1983), *Responses to Poverty*, London: Routledge.

Training Commission (1988), *Annual Report 1987/88*, Sheffield: Training Commission Publications.

TRAVERS, T. (1986), *The Politics of Local Government Finance*, London: Allen and Unwin.

TRINDER, C. (1987), 'Public Service Pay', in M. S. Levitt (ed.), *New Priorities in Public Spending*, London: Gower.

UCCA [Universities Central Council for Admissions] (1987), *Statistical Supplement to the Twenty-Fourth Report 1985–86*, Cheltenham: UCCA.

UGC [University Grants Committee] (1987), *University Statistics 1985–86*, iii. *Finance*, Cheltenham: University Statistical Record.

WALENTOWICZ, P. (1988), *Room for Improvement*, London: SHAC.

WALFORD, G. (1987), 'How Dependent is the Independent Sector?', *Oxford Review of Education*, 13 no. 3: 275–95.

WALKER, A. (ed.) (1982a), *Public Expenditure and Social Policy: An Examination of Social Spending and Priorities*, London: Heinemann.

——(ed.) (1982b), *Community Care: The Family, the State and Social Policy*, Oxford: Blackwell.

WARNOCK, M. (1975), 'The Concept of Equality in Education', *Oxford Review of Education*, 1 no. 1: 3–8.

WEBB, A., and WISTOW, G. (1982), 'The Personal Social Services', in A. Walker (ed.), *Public Expenditure and Social Policy*, London: Heinemann.

——(1983), 'Public Expenditure and Policy Implementation: The Case of Community Care', *Public Administration*, 61 (Spring), 21–44.

——(1986), *Planning, Need and Scarcity*, London: Allen and Unwin.

——(1987), *Social Work, Social Care and Social Planning*, London: Longman.

WEBSTER, C. (1988), *The Health Services since the War*, London: HMSO.

WEINER, M. J. (1981), *English Culture and the Decline of the Industrial Spirit, 1850–1980*, Cambridge: University Press.

WELSH OFFICE (1979), *Health and Personal Social Services Statistics for Wales*, Cardiff: HMSO.

——(1982), *1981 Welsh House Condition Survey*, Cardiff: Welsh Office.

——(1987), *Welsh Housing Statistics 1987*, Cardiff: Welsh Office.

——(1988), *1986 Welsh House Condition Survey (Revised Edition)*, Cardiff: Welsh Office.

——(1989), *Welsh Housing Statistics 1989*, Cardiff: Welsh Office.

WEST, E. G. (1965), *Education and the State*, London: Institute of Economic Affairs.

——(1975), *Education and the Industrial Revolution*, London: Batsford.

WHITEHEAD, C. M. E. (1977) 'Neutrality between Tenures: A Critique of the HPR Comparisons', *CES Review*, 2 (Dec.), 33–6.

——(1978), 'The £25,000 Limit', *CES Review*, 4 (Sept.), 12–15.

WHO [World Health Organization] (1958), *The First Ten Years of the World Health Organization*, Geneva: WHO.

WILDAVSKY, A. (1964), *The Politics of the Budgetary Process*, Boston: Little Brown and Co.

WILDING, P. (1986), *In Defence of the Welfare State*, Manchester: University Press.

WILLIAMS, G., and GORDON, A. (1981), 'Perceived Earnings Functions and Ex-

Bibliography

Ante Rates of Return in Post Compulsory Education in Eng
Education, 10: 199–227.

WILLIS, J. R. M., and HARDWICK, P. J. W. (1978), *Tax Expenditures i.
Kingdom*, London: Heinemann.

WILLMOTT, P. (1986), *Social Networks, Informal Care and Public Poll.
Studies Institute, Research Report No. 655), London: PSI.

WINTER, D. (1989), 'Self-Reported Morbidity: A Time Series and Coho
lysis', paper presented to Conference on the Analysis of Social and F
Change, Oxford, May 1989 (mimeo).

WOLFENDEN COMMITTEE (1978), *The Future of Voluntary Organisations*, Lon
Croom Helm.

WOOLLEY, F., and LE GRAND, J. (1990), 'The Ackroyds, the Osbornes and
Welfare State: The Impact of the Welfare State on Two Hypothetical Famili
over their Life-Times' *Policy and Politics*, 18 no. 1: 17–30.
London: London School of Economics.

WORSWICK, G. D. N. (1985), *Education and Economic Performance*, London:
Gower.

WRIGHT, M. (ed.) (1980), *Public Spending Decisions: Growth and Restraint in the
1970s*, London: Allen and Unwin.

Index

Note: Authors of cited publications are entered under name of the first author only.